Downfall

Alan McCombes is a freelance writer and journalist and previously editor of the *Scottish Socialist Voice*. A founder member of the Scottish Socialist Party, he was an executive member of the party and also its national press and policy co-ordinator. He lives in Glasgow.

Contents

Foreword

This is a book I never wanted to write. The subject matter was too raw, too painful, too emotionally draining. It involved delving into dark corners of the human psyche. And it meant laying bare some of my own skeletons, if only to lay to rest any suspicion that this conflict was between narrow-minded Calvinist-Catholic sexual morality on the one side and tolerant liberalism on the other. This was about a deeper, more fundamental morality, in the broadest sense of the term.

I didn't want to be the person to bring out into cold daylight the whole sickening, sordid, destructive account. I wanted to be writing about other things – the disintegration of free-market capitalism and the potential resurgence of a new socialism for the twenty-first century; the tragedy and shame of the West's role in Afghanistan, which I covered as a campaigning journalist from the North West Frontier Province in the weeks after 9/11; and the progressive, left-wing case for a free, independent Scotland.

But, first, this story had to be told. It has generated too much division, too much hatred, too much confusion. It has fascinated the public but it stands in the way of politics. The mysteries of the Tommy Sheridan legal drama have to be cleared up before the Scottish socialist Left can move on and recover the ground it has lost.

This is a complex story. It requires a full, in-depth account of the incidents, the personalities and the politics that shaped this shocking saga of sex, lies, libel, forgery, perjury and imprisonment.

Those who found themselves near the centre of these events were damaged by the experience. Lifelong friendships turned into savage enmity. Some people were jailed. Others suffered mental health problems and psychological scars. Some individuals were unfairly maligned, demonised even – victims of prejudice, the ugly twin of ignorance. The fall-out affected hundreds and probably thousands of people across Scotland to one degree or another.

The media always focussed on Tommy Sheridan and his photo-genic family and their ordeal at the hands of the law. But innocent people had families too – mothers and fathers, daughters and sons – whose lives were tarnished by what turned into a sustained crusade by one man to deceive everyone else. Some of these mothers and fathers left this world with a shadow over their graves.

On the scale of atrocities against humanity, the Thomas Sheridan Affair was a fleabite. Measured against the tumultuous global events which were raging in the background, it is a grubby, trivial tale of deceit, selfishness and cowardice. But the specific can illuminate the general. The story of the rise and self-destruction of Tommy Sheridan can, I believe, help us understand far greater historical tragedies better.

From my point of view, the biggest tragedy was the damage wreaked on a noble political cause. Tommy Sheridan, as this book recognises, played a vital, even heroic, role in helping to advance the cause of a socialist Scotland. But others played an equally heroic role, well away from the spotlight and thousands gave time and money to that cause. Sadly, Tommy tore his ideals to shreds with the same casual contempt he once famously tore up a court order banning him from attending a Poll Tax protest.

The record had to be set straight – and not by a detached journalist but by a central participant in the events at the heart of this story. For two decades, during the glory years, when he became the most famous and most popular politician in Scotland, I worked with Tommy Sheridan on a day-to-day basis. As the introduction to the book *Imagine*, published in both our names, states, 'We've laughed together, been locked up together, marched together, and been on hunger strike together.' For all these reasons, I was best placed to tell this story. It helped that I am a journalist. I have spent decades working with words and ideas – writing, editing, speaking, reporting, analysing, interpreting – and this was a story I knew inside out.

This book is not about settling scores. I have tried to describe what happened with calm and restraint, even though the events have generated much anger and pain. But I make no claim to neutrality in what I believe has been a conflict not between right and left but between right and wrong. We all make mistakes but some mistakes have greater consequences than others.

In telling the story, I have pulled no punches. I have not spared those who have, in some way, been complicit in a shameful legal and political scandal. Some of these people I still like and respect despite everything. I hope that some of them, at least, will be strong enough and brave enough to retrace their steps and acknowledge that, if they had to do the same again, they wouldn't.

Before the wounds of five years of conflict can even start to heal, truth has to prevail. Without truth, redemption and reconciliation are unattainable. Truth means first bringing all the relevant information out into the open, in full and in context, and then understanding the significance of that information.

People are free to disagree with my opinions, interpretations and conclusions. But the facts are the facts. They are unalterable. Stubborn, obstinate, unyielding. As Robert Burns put it, 'But facts are chiels that winna ding/An' downa be disputed.' He might have put it if he was writing in the modern Scots idiom, 'Ye cannae argue wi' facts.'

Finally, I want to thank the following people for their help. My agent Mark Stanton ('Stan') for getting this project off the ground; Hugh Andrew and his team at Birlinn for having the courage to take on this book at a time when other publishers were, perhaps understandably, running scared; Andrew Simmons, the editorial manager at Birlinn, for his professionalism, commitment and courtesy; Patricia Marshall for her patient and meticulous copy-editing; Roz Paterson, a superb writer, who diligently went through the manuscript line by line, her sure and subtle touch with the written word improving every chapter; Davie Archibald, a veteran activist from the early days of the Thatcher Government and now a lecturer in film and media studies at Glasgow University, whose expert advice helped me develop a coherent structure for this complex story; Pauline Goldsmith, a supremely talented playwright and actor whose advice on tone, language and presentation was spot on; Eddie Truman, for procuring, selecting and optimising the photographs; and Pam Currie and Carol Hainey for their detailed, painstaking transcripts of the defamation trial in 2006.

I also want to thanks all of those who provided me with insight and information, either directly or indirectly. Although for reasons of space I'm unable to list them all by name, I do want to specifically mention Anne Colvin and Helen Allison who, for no personal gain or political benefit, gave up hours of their valuable time to talk to me in January 2011.

Most of all, I want to thank everyone who had the strength of character to stand firm, loyal and faithful to their principles throughout these strange and difficult times. They can forever hold their heads high.

1

1984–1988

The Graduate

'Bliss was it in that dawn to be alive/But to be young was very heaven!' wrote the English poet William Wordsworth about the French Revolution. The long hot summer of 1984 was neither bliss nor heaven in Margaret Thatcher's Divided Kingdom. But, if you were young and left-wing, it sometimes felt like revolution was in the air. On one side stood the most right-wing government since the 1930s, backed by the full might of the British state. Dixon of Dock Green had been pensioned off and replaced with paramilitary-style Robocops tooled-up for war. The government had a blank cheque in one pocket and most of Britain's newspaper editors in the other.

Ranged against them were 100,000 miners and their families. They lived off charity soup kitchens and street collections. Their communities had been turned into mini-police states. But they stood together, as rock solid as the Grampian Mountains. It was the irresistible force versus the immovable object. Someone said it was like a civil war without bullets.

One Sunday afternoon, I had a call from a strike leader in Ayrshire asking me to try to get a carload or two down from Glasgow to help out with some action they were planning at dawn the next day. In my small ground-floor flat, across the road from the main gates of Govan shipyard, I talked it over with Jack and Willie. Jack Harvie was a tough, hard-drinking building worker in his late twenties, with a hilariously surreal sense of humour and an awesome mastery of the English language. Years later, he went to university and then became the head of the English department in a tough secondary school in Essex. Willie Hamilton was a laid-back, easy-going artist from Govan's own mini-version of the Bronx. Plenty of graffiti artists had emerged from the Wine Alley but Willie was a genuinely talented painter, who had designed and supervised the biggest art mural in Scotland. For decades it stood in the back streets of Easterhouse unblemished by vandalism.

From Easterhouse itself, over on the Wild East of the city, we roped in Gary Stevenson, a multi-talented, razor-witted guy who had done a bit of acting. While still in his early twenties, he had played the role of John MacLean, the legendary icon of Red Clydeside, in the late Freddy Anderson's play *Krassivy*, which was acclaimed the best drama of the Edinburgh Fringe in 1979. Later – under his Equity name, Gary Lewis – he became one of Scotland's great actors, appearing in a string of Ken Loach films and in Martin Scorsese's *Gangs of New York* alongside Daniel Day Lewis, Cameron Diaz and Leonardo DiCaprio. In *Billy Elliot*, set in 1984, he played a desperate and broken striking miner, torn by conflicting loyalties to his union and his family. It was a strange experience watching Gary's performance in that memorable film – I had stood beside him on these picket lines in the real world fifteen years before. I almost stood up and cheered in the cinema when, after crossing the picket line, he changed his mind and turned back.

We needed transport to get down to Ayrshire but these were hard times and cars were scarce among the people we knew. Eventually we managed to track down a driver – a young Stirling University student who was back home in Pollok for the summer. With his Italian good looks and slim physique, he looked as though he'd be more at home singing with a pop group than standing on a miners' picket line but, that evening, he drove us down to the Netherthird Miners Social Club on the edge of Cumnock. It was a warm summer's evening and, outside in the car park, we played football with some of the local striking miners and then stayed over for the action the next day. That's how I first got to know Tommy Sheridan.

Tommy and I went on to forge a close political alliance that was to last for twenty years. I was impressed by his raw talent as an orator and his pulsating energy. After he'd left university a couple of years later, towards the end of 1986, I pushed for Tommy to be taken on as Militant's Scottish youth organiser. The decision was taken by a small group of Militant organisers in a dingy office next to Queen Street Station in Glasgow. The vote was on a knife-edge, split three ways between Tommy, Davie Archibald, then a young engineering worker in Clydebank, and Patricia Moore, a popular young activist from Motherwell who was still in her teens. All the three had ability and I'd have been happy with any of them but I felt that Tommy had the edge. Even back then, he had a touch of the flamboyance and charisma that would later take Scottish politics by storm. Some people found him a little bit too pushy but I was attracted to his bravado. He was like a breath of fresh air in these left-wing circles where the culture, strangely enough, could often be quite staid and conservative.

For better or worse, my arguments swayed a few people and

Tommy was duly appointed. From that day onwards, Tommy was a full-time political campaigner until his defeat in the May 2007 Scottish elections. If it hadn't been for that fateful, wafer-thin vote, I suspect Tommy may have moved on, like thousands of other talented young working-class men and women who went in and out of the revolving door of the Militant organisation in the 1980s. We used to joke that the biggest party in Scotland was the ex-Militant Party.

Maybe that decision affected the future march of Scottish political history. Would the Poll Tax campaign have spread across Scotland and then throughout Britain if Tommy had gone off to work in an office or into teaching? Would a party like the Scottish Socialist Party (SSP) have scaled the heights it did in 2003 without him? I believe others would have emerged to play that role – probably less flamboyantly, more collectively and less recklessly. But who knows?

Back then, the main figurehead of Militant in Scotland was Bob Wylie, a powerful and entertaining speaker, who later went on to become a BBC reporter and a kind of cult figure for his eccentric on-screen style. In the mid-80s, he went to South Africa to assist Militant's sister organisation in the South African townships during the uprising against apartheid. It was a brave move but it took him out of the picture in Scotland for a couple of years. On his return, he moved gradually out of political activity into mainstream journalism.

When I first met Tommy Sheridan, he was barely out of his teens yet brimful of confidence. Most people from our kind of working-class background tended to appear slightly uncomfortable speaking in front of an audience – even Bob Wylie who was 15 years older and an outstanding orator – but Tommy flourished in the limelight. He was good and he knew it.

Eventually, he would develop into one of Scotland's most accomplished public speakers with the ability to set audiences on fire. He had natural talent but he also worked hard at polishing his technique. In the early days, he would write out his speeches word for word, in block capitals. His delivery was strong but his voice was untrained. He'd begin by bellowing out his speech at full volume. Then, somewhere in the middle, his voice would begin to crack and start to trail away into a hoarse croak but, as he gained experience and mastery of breathing techniques, his voice grew strong and resonant.

The American writer, Malcolm Gladwell, of *The Tipping Point* fame, argues persuasively in his 2008 book, *Outliers*, that the key difference between mere talent and outstanding brilliance in any field is practice, repetition and dedication. The Beatles, for example, played 1200 live concerts in the German city of Hamburg between

1960 and 1964, more than most bands would perform in their entire careers. 'The Hamburg crucible is one of the things that set the Beatles apart,' insists Gladwell.

The Poll Tax crucible was one of the things that eventually set Tommy Sheridan apart. In the 1980s his talent for oratory was already beginning to emerge. He always made himself available to speak to any kind of gathering, large or small, honing his oratory as diligently as he would tone his body in the gym. According to an ex-girlfriend, he would practise his body language and gestures for hours on end in front of a mirror. When the campaign against the Poll Tax took off, he was in his element. Thousands of public meetings later, in community centres, schoolrooms and public halls across Scotland, his skills blossomed. His style was stamped in the mould of the 1970s generation of Scottish working-class rebels, such as the fiery nationalist Jim Sillars, the Upper Clyde Shipbuilders (UCS) hero Jimmy Reid, and the Scottish miners' leader Mick McGahey.

Although Tommy would never attain either the intellectual breadth or depth of these speakers, or match the eloquent command of language of people like George Galloway and Tony Benn, he would become a master of oratorical technique with an ability to move audiences in a way that few could ever hope to achieve. Like an evangelical preacher, he knew which buttons to press, when to pause and when to slow down, when to raise or lower his voice and how to synchronise his facial expressions with the content of his speech.

In the late 1980s, he also began to grasp the power of the media. In his first tangle with a TV interviewer, on a Scottish current affairs programme, during a series of school student strikes against conscription onto government training schemes, he looked more like a send-up of a far-left activist than a future media maestro. His eyes darted shiftily from side to side, while his jacket was festooned with a kaleidoscopic mosaic of political badges and stickers – Coal Not Dole, Fight Fascism, Jobs Not Bombs, Tories Out and many more. Gary Stevenson later devised a sketch which depicted Tommy taking part in a TV interview with political stickers plastered over his forehead, nose and cheeks and across every inch of his clothing.

Nonetheless, in the decades to come, he was to grow into a consummate media performer, his quick-fire responses sharpened close to perfection in hundreds of TV and radio jousts. He also learned to utilise the print media to maximum effect. Courteous, friendly and approachable, he went out of his way to make time for journalists, never failed to return a call and was always willing to supply the kind of short, snappy quotes reporters love.

One of the decisive turning points in the rise of Tommy Sheridan as a political powerhouse came when George McNeilage became involved with the local branch of Militant. Today, George is something of a legend in Pollok. As streetwise as an alley cat, hard as a concrete pavement and fearless as a guerrilla fighter, George is hugely respected in the housing scheme for his work with the local community, his courage and his generosity. George had gone to school with Tommy. They shared a desk during their second and third years at Lourdes Secondary and they regularly stood together in the old 'Jungle' at Celtic Park. But their paths soon diverged. While Tommy went to university, George, like many other young people brought up on Glasgow's bleak council housing schemes in these poverty-stricken times, drifted into a life of crime.

After serving a jail sentence in 1985, he decided to sort himself out. Intelligent and well read, he enrolled at the local Cardonald Further Education College. There, by chance, he met Davy McDickens, an old acquaintance from the scheme who had become involved with Militant and the Labour Party Young Socialists in Pollok. One day, he removed a copy of *Militant* newspaper from Davy's bag and read it from cover to cover. It blew George away. Although he didn't understand everything, it was expressing the kind of politics that he had always instinctively believed in.

When George attended his first meeting of the local Militant branch, there were four other people there and one of them was lying drunk on the floor, while another was emptying a can of lager. But George's involvement changed everything. Unlike Tommy, who had left the scheme to go to university, George was rooted in Pollok. He had connections aplenty. Among the local youth, he was held in awe. In Glasgow's council housing schemes in the 1980s, it was no shame to be an outlaw. George's criminal exploits made him one of the boys and someone they could look up to – a role model.

George could look after himself but he also had a brain and a hunger to understand the world around him. He especially identified with the simmering revolution against apartheid in South African. With George McNeilage involved, Militant now held a magnetic attraction for hordes of young people in Pollok who might easily have become involved in drug dealing and general criminality instead.

In one of his first brushes with the law, in early 1987, Tommy, together with Davie Archibald and George McNeilage, led a youth occupation of a Benetton clothes store in Argyle Street in Glasgow city centre to expose the hypocrisy of its high-profile advertising campaign, 'United Colours of Benetton', which depicted black and white young people mixing harmoniously, while the same multinational was heavily investing in the rogue racist state of South Africa. The police moved in and the protestors were arrested. The resulting press coverage impressed on Tommy the lesson that you don't generate publicity by meekly pleading your case.

The next time Tommy found himself stuck between two police officers was in 1989, when Margaret Thatcher visited the Volvo Truck plant in Irvine. Leading a small band of anti-Poll Tax protesters, Tommy hurled an egg at the Prime Minister. He was instantly huckled away by the police and charged with breach of the peace. Some anti-Poll Tax activists, including members of Militant, thought the action a bit childish and embarrassing. It wasn't exactly a spontaneous outburst of anger – not unless Tommy had been carrying the egg in his pocket with the intention of boiling it later for lunch. Others, though, criticised him for being off target and quite a few people suggested it might have been more effective if he had lobbed a hand grenade rather than an egg.

George became a close friend of Tommy and a key political ally. Ten years later, in 1996, Tommy was to be the best man at George's wedding and then, in June 2000, George became best man at Tommy's wedding – or, more accurately, one of three best men. But, on first resuming his acquaintance with his old classmate, George was struck by a few peculiarities of the post-Stirling University Tommy Sheridan. One was his merciless hostility to any form of charity. George remembers Tommy dressing him down for giving money to beggars and down-and-outs. For George, socialism was more than just a textbook theory – it was the way he wanted to live his life. Wealth redistribution wasn't just an ideological doctrine – it was about helping out people who had nothing. Yet, when he gave cigarettes or money to someone in dire straits, Tommy would wag his finger and lecture him about the futility of charity, which encouraged people to beg rather than become politically active.

Tommy was really just reflecting the culture of doctrinaire disdain that was, and remains, a characteristic of some far-left socialist groups but George could never get his head round it. 'Here was somebody preaching socialism and wanting to change the world. Yet, if you had a guy wi' the arse hanging out his trousers and you gave him a fag, Tommy would lash into you: "What are you giving him that for? You shouldn't be doing that."'

Later, as his celebrity status soared, Tommy would forget his ideological antagonism towards charity as he bestowed his presence repeatedly on charity football matches and charity boxing matches, and other fundraising events. He also insisted that the payment for his weekly column in the *Scottish Daily Mirror* – usually written by other people – should go to a different 'good cause' every week, chosen by himself, rather than into the funds of the SSP as many party members had expected. At the end of 2003, the *Mirror* boasted that it had showered thousand of pounds on Scottish charities via the £200-a-time fee Tommy was paid for his column. The beneficiaries had included 'abandoned animals, epilepsy charities, burns victims and the brave men and women who have fought for their country'.

George McNeilage was also puzzled by Tommy's mystifying conversion to the cause of Glasgow Rangers Football Club. In the days when they used to go to Celtic Park together as part of a large group from Pollok, Tommy had often draped himself in a large green, white and gold Irish tricolour. When George discovered Tommy was now a Rangers fan, he was amazed. People who don't follow football might not grasp the sheer abnormality of such a switch. In the Ken Loach–Paul Laverty movie, *Looking for Eric* (2009), one Manchester United football supporter makes the point emphatically when he says, 'You can change your wife. You can change your religion. You can change your job. But you can never, ever change your football team.'

In the years to come, Tommy would get himself into a fankle over his football allegiances. In the late 1990s, Tommy's future QC, the Rangers-mad Donald Findlay, cracked a gag on the STV football quiz programme, *A Game of Two Halves*: 'What's red on the outside and orange on the inside?' The answer? Tommy Sheridan. Boom, Boom! Then, in 1999, the Glasgow *Evening Times* asked in a headline, 'Whose side are you really on, Tommy?' Tommy had told the newspaper of an incident when he had been threatened by a Rangers fan after an Old Firm match and the newspaper was flooded with letters making the point, 'But Tommy *is* a Rangers fan.' It had been no big secret. On one occasion in 1989, we raised a fortune outside the Old Firm Scottish Cup Final by selling 'Pay No Poll Tax' stickers in blue and green. We divided into two teams according to our own allegiances. I went with one group to the Celtic end of Hampden with green-and-white stickers, while Tommy led the blue sticker brigade at other end of the stadium.

In the 1980s, he regularly wore a royal blue football scarf around Glasgow. At a glance, it looked like a highly visible display of his support for Rangers but it was actually an Everton scarf. His affinity with the Merseyside club was probably a political gesture more than anything else. During the mid- and late 1980s, the city of Liverpool became a focal point of resistance to Margaret Thatcher's government and the struggle was led by Militant. As it happened, both Peter Taaffe, the leader of the Militant Tendency across the UK, and Derek Hatton, the Liverpool City Council front man, were avid Everton supporters.

The council's battle divided the Left across the UK, including in Scotland. In his 2004 book, *I'm Not the Only One*, George Galloway is scathing of the stance of Liverpool council in the mid-1980s. But, for others, it became a major cause célèbre. The idea of socialism was no longer just a broad philosophical theory. It was also about action, about making an instant impact on people's lives. The much-maligned Liverpool City Council managed to build 5000 brand-new council houses, construct dozens of new sports and community centres and create tens of thousands of jobs even in the midst of the biggest economic depression the city had suffered since the 1930s.

Derek Hatton was not the architect of the campaign – only its charismatic figurehead. Tommy was inspired by the flamboyant, fast-talking Scouser. In political terms, they were a generation apart. But the Liverpool councillor became something of a role model for the future Glasgow councillor. Both men shared an obsession with their appearance. Derek was the original 'sunbed socialist' and, like Tommy, spent long hours in the gym building up his physique. In the years to come, the parallels would become even more glaringly obvious. Before his election to the Scottish Parliament in 1999 at the age of 35, Tommy had generally stuck with the conventional working-class uniform of jeans, T-shirts and leather jacket but, from the day of his inauguration as an MSP, he began to flaunt the expensive designer suits which had been Hatton's trademark more than a decade earlier.

Both were highly skilled political operators with a strong populist instinct. Yet neither Derek nor Tommy had any serious interest in broad political ideas, theory, philosophy, history or culture. Twenty years before Tommy entered the infamous *Big Brother* house, Derek was already breaking with politics and starting to dabble in the glistening waters of celebrity self-infatuation. By the early 1990s, he was appearing on game shows, advertising Sekonda watches, hosting radio programmes and trying his hand at stand-up comedy.

Yet, as one star of the far Left began to fade, another began to rise. In 1986, at the same Labour Party conference in Blackpool which had expelled Hatton, an unknown young delegate from Glasgow Pollok constituency moved a resolution calling upon a future Labour government to arm the ANC's struggle against apartheid in South Africa. He electrified the hall.

Tommy Sheridan had bags of energy, drive and political ambition. Political superstardom was still somewhere in a distant galaxy but, by the early summer of 1988, the angry young university graduate from the backstreets of Glasgow was on his way.

1988–1992

A Taste of Fame

'Militant Poll Tax Plot – Extremist Group In City Power Bid' screamed the front-page headline in the *Evening Times* of 31 May 1988, alongside a photograph of a young man – now with rippling biceps – posing in a sleeveless vest in front of an anti-Poll Tax poster. A two-page spread prophetically forecast that 'Mr Sheridan is poised to become the working-class hero of the city's poll tax struggle'.

Tommy's discovery by Glasgow's evening newspaper wasn't quite the equivalent of winning *The X Factor* but it was the first step on a long road that led him to become one of Scotland's best-known celebrities. If the Poll Tax broke Margaret Thatcher, it made Tommy Sheridan. This was a tax on the poor for daring to exist. And it was tested out first in Scotland, the part of Britain that had most resoundingly rejected Toryism over and over again. It was explosive. Scotland had a defiant history of working-class resistance, from Red Clydeside in the period after the First World War to the UCS work-in of 1971–72. It also had a parallel tradition of community solidarity, usually led and organised by women, going back to the Glasgow rents strikes in 1915.

Across Scotland, community councils and tenants' associations were preparing for war. An amorphous coalition began to emerge, loosely pulling together a colourful hotchpotch of forces, from be-draggled anarchists to respectable church ministers. In Glasgow, old rivals on the political Left began to work together for the first time in a campaign that included Militant, the Communist Party, Labour Party activists, SNP members, trade unionists, anarchists and hundreds of women and men with no political affiliation at all. The goal was to build a mass non-payment campaign across Scotland, backed up by physical resistance to the debt collectors. It went far beyond the plans of some rebel Labour MPs and the SNP leadership for a more limited, token non-payment campaign by prominent individuals. There was no single architect of the strategy to combat the Poll Tax – least of all Tommy whose strengths were as a campaigner rather than a strategist.

Months before he became involved, there were already local campaigns in existence around Glasgow and Edinburgh. Within Militant, the late Chic Stevenson, then a Labour councillor – and father of Gary Lewis – had been the first to propose that resistance to the Poll Tax should be a top priority. Another Glasgow Militant Labour councillor, Larry Flanagan, had written a small photocopied pamphlet in early 1988 calling for the Labour Party to lead a community-based non-payment campaign.

In April 1988, I tried to set a strategy down in writing in a pamphlet, with the slightly condescending title, *How to Fight the Poll Tax*, which sold thousands. Before it was publicly launched, the text of the pamphlet was endorsed by a Scottish Militant all-members meeting in the Daisy Street Neighbourhood Centre in Glasgow's southside. But not everyone on the Left supported the mass non-payment campaign. In the same issue of the *Evening Times* which had catapulted Tommy into the public eye, a spokesperson for the Socialist Workers Party dismissed the grassroots movement, telling the *Evening Times*, 'Militant's strategy is diverting attention away from the Labour Party/STUC campaign. Militant is going to carry the can for the thing going down the plughole.'

It was an exaggeration to present it as Militant's campaign. Nonetheless, the organisation, with a network of committed activists across urban Scotland, was central to galvanising the campaign at local level. We provided many of the direct action shock troops which made collection of the Poll Tax impossible and pulled out all the stops to deliver tens of thousands onto the streets in a series of protest marches – the biggest in Scotland for generations. At the same time, within Militant, we made a calculated decision to release Tommy from his other responsibilities to become a full-time front man for the anti-Poll Tax movement in Scotland. I worked with him closely behind the scenes on tactics, strategy, direct action initiatives and publicity. Ronnie Stevenson, a former social worker and trade union official, took charge of the nuts and bolts operations of Militant in the West of Scotland.

Tommy became the main figurehead of the campaign. Most nights of the week he would speak at public meetings in local community halls. His delivery was superb. He would combine barnstorming denunciation of the Tories and their 'Labour lapdogs' in the councils who were implementing the Poll Tax with practical advice, including information on the legal rights of non-payers. Tommy wasn't the only anti-Poll Tax agitator – day in, day out, a sizeable team of speakers would criss-cross Scotland, rallying support for mass non-payment.

Tommy was indisputably the star performer. In some areas, he would be mischievously advertised as the speaker to attract a bigger crowd, even when he was unavailable. Jim Cameron, the chair of the Strathclyde Anti-Poll Tax Federation – and himself an eloquent speaker – used to joke that he was fed up opening all his speeches with an apology 'for not being Tommy Sheridan'.

Keith Baldassara came to Pollok from London in 1988 from the Militant HQ. Born and bred in Clydebank, where the great ocean liners were built, where the workers had seized the shipyards in the famous UCS work-in of the 1970s, where communism red in tooth and claw was mainstream politics, Keith's socialism was rooted in poverty and struggle. He had tangled with gangsters, lived in squats and raised five children, while Margaret Thatcher's market forces wreaked destruction upon his town on a scale unseen since the Luftwaffe blitz forty years before. Selfless, courageous and incorruptible, Keith is one of those people that you'd trust with your life, one hundred percent. He became Tommy's closest friend and staunchest political ally and remained so right up until November 2004. Back then, he worked tirelessly across the Greater Pollok area, building up the most densely concentrated network of anti-Poll Tax unions anywhere in Scotland and involving thousands of people of all ages.

In early 1989, we began renting a tiny office in Renfield Street in the centre of Glasgow, which became the nerve centre of the anti-Poll Tax movement in the West of Scotland. Our equipment consisted of a single telephone and a photocopier, though we later acquired an intriguing piece of cutting-edge technology known as a fax machine. From the office, we organised pub and street collections to fund the campaign and arranged a series of mass demonstrations to galvanise the non-payment movement.

A vast network of activists organised the campaign on the ground and staffed the advice hotlines. Jack Harvie, who had been working down south, returned to Scotland to work closely with Tommy and me on the central campaign. A grizzled building worker, Jack took great delight in winding Tommy up about his vanity. On one occasion, when Tommy was lashing on the moisturiser and drenching himself in aftershave in the office, Jack warned Tommy that he was going to rename him Narcissus.

Tommy swallowed the bait. 'Narcissus? What are you talking about, big man?' Greek mythology had never been Tommy's specialist subject.

'You know, the Greek god. That's who you remind me of,' said Jack.

'So you reckon I'm like a Greek god?' asked Tommy, flattered at the extravagant comparison.

'Aye, definitely. Narcissus. In fact, I'm going to call you that from now on.'

At the time, it was all dished out and taken in good humour.

By the end of 1989, over a million people in Scotland were refusing to pay. This was a campaign of civil disobedience to rival the suffragettes and the Chartists. We then began to send missionaries south of the border to spread the word, in preparation for the introduction of the tax in England and Wales a year behind Scotland. By the time it hit London, Cardiff, Liverpool and the rest, the Poll Tax was already on its last legs in Scotland, with a million and half people refusing to pay and the numbers growing week by week. By the time the Poll Tax riots swept through England, Tommy was chair of the All Britain Anti-Poll Tax Federation. On the day of the famous Trafalgar Square riot, on 31 March 1990, he spoke first at a 50,000-strong demo in Glasgow, which then marched to Queen's Park, before flying to London. It was on the flight down that he resumed his acquaintance with a girlfriend from his schooldays, Gail Healy, although it would be another couple of years before they were to get together again in a relationship.

He arrived to speak in Trafalgar Square just as mayhem was descending on central London. As TV news bulletins broadcast scenes of destruction and violence that could have been filmed in a war zone, Tommy told a press conference that the All Britain Anti-Poll Tax Federation would hold its own inquiry to identify individuals involved in violence, theft and criminal damage. He said, 'If any of those who climbed the scaffolding in Trafalgar Square and threw blocks of concrete, metal and fire extinguishers into the crowd are identified, we will have no qualms about informing the police.' Because of his comments, Tommy became a figure of hate for some fringe groups. I remember being furiously heckled at an All Britain Anti-Poll Tax Federation conference in Manchester by members of the Socialist Workers Party for defending Tommy against people who were denouncing him as a 'police informer' and a 'grass'.

On another occasion back in the early 90s, some of the other guys from Glasgow and I got involved in a skirmish at an anti-Poll Tax rally at a park in London, when a group of apparently drunken, hysterical anarchists refused to stop heckling Tommy while he was speaking. Eventually a scrap broke out. Bizarrely, one of the guys from Glasgow ended up with a long black wig in his hands, as the now short-haired 'anarchist' he had been grappling with melted away into the crowd. Had we just rumbled an agent provocateur?

At the time, the Tories were running rampant in Scotland without a shred of democratic legitimacy. The Labour Party had hoisted the white flag, even though it controlled almost every council and had two thirds of Scottish MPs. Even sections of the press began to dub them 'The Feeble Fifty'. We confronted the law not gratuitously but in the spirit of peaceful civil disobedience. We occupied sheriff officers' premises and blockaded the homes of people threatened by warrant sales. On 14 February 1991, we stormed the debt department of Strathclyde Regional Council and tore up thousands of files on Poll Tax non-payers, turning the back lane below into a winter wonderland of ripped-up pieces of paper. The Valentine's Day Massacre, we called it.

These were hard, angry days of discontent – *A Time to Rage*, as it was summed up in the title of Tommy's memoirs of the period, brilliantly written by the then *Scotsman* journalist, Joan McAlpine. Scotland was on the march – and not just against the Poll Tax. The Proclaimers had sung poignantly of Scotland's industrial disintegration, while evoking bitter historical memories of the Highland Clearances: 'Bathgate no more, Linwood no more, Lochaber no more.' The whole country was becoming more entrenched in its separate national identity. After the victory of Jim Sillars in the 1988 Govan by-election, young people on the political Left had begun to abandon Labour and gravitate towards the SNP, whose socialist rhetoric at the time was reminiscent of the old Red Clydesiders.

We began to feel imprisoned within the Labour Party. In February 1991, I wrote an internal Militant document calling for the organisation to break with Labour in Scotland and launch a new left-wing party which would advocate a Scottish road to socialism. Before the end of year, Militant and its international organisation, the Committee for a Workers' International (usually shortened to CWI) had been split asunder over the proposal, with the two most powerful figures in the movement on opposite sides. Peter Taaffe, the Merseyside-born general secretary of Militant, had strongly backed our strategy while Ted Grant, the veteran Afrikaner who had founded the movement, was equally vehement in his opposition. The new party, Scottish Militant Labour, was launched just as the anti-Poll Tax campaign reached a crescendo.

The first day of October 1991 was a grey Tuesday morning with bit of drizzle in the air. The day before, Tommy had been banned by a court order from venturing within 200 yards of the scene of Scotland's first attempted Poll Tax warrant sale. Sheriff Officers had uplifted the household goods of a Greenock family – a portable TV, a coffee table, a rosewood veneer wall unit and a display cabinet, altogether valued at £360. Now they were to be auctioned off publicly. Fearing disruption, every firm of auctioneers in Scotland refused to handle the warrant sale so the humiliating ritual was scheduled to be performed instead in the courtyard of a police detention centre in Glasgow's Turnbull Street, just a few hundred yards from the Scottish Anti-Poll Tax Federation's shop in London Road.

Tension had been building for days as the media drooled at the prospect of reporting the inevitable battle. Reporters, photographers and TV crews from all over Britain gathered outside the yard from early morning. Then at 9.30 a.m., five hundred of us marched the short journey from the shop to the forbidding iron gates of the detention centre. We tore them open and poured into the courtyard. For the next hour, there was a stand-off. A dense cordon of police guarded the transit van holding the disputed goods, while the two sheriff officers sat impassively in the front seat looking out at the protesters. 'We've had our Weetabix,' chanted the anti-Poll Tax army, parodying a TV advert of the time. The part of the yard where the police were massed was under cover but the rest of us were in the open air and now the Glasgow rain began to tumble down in earnest. 'Why is it we always get the Celtic end?' someone shouted.

As the 11.00 a.m. deadline for the symbolic ceremony crept closer, the police looked none too happy at the role they had been asked to perform. A few others and I helped Tommy up on to a crush barrier to address the crowd. As he got ready to speak, on the spur of the moment I handed him the court papers – the interim interdict, as it's called in Scotland – and suggested he rip them up for the TV cameras. It turned out to be an unintentional PR masterstroke and, for years afterwards, the footage became the defining image of Tommy Sheridan – the angry young rebel in a leather jacket, fearlessly flouting the law. The crowd now surged forward, overwhelming the police by sheer weight of numbers. As the first wave subsided, panic-stricken consultations got underway between the police, the sheriff officers and council officials. Then a spokesman appeared with a megaphone to announce, 'The warrant sale scheduled to take place at 11 a.m. today has now been cancelled.' Jubilation swept the yard and the surrounding streets. 'VICTORY' proclaimed the banner headline in the *Evening Times*, which had been so hostile to the Scottish Anti-Poll Tax Federation a few years earlier.

It was a turning point. Before the end of the year, sheriff officers in Glasgow made one last-ditch drive to smash the wall of resistance they had run into. A one-day blitzkrieg, spread across a number of housing schemes on the north side of Glasgow, turned into a rout when a thousand local people, led by Kenny Weir, Militant's organiser in the north of Glasgow, and Willie Campbell, from Springburn, drove the sheriff officers out empty-handed – though it was at the cost of twenty-nine arrests. That same week, hundreds marched through Pollok, on the other side of the city, in solidarity with the first-ever Poll Tax prisoner in Scotland, George McNeilage, who had been jailed for sixty days for obstructing sheriff officers in the Priesthill area.

Tommy was soon to become the second martyr of the anti-Poll Tax campaign. He appeared at the Court of Session in early December 1991, charged with contempt of court. We all expected a jail sentence but the punishment was severe – six months in Edinburgh's Saughton Prison. A crowd of anti-Poll Tax activists had gathered outside the Court of Session for the verdict and applauded Tommy as he was taken from the courtroom in handcuffs to a black prison van. Immediately his lawyers lodged an appeal and, a few days later, he was released pending the decision of the three appeal judges.

The night before he returned to the Court of Session for the appeal in March 1992, Keith Baldassara organised a series of street meetings across the sprawling collection of housing schemes that made up Greater Pollok. That night, up to two thousand people turned out to hear Tommy before he set off to face three appeal judges in Edinburgh the next morning.

As expected, the appeal ratified the initial sentence – six months in Saughton Prison for contempt of court, with two months remission for good behaviour. I felt more than a twinge of guilt as Tommy was bundled into a police van outside the High Court. Throughout the anti-Poll Tax campaign, I had discussed tactics with him at every turn, including during the run-up to the Battle of Turnbull Street. Tommy didn't have to be there. The warrant sale would have been stopped anyway by the five hundred solid and determined activists from the housing schemes mobilised that day by the Scottish Anti-Poll Tax Federation. Nor had it been necessary for me to urge him to publicly rip up the interim interdict. Pronouncing sentence, Lord Caplan had made a great song and dance of what was essentially a piece of theatre. 'He contemptuously tore up what appeared to be the interim interdict, which could only be taken as a representation to the crowd that they should ignore the law,' the judge had thundered.

Yet I knew also, in my heart of hearts, that if I or Keith or George or any one of hundreds of other activists had been in Tommy's shoes, we'd have done exactly the same thing. Symbolism can be potent. And, as it happened, Tommy's spell in Saughton turned him overnight into a working-class hero. Although not everyone saw it that way. The following morning, the *Daily Record* splashed a photo of Tommy in handcuffs alongside the headline: 'Downfall of a Dodger'.

Many years later, after his defamation victory, the same newspaper paid Tommy £20,000 to denounce some of his oldest allies from the Poll Tax days as 'scabs', 'rats' and 'liars' who had conspired to ruin him.

But back in the early 1990s and for many more years to come, we were like a close-knit family. We could never have dreamed how things would eventually turn out – not even in our worst nightmares.

3

1992–1998

Jailhouse Shock

Amidst the gloom of yet another Tory victory, one result of the 1992 general election stood out like a red flag. In the Glasgow Pollok constituency, a brand-new party, just six months old, had stormed into second place, defeating the SNP, the Lib Dems and the Tories. Even more sensationally, the candidate who had taken 6000 votes was Civil Prisoner 2/92 from HMP Saughton.

In the future, feature writers would paint a picture of Tommy organising his election campaign from a lonely prison cell in Edinburgh. It was a romantic story but a fairy tale. He served most of his sentence in the Training For Freedom unit, where prisoners could move freely around in a self-contained two-storey building with their own cooking facilities and a large degree of autonomy and control. They also had the right to wear their own clothes. Tommy, however, was always photographed in a prison-issue striped shirt. According to one old lag, he was the first convict in history to demand the right to wear prison uniform. To be fair, we encouraged him – I splashed the photographs of Tommy wearing a prison uniform across the front page of a four-page freesheet we distributed during the 1992 general election in April.

Support for Scottish Militant was already strong in the Pollok area, even before Tommy's jailing. He had played a part in building the movement in Pollok but others had played an even bigger role. Between 1988 and 1992, Tommy had operated mainly at a Scottish and then a British level, rather than as a local activist. While he was touring the country, speaking at meetings and rallies and conducting press interviews, his future political base in Pollok was expanding rapidly. That was mainly through the work of people like George McNeilage, Keith Baldassara and Kirsteen Walker, who lived with Tommy for a time in the late 1980s but, for whatever reason, failed to receive a mention in his memoir, *A Time to Rage*.

When Keith Baldassara arrived in Pollok back in 1988, he had intended to stay for only a few months but he never got round to leaving. Instead, he poured body and soul into building up what became the strongest, most dense network of anti-Poll Tax unions anywhere in the UK, across the sprawl of council housing schemes that made up the Greater Pollok area. In a parallel operation, George McNeilage turned the more localised community of North Pollok into a socialist stronghold. He had used his influence to encourage scores of young people to get involved in local community action. At their core was a group of fearless, streetwise young men with their origins in the local Bushwhackers gang – Colin McGregor, James McGregor, Brian Kydd and Tam Dymond. They took over the running of the local community centre and put on regular raves, charging just £2 a head. They then used the profits to fund children's Christmas parties, summer playgroups and pensioners' outings.

At a time when criminal drugs gangs were flooding the housing schemes of Glasgow with smack and jellies – heroin and temazepam – George and the young team around him organised anti-heroin rallies and concerts in the heart of North Pollok. In contrast to other deprived schemes in the city, gang-related crime, housebreaking and drug abuse started to plummet in the area. Southside gangland figures soon used intimidation to try to break into the potentially lucrative North Pollok heroin market. George's car was blown up. The community centre was set alight. On one occasion, George had a gun held to his head in front of a group of local youths. He calmly walked away, taunting the gunman for lacking the bottle to pull the trigger in front of the Pollok young team. It was a wise retreat by the would-be assassin.

During the election, Keith became Tommy's stand-in, speaking at the rallies, the debates and the street meetings and doing the rounds of the local community organisations across the vast sprawl of the Pollok constituency. Richie Venton, a dynamic Irishman originally from Fermanagh, who had been a Militant organiser in Liverpool during the Derek Hatton era, came up to Scotland to assist the Pollok general election campaign – and never went back. Richie brought a wealth of campaigning experience into the socialist movement in Scotland and, in the future, would become one of the key organisational driving forces behind the SSP.

We had a strong machine on the ground and, by polling day, literally thousands of Scottish Militant Labour window posters were on display the length and breadth of the constituency. Without that machine, Tommy would just have been another fringe candidate for yet another fringe party. When the votes were stacked up, the political journos could hardly believe what they were seeing. In a general election under the Westminster first-past-the-post system, a new party on the scene might expect to get two or three per cent of the vote at best. To get 20 per cent was unheard of.

And there was more to come. Within a month of the general election, we had made an even more startling breakthrough. From Saughton Prison, Tommy had been elected to Glasgow City Council. 'With politicians, it's usually the other way round,' we joked. It seemed amusing at the time. Nicky Bennett, another Scottish Militant Labour candidate, had also been elected in an adjacent ward. In the East End, two popular sitting ex-Labour councillors – the late Chic Stevenson and Jim McVicar, now the National Treasurer of the SSP – were re-elected against their old party with thumping majorities. The four went on to form a Scottish Militant Labour group on the council. In Drumchapel, Ann Lynch was just forty-six votes short of victory; if she had won, a coin would have been tossed to decide whether the Tories or Scottish Militant Labour should form the official opposition in the City Chambers.

At the count in the Scottish Exhibition Centre, the other parties looked shell-shocked. Dressed in their best suits adorned with brightly coloured rosettes, they could hardly believe that this ragged band of activists from the housing schemes were now storming the City Chambers. It was like the French aristocracy gazing with horror at the revolting peasants. The rafters rang as left-wing songs and chants reverberated around the cavernous hall.

Meanwhile, the press photographers focussed on Alice Sheridan, as she wandered up and down the aisles displaying a huge framed photograph of her son. It evoked the mothers of 'Los Desaparecidos' – the disappeared victims of the vicious military junta of 1970s Argentina which abducted and murdered opponents, before dropping their corpses from aeroplanes into the Rio Plata. Some of us were uncomfortable with the comparison. I was a good friend of Alice back in those days. She had been a stalwart of the anti-Poll Tax campaign and became a key Scottish Militant Labour activist in Govan, where I also lived. She was great on the streets – warm and able to connect immediately with total strangers. I admired her courage and audacity and always liked her personally. Others were less patient with some of her eccentricities. She was a spiritualist who attended séances and believed in communicating with the dead. She also doted on her son and would tell everyone that there had 'always been something very special about Thomas'. Alice made no bones about her conviction that he was destined to become some kind of political messiah.

While Tommy was in Saughton Prison, Alice set up a vigil in the grounds of the prison. One of the people who came to sleep over in the tent was Catriona Grant, a young Edinburgh woman in her early twenties who had just become involved in socialist politics. Extrovert and easy-going, she was later to become a political powerhouse within the Scottish socialist movement, driving forward progressive equality policies around women's rights and gay rights. She was one of a group of younger Militant activists, including Pam Currie, a stalwart of the Vigil for a Scottish Parliament, who were strongly in favour of Scottish independence long before Scottish Militant Labour finally shook off the old Left theology that preached the British road to socialism. Back then, Catriona admired Tommy as a brave, heroic figure. At the prison vigil, she and Alice hit it off instantly. Alice taught Catriona to jive and told her ghost stories. They became friends but, after Tommy's release, Catriona found herself unwittingly embroiled in a bizarre salvage operation to rescue him from an embarrassing debacle.

I was vaguely aware that Tommy had been juggling a handful of relationships with various young women in Scotland and south of the border. I remember laughing at a profile of Tommy in the *Guardian* at the time, which reported that 'Mr Sheridan is said to lead a fairly monastic life. He does not drink, and is not known to have any personal relationships.' I wasn't that close to Tommy socially but I had a fair idea his lifestyle was not quite that of the average Franciscan brother. Twelve years later, he would boast to the press of his early sexual exploits, telling the *Scottish Mirror* that, when he was younger, he 'was very sexually active and . . . slept with lots of women'. On *Celebrity Big Brother* in 2009, he went further, boasting how he would set himself a target for how many women he could sleep with in a single day.

From prison, he was writing to a string of women, including a nurse from Edinburgh, with whom he kept up a constant stream of correspondence. The day he came out of jail, she finally met him in the flesh. But, for Tommy, it wasn't so much love at first sight, as time to make a sharp exit. It wasn't quite what he had been expecting. But his pen pal wasn't giving up so easily. She would follow Tommy every-where – and he would go into hiding whenever she appeared. It was like one of the old Ealing comedy farces. Ominously, the young woman had kept a thick file of letters from Tommy and started threatening to go to the *Sun* newspaper. Tommy began to sweat. Catriona was dispatched by Maureen Hearns, the Scottish Militant organiser in Edinburgh, to find out how damaging the letters might be and, if possible, return them to Tommy. Using all the wile and diplomacy she could muster, Catriona persuaded the woman to show her the letters from Tommy – an excruciating mixture of gushing adolescent romance and triple-X-rated porn. Eventually, she persuaded her to hand them over.

When she gave them back to Tommy, Catriona expected a sheepish apology or perhaps a few self-deprecating jokes about the perils of enforced abstinence but his reactions mystified and disappointed her. He turned hostile and contemptuous, rarely speaking to Catriona again, even when she was elected co-chair of the SSP, except in a brusque, offhand manner. It was as though Tommy now saw Catriona as some kind of threat to his self-image.

Within Glasgow City Council, Tommy and the other three Scottish Militant Labour councillors became the voice of Glasgow's disaffected housing schemes. In 1990, the year the city was designated the European Capital of Culture, a friend of mine, John Herron, who ran a stall at the Barras, captured the mood of the schemes brilliantly. Referring to the much-hyped visit to Glasgow of the world's top opera singer, he produced thousands of T-shirts emblazoned with the immortal slogan: 'There's Not a Lot of Pavarotti for the Poveratti'.

The late Robin Cook astutely observed that 'Labour is the establishment in Scotland – but the electorate is looking for a resistance force'. In Glasgow, at least, a resistance force was beginning to take shape. By the end of 1992, another two Scottish Militant Labour councillors – Christine McVicar and Willie Griffin – had won landslide victories in regional by-elections in the sprawling jumble of decaying postwar housing schemes that made up Greater Easterhouse.

I stood in another by-election in the Govan-Drumoyne seat, a more traditional working-class shipbuilding area with an older population, and took 1771 votes – 30 per cent of the total. In other council by-elections in Glasgow and Dundee during 1992 and 1993, we came second, in front of the SNP, the Tories and the Lib Dems.

During one election campaign, in Barlanark – the scheme which gave its name to Glasgow's most notorious underworld gang – a man in his late 30s or early 40s had flaunted a large wad of cash in front of one of our canvassers, promising a £500 donation to our campaign on condition that our candidate, Willie Griffin, came personally to see him. It was a sizeable sum in those days, especially for a small, impoverished political party operating on a shoestring. Our canvasser didn't recognise the benefactor's name but Chic Stevenson, the election agent, did. Tam McGraw, also known as 'the Licensee' – a major player in the Glasgow underworld – was trying to put Scottish Militant Labour on his payroll. We politely declined.

Eventually, the SML surge began to subside. By the mid 1990s, the bitterness generated by the Poll Tax had begun to fade. And, with the Tories engulfed in one sleaze scandal after another at Westminster, it started to look as though Scotland was no longer condemned to another generation of Tory rule. There was a drift back to Labour and political passivity. Although Scottish Militant Labour continued to win an impressive minority vote, the early momentum had begun to run out of steam. By May 1995, we were down from six councillors to just one, in our North Pollok stronghold. Tommy was now the last man standing – our sole elected standard-bearer. And it stayed that way until 2003. He was an outstanding public figurehead – articulate and inspirational – and, for the next eight years, Scottish socialism came to be personified in the eyes of the public by one man.

That summer, we began to take the first tentative steps towards creating a bigger and broader movement of socialism in Scotland. Since time immemorial, the radical Left had been segregated into hostile tribes as numerous as the proliferation of Glasgow street gangs I grew up with. Their weapons were newspapers, pamphlets and verbal polemics. But some of us, at least, had begun to chill out and leave behind the entrenched political sectarianism that had historically paralysed the Left. Scottish Militant Labour had launched the Hands Off Our Water campaign in 1992, fronted by Tommy. Threatened with a rerun of the kind of mass campaign that had wrecked the Poll Tax, the Tories backed away from their privatisation plans. Scotland and Northern Ireland are still the only parts of the UK where water remains publicly owned.

Then, in 1994, we initiated a campaign against the Tory Criminal Justice Act, which threatened to open the door to the banning of protest marches and the criminalisation of gypsy travellers, hunt saboteurs and even ramblers trespassing on private land. The campaign involved almost everyone on the broad Left except the Socialist Workers Party who insisted on organising their own little rival campaign, directed from London. It brought us into contact with people we saw as quite exotic – anti-fox-hunting saboteurs, people involved in organising illegal raves and tree dwellers from 'Pollok Free State', which had been set up in the path of the M77 motorway construction site. One of those Pollok Free State eco-warriors was a quiet young woman called Rosie Kane.

One dreich December morning, with waterfalls pouring out of the skies, Scottish Militant Labour brought a team of young activists from Glasgow to the opening day of the Renfrewshire Fox Hunt to show our solidarity with the hunt saboteurs who were facing arrest under the new laws. 'Basil Brush, Basil Brush, Basil Brush,' chanted the baseball-capped young team from Pollok, Govan and the East End. The bedraggled hunt sabs looked almost as intimidated as the tally-ho brigade in their John Peel clobber.

Out of that mishmash, a new political force began to take shape. The Scottish Socialist Alliance was born in Glasgow City Halls on the morning of 10 February 1996. The journalist Ian Bell, then with *The Scotsman*, grasped the potential significance of the event more than most. Under the headline 'Rainbow Left Unites Under the Red Flag', he asked:

> Where had they all come from on a grim grey afternoon? I counted upwards of 400 spilling from one packed hall to another. And why – since socialism is now defined as the property of the passé – were so many of them so young? Come to that, why were so many of the left's lost tribes, who lived to tear lumps out of one another, sitting down amicably together? If nothing else, we now have the glimmerings of five party politics in Scotland. The fun is just beginning.

At that stage, the one-man-band myth hadn't yet taken root. It was significant that, in Ian Bell's sympathetic 1000-word report, there was just one fleeting – and vaguely disparaging – reference to the man who would become Scotland's most famous political celebrity: 'If you've seen Tommy Sheridan spit venom you don't need to be told again that righteous anger is, brothers and sisters (as he likes to say), his reason for living.'

The Scottish Socialist Alliance began as a small-scale operation, mainly based in Glasgow, Edinburgh and Dundee. At its core were several hundred battle-hardened campaigners from Scottish Militant Labour, with strong roots in some of Scotland's most deprived working-class communities. But the strength of the new movement was its diversity. It included left-wing nationalists who wanted a socialist independent Scotland, Labour left-wingers who believed their old party had sold its soul to the free market, former Communist Party stalwarts and a few ex-Green Party activists.

In 1997, the Scottish Socialist Alliance led mass movements in a number of local areas against the closure of schools and community centres. Our campaign forced the council to reprieve seventeen closure-threatened schools and, after long-drawn-out occupations, saved several community centres from the axe, including the Ladymuir Community Hall in Pollok – now the Jack Jardine Centre – and Easterhouse Community Centre. In Pollok, the campaign was led by George McNeilage and Keith Baldassara while, in Easterhouse, the two main figureheads were Frances Curran, who later became an MSP, and Jim McVicar.

On one memorable occasion, the night before Glasgow City Council's 1997 budget meeting, George McNeilage and I, along with dozens of others, gained access to the City Chambers and barricaded ourselves into the main council chamber. When the councillors arrived the next day to vote through a draconian package of cuts, they were confronted by the sight – beamed live on TV – of socialist banners draped from the balconies of their HQ, while thousands of striking council workers protested outside. The forced relocation of the council meeting was an electrifying victory, charged with symbolism. These councillors were only locked out of their palace for one day yet their package of closures would have locked tens of thousands of Glaswegians out of their local schools and community centres for all time.

As a Glasgow city councillor – and therefore the only elected public figurehead of the new movement – Tommy had been elected unopposed, almost by default, to the post of national convenor of the Scottish Socialist Alliance. But Allan Green, the national secretary became the lynchpin of the new movement. Allan was also a shrewd tactician and strategist. Sometime in late 1997, after it became clear that the new Scottish Parliament would definitely be established under proportional representation, Allan began to float with me the idea of transforming the Alliance into a cohesive political party. Allan Green had never been a member of Scottish Militant Labour so it was left to me to convince the organisation – the biggest single group within the Alliance – to make the move. In March 1998, I wrote a document entitled 'Initial proposals for a new Scottish Socialist Party'. All hell broke loose. The membership of Scottish Militant Labour overwhelmingly supported the proposal but it was resisted with venom and fury by the international organisation we were affiliated to – the London-based CWI led by Peter Taaffe.

In the future, the media would invariably describe the SSP as 'Tommy Sheridan's party'. Tommy – a councillor and the only elected politician in the new party – was the natural choice to be the party's figurehead or convenor, as we called it. Yet Tommy played only a minor role in the establishment of the new party.

Tony Blair once advised David Miliband to 'go around smiling at everyone – and get other people to shoot them.' It had some similarities with Tommy's approach. To protect his personal popularity, he tended to steer clear of internal political conflict or at least stay well back from the firing line. It was left to others, particularly Frances

Curran and me, to face the bullets. And there were plenty of them.
Peter Taaffe was a formidable operator. Originally from the shipbuilding town of Birkenhead, five minutes across the Mersey from
Liverpool, he kept himself super-fit and was a fine footballer well into
his fifties. For a long time, I had respected him and found that he
understood the nuances of Scottish politics better than most English
socialists. He was also a powerful orator, with a rich resonant Merseyside accent and a lacerating wit. But Peter was also a classic control
freak and was often on a short fuse. Some of those who used to work
alongside him in the Militant HQ nicknamed him Don Taffeone. The
CWI itself was a rigidly hierarchical organisation, directed by a ten-
strong full-time executive committee. Secret ballots were taboo. Like
the politburo of the old Soviet Union, the leaders of the CWI were
re-elected, year after year, by a show of hands. There was never any
dissent.

Frances Curran herself had once been part of Peter's inner circle.
From 1983 to 1995, she worked in Militant's fortified HQ in East
London – a vast labyrinth with its own canteen, a couple of bedrooms,
a print factory, a conference hall, a boardroom and dozens of
individual offices, all protected by high perimeter fencing, sophisticated alarms, closed-circuit TV and twenty-four-hour volunteer
guards. But she had never quite fitted the mould. For a start, she
was always easy-going, open-minded and sociable, with an effortless
charm that immediately put people at their ease. She returned to
Scotland in 1995, vaguely disillusioned with the Militant/CWI leadership in London – its dogmatism, its intolerance of dissent and its
hierarchical mindset. Yet she was as tough as they come politically.
Born and bred in Barlanark, the East-End council housing scheme
which you won't find in any tourist brochure, she had never gone to
university but, over the years, she acquired an encyclopaedic knowledge of international politics and an ability to think lucidly – a useful
asset in politics.

Frances and I had always been on the same wavelength. From 1995
onwards, we worked together to gradually push Scottish Militant
Labour towards a more clear-cut pro-independence stance, which
the CWI leaders in London tolerated with gritted teeth. We also
launched the *Scottish Socialist Voice*, the first socialist newspaper for
fifty years, which was written, edited and printed in Scotland. The
CWI leadership privately fumed at the newspaper's irreverence. They
wanted a dull propaganda organ whereas we established a lively
newspaper with humour, controversy and human interest. But it
was the proposal to wind up Scottish Militant Labour in favour of

a broader socialist party which finally provoked the CWI leaders to move to crush their rebellious Scots. For six months solid, we came under siege as they denounced our plan as reckless, irresponsible and disloyal. We stood firm and, in September 1998, with the backing of 95 per cent of the membership of Scottish Militant Labour, the Scottish Socialist Party was founded. The CWI World Congress, no less, issued a thunderous condemnation: 'This World Congress of the CWI places on record its strongest opposition to the decision to launch the Scottish Socialist Party.'

On Sunday 20 September 1998, a few hundred Scottish Socialist Alliance activists gathered in India House, the old HQ of Strathclyde Regional Council in the Charing Cross area of Glasgow, and agreed unanimously that the group should transform itself into a fully-fledged political party. There was no media fanfare but, within five years, the newly founded Scottish Socialist Party would grow into one of the strongest left-wing organisations anywhere in Europe.

Our old friends in the CWI never forgave us for this act of gross disobedience. For eight long years, they nursed their wrath to keep it warm. Then, with a few unlikely allies in tow, they came back for revenge.

4

1999–2002

The Clenched Fist Politician

Tinto Park in Govan, home of the mighty Benburb Juniors, had never seen a match quite like this before. The oldest player on the pitch was an 81-year-old woman with a twinkle in her eye. And while one of the sides was kitted out in the black and gold stripes of the local team, their rivals were elegantly attired in grey suits and sombre ties.

It was the workers versus the bosses, the socialists versus the capitalists, the people versus the fat cats. And it was possibly the most effective party political broadcast ever filmed in Scotland. It had colour, humour, passion and vision. When the five-minute tour de force was screened a week or so later, the phones were burning hot as hundreds of people from every corner of Scotland deluged the SSP headquarters with calls wanting to know more about this new political party.

Peter Mullan, who had just won the Best Actor Award at the Cannes Film Festival for his starring role in Ken Loach's *My Name is Joe*, was involved in pulling together the four-minute film. Frank Gallagher, who is best known as *River City*'s resident villain Lenny Murdoch, was there too. It was directed by the multi-talented, likeable and down-to-earth actor and film-maker Davy McKay. But, although there was no shortage of talented artists there that day, the mini-drama was to launch a much bigger celebrity on to the national stage. Tommy Sheridan was then a local councillor and reasonably well known around Glasgow for his role during the anti-Poll Tax campaign a decade earlier. He was no stranger to TV either but his appearances had generally been confined to obscure, late-night current affairs programmes. His name was mentioned in the press from time to time, though usually buried deep in the political pages of the heavy-weight broadsheets. But for the broad mass of the Scottish population, he was still an unknown quantity. All that was about to change. I had written Tommy's script to accompany the surreal football footage. He delivered it from the trackside with power and aplomb. And it was broadcast on prime-time TV. It was a revelation. One journalist hailed

Tommy as a young Sean Connery. Another described him as 'the embodiment of heroic Scottish integrity. Lantern-jawed. Cool as a fridge. Gallus.' Within a few weeks, Tommy was promoted to the new Premier League of Scottish politics – the national parliament, reborn after 300 years. Inside Holyrood, he was instantly and justifiably marked out as a star.

Some people in the SSP had argued we should take the same stance as Sinn Fein MPs and refuse to take the oath of allegiance to the crown at the swearing-in ceremony. Such a stand would have been consistent with our egalitarian, republican principles but it wouldn't have been understood by the tens of thousands of people who had voted for a socialist MSP to represent them in Holyrood. Any SSP members elected to the parliament would be instantly disbarred from taking part in any further proceedings in the parliament. Nor would they have received any salaries and allowances. We decided instead that our elected MSP, Tommy, should boycott the opening ceremony, with its medieval pageantry, its royal procession and its 21-gun salute. But, when it came to the crunch, he'd take the oath under protest, as Tony Benn and others had done in Westminster.

When the time came for Tommy to step forward, over 100 of the 129 newly elected MSPs had already sworn allegiance to the British Crown by saying, 'I [MSP's name] do solemnly, sincerely and truly declare and affirm that I will be faithful and bear true allegiance to Her Majesty Queen Elizabeth, her heirs and successors, according to law.' Tommy made his objections clear by prefacing his recital with the assurance that his oath was to the people of Scotland. He then raised a clenched fist in the air, the symbol of opposition to oppression, as he repeated the archaic words through gritted teeth. His simple gesture of defiance at the swearing-in ceremony became the most memorable image of that historic day. The Scottish political editor of *The Herald* reported that one pub in the centre of Edinburgh erupted in spontaneous applause as the image flashed across the TV news. It was splashed over the front pages of every newspaper in the land, broadcast on TV channels across five continents and reproduced on T-shirts, posters and book covers.

Inside parliament, Tommy was in his element. Over the previous decade, he had spoken at thousands of public meetings, conferences, rallies, street meetings and demonstrations. He had been a significant figure in Scotland's biggest council for the previous seven years. And, as the front man for a series of high-profile campaigns from the Poll Tax onwards, he was by far one of the most experienced orators and media operators in Holyrood. He had learned how to immerse himself single-mindedly in a campaign and master his brief to perfection. Original thinking was never his greatest strength but he knew how to tap into other people's expertise and deliver the message with confidence, power and conviction.

Tommy had also developed the acumen to build alliances across traditional political boundaries. He employed these tactical skills to devastating effect when he steered the Abolition of Warrant Sales Bill through the parliament at the end of 2000, having pulled together an influential alliance of key individuals, including the wily SNP MSP Alex Neil, the fiery independent Denis Canavan, and the Labour left-winger John McAllion, probably the most respected member of the parliament. In the final debate on the bill, McAllion delivered the killer blow to the hated and archaic debt collection procedure, his scintillating summing-up speech splitting asunder the Labour monolith. For Tommy, it was a sweet victory. In 1992, he had been dragged out of the Court of Session in handcuffs and bundled into a van bound for Saughton Prison for his part in resisting warrant sales. Here he was, seven years later, just along the road from the Court of Session, surrounded once again by TV crews, photographers and journalists. But now he was being hailed as a statesman for abolishing warrant sales, rather than being denounced as a delinquent for defying them.

Tommy came close to pulling off an even bigger coup in 2002 with his Free Schools Meal Bill. The idea had been floating around anti-poverty groups for some time and was taken up by the SSP. Although the bill failed to get through the first stage, it did force the mainstream parties to take the link between school meals, nutrition and child poverty seriously. It was in direct response to the impact of the bill that Labour and the SNP began to roll out their own, more timid schemes for extending free school meals.

Similarly, the SSP's anti-Council Tax campaign, fronted by Tommy, forced the injustice of the local tax system onto the mainstream political agenda. Again the SSP was ahead of the game by making the running on an issue that, years later, began to be taken up seriously by some of the big parties. Tommy hadn't devised the idea but he fronted the campaign in parliament, in the media and at public meetings in community halls the length and breadth of Scotland. It was Sheridan at his best. He absorbed all of the facts and figures until he could recite them in his sleep. And, as always, he argued his case with passion.

Tommy also displayed an unnerving populist instinct that, at times, verged on double standards. At a petty level, it would amount to no more than harmless political posturing. For example, he publicly lambasted Glasgow City Council's plan to build an ice rink in

Glasgow's George Square over the festive period in 2000, telling the *Evening Times*:

> The council has already made a mess of George Square. You would have thought it had learnt its lesson. It ripped out the grass without asking the public what they thought, now it wants to spends thousands of pounds on a temporary ice rink – it's a disgrace.

It was typical Tommy, pressing the buttons he knew would wind people up – wasteful public spending, lack of consultation and discontent at the civic vandalism that had recently been inflicted on Glasgow's great public gathering place. Conveniently, he had omitted to mention that he had been one of those councillors who voted to replace the grass and flowerbeds with Moscow-red concrete paving. He said to me at the time – only half-jokingly – that it would allow bigger crowds into the square to hear him speaking at demonstrations.

During his time in Glasgow City Council, Tommy had learned how to generate favourable publicity for himself by denouncing the junketing of other councillors. His popularity derived, in part at least, from his relentless campaigning against the squandering of taxpayers' money. He thundered, justifiably, against MSPs' second homes, the use of ministerial limos and the costs of the new parliament building – even calling upon Donald Dewar to resign as First Minister over the spiralling costs: 'If he's an honourable man he should fall on his own sword.' Following the Henry McLeish fiasco in November 2001, when the second First Minster was forced to resign after being caught between a 'muddle and a fiddle', Tommy boasted of firing the silver bullet. He did indeed expose an irregular office sublet that was to become the final nail that crucified McLeish. After his resignation as First Minister, other political opponents, such as John Swinney of the SNP and David McLetchie of the Tories, expressed a degree of pity for McLeish – but not Tommy. He never failed to exploit any weakness or error on the part of political opponents. 'He had to fall on his sword. He misled parliament and by misleading parliament he misled the Scottish people.' The following March, Tommy put down a motion to the Scottish Parliament calling for the former First Minister to resign as an MSP. In August 2002, he made an official complaint to the Holyrood Standards Committee alleging that McLeish had misled parliament by failing to declare allowances. And, in December 2002, he lambasted the Standards Committee's report as 'a whitewash' and ripped into McLeish for misleading Parliament:

'He made a clear statement to Parliament, then did the exact opposite. To most ordinary Scots that constitutes lying. This kind of behaviour brings all politicians and the Parliament into disrepute.'

From 1999 onwards, the Scottish Socialist Party was surging ahead. The new Scottish Parliament had created a buzz and now at least some of the big debates were taking place closer to home, under the full glare of the Scottish media spotlight, rather than behind closed doors in the obscure back corridors of Westminster. For the SSP, having a toehold in the parliament was vital – especially when our representative was such a talented and experienced operator.

Outside parliament, the SSP was building up a vibrant network of branches from the far-flung Shetlands across to the Western Isles and down to the English border. Tommy toured Scotland tirelessly and, in community centres and village halls across the country, people packed into public meetings to hear what all the fuss was about. Several Labour councillors in Glasgow defected to the SSP. SNP activists were also signing up in significant numbers, including an entire branch in the East End of Glasgow. Jim Sillars wrote in his column in the *Scottish Sun* that 'the SSP has the kind of elan, flair, and infectious enthusiasm that was once the hallmark of the SNP.'

A parade of actors, writers and academics publicly backed the party, including: the Fife-born Hollywood heart-throb, Dougray Scott; the Glasgow cult band, Belle and Sebastian, who played some fund-raising gigs for us; Peter MacDougall the playwright; and Jackie McNamara Sr, the Hibs football legend. In November 2000, the writers James Kelman, Tom Leonard, Alistair Gray and William McIlvanney all came to the Glasgow launch of *Imagine*, the book published by Canongate under the joint names of Tommy and me. Support came from some improbable quarters. Orkney-based Peter Maxwell Davies, the Queen's official composer – the musical equivalent of the poet laureate – came out in support of the SSP. The radical Edinburgh priest, Steve Gilhooley – who later left the Catholic Church – joined the party and, in his Edinburgh *Evening News* column, described how he had chatted to a group of priests outside a funeral and discovered that every one of them had now switched their vote from Labour to the SSP. Richard Holloway, a former Episcopalian bishop – now Chair of the Scottish Arts Council – compared Tommy Sheridan to Jesus Christ. Colin Bell, a former Executive Vice-Chair of the SNP and distinguished BBC broadcaster, also signed up, contributing a weekly diary piece to the *Scottish Socialist Voice* and hosting media workshops for our election candidates.

Steve McGrail, a major shareholder in his family's brass manu-facturing company, ploughed £30,000 into the party in the year running up to the 2003 election. There was even press gossip that the aristocratic celebrity chef Lady Claire MacDonald, from the Isle of Skye, was backing the SSP. And the SNP icon, Sean Connery, praised Tommy Sheridan in glowing terms: 'He's remarkable. That's the kind of fella, the spirit one wants to see.' But that was just the icing on the cake. It helped to give us a bit more kudos with the media – but much more important was what was happening on the ground. The party was vibrant and growing stronger by the day. A university study of our 2001 general election candidates found that more than half had only joined the SSP in the previous two years, after the party had already been launched. The old Marxist-Trotskyist-Communist Left still had influence in the leadership but the SSP had grown much larger than the sum total of the combined old Left. It was a brand-new party, made up overwhelmingly of people who had never before been active in politics.

With the bandwagon at full throttle, even the Socialist Workers Party began to make overtures. They had been hostile to the SSP from its first incarnation as the Scottish Socialist Alliance. In November 1998, just after the SSP was launched, I had debated with the SWP's national organiser at an all-Britain conference they held in Glasgow. Chris Bambery, who had been a pupil at Loretto, an exclusive private school in Musselburgh just outside Edinburgh, at the same time as Alistair Darling, told his stamping, cheering supporters:

> The difference between Alan and myself is what sort of party we need. There is a fundamental divide between reform and revolution. There is a river of blood between them. The attempt of the Scottish Socialist Party to bridge this divide, to have people from the social democratic tradition, the reformist tradition and the revolutionary tradition in the same party, is fundamentally wrong.

Two years later, they were knocking at the door. We held a series of face-to-face meetings in Glasgow, involving representatives from the SSP executive and the SWP's British Central Committee. Tommy was especially enthusiastic about bringing the SWP into the fold not because he had any respect for them but because it would be a financial boost for the SSP. He was desperate to employ more organisers in the regions to help us build for the 2003 Scottish general election. Allan Green and I were more cautious and insisted on conditions. Others in the party were convinced that this was a Trojan horse raid and wanted to keep the gates barred to what they regarded as a zealous, self-righteous sect.

The SWP agreed to every condition. Yes, they would go along with Scottish independence which they had always haughtily derided. Yes, they would stop selling their own newspaper, published in London, and would start selling the Glasgow-based *Scottish Socialist Voice* instead. Yes, they would stop organising as a rigid, monolithic bloc and become a loose grouping of kindred spirits, breaking from the robotic regimentation which had always been their hallmark – they called it discipline; we called it mind control.

Eventually they were admitted into the SSP, though there remained more than a few sceptics in our ranks. Their scepticism was well founded. They came to meetings in a pack, determined to foist their own priorities on everyone else. These priorities were always decided in London and conveyed down the hierarchical pyramid. The duplicity of the faction was lampooned by *The Scotsman*'s Robert McNeill when, after the libel case in 2006, he recalled an SSP conference he had once reported on:

> The people behind me kept sniggering at the various speakers and saying how awful it all was. I thought they must be from some reactionary media outfit. Then one of them strode forward to the microphone to declare how impressed she'd been with the various contributions and how glad she was that her faction was now joining them. That was the Socialist Workers.

It had been an amazing feat to pull together such a disparate party. The SSP now included people who had lived and worked in Cuba alongside Che Guevara and Fidel Castro, and groups like the Socialist Workers Party who dismissed the revolutionary Caribbean island as just another capitalist state. It included British centralists who had, in the past, opposed even mild devolution, alongside hard-line nationalists, such as the small Scottish Republican Socialist Movement, who had been preaching the cause of independence back in the days when almost the entire Left was advocating the British road to socialism.

By this time, Tommy, Frances and I, together with the vast majority of the old Scottish Militant Labour group, had broken completely with our old friends in the CWI. After May 1999, we had tried to get on with things. The debate was over. But not for them it wasn't. The success of the new party was living, breathing proof that the cardinals of Marxism in London were not infallible. But, instead of admitting that they had been mistaken, the CWI began to pretend to themselves and anyone else who would listen that the SSP was a flop. They belittled every success and exaggerated every weakness. While Labour and the Tories attacked our proposal to replace the Council Tax with a redistributive Scottish Service Tax as a revolutionary fantasy, the CWI ridiculed it as a paltry reform. They denounced us for 'pandering to nationalism'. Every week they would scour Tommy's columns in the *Daily Record* and, later, the *Mirror* to sniff out any words or phrases that might deviate from their dogmatic Trotskyist orthodoxy. They'd then quote these heresies with glee in their party newspaper as evidence of the 'political degeneration' of Tommy Sheridan and the SSP. They even publicly attacked Tommy in a press release – carried in the *Record* – as a 'neo-Stalinist' because he had expressed sympathy for the Cuban government.

Tommy was furious and he fired off a letter to Taaffe:

It is with a mixture of sheer astonishment and deep disappointment that I feel compelled to write this letter to condemn your actions. You have committed a cardinal sin within the socialist movement. You have put our disagreements into the hands of the anti-working-class, anti-democratic and anti-socialist press and media. You and the CWI stand condemned for your anti-socialist actions. You don't run to our enemies when you fall out with socialists. You should be ashamed of your actions.

It was an over-the-top response, like using a machete to swat a fly. Yet it's a funny old world, as Margaret Thatcher once observed. Five years later, Tommy would join forces with the CWI and their arch-enemies, the Socialist Workers Party, to split the SSP asunder and found Solidarity. It was a strange threesome, even for Tommy, noted our press officer Ken Ferguson.

During the early days of the Scottish Parliament, Tommy began to cultivate a more respectable persona. He would rarely be seen in public without a collar and tie – not just inside the parliament or in the TV studios but everywhere he went. At SSP meetings and conferences, he would stand out like a well-manicured chief executive strutting around the shop floor. It never really bothered us though. Vanity was just one of Tommy's harmless foibles – or so we thought at the time.

For the media, Tommy was hot property. He gave interviews galore to glossy magazine supplements. These were rarely about politics.

Instead he poured out the details of his private life – his undying love for Gail, his childhood, his relationship with his mother, everything. He nurtured an image of himself that made John-Boy Walton look like the gangsta rapper from hell. A typical profile in the *Sunday Herald* in 1999 had described the non-smoking teetotaller, whose only vice was a penchant for ultraviolet rays, as 'so clean-cut your mother would do back-flips if you brought him home . . . He is pleasant and respectful, showing people to the door as they leave, shaking their hands and thanking them for coming.'

In contrast to other prominent Scottish political figures of the time – Alex Salmond, Donald Dewar, Jim Wallace, David McLetchie, Robin Harper – Tommy's family life was as public as a shopping mall and as sugary sweet as a stick of candyfloss. In February 2000, he even paraded down the catwalk hand in hand with Gail at the National Wedding Exhibition, where he cut the ribbon. Four months later, I was among the 200 guests at their wedding in Our Lady of Lourdes Church in Glasgow, where a battery of press photographers waited outside to photograph Gail and Tommy, resplendent in his Maclean tartan, before we headed off for the reception in the Moir Hall, which is now part of the refurbished Mitchell Library.

It was all a facade, as we were later to discover. I had a fair suspicion that Tommy's personal life wasn't quite as squeaky clean as a Fairy Liquid advert but, then, I wasn't too concerned. The old sleaze scandals of the 1980s when Tory MPs were regularly caught in compromising positions with Dalmatian dogs while their friends jammed tubes of Smarties up their orifices generally left me shrugging my shoulders. I couldn't care less what they got up to in private – it was what they got up in parliament that was the problem.

But a few dim warning signs began to flash. At the SSP's Socialism 2001 event, in November, Nick McKerrel, a party member in Glasgow, approached me about a tip-off he had received indirectly from a Glasgow *Evening Times* journalist through a mutual acquaintance. Someone had claimed to have spotted Tommy in a sex club in Manchester and had contacted the newspaper. In the cafeteria of Glasgow Caledonian University, where the event was being held, I asked Tommy point-blank if he had been in Manchester recently. He told me that he had visited the city the previous month to speak at an anti-war meeting.

'And did you visit a sex club while you were there?'

Tommy angrily dismissed the suggestion as ridiculous. 'Do you think I'd be so stupid? I'd be crucified. This is just another concoction – probably from someone looking for easy money.'

I had no reason to disbelieve Tommy's denial. It was convincing. And he was right – the *Daily Record* in particular had been running a vendetta against Tommy and the SSP all year. A visit to a sex club would be just what the editor ordered. Tommy was a smart operator – he wouldn't be so crazy. But, then, he had admitted that he had been in Manchester. A glimmer of suspicion lingered.

2002–2003

Warning Signs on the M8

Keith Baldassara sounded unnaturally agitated. 'I need to meet you right away, face-to-face,' he told me. It sounded like trouble ahead.

Driving through the grey November morning, I pondered the possibilities. Maybe Keith wanted out. That would be understandable. For years, he had shouldered a heavy burden as the main organisational driving force in our Pollok heartland and as Tommy's caseworker. Over the previous couple of years, Tommy's fame had grown rapidly and the SSP had benefited politically. But, as his celebrity status soared, his caseload had expanded, like a river bursting its banks, and Keith's workload had escalated out of control.

In a hostile analysis of the SSP in the *New Statesman* in 2001, Tim Luckhurst, a former editor of *The Scotsman*, had pinpointed one of the key reasons behind the rising tide of Scottish socialism in 2001. It wasn't so much the political programme of the party, he suggested, it was '[g]etting housing benefit claims sorted, arranging new tenancies, cleaning stairwells and organising repairs'. I never actually saw Keith with his mop and bucket cleaning a stairwell but he was the man sorting out benefits, housing exchanges, repairs, debt problems and complaints about crime and antisocial behaviour. He was the man hounding the officials, making the phone calls, writing the letters, arranging the meetings, negotiating with the authorities, listening to the grievances.

Tommy would get flooded with thank-you cards, praising him for the help he had given and the problems he had solved. He displayed them proudly on the walls of his office. For the senders of the cards, it was an excusable case of mistaken identity. Almost all of their problems had been sorted out by Keith Baldassara. While Tommy was making eloquent speeches in parliament, and cultivating journalists and celebrities, Keith was neck-deep in the raw sewage of human misery.

On top of that, Keith was also the national treasurer of the SSP, which meant juggling with the bills daily, dealing with the banks and the accountants, organising fund-raising events and sorting out wages and expenses. If he now decided he'd had enough, it would be out of character but who could blame him? Yet, at that point, he was irreplaceable. If Keith were to walk, it would leave a gigantic void at the heart of the organisational structure of the party.

As it happened, I was half right. Keith was on the point of resignation but not for the reasons I had imagined. When we met in the Costa cafe attached to Harthill Services on the M8, halfway between Glasgow and Edinburgh, I could see anger and disappointment tattooed all over his face – and the target of his fury was Tommy. The two were close friends. One of three best men at Tommy's wedding a couple of years before, Keith was also close to Gail, to Tommy's mother Alice and to his sister Lynn – a member of the SSP and gay rights activist. He was virtually an honorary family member. And what he was telling me made my blood run cold. It wasn't the morality that bothered me so much as the reckless stupidity of Scotland's favourite clean-cut boy next door.

The May 2003 elections were just six months away and we were running high in the polls. We knew we were within reach of the biggest socialist electoral breakthrough since Jimmy Maxton and the Independent Labour Party won six parliamentary seats in Glasgow in the 1930s. Hundreds of people, maybe even thousands, had given their time, their money, their sweat and their tears to this new force for socialism. Not just in Scotland but across Europe and even worldwide, people were inspired by the success of this red-blooded socialist party and its charismatic figurehead. Despite the polls, we knew we had a tough battle on our hands. Sections of the media, especially the hostile, pro-Labour *Daily Record*, would be out to stop this bandwagon. They'd ridicule our politics and, if that didn't work, they'd begin digging the dirt. But up until now, there hadn't been much dirt to dig. Then, as though a tsunami had just swept in over Portobello Beach, the landscape had changed. Tommy, it now transpired, had been living a semi-secret life more akin to that of a 1970s porn star than the leader of a socialist party challenging inequality and exploitation. Live sex shows – with the boy wonder himself in the starring role. Three-in-a-bed sex sessions in a hotel suite with his brother-in-law and a woman flown up from England. Repeated visits to a seedy Manchester sex club. In these naive days, I would have guessed that Cupids swingers' club was a dating agency for lonely golfers. Keith put me in the picture. I began to wonder if I'd led a sheltered life.

His story began back in 1995, when he had stormed out of a stag night organised by Tommy in a Pollok bar. The local socialist councillor for Pollok, as he was then, had laid on the evening's entertainment – a hardcore stripper performing live sex acts in front of an all-male but suitably mortified audience. While others cringed, Tommy, as a man of the world, was in his element. He would later boast in football shower rooms of his prowess in front of a live audience. And he wasn't talking about public speaking or karaoke.

Years later, in 2002, the embarrassing episode reared its ugly head once again. Andy McFarlane, a social care worker from Glasgow, had just tied the knot with Gail's sister, Gillian. Keith and Tommy were there at the reception – and George McNeilage too – in the lush Winter Gardens of the People's Palace in Glasgow Green. The table they shared included a mysterious businessman, known to Keith at that time only as Hadgie.

'Just watch what you say in front of Keith – he's a bit of a puritan,' mocked Tommy. 'This is the man who walks out of stag nights when a stripper comes on.'

At first, Keith was irritated. He thought this was just a gratuitous attempt by Tommy to belittle him in front of the lads. Later that night, as the drink flowed and the tongues loosened, the reason for Tommy's comment became clear. His jocular taunt had a calculated purpose. It was a warning to the others at the table – no loose talk in front of Keith.

According to Keith and several others present, Andy boasted of the previous evening's 'night of madness' in a Glasgow hotel involving 'a woman who had been flown up from Birmingham'. Hadgie – later to be revealed as Matt McColl, the coach of Arthurlie Junior Football Club – described the events of the night before as 'unbelievable'. Tommy and Andy had been 'unleashed', he explained, and were 'absolutely demented'. It had been too much even for Hadgie who had to get out of the way.

Challenged by Keith, Tommy's attitude was supercilious – he behaved like an irritated schoolteacher sarcastically reprimanding a recalcitrant pupil. 'Yes, Keith, you're right. I was in the hotel with Andy and these women. I am an adult. And so are the women. And, no, they're not prostitutes. They're swingers. They do this because they enjoy it. So it was consensual.' Anyway, he added lamely, 'I didn't participate.' In the face of this implausible denial, there wasn't much Keith could do. But he refused to speak to Tommy for a fortnight and began to write a letter of resignation. 'I can't work with this guy,' he thought.

There was pattern emerging. Eight months before, Tommy had boasted to friends about a trip he had made to a sex club in Manchester. Through mutual friends, the word had got back to

Keith. When he challenged Tommy about it, he was evasive – neither confirming nor denying it. But Keith knew it was true. He later tore up his resignation letter. He had only recently taken on a mortgage and he wasn't just Tommy's employee – he was working for the party, for the cause. He gritted his teeth and got on with it.

Then, in November 2002, Tommy had asked Keith to travel with him by car to Lanarkshire to a vigil for the Chhokar family, whose son had been murdered in a racist attack. Instead of getting the bus with everyone else, he wanted to talk privately to Keith. In the car, Tommy hinted darkly that something might soon be appearing in the press.

'You've not been back down Manchester?' asked Keith, incredulously. He had – this time with a different group. 'Here we go again,' thought Keith. He lashed into Tommy for his selfish irresponsibility. Tommy was none too happy either. As far as he was concerned, Keith had no right to be angry or ask awkward questions about his employer's conduct. On the way home, they sat in silence.

The next morning, Keith was in a committee room in the City Halls in Glasgow where a group of SSP activists were meeting to organise the distribution of a special four-page election broadsheet we had produced. Tommy arrived, accompanied by Paul Holleran, the Scottish Organiser of the National Union of Journalists. Tommy explained to Keith that they were planning to take legal action against the *Daily Record*.

Although I never made any connection at the time, the strange political invective that the newspaper had begun to direct against Tommy hinted that it had something on him. A couple of weeks before Tommy's conversation with Keith, the paper had carried an article about Tommy under the byline of political editor Paul Sinclair headlined 'NO WHORE LIKE AN OLD WHORE'. He wrote, 'So much for him [Tommy Sheridan] trying to play the virgin in the brothel. He's a whore like the rest of them – or maybe slightly worse.'

Two years later, when Tommy did begin legal action to prevent publication of the story, it was mythologised as a battle against the Murdoch Empire. But his initial target was neither the *News of the World* nor the *Sun* but the *Daily Record*.

'This man is seriously unhinged,' thought Keith. He left the City Halls and walked the short distance to Tommy's top-floor office in the City Chambers, where Keith also sometimes worked. From there, he phoned me in Edinburgh and arranged to meet me on the M8 later that day. A few days after we met, Keith told Tommy he had spoken to me and Tommy was furious. 'You've what? You've broken my confidence,' he raged. He stormed off and went into a sulk, refusing even to speak to Keith for a few weeks. It was the beginning of a slow cooling in their relationship, which eventually turned into a cold war.

The following week, I met Tommy in the deserted members' lounge of the City Chambers. We faced each other tensely across the plushly carpeted room, the smell of fresh coffee mingling with the scent of his cologne. The lounge looked out over George Square, an iconic site for the Scottish socialist movement. This was the scene of the Battle of George Square in 1919, when the tanks rolled in, backed up by 12,000 English troops, on the day the Red Flag was hoisted over the City Chambers. From here, the great Poll Tax marches set off, 50,000 strong, on 31 March 1990, led by a band of self-styled 'mad pipers' in ragged Highland dress. It was from here, too, that we marched illegally against the Tory Criminal Justice Act three times over – Nicky McKerrel and I were charged with organising the illegal demos but we were never prosecuted. On the day he had been released from Saughton Prison in 1992, Tommy had been carried shoulder-high across George Square by George McNeilage and Matt Smith, from Queen Street Station into the City Chambers. And it was down there on George Square that seven of us – Linda Thompson, Tommy, Keith, me, Andy Lynch, Paul Couchman and Tam McGhee – had camped out on a seven-day hunger strike against Poll Tax benefit deductions during the Italia 1990 World Cup.

And here we were older, greyer and more battle-scarred. We had come a long way together through hard times and exhilarating times. The party that had been forged out of these campaigns was now a credible national force. In the latest opinion polls for Holyrood, we were now running at 9 per cent, just one point behind the Tories. Tommy had been a fantastic asset, indispensable to the rise of the new party. Indeed, for the wider public, Tommy Sheridan *was* the SSP. Since his election on 6 May 1999, he had come to personify not just the socialist politics of the SSP but a new kind of politics based on straight talking, decency and self-sacrifice in pursuit of a noble cause. 'The eyes are deep pools of integrity,' wrote the veteran pro-Labour commentator, Tom Brown in a smitten profile in the *Daily Record*. His only flaw was 'a surfeit of sincerity'.

Tommy was a practised maestro in the art of body language. He could turn on the charm like a light switch, especially with journalists and other people he considered valuable acquaintances. He could transmit sincerity with the professional efficiency of a BBC newsreader reciting lines from an unseen autocue. He was equally capable of conveying a subtle hint of menace when he felt under threat.

In the City Chambers, he stared across the room, holding my gaze unblinkingly, like an oncoming vehicle with full-beam headlights on a dark road. His lips were pursed, his shoulders pushed back and his chest thrust out defiantly. He responded to my questions with long silences. I had seen him throw people off their stride, making them stutter and stumble when confronted with this machine-like will. But I knew it was a well-rehearsed act, a dominance display designed to intimidate.

I restrained my anger and calmly expressed my sense of betrayal and disappointment. I asked him where his brains were located, though I put it rather less politely that. I reminded him that, back in 2001, I had warned him that someone was trying to sell a story to the media about his visit to a sex club and he had denied it. Now I had discovered, first, that his denial had been dishonest and, second, that he gone back to the same club six months later and with a group of friends in tow, who were now bragging to others. Unbelievable.

Tommy knew better than anyone that the SSP and socialism had many sworn enemies. They would dearly love to get their hands on this information and they would use it mercilessly. What if this information was to explode into the public domain in the middle of the election campaign? Our policies on the Council Tax, free school meals, the wars in Iraq and Afghanistan, nuclear weapons, independence and socialism would be forgotten amidst the general hullabaloo over Tommy's bizarre behaviour. Tommy himself would be engulfed in a tidal wave of derision, ridicule and contempt. It would eventually die down but it could blow apart our election campaign. His behaviour had been reckless, selfish and irresponsible. He owed his fame to the sacrifice of hundreds of others. Yet now he was playing Russian roulette not just with his own reputation but also with the prospects of the political party he had come to personify. Our members deserved better and I pulled no punches.

But, at that stage, I made no moral judgement. In the book *Imagine*, published under both our names, I had torn into 'the moral Gestapo' of the tabloid press. They were the modern equivalent of the eighteenth-century Kirk ministers – the Holy Willies – who would force 'sinners' to sit on the 'creepie chair', where they were mercilessly denounced for offending the rigid sexual codes of Calvinism. Tommy thanked me for concentrating on the potential damage to the party. 'You're taking a political stand on this and I accept everything you're saying,' he said. 'But wee Keith – he's just on his moral high horse.'

Keith had a perfect right to be on his moral high horse. Although our primary concern was the political consequences, this wasn't just about what some people later mocked as 'bourgeois morality'. It was rather more than just a matter of marriage vows and personal infidelity. It was about the commercial sex industry and the exploitation of women for personal gratification. It was also about hypocrisy – not only in the sense that Tommy's secret life stood in stark contrast to his brashly advertised marital status but because, as a Glasgow city councillor and an MSP, Tommy would be called upon to vote on issues such as the licensing of lap-dancing clubs and the outlawing of kerb-crawling.

Back in the City Chambers, Tommy's defiance had evaporated. He was now sheepishly accepting that his behaviour had been out of order. But he projected no sense of contrition – only supreme confidence that his escapades would never be revealed. 'There's no photographic evidence and none of the people who were with me will ever talk. They're all close friends.' I didn't press him to name any of the other names.

I returned to our conversation of the previous year, when I had warned him about a story circulating around the Scottish Media Group, the publishers of *The Herald* and the *Evening Times*. If this was so watertight, why was it being discussed in media circles back in November 2001? Tommy did admit that he had spoken to a Scottish guy – from Edinburgh, he thought. 'He might have then tried to sell a story but how could he ever back it up without revealing his own identity? People who go to these kind of clubs can't go around advertising it to the rest of world.' Despite Tommy's lack of any trace of concern, I had a gnawing fear that this might well come back to haunt us. We left it at that. For the next six months, Keith and I kept our lips sealed – and our fingers crossed.

Meanwhile, the war drums were beating on the other side of the Atlantic, and in Downing Street dodgy dossiers were being cobbled together. Within a few months, millions of people would march on the streets in a vain attempt to stop the coming slaughter.

As the days rolled on towards the May Day election, support for the SSP was growing but a nagging fear gnawed away somewhere deep inside me. A single front-page splash in the *Daily Record* or the *Sun* could turn our hopes to ashes overnight. However, as it turned out, Tommy was right – they had nothing. And, by the close of polls, we were confident that we had made a mighty leap forward. That night, as the ballot papers were being counted, I made my way to the old BBC studios in the West End of Glasgow. As the party's election coordinator, I hadn't been a candidate in the election so I didn't have to be present at any of the election counts. More or less by default, I was sent along as the voice of the Scottish Socialist Party for the election night special, hosted by Kirsty Wark. All through the night a rotating parade of high-ranking politicians from the big parties paraded in and out to do their stint in front of the cameras. Alex Salmond, Menzies Campbell, Douglas Alexander, Brian Wilson and a host of others came and went as the night wore on. I had no replacement. All our people were tied up at their election counts. But the small parties had become the most interesting show in town and the producers wanted me to stay. In the depths of the old BBC HQ, I couldn't get a mobile phone signal so, by the time I finally escaped from the studio, well after dawn, I still had no idea of the sheer scale of our breakthrough. I thought we might have won three seats, maybe four at a push.

I knew that, in Glasgow, Tommy had been re-elected and joined by Rosie Kane, the number two on our list for the city-wide seat. Word had also come through on the BBC that Frances Curran had been elected in the West Scotland and Carolyn Leckie in Central region. As I was leaving the studios, I got a phone call from an excited Catriona Grant telling me that Colin Fox had just been elected in the Lothians. One of the most memorable images on the TV news that night was of Colin leaping around the counting hall in Meadowbank, intoxicated with victory. Based on that performance, I'd have bet on him to win the Grand National.

Later that morning, I went to the Scottish Exhibition and Conference Centre where they were now counting the votes for the Glasgow City Council elections. Across Scotland's biggest city, the SSP had annihilated the Tories, the Lib Dems and the Greens and had come within a whisker of replacing the SNP as the main opposition force in the city. Keith Baldassara had won Tommy's old council seat in Pollok resoundingly and, out in the Vale of Leven – the old industrial belt that runs almost to the shores of Loch Lomond – a sitting SSP councillor, Jim Bollan, had been re-elected by a landslide onto West Dunbartonshire Council.

We had narrowly failed to make the breakthrough in Fife, the Highlands and North-East Scotland. Still, for a small party, less than five years old, to win five seats was glorious achievement. The votes across the South of Scotland had still to be counted but, realistically, few of us expected to win a seat from the vast and predominantly rural region. It wasn't until late in the afternoon, as we were gathering for a victory press conference in the Glasgow Film Theatre, that the shock news came through – Rosemary Byrne had been elected in the South of Scotland. It was a political earthquake. Six Scottish Socialist MSPs

– and the Greens had done even better with seven. Scotland's grey-suited parliament had been daubed with a large splash of scarlet and emerald.

Even the hardened hacks of the Holyrood press pack looked impressed. They certainly brightened up when Rosie Kane promised madness and mayhem. 'It'll be like the *Big Brother* house,' she predicted, tongue-in-cheek. It was meant as a joke but, by the end of the following year, even Rosie had stopped joking.

6

1999–2004

Behind the Scenes

In the drab and dusty world of party politics, Tommy stood out like the aurora borealis. He had the matinee idol looks of a Hollywood star, the vocal power of a Christian fundamentalist preacher and the persuasive techniques of a door-to-door salesman.

The TV cameras and the political journalists loved him – and the love affair was mutual. Only the crème de la crème of celebrities anywhere achieve the level of fame that allows them to be instantly recognisable by their first name. For headline writers in Scotland, Tommy, like Elvis and Kylie, needed no surname.

Apart from politics, his big passion was football. Gail used to complain that, when they went on holiday to exotic locations, Tommy only wanted to sit in his hotel room watching football on satellite TV. He was good footballer though, by his own admission, a bit slow. Even as an MSP, he continued to train a couple of nights a week and played in the Junior League with Baillieston and East Kilbride Thistle and as player-coach of St Anthony's.

For all his gifts and skills, Tommy looked more impressive from a distance than up close. Those of us who knew him well were always aware of his lack of breadth. That wasn't a problem. Just as a football team requires strikers, midfielders, defenders and a goalkeeper, so a political movement needs a range of different skills and talents. Tommy had studied political economy at university and could comfortably plough through documents on the Council Tax, for example, or on poverty and had a good memory for statistics but, otherwise, he read very little – perhaps the occasional political book by someone like John Pilger or Tony Benn. He had zero interest in fiction, poetry, drama, art, science or philosophy. One time, back in the 1990s, he opened his briefcase beside me at a press conference in Dundee and out spilled a copy of the fashionable women's magazine *Cosmopolitan*, which he had been reading on the train. I quickly slipped it back inside bag before it became an embarrassing diary item in the next morning's edition of the Dundee *Courier*.

His favourite films were Hollywood blockbusters of the *Mission Impossible* genre. In a 2007 interview, he singled out *Shrek* as his favourite movie, typically highlighting the fact that, in *Shrek 2*, the trade union movement got a mention. He also said that he had watched *Spartacus* and *Gladiator* many times – and it wasn't difficult to imagine Tommy visualising himself in the Kirk Douglas and Russell Crowe roles. His musical tastes centred on middle-of-the road, mainstream pop – Rod Stewart, Billy Joel and The Eagles.

Later, he hung a portrait of Burns in the hallway of his home but it was something of an affectation. When the *Daily Record* gave sixteen Scottish MPs and MSPs a line from some famous Burns' poems and asked them to recite the next line, Tommy came bottom of the class with just one out of five. He did manage to guess what the next line was after 'Should auld acquaintance be forgot', in the song 'Auld Lang Syne'. One of his favourite quips was, 'For most Glaswegians, culture is something that grows on your walls.'

This narrow, utilitarian focus had its advantages. He was a powerful parliamentary performer and gave the political journalists exactly what they wanted. His formidable skills led sections of the political media to overestimate his stature in relation to his own party. According to the folklore created by the small knot of political journalists based in Holyrood, the SSP was a one-man band with the rest of the membership only there to make up the numbers. The media has always preferred to focus on colourful personalities, rather than allowing life to become cluttered with complications. That's what sells papers. People love to read about larger-than-life characters, celebrities, heroes and villains.

That impulse to oversimplify history was strikingly illustrated in the aftermath of the Glasgow airport terrorist attack in 2007, when the baggage handler John Smeaton became lionised as a kind of William Wallace meets Forrest Gump character. Later, an anti-John Smeaton backlash erupted with claims he had exaggerated his own role and diminished the role of others. It wasn't really fair – Smeato never claimed to have taken on the suicide bombers single-handedly. But, for the media, there was only room for one Batman or Superman so they created a legend. It wasn't so much what John Smeaton had done – it was what he had said and how well he had said it. It was pretty much the same story with Tommy Sheridan. Other political parties – even small parties – were never dismissed so lightly as the personal property of one individual. The Scottish Green Party, for example, which also had one MSP elected in 1999, was rarely described as

Robin Harper's Green Party but, then, Robin didn't quite fit the bill of swashbuckling superhero.

Far from being a one-man band, the SSP, by 2003, was an ensemble of individuals with a broad range of skills and talents that had begun to blend together into a powerful sound. Unlike the Berlin Philharmonic and the rest, this was an orchestra without a conductor. There never was a single commanding figure directing operations. Although the term 'leader' was used by the media to describe Tommy's role, his official title within the SSP was 'convenor'. The leaders of Scotland's four biggest political parties all have the power to make appointments and to take policy decisions. The resulting hierarchical structure, with its echoes of feudalism, tends to generate a culture of subservience, particularly among ambitious MPs and MSPs who hanker after the prestige of ministerial portfolios and suchlike.

As SSP convenor Tommy had neither the power of patronage nor the authority to change party policy. He rarely even convened meetings. In practice, his role was as a mouthpiece for the party. Policies were decided democratically by the annual party conference or the bi-monthly national council and were binding on all elected representatives. In between times, leadership was exercised collectively by the executive committee, which is elected annually by secret ballot. Tommy, like any other party member, could only exert influence through persuasion and example. In some spheres, he did command influence – for example, between 1999 and 2003, when he was the SSP's sole representative in Holyrood, he was left to take many of the routine daily voting decisions within the parliament. But, when it came to general strategy, others played a bigger role.

The five new MSPs who joined Tommy in 2003 were each formidable political figures in their own right. Rosemary Byrne was the oldest – and probably the quietest – of the six. Prior to her election, she had been Head of Learning Support at Irvine Academy. She had been a co-chair of the Scottish Socialist Alliance though she tended to concentrate her political activity on her home patch of Ayrshire. I never really got to know Rosemary well. Back in 1998, when we were trying to turn the ramshackle Alliance into a cohesive pro-independence Scottish Socialist Party, Rosemary had initially been sceptical.

In contrast, Frances Curran had been a major driving force for change. She had played a much greater role than Tommy, albeit behind the scenes, in the battle to establish the SSP. She was an experienced and astute political operator. Back in 1984, just as

Tommy was first becoming active in politics, Frances was elected to serve as the youth representative on Labour's National Executive, where she sat alongside some of the great beasts of the political jungle, including Tony Benn, Denis Healey, Arthur Scargill and Neil Kinnock.

Colin Fox was another youthful veteran. Colin had grown up in the shadow of the gigantic Ravenscraig steelworks and joined the Labour Party Young Socialists in the early 1980s just as the Thatcher government was laying waste to Scotland's industrial heartlands. Like Frances, he had been politically active without interruption for more than two decades before he became an MSP in 2003. Personable and witty, Colin's laid-back style could be deceptive as behind the cheerful exterior was a methodical political operator. He also became something of a cultural impresario and the main driving force of the annual established Edinburgh Peoples Festival, a kind of fringe of the fringe, which takes music, drama and art out to the neglected communities tucked away behind the city's grandiose facade.

In her early days in Holyrood, Rosie Kane became a target for some cynical, sexist and downright nasty abuse. The fact that she wore a blouse and jeans to work and spoke in working-class Glasgow accent seemed to irritate some journalists. When she frankly admitted that she had only ever read a handful of books, the sneering grew even louder. Bookworm she may never have been but Rosie has one of the sharpest wits and the most eloquent tongues I've ever known. She's also warm and generous and uproariously funny with a Billy Connolly-style instinct for spotting the absurd and hilarious in everyday life. Rosie was never really comfortable as a conventional politician. She despised the pomp and pretentiousness and disliked the contrived university debating club atmosphere of the parliament. Just months after her election, she plunged into a clinical depression. After she had been ill for a few months, Tommy started to become impatient and tried to persuade me that Rosie should be told to stand down and make way for someone else. There was no evident tension between the two so I put it down to Tommy's lack of understanding that fighting depression takes time.

Rosie made a phenomenal impact from the day she was sworn in. Wearing jeans and a brightly coloured blouse, she raised her right hand aloft, with the words 'My oath is to the people' inscribed on her palm. Some of the traditionalists would gladly have dragged her up the Royal Mile to the dungeons of Edinburgh Castle but, for younger people, she was a breath of fresh air. Not long after her election, I went with Rosie to meet Allan Rennie, the editor of the *Sunday Mail*, in the

Balmoral Hotel in Edinburgh. Allan was a decent, down-to-earth bloke who told us that he had walked from Glasgow to London in the early 1980s on the Peoples March for Jobs, during the heyday of Maggie Thatcher. Now he was a middle-class newspaper executive living in suburbia but he was impressed by Rosie's idealism and flair and offered her a column in the newspaper. When I told Tommy, he hesitated fractionally, then loudly responded with 'Brilliant!' But I had an instinctive feeling that there was a false note to his response. It wouldn't have helped when I then began to wind him up about the fleeting nature of celebrity by saying, 'The problem with fame is that the media soon get bored with you and move on to someone else. And now they've discovered a new kid on the block.'

In common with many Glaswegians, Carolyn Leckie didn't fit neatly into any mould. Brought up in the Gorbals in an Orange-loyalist family, she was already a feminist and a Scottish republican socialist in her teens. Her father had died young and she had been raised in a one-parent household in serious poverty. After leaving school at sixteen, she had steeped herself in literature and had become as widely read as many a university professor, while raising two daughters on her own. Like her friend, Rosie, Carolyn had never been involved in traditional Labour politics. She had always been pro-independence and, up until the formation of the Scottish Socialist Party, had voted SNP. Yet she had also been an active trade unionist. As a midwife and UNISON official representing thousands of health workers, she led two victorious strikes in 2001 and 2002, one of them involving low-paid laundry and catering workers against the French-based multinational, Sodexho. A tough negotiator, Carolyn became the SSP representative on the powerful business bureau of the parliament, which involved trawling through masses of motions, amendments and resolutions every day and deciding how the SSP group should respond. No one ever questioned her judgement.

All six MSPs abided by the SSP's constitutional requirement that they should live on no more than the average wage of a skilled worker, plus essential expenses. It meant they donated half their salaries to help to fund the campaigning of the party. Two MSPs, Rosemary Byrne and Carolyn Leckie, were eligible for second-home allowances because they lived beyond the qualifying boundary but, while scores of MSPs from other parties took advantage of the offer – and made lucrative profits as a result of Edinburgh's property boom – Rosemary and Carolyn spurned this opportunity to boost their bank balances.

The six MSPs were the public faces of the SSP and became well known, at least to those who paid attention to politics. Others, working behind the scenes, played an equally vital role in turning the SSP into a force to be reckoned with.

Inside Holyrood, Tommy relied heavily on his office manager, an organisational dynamo called Felicity Garvie. Fiz, as she was known to everyone in Holyrood, was respected right across the political spectrum by everyone – the canteen staff, the MSPs of all parties and their political backroom staff and the security guards. Brought up in Oxford and speaking with a cut-glass English accent, Fiz combined ardent support for Scottish independence with a broad internationalist outlook. She had lived in Germany for 20 years and spoke four languages. One former SNP MSP said of her, 'Sheridan gained the glory but Fiz is the cleverest person I ever knew in that parliament.' Her formidable organisational drive and campaigning flair were vital ingredients of Tommy's rising stature after 1999. Without the background work undertaken by Fiz, neither of Tommy's first two parliamentary bills – to scrap warrant sales and to bring in free school meals – would ever have reached the stage of even being debated in Holyrood.

Outside of the parliament, a team of organisers, led by Richie Venton and Kevin McVey, built the party on the ground to a high point of over 3000 members across every corner of Scotland. That made the SSP bigger than the entire myriad of socialist parties and organisations across the UK put together. This was a volunteer army and most of them had full-time jobs during the day. They came from all walks of life – nurses, firefighters, building workers, teachers, clerical staff, technicians, students, mechanics, joiners, bank workers, civil servants, charity workers, journalists, postal delivery staff, actors, musicians, housewives, pensioners, bar staff, waiters, security guards – though there was a woeful shortage of landowners, investment bankers and stockbrokers. These were people who worked by day and gave up their precious time in the evenings and weekends – and many of them donated hefty portions of often-meagre salaries to aid the cause.

Allan Green was the founding national secretary of both the Scottish Socialist Alliance and the SSP. Low key, with a dry sense of humour, Allan was a great administrator and an astute tactician. Meticulous and methodical, he had an intricate understanding of the mechanics that held everything together. His scrupulous honesty, his competence, his sense of fairness and his formidable diplomatic skills lent Allan a moral authority within the SSP unsurpassed by anyone.

One of the more flamboyant characters who hung around Tommy from 1999 onwards was Hugh Kerr, a former Labour Member of the European Parliament (MEP). I had first met Hugh in Edinburgh a few days before New Year 1998, just as he was about to be expelled from the Labour Party, along with another Labour MEP, Ken Coates. Hugh had been in contact with Allan Green and now wanted to get involved in the Scottish Socialist Alliance. We met in an opulent townhouse belonging to two artist friends of Hugh – the same house that Naomi Mitchison had been brought up in and had vividly described in her memoirs. Hugh had always kept his own pied-à-terre in Edinburgh's New Town, as well as his homes in Essex and Brussels. Although originally from a working-class town in Ayrshire, he spoke in a rather affected accent and sounded more like a luvvie than any actor I ever met.

Hugh had already been deselected by Labour as its candidate in Essex for the Euro elections in 1999 and stood in Scotland for the SSP instead. Afterwards, he offered his services, unpaid, to Tommy as full-time press officer in the parliament. Hugh loved to indulge in the dark arts of media spin – a hobby that was to wreak havoc on the SSP after 2004. He was hard working and generous with his cash, regularly wining and dining broadsheet journalists and feeding them a steady stream of parliamentary gossip. Some liked him as a sociable companion though others found him embarrassingly loud and tiresome.

He would occasionally appear at Holyrood awards ceremonies and other social events slightly the worse for wear and noisily heckle the speakers. Sometimes he would even get to his feet uninvited and bore everyone rigid with a rambling speech. On one occasion, he accompanied Gail Sheridan to a Scottish Politician of the Year award dinner, which Tommy had boycotted. Embarrassed by his non-stop, full-volume commentary, Gail leaned across their table and said, with a grim smile, 'Hugh, if you don't shut up, I'm going to kick your head in.'

At the time Hugh was married to a woman from Denmark and had ambitions to return to the European parliament. He had topped the SSP list for the Euro elections in 1999 and, with Tommy's backing, fully expected to be reselected for the number one spot in 2004. Instead, in a secret ballot of all party members, he was relegated to third place, behind Felicity Garvie and Nicky McKerrel. Hugh seemed eaten up with resentment towards three of our MSPs – Frances, Carolyn and Rosie – because they had openly supported Felicity's campaign. They had no confidence if Hugh's judgement and had complained of what they delicately described as 'inappropriate behaviour'. He left Edinburgh later that year to spend part of his time in Brussels – but he would never forgive or forget those he blamed for thwarting his political ambitions. Eddie Truman and Ken Ferguson took responsibility for our media operation. Eddie was a talented communicator, with a superb understanding of the power of technology and how to harness it. Unlike Hugh, he knew how to write a press release and organise a press conference and was widely respected within media circles. So too was Ken Ferguson, a wily old-school socialist from a Communist Party background. As a mature student, Ken had gone to Stirling University and shared a flat with another communist, John Reid, who was to become a future Home Secretary, Minister of Defence and chair of Celtic Football Club. Ken was a heavyweight journalist with decades of experience working in newspapers and press agencies and as a press officer for both the old Greater London Council and for Dundee City Council. Some of the big political parties would have paid handsome cash to have such a skilled double act as Ken and Eddie fronting their media operation.

The SSP also had its own newspaper, the *Scottish Socialist Voice*. The twelve-page tabloid of which I had been founding editor was produced on a shoestring with an editorial team of just four – Kath Kyle, Jo Harvie, Roz Paterson and Simon Whittle – plus Lisa Young who ran the business side of the operation. These were highly talented people and worked with me to produce the election and campaigning material for the party. Some of the memorable leaflets and posters broke new ground for political literature by being readable and sometimes even entertaining. One SSP election leaflet, which was delivered to every household in Scotland during the 2003 election, was praised by the tabloids and broadsheets alike for its wit and originality. Some journalists imagined that Tommy had personally written, designed and possibly even printed all this stuff himself. 'Sergei Platt', the political diarist for *The Sun*, commended Tommy for finally finding a sense of humour – 'rarely the province of grim-minded commies'. Alan Taylor in the *Sunday Herald* praised our brochure lavishly and added, 'Tommy Sheridan, we salute you.' As with much of the SSP's election material, the first time Tommy saw the leaflet was when it dropped through his own letterbox.

This was all a source of amusement rather than resentment. Political commentators would later rush to defend Tommy against those SSP members they assumed were driven by envy and malice. Steeped in a media and parliamentary culture dominated by individual ambition and personal jealousy, they got it spectacularly wrong. There was never any resentment within the SSP over Tommy's fame – not a trace. If anything, SSP members at every level of the party were proud of the fact that he was the best-known and most-recognised politician in Scotland. Some of us had played a big part in turning him into a household name. We had churned out enough press releases in his name to fill the archives of the British Library. I had written some of his key speeches in the parliament and churned out more words under the byline Tommy Sheridan than either of us had ever written under our own names. Although an exceptional orator, writing had never been Tommy's strong point. Much of his charisma on a public stage or in a TV studio was based on technique rather than content. His autobiographical memoir of the anti-Poll Tax campaign, *A Time to Rage*, was brilliantly written but not by Tommy. Joan MacAlpine, *The Scotsman* journalist, had written the text based on interviews with Tommy and others.

For the first six months after he was elected in 1999, I wrote all his weekly *Daily Record* columns and his fortnightly sports column for the *Sunday Herald*. Later, between January and May 2003, I wrote his weekly page in the *Scottish Mirror*. When he did write his own material, Tommy had an exasperating habit of cramming his articles full of facts, figures and statistics until they read like a railway time-table. His more light-hearted pieces were invariably laden with la-boured and cheesy banter, usually about Gail or his friends, along the lines of 'My fourteenth – oops, sorry – fourth wedding anniversary is tomorrow. It just seems longer . . . only kidding.' Nor did Tommy make any significant contribution to the book, *Imagine*. I had written virtually every word, including most of Tommy's personal introduc-tion. The book reached the top ten of bestsellers in Scottish bookshops in late 2000 and early 2001, which was not bad going for a political book arguing the case for socialism at a time when the free market appeared to have vanquished all ideological opposition. Favourable reviews, including glowing praise from people like Tony Benn, John Pilger, George Galloway and Ken Loach, helped the sales but I was under no illusions – it was Tommy Sheridan's name more than anything that shifted those thousands of copies from the bookshelves. After Tommy's victorious defamation action, one of the dark jokes that began to circulate around the Scottish Socialist Youth posed the question, 'What's the difference between Tommy Sheridan and Jeffrey Archer?' The answer? 'Jeffrey Archer's written a book.'

Did we create a personality cult around Tommy Sheridan, as some people later suggested? Over fifteen years, we had plastered Tommy's face and name on countless millions of leaflets and hundreds of thousands of posters. Perhaps, at times, we inflated Tommy's abilities and exaggerated his role as an individual. None of it was dishonest but it was embellished or, to use the political buzzword, spun. Why? One reason was that, for eight years between 1995 and 2003, he was our only elected representative – first in Glasgow City Council and then in Holyrood. He had a public platform that wasn't available to the rest of us so we exploited it mercilessly to get our political ideas out to as wide an audience as possible. And, secondly, people find it easier to relate to personalities than manifestos. Focussing on an individual keeps things simple for the media and makes it easier to connect with people and get the political message across.

One myth, however, grew arms and legs – and is still racing around Scotland to this day. According to this piece of fiction, the SSP only won six seats in the 2003 election because we put Tommy Sheridan's name on every ballot paper. In fact, the SSP executive took a decision before the election *not* to put Tommy's name on the ballot paper alongside our party name and logo, except in Glasgow where he was a candidate. Two regions defied the decision – the South of Scotland, where we won a seat, and the Highlands and Islands, where we didn't. We won in Central Scotland, West Scotland and Lothians without Tommy's name on any of those ballot papers.

Yet, in the eyes of the media and the general public, Tommy Sheridan was bigger than the cause he represented. By 2003, he had become Scotland's best-known politician, with a 91 per cent recognition rating, according to one opinion poll. And he loved being the centre of attention. Back in the late 1980s and 1990s, I used to travel regularly to London with Tommy for UK-wide Militant Central Committee meetings. As he grew more famous in Scotland, he came to loathe these trips more and more. He used to joke that he hated London because nobody recognised him down there – though, as the old cliché goes, there's many a true word spoken in jest.

But I wasn't sanctimonious about it. He certainly wasn't the first conceited politician to strut the political stage in Scotland and he won't be the last either. At the level of a national parliament, politics is close to a performing art. And like most public performers, from stand-up comics to opera singers, politicians often thrive on the applause and the fame. Some would love to be Shakespearian actors – although, based on talent alone, few of them would get a part in the school play.

Like it or lump it, Tommy's public popularity was important to the success of the SSP. No political movement can be faceless. Like everyone else, the socialist Left needs effective communicators who

can inspire people. But we went too far. With the best of intentions –
and with Tommy's enthusiastic acquiescence, it has to be said – we
created an unhealthy and imbalanced relationship between the individual and the movement.

No one knew it at the time but we were to discover the hard way that
Tommy Sheridan's fame was to be our Achilles heel.

31 October 2004

Cupid's Poison Arrow

As the midnight hour struck to usher in Halloween 2004, I stood rooted to the spot, gaping in horror. There, in the twenty-four-hour shop, one headline blazed out from the news-stand, as though it had been typeset in neon lights, 'Married MSP Is Spanking Swinger'. I grabbed the early edition of the *News of the World*, threw a few coins on the counter and rushed outside to read the full story.

My stomach churned as I glanced at the sub-headline, 'Lusty *News of the World* sex columnist Anvar Khan has told how she had a kinky fling with a married Scots politician'. The story, based on the journal-ist's 'new X-rated diary-style autobiography, *Pretty Wild*', described a visit to Cupids, a club in Manchester, with 'Patrick' – an MSP whose real name could not be revealed 'for legal reasons'. Also in the company were two men, Gerry and Drew, and a woman called Hilda 'who was definitely NOT his wife'.

The columnist described a club 'crawling with middle-aged couples openly having sex while others watched'.

> I saw a fat, bespectacled woman lying naked on a bed in the corner of the main bar, with one man stroking and kissing her nipples, another snogging her, a third performing a sex act on her and a fourth looking for something to do. Everyone was naked or wearing just skimpy underwear. Guys were walking up to women and asking to grope them as their hubbies looked on.

The paper lingered over further detail, including games of naked snooker and incidents involving pink rubber gloves. I scanned the article again. Maybe it was sexed up, as they used to say of certain government dossiers. Certainly, some of the details didn't ring true. In twenty years, I had never seen Tommy touch a drop of alcohol yet this story described a drunken sexual encounter with the MSP. But there was no arguing with the fact that the substance of the article tallied with the facts Tommy had already admitted to Keith and me a couple of years before. He had insisted that none of his companions would ever talk. These three people, he said, were 'rock solid'. The Mediterranean would freeze over before this story ever leaked out to the press. Keith and I had believed him. Now I was just incredulous. One of those involved in the escapade had been the self-styled 'sex columnist' with the *News of the World*. On the Beaufort scale of recklessness, this was Hurricane Anvar.

I remembered a conversation I'd had on an Edinburgh local train with the associate editor of *The Scotsman* newspaper, George Kerevan, a few days after the 2003 Scottish election. George had been a revolutionary Marxist in his younger days but was now an SNP member and a staunch free marketeer. He warned me that morning, 'You realise that the SSP has become dangerous. You are now a target for the state.'

Could anyone seriously imagine, say, Gerry Adams or Martin McGuiness attending a swingers' club in the company of a *News of the World* journalist? Or, for that matter, former loyalist political leaders such as David Ervine, ex-leader of the UVF-linked Progressive Unionist Party? Whatever you thought of their politics, these people took their responsibilities seriously. Yet here was Tommy Sheridan, the figurehead of a rapidly rising left-wing party, whose aim was to break up the British state and move towards a Scottish socialist republic, delivering a gift-wrapped weapon to our enemies.

I called Tommy's number. No answer. I left him a message to call me back urgently, then phoned Keith Baldassara. I read him the main points of the story. He was aghast. Although Tommy wasn't named, we knew the secret we had suppressed for two years was about to come spilling out like an oil slick. It could be cleaned up – although it would certainly be messy – but it couldn't be covered up. It was clear the *News of the World* already knew the identity of the wayward politician. In a sidebar to the main piece, the paper's political editor, Euan McColm, had offered betting odds on the real identity of Patrick. Could it be John Swinney of the SNP? Or Labour's Jack McConnell? The Tories' David McLetchie perhaps? Maybe Jim Wallace of the Lib Dems? Or even Robin Harper of the Greens? So they knew it wasn't just an anonymous backbench MSP. It was a party leader. And, of the six party leaders in Holyrood, one name was glaringly absent from the list of suspects. It was now just a matter of time before the story blew up. We had to move fast.

When Tommy phoned back, I exploded. Could he really have been so stupid? And why hadn't he told us that the *News of the World* resident sex columnist had been there too? During the conversation, he told me the names of the other three people he had been with. The two men were his brother-in-law, Andy McFarlane, and his friend, Gary Clark. That figured – 'Drew and Gerry'. Some of the more lurid details about what they had got up to in the club was fictionalised. But they had all been to Cupids together – there was no doubt about that. At the time of the incident, Gary had been separated from his wife and Andy was married to Gail Sheridan's sister. Through Tommy, I knew both men vaguely though neither had ever been involved in politics. The other person – the mysterious 'Hilda' – was actually Katrine Trolle, a Danish-born SSP activist in her late twenties, who had lived in Aberdeen and then moved to Dundee. I hadn't known of any relationship between her and Tommy but I was now rapidly finding out more than I ever wanted to know. After a tense 15-minute exchange, we arranged to speak to Keith at an SSP National Council meeting in Edinburgh the next day to thrash out a damage limitation strategy.

Keith failed to show. He was pole-axed by the revelations. Tommy, in contrast was remarkably unfazed. At one point on the agenda, he stood up to give a report to the hundred or so delegates in a University of Edinburgh students' hall. I had sat at the back of the hall, too distracted to concentrate on the meeting. As Tommy spoke, I gazed around the meeting, sick to the pit of my stomach. It was like watching the movie *Titanic*, where you know what's about to happen but Kate and Leonardo are cheerfully oblivious to the calamity about to fall around their heads.

The general public are often slightly suspicious of political activists but I knew that most of these delegates and the people they represented back in the localities were driven by idealism. They gained neither cash nor glory from their involvement. As a brave minority have done down through the ages, they dreamed of a better world and were doing their best to try to build it. They trusted Tommy as a faithful parishioner would trust their priest or minister. He had betrayed that trust – and now their hopes and dreams were about to be shattered.

No one at the meeting mentioned the *News of World* front page. Most of these left-wing activists would be more likely to read the Sunday broadsheets or maybe the *Sunday Mail* rather than the red-top scandal sheet. And, even if they had read about the antics of the unnamed MSP, they'd probably guess it would be a Tory. In fact, as it happened, Rosie Kane had spoken to a man she knew who ran a small business and who was also a regular Tory candidate. 'Rory the Tory', as she called him, feared that, when the name was revealed, it would be one his own party's MSPs because 'it's always Tories who get caught up in these tabloid sex scandals'. Rosie cheerfully agreed but told him not to worry as 'it'll just become yesterday's fish-and-chip paper'.

Tommy left the National Council meeting before the end, as he often did. I raced after him and exchanged some words. Catriona Grant, who was chairing the meeting, noticed an animated conversation through the glass doors at the back of the hall. Even from a distance, she could see that something was seriously amiss. It was the first time she had ever seen Tommy and me in dispute.

Tommy was dismissive about the article. 'I'm just going to deny it,' he shrugged. I wasn't happy and wanted to meet him privately, with Keith there too. He could survive these revelations if he handled them with contrition and honesty but, if he denied the allegations and was then caught lying, it could be political suicide. Tommy himself had been merciless with other politicians who had been caught out lying. In one of his favourite quips, which he repeated endlessly at public meetings – with the name changed depending on which less-than-candid politician he was lambasting – he would tell the audience that Walt Disney were making a sequel to the *Lion King*. 'It stars Tony Blair/George Bush/the local MP/the local council leader/the First Minister/whoever and it's called the *Lyin' Bastard*.' It was guaranteed a laugh.

Four months earlier, Tommy had even called for the resignation of a Labour minister, Frank McAveety, for misleading parliament over a plate of pie and beans. The Culture Minister had arrived late a ministerial question time, muttering that he had been delayed at a book award. He later had to apologise when it emerged that he had, in fact, been eating lunch in the parliament canteen. Tommy's reaction was severe: 'He has been caught out being less than frank over his late appearance at questions. Mr McAveety's days as minister must surely be over now.' On another occasion, he had ripped into another Labour minister, Wendy Alexander, for misleading the public. 'I checked my mini-dictionary,' he wrote in the *Daily Record*. 'The definition of a lie is straightforward. It says: "Statement speaker knows to be untrue." Integrity and honour are two commodities which are sadly lacking in politics. If she has any honour left she will now resign'.

At Tommy's suggestion, we met the following afternoon in the upper area of Cuba Norte, a fashionable cafe bar close to Glasgow City Chambers. The bar was small and there were several groups of people easily within hearing distance. I wanted to move somewhere more private but Tommy was resistant. He obviously wanted this to be a short, muffled meeting, a whispering huddle rather than a straight-talking exchange of views. Under pressure, he reluctantly agreed to retreat to Keith's office across the road in the City Chambers.

Keith had been elected to Glasgow City Council the previous summer, when Tommy stepped down as a councillor to concentrate on his MSP's role. A year and a half later, the walls of the office were still plastered with newspaper cuttings of Tommy's exploits over the years and thank-you cards from constituents. Keith had always been an unassuming guy. I couldn't have imagined him ever plastering his own photos on the walls but it hadn't even crossed his mind to take down the cuttings glorifying Tommy.

Tommy said his piece. He would fight this all the way, including through the courts. Anvar Khan had behaved despicably by writing a book revealing the incident and now he was going to destroy her. There was no photographic or forensic evidence of his visit to the club. The others who had been there would back up his story if necessary. It was her word against his.

Keith seethed. I challenged Tommy's strategy. How could he guarantee there was no other evidence? Following the collapse of his libel action against the *Guardian* five years earlier, the Tory Cabinet Minister Jonathan Aitken had been jailed for perjuring himself. A few fragments of evidence that he never knew existed had suddenly emerged – a couple of plane tickets and a hotel receipt. Another leading Tory politician, Jeffrey Archer, had also been jailed a few years before when his closest friend blew away his alibi, twelve years after a libel trial which he had won. How could Tommy know for sure his friends would never talk? At least one of them had already been spilling the beans to his mates like a guest on the Jerry Springer show.

Then there was the questionable morality involved in seeking to destroy someone else to cover up your own hypocrisy. But I would have been as well attempting to explain the laws of quantum physics in Swahili as trying to convince Tommy to back away on moral grounds. Destroy or be destroyed – that was his attitude. 'I'll be finished politically if this comes out,' he said.

I suggested that, provided he handled the allegations with suitable remorse and honesty, he would be forgiven – though he would have to endure an incessant stream of jibes and taunts from the likes of Tam Cowan and other TV and radio pundits. If necessary he could stand down from his frontline role for six months, saying he had to spend more time with Gail and his family, until the storm blew over.

We put forward a couple of options. Personally, I was in favour of him going to Mike Graham. The garrulous Londoner edited the

Scottish Mirror and he and Tommy had become friendly. Maybe Mike could pre-empt the *News of the World* by bringing out the story on Tommy's terms. It would still be damaging but people admired honesty. If Tommy took it on the chin, expressed his contrition, sought to patch things up with Gail and apologised to his friends, political colleagues and supporters, any feelings of disappointment would be mingled with sympathy and respect. If that was a step too far, he could ignore it – perhaps issuing what is known in media circles as a 'non-denial denial' along the lines of 'I refuse to even dignify this nonsense with a response'.

We offered him total support. We'd speak to Gail and to his mother Alice if he wanted. Both Keith and I were friends of the family. Gail used to say that there were only two people in the world Tommy would ever take advice from – Keith Baldassara and Alan McCombes. But he wasn't taking our advice now. He was having none of it. The political damage would be irreversible, he insisted. He would be finished.

We all knew that there was an added, heart-rending dimension to this already agonising state of affairs. Gail was pregnant. Keith and I both knew Gail well and liked her, as most people did. She was friendly, generous and as gallus as they come. She was also funny, not least when she was sending Tommy up: 'He's a total bore. All he ever does is drone on about politics and watch football.'

Many people were amazed when, just a few weeks into Gail's pregnancy, Tommy had announced that he was going to be a father. Most women prefer to wait until the critical three months deadline is over before they reveal the news. It wasn't just a quiet word in a few ears either – he gave the *Scottish Mirror* a front-page exclusive. A few days later, at a Scottish Republican rally on Calton Hill, some people squirmed when, midway through his speech, Tommy paused dramatically to make the oddly worded announcement, 'Gail and I are expecting a very young child.' With hindsight, I now suspect that he had known about the Anvar Khan book for weeks. Tommy was sufficiently cynical and calculating to use the pregnancy announcement to bolster his image as a doting family man.

Around that time, he had been acting strangely in other ways too. Just four days before the Cupids story broke, he had written a piece in his *Scottish Mirror* column publicising two meetings in Glasgow and Dundee that the small CWI faction had called to celebrate the fortieth anniversary of the founding of *Militant* newspaper, where his old foe Peter Taaffe would be speaking. A few weeks before, the CWI had boycotted the Calton Hill rally and just two days earlier, Philip Stott, the faction's leader in Scotland, had published a lengthy article highly critical of the 'nationalism' of Tommy Sheridan, myself and the rest of the SSP leadership. I had also been slightly incredulous when he had arrived back in Glasgow from London, just before the crisis broke, and suggested to me that the SSP might publish a pamphlet on the Iraq war by Chris Bambery, one of the leaders of the Socialist Workers Party – a faction within the SSP that Tommy despised.

It had been a suspiciously long trip to London. Later events suggested he may have spent his time schmoozing the UK leadership of the SWP and the CWI, and possibly also some individuals such as George Galloway and Bob Crow, the leader of the railworkers' trade union, to get them onside in preparation for the earthquake that was about to erupt. But he hadn't even been honest with them, as we'd later discover. In the months to come, my blood pressure would shoot into the stratosphere whenever I heard Tommy's friends in the south condemn the SSP executive for our rigid moral intolerance. Immediately after his resignation, George Galloway would denounce the SSP executive as 'Calvinist-Trotskyist' for daring to challenge Tommy's behaviour. George then went on to campaign for the closure of local 'dens of iniquity' in his constituency – even threatening that his Respect Party would take photographs of men going into strip bars and lap-dancing clubs and post them on the Internet. Meanwhile, the Socialist Workers Party complained that we had 'bowed down before bourgeois morality'. The only person who was 'bowing down before bourgeois morality' was Tommy. He was ready to stop at nothing to preserve his wholesome image. Within a few weeks, he would initiate a legal battle that was to consume him for years on end before eating him alive. At the time, it seemed inexplicable. It was like treating a painful open wound with toxic uranium.

We told Tommy that we'd have to consult further. Neither Keith nor I were prepared to dupe the rest of the party. I could see the grisly scenes unfolding in the future weeks and months – our press team launching a media offensive to clear Tommy's name; the party's newspaper, the *Scottish Socialist Voice*, denouncing the outrageous frame-up of Tommy Sheridan by the tabloid press; our MSPs joining the fray to defend him, oblivious to the truth; the grassroots members of the party out on the streets with petitions, burning with rage at the tabloid lies; and Keith and me complicit in the whole wretched charade. If and when the truth did finally emerge, it would be calamitous for the party.

Damage limitation had to be the name of the game. I spoke to a few people in Glasgow individually. By that time, I was involved in a relationship with Carolyn Leckie and spoke to her in the early hours of the morning, in between irate phone calls to Tommy and Keith. Now Allan Green, Richie Venton, Frances Curran and Rosie Kane were all put in the picture. Colin and Rosemary were in Edinburgh, so I left them till later in the week, because I wanted to talk to them face to face. We were slightly paranoid about talking over the phone, in case there were prying ears listening in.

During these discussions, I candidly explained the circumstances of my own marital break-up the year before. Over a number of years, I had been living between two different cities and I'd become so immersed in politics that my marriage had hit the rocks. Instead of dealing with it, I just threw myself even deeper into political work. Eventually, I became involved in a relationship with Carolyn. I completely accepted the blame for the damage caused. Everyone assured me my situation was irrelevant as it was an everyday private heartbreak. Tommy's behaviour was of a different order.

It was an open secret that Tommy had affairs – or 'flings' as he preferred to call them – but these were off-limits politically. That was his private life and any fall-out would be a matter for him and Gail. In any case, I was in no position to make moral judgements about infidelity. But repeatedly driving down to England with a carload of friends – including a tabloid sex columnist – to a commercial sex club whilst publicly masquerading as devoted family man was quite a different order of transgression and could drag down the party as well as Tommy. And to then mount a marathon, high-profile political and legal campaign to deny the facts . . .? That would magnify the damage umpteen times over. Still, I was uncomfortable. I suspected – rightly, as it happened – that Tommy would use my own problems to muddy the waters over his behaviour.

When they heard about Cupids and Tommy's insistence on lying, the reaction of everyone was pretty much identical. Incredulity. Shock. Bewilderment. Desolation. The women MSPs, including, at the time, Rosemary Byrne, were outraged. This was not just about handing our enemies a loaded gun – it was also about the most famous socialist figure in the UK getting involved in the notoriously exploitative commercial sex industry. Increasingly, the party was being forced to decide where we stood on issues such as prostitution, the licensing of lap-dancing clubs and pornography. Party members had expressed conflicting views. Some favoured prostitution tolerance zones and a more laissez-faire attitude towards pornography (child pornography excluded) and lap-dancing clubs. Others argued that the commercial sex industry inevitably involved the exploitation of women for profit – including, at its most extreme level, human trafficking and sexual slavery – and undermined the wider cause of women's equality. Gradually, the party had been shifting towards the Swedish model of dealing with prostitution – now partially adopted in Scotland – which is based on deterring men from using prostitutes by making it a criminal offence. How could we be taken seriously as a party on these questions when our most famous figurehead regularly frequented sex clubs? As some of our women MSPs pointed out, Cupids, at that time, carried links from its home page that were not just sexist but racist – 'Fuck a Negro', 'Fuck a Filipino' and 'Fuck a Chinese'.

Equally inflammatory was Tommy's contempt for the collective principles upon which the SSP had been built. Keith, Richie, Allan, Frances and many others had, over the years, run ourselves ragged to put Tommy where he was. Whenever he asked for our support, he got it without question or complaint. Back in January 2004, after watching the film, *Lord of the Rings: The Return of the King*, Tommy had written a rather vainglorious piece in the *Mirror* comparing himself to Frodo. 'I couldn't help reflecting how the film sort of mirrored my own life,' he gushed. Speaking of Frodo's reliance on Sam, he said, 'I've got so many "Sams" in my life – from Keith to George, Richie and Alan, Fiz and my mum to name only a few.' It was illuminating that, of the six people he mentioned, the only one to back him in his court case and follow him out of the SSP was his mother. We were all destined to be branded as plotters who were out to get Tommy. But the analogy was also patronising – Sam is the loyal servant who runs errands for Frodo, cooks for him, carries him and carts around his baggage. It certainly revealed how Tommy pictured himself in his own imagination and how he viewed his relationship with his closest collaborators.

Now we were in a mess of Frodo's making and I asked him to meet a group of executive members from the Glasgow area to try to sort things out informally. He refused point-blank. There was nothing to discuss, he told me in a heated phone conversation. He had made up his mind how he was going to deal with this. His attitude towards these people was one of shocking hostility and contempt. I told him that these people worked their socks off to put him in the limelight. It was a mistake. Tommy wilfully misinterpreted my comments as evidence that I was motivated by envy. It was nonsense and he knew it. The limelight was the last thing I wanted or needed. But the conversation planted in his mind a seed that he would cultivate and nurture until it became a full-grown conspiracy theory.

We went ahead with the meeting anyway. It was another mistake. Tommy would later claim that this private meeting proved the existence of a 'secret cabal' plotting against him. It was nothing of the sort. It was a meeting of Tommy's closest political friends allies to which he himself had been invited. Its purpose was to find a way out of the crisis without having to take these delicate matters through the formal structures of the party. Its purpose was to find a way out of the crisis without having to take these delicate matters through the formal structures of the party.

Everyone there was disappointed at his attitude. The greatest test of anyone's character comes not during the good times but when the going gets tough. And Tommy was starting to look like a self-centred prima donna, too cowardly to face up to the consequences of his own behaviour and focussed only on protecting his own halo, regardless of the consequences for everyone else.

Tommy's refusal to discuss the crisis informally forced us to call an emergency meeting of the executive. Those of us who knew what was on the agenda arrived at the SSP headquarters on the evening of 9 November 2004 with heavy hearts. Others were curious, expecting that the meeting had probably been called to discuss our seemingly never-ending financial crisis.

They were in for the shock of their lives and, for years afterwards, we would look back wistfully at the good old days when we thought that bankruptcy was the worst thing that could ever happen to us.

Early November 2004

Showdown

In the semi-derelict backstreets of Glasgow's Kinning Park, the brightly painted murals of the single-storey building stood out like a rainbow against a grey sky. Just round the corner from the SSP HQ was News International's grimly imposing offices and factory where the *Scottish Sun*, *The Times*, *The Sunday Times* and the *News of the World* were edited and printed. Production first began there in 1986, coinciding with Rupert Murdoch's onslaught against the print trade unions, when thousands of workers were sacked in Fleet Street to be replaced by the new computerised technology that would transform the media industry. I used to stand outside these gates, late on Saturday nights, alongside Tommy and hundreds of other socialists and trade unionists, jostling with massed ranks of police officers. Our goal was to hold up the distribution vans laden with copies of the newly launched Scottish editions of the *News of the World* and *The Sunday Times*. Sometimes we delayed the lorries but no one could stop the juggernaut of new technology. It was an honourable, last-stand battle of a proud trade union representing some of the most skilled workers in the world.

Now, just a few hundred yards from the scene of these weekly clashes, we sat in a tight circle facing each other across the oblong office, around eight metres long and five metres wide. There were twenty-two people present on that Tuesday evening. The atmosphere was tenser than any picket line. Carolyn Leckie – at the time co-chair of the party with Catriona Grant – opened the meeting and invited Tommy to explain the background. As the silent huddle listened intently, Tommy referred to the front-page splash in the *News of the World* nine days before. Tommy admitted that he was the unnamed MSP, adding that some of the secondary details had been embellished. He went further, saying that he had visited the club on two occasions – once in 1996 and again in 2002. I was surprised. I knew he had visited the club in 2001 and 2002. I wasn't going to quibble over the exact dates or even the frequency of the Cupids expeditions but now

Tommy was telling the meeting of a trip to Cupids eight years earlier. It was more information than we needed to know. I would soon discover why he had thrown in this red herring.

He apologised for his reckless behaviour, offering the excuse that he had gone to the club for 'a cheap thrill'. He then insisted that no evidence existed of his participation. He acknowledged, however, that there were no guarantees. If proof did emerge, he 'would take the silver bullet, apologise and resign'. He told the meeting he had already taken legal advice from NUJ solicitors. Based on this advice, he had made up his mind: 'I will fight it out in court.' In the meantime, he wanted to remain convenor.

The meeting was stunned. Some people were hearing this for the first time and could hardly believe that it was for real. This icon, this hero of the socialist movement, this figurehead, around whom a wildly successful socialist party had been built, was confessing to behaviour that was off the scale of reckless irresponsibility. And, if that wasn't enough, he was announcing his intention to embark on a media crusade to deny the facts he had just acknowledged. To cap it all, he was planning to fight a legal battle to disprove the truth. It felt like the walls had just caved in.

I then spoke, noting that this was the most painful discussion I had ever been involved in and stressing that Tommy, Keith and I went back 20 years without any trace of acrimony. I went on to explain the chronology of the crisis and suggested that 'people will forgive sexual misconduct but not the leader of a party lying about it and refusing to take the consequences'. As a member of the NUJ, I expressed concern that the union and its lawyers had been enlisted under false pretences in Tommy's campaign to clear his name. I asked him to manage the fallout in the media as soon as he was named. He should then acknowledge his stupidity, apologise to those he had let down and resign as convenor to spend more time with his family. In my view, the executive could not and should not be party to a fraudulent campaign of denial that, sooner or later, would backfire on us. If your enemy is pointing a loaded gun to your head, the best course of action is to try to disarm him, even if it means being wounded in the process. There was no painless way out of this.

As an open discussion began, Barbara Scott, the minutes secretary, scrawled in the margin of her handwritten notes a message to Catriona Grant, who was sitting beside her. 'Is this a dream?' Catriona jotted back: 'Now you know now how bad it is!' Barbara wrote back: 'I hope my bag doesn't get stolen on train!' These scribbled comments offer a glimpse of the shell-shocked mood of the meeting. It was portrayed later by Tommy – and some of his more gullible friends in the media – as a cold, calculated coup. It was nothing of the sort. A few people were literally in tears. Others spoke with the anger that springs from a heartfelt sense of betrayal. Yet at no stage did the meeting descend into heckling or interruptions. Everyone voiced their opinions strongly and clearly, apart from Duncan Rowan, the North-East organiser from Aberdeen, who looked to be in a state of extreme distress. He had phoned me the night before to ask my advice because several journalists from the *Sunday Mail* and the *News of the World* were hounding a woman party member who lived in the fishing port of Peterhead. The name, Fiona McGuire, meant nothing to me. Duncan explained that she was a former escort girl who was known to the media and was now being harassed over an affair she was alleged to have had with Tommy Sheridan. Duncan was upset because she had taken an overdose of painkillers and had been rushed to hospital.

Katrine Trolle had lived in Aberdeen, though she had since moved to Dundee. Maybe the journalists had been tipped off that one of the women on the Cupids expedition had been from the Aberdeen area and had guessed it might be Fiona McGuire because of her background as an escort girl. I was wrong – the two Sunday newspapers were pursuing Fiona McGuire over an entirely different story.

Duncan was agitated and clearly worried that Fiona McGuire may not survive. I didn't know it then but he had been in a personal relationship with her. He held Tommy responsible for the potentially tragic incident and verbally lashed into him. The rest of us weren't quite sure what this was all about. We wouldn't have recognised Fiona McGuire if we'd met her in the chip shop. It seemed like a baffling diversion but Duncan looked as though he was on the verge of having some kind of breakdown.

The rest of the meeting concentrated on the Cupids crisis. Some of the women expressed revulsion towards the sex industry. They recognised that Tommy may have genuinely believed that this was harmless fun involving people with a libertarian approach towards sex but there was a murky line between consensual sex and abuse of women. Carolyn Leckie and Catriona Grant suggested that women were often coerced, psychologically or physically, by their male partners into participating in orgies in sleazy, backstreet clubs such as Cupids. There was also suspicion that some of these swingers' clubs, like saunas and massage parlours, doubled as fronts for prostitution. Was this the kind of club where the female staff were expected to have sex with male customers? None of us knew for sure but Rosie Kane had been heavily involved in fighting asylum cases on behalf of trafficked women from Russia and the Philippines. She had a better insight than any of us into the personal misery suffered by young women who had been conscripted into the sex industry. Earlier in the week, she had been joking in the parliament with some of the SSP's parliamentary staff about the identity of the swinging MSP. Carolyn Leckie had to gently take her aside and advise her to steer clear of the subject. When she heard of Tommy's involvement, she could hardly breathe.

Just a few months before, Tommy had supported the sacking of seven Scottish executive civil servants for surfing pornographic sites at work and disciplinary action just short of sacking against a number of others. He had told the press then that, if there was evidence they deliberately accessed porn sites, 'then disciplinary action is justified'. So would disciplinary action be justified against the leader of a political party who had not just viewed pornography but had actually participated in what many people would regard as live pornography? These were difficult questions that we didn't even attempt to answer.

Our immediate concern was Tommy's determination to march blindfold towards the edge of the cliff. If that's where he was going, then he was on his own. Tommy's popularity with working-class voters derived not just from his verbal skills but from his reputation as a man of shining integrity, someone that ordinary people could trust in the devious, double-dealing world of party politics. In the first few months after he started his column in the *Daily Record* in 1999, the paper had been inundated with letters of praise for Tommy – and there was a single unifying theme running like a pure white thread through all of the comments. 'I really admire his honesty and integrity and may he continue to champion the cause of the underdog for many years to come,' wrote an Aberdeen man. 'He is most definitely a man of worth and integrity,' wrote a Glasgow woman. 'The man's honesty, integrity and dedication shine through,' wrote a twenty-year-old man from Clackmannanshire. 'He radiates honesty,' wrote a woman from Larkhall.

Tommy had become a national institution. It was almost obligatory for journalists to poke gentle fun at his burnished, coffee-coloured skin and his twice or thrice weekly sunbed habit. After a time, the jokes became tedious and predictable though there were a few originals. The *Herald* diary reported that Tommy was on holiday when he suddenly remembered he had left his sunbed switched on. He called Strathclyde Police from his hotel and was told he was too late – 'Your house has been tanned.' It probably wasn't good for his health but it was an amusing chink of vanity, revealing that he had at least one human weakness. Tommy was always happy to go along with the fun. But no one ever questioned his honesty. It would have been like accusing Cliff Richard of Satanism.

If the truth was brought out, his reputation would be battered. That was unavoidable but it would heal. But, if he lied repeatedly to the media and committed perjury in the courts, who would ever trust Tommy Sheridan again? And, if the rest of us were complicit in this, who would ever trust the SSP again? We asked him either to work with us collectively on this or to stand down as convener. It was an extraordinary situation that none of us had ever anticipated. We were in an impossible position. We knew that you can't erase facts no matter how silver your tongue. You might hoodwink some people, you might hoodwink many people, you might hoodwink yourself but you can't change the past. If something's happened, it's happened. You can ignore it, you can forget it, you can put it behind you but you can't undo it.

A few others spoke before Tommy left the meeting at 8.15, including Richie Venton who made the point that the actor Hugh Grant had been caught in an embarrassing encounter with a prostitute but had managed to escape relatively unscathed because he handled the fallout with a degree of honesty and humility. After Tommy left, the meeting continued until 10.30. Rosemary Byrne said she was 'devastated'. She said she was 'worried about the reactions of people, relatives etc.' and insisted that the SSP needed a 'commitment from him not to lie'. She went on to say, 'If we can't get assurances, he'll have to go.'

Graeme McIver, the SSP's South Scotland organiser, said:

> Tommy is in denial – his normality is a sign of this. I'm disappointed and sad about the situation. It's also a personal tragedy. The party is based on a rock of honesty and integrity. We need to give him one or two weeks to own up.

Out of misplaced loyalty, Rosemary and Graeme later changed their stories, as did Jock Penman and Pat Smith – neither of whom had spoken at the meeting. Three years later, all four would be charged with perjury.

We still wanted to give Tommy a chance to reconsider. The only minor dispute was over the timing. The best way to get the news out to the party and our closest supporters would be through an agreed statement in our own newspaper, the *Scottish Socialist Voice*. It would protect Tommy's confidentiality and praise his record as convenor, while skilfully distancing the party from any legal action he was planning. It would allow us to bring out the story on our terms. On the Monday, I had warned Jo Harvie and Roz Paterson – the editor and deputy editor of the *Voice* – about the storm to come and asked them to delay publication of the paper until the Wednesday. At the executive meeting, some argued that one day wasn't enough and we should give Tommy a few more days in the hope he could be persuaded to change his mind. By nine votes to seven, we decided to extend the deadline until Saturday 13 November.

The meeting agreed to send Frances Curran and Colin Fox to explain our decision to Tommy and put the options before him once again. They met him the next morning in the foyer of the Macdonald Hotel in Edinburgh, across the road from *The Scotsman* HQ. Tommy was still not for turning. He was determined to pursue the same strategy that had landed Jeffrey Archer and Jonathan Aitken in jail for perjury. It was stalemate.

That afternoon, events beyond our control accelerated everything. I was in the cafeteria of the Glasgow Science Centre, on the banks of the Clyde, discussing the crisis with Allan Green, when I took a call from Paul Sinclair, the political editor of the *Daily Record*. He was a hard-line New Labourite even though he had been president of the University of Glasgow Tory Society in his student days, during the heyday of Thatcherism. He had never been a friend of the SSP. He wanted to run some information past me which, he explained, had been supplied by a source within the SSP who was normally reliable. Had Tommy been forced to resign as party convenor at a meeting the previous evening? Had Colin Fox been elected interim convenor in his place? Had we examined CCTV footage of an unspecified incident? I didn't respond in detail, except to tell the journalist that he had been misinformed which, strictly speaking, was true. Tommy hadn't been forced to resign at the meeting – it had been decided to present him with options. There had been no discussion on an interim replacement for Tommy. And no one had mentioned, let alone examined, CCTV footage.

The source of the information may well have been an SSP member who had picked up some rumours but it was also clear that it wasn't someone who had attended the meeting. When twenty-two people participate in a meeting with such dramatic consequences, it's likely that within a few hours another 22 people will have been told. They will then tell others and they, in turn, will spread the word wider. Within a day, people begin to hear the story third-, fourth- or fifth-hand, by which time embellishment and speculation have been turned into facts cast in concrete.

I tried to put Paul Sinclair off the scent but I knew the word was out. Later that afternoon, he spotted Tommy in Waverley Station in Edinburgh and confronted him with the same information. At ten o'clock that night, I bought the early edition of the *Daily Record*. 'Sheridan to Quit as Leader of the SSP', ran the headline. 'The shock move comes amid rumours about his private life and concerns over his party's ailing finances,' continued the story, under the bylines of Paul Sinclair and James Moncur. 'Sheridan has angrily denied whispers sweeping Holyrood suggesting he may have been involved in a sex scandal.'

We knew we had to act fast. Paul Sinclair, an old adversary of the SSP, had forced our hands. Late that night, I cobbled together a statement from the SSP executive and ran it past Tommy over the phone. The statement praised Tommy's historic role, from the anti-Poll Tax campaign to his work in the Parliament, and made only oblique reference to the fact that 'as a larger-than-life public figure, Tommy's personal life has come under intense personal pressure and scrutiny . . . recently aggravated by changes in his personal circumstances which have been widely reported'. It looked forward to Tommy 'continuing to play a role in the success of the party and the movement that he played a central role in bringing to the position it is in today'. At 12.45 a.m., Eddie Truman sent out the press release. It was late but the phones went on fire as the word spread.

The next morning, I appeared on BBC Radio Scotland's flagship news programme, *Good Morning Scotland*, to be grilled for breakfast by Andrew Cassell. My message was simple – this was a private matter and we were not prepared to talk about it. No, there was no political friction. Tommy was no Berti Vogts, I pointed out – a reference to the resignation the previous week of Scotland's national football team coach after a string of defeats. Measured by results, Tommy had been the most successful party leader in Scotland.

Later that same day, Tommy appeared on BBC Two's *Newsnight Scotland* while, over on BBC One, Rosie Kane was on the *Question Time* panel. After the trauma of the resignation crisis, she had tried to pull out of the show, at one point even phoning up to cancel. She had visions of being interrogated over Tommy's resignation on near-live TV, broadcast UK-wide. I persuaded her to cancel her cancellation and go ahead with the show but we did first tell the producers that she wasn't prepared to answer any questions about Tommy's resignation. As it happened, Yasser Arafat died that day and much of the discussion centred around the Israel–Palestine conflict. Rosie grew more and more confident and more and more eloquent as the debate raged on. The final question was about taxation and Rosie began to work out her reply as David Dimbleby went round the table for the 'drop the dead donkey' question. She could hear the countdown in Dimbleby's earpiece as he turned to Rosie for the last word. Twenty seconds to go.

'Rosie, the Scottish Socialist Party is looking for a new leader. Will you be throwing your hat in the ring?' asked Dimbleby.

'Aw, naw,' thought, Rosie before blurting out her response of 'You wee rascal, David!'

Ten seconds to go. The Glasgow audience laughed and cheered. The applause meant that veteran broadcaster had no time to come back. He did though remove his spectacles – the gesture he uses to warn his production team that this part may have to be speedily edited out before going live. David explained to her later that he had misheard her – he thought she had called him 'a wee bastard'!

In the weeks to come, some people would condemn the SSP executive for discussing Tommy's private life. The Liberal Democrats were to become the target of similar criticisms when Charles Kennedy was deposed as party leader. I'm in no position to judge whether the Liberal Democrats were right or wrong to remove Kennedy on the grounds of his alcohol problem. But I would defend the right of any political party to discuss problems that might impact on it politically, no matter how distasteful or delicate these problems might appear. This is not the 1950s when the press had a 'gentleman's agreement' to cover up damaging or embarrassing information about the private lives of famous politicians, Hollywood stars and the royal family. Tommy himself had recently signed up to support a 'Free Speech' campaign waged by the *Sunday Mail* to defend its right to publish details of Prince Charles's personal life. The Prince had banned newspapers from carrying extracts of a book published in the US by his former housekeeper, arguing it was an invasion of his privacy. He then used an interim interdict to stop the *Sunday Mail* carrying extracts in Scotland and Tommy leapt to the paper's defence, attacking 'the gagging order' on the *Sunday Mail*.

Like it or lump it, people in the public eye are under scrutiny. Their finances, the houses they live in, the holidays they take, the schools they send their children to and the details of their personal relationships are all now seen as fair game by the media. It was absurd and naive to imagine that the SSP executive should refuse to discuss the impact on the party of a potentially sensational story which would have the whole of Scotland agog. Within days of the Cupids story appearing in the *News of the World*, Eddie Truman had attended a drinks reception for a Press Association journalist who was about to emigrate to Australia. Pinned on the wall was a pink rubber glove, accompanied by the caption 'Who is the mystery MSP?!' The hunt was on. Journalists were asking Eddie point-blank, 'Tell us – is it Tommy?'

The day before the SSP executive meeting, Tommy had already brought in National Union of Journalist lawyers to clamp down on a pro-SNP website for naming him in connection with the Cupids story. That information had then seeped into the mainstream media and, on the morning of the SSP executive meeting, the *Daily Mail* had carried an item stating, 'Holyrood gossip about an unnamed MSP's private life became public yesterday when a website published an email speculating that the politician in question was Mr Sheridan.'

In Holyrood, everyone was talking about it – the press pack, the MSPs, the staff. Outside the political bubble, Tommy's footballing friends had been talking about it for years. And we knew that, if he was named in the *News of the World*, the whole of Scotland would be talking about it.

Was it right that the SSP executive tried to pre-empt the looming crisis or should we just have closed our eyes and stuck our fingers in our ears? As the Americans say, it was a no-brainer.

9

Mid-November 2004

Smoke and Mirrors

It was a scintillating performance worthy of Marlon Brando at the peak of his powers.

Tommy sat in the cafeteria of the newly opened Scottish Parliament surrounded by a throng of scribbling journalists. He looked each of them straight in the eye, one by one, holding his gaze steady as he explained that he was 'standing down for Gail – there's no way I can fight a general election with a wife who will be six months pregnant by then.' This was vintage Sheridan and the hard-bitten hacks were eating out of his hands, some with a hint of moisture in their eyes. He scorned suggestions that he might be the unnamed MSP who had visited Cupids, telling the *Sun*, 'Rumours about my private life have been around for two or three years – a lot of tittle-tattle and garbage and anyone who wants to peddle this rubbish should be man or woman enough to say it to my face.'

On the TV news bulletins that evening, Tommy turned in several more Oscar-winning routines. Virtue and decency oozed from every pore. Who could fail to be moved by this New Man, selflessly sacrificing his political ambition for the sake of his wife? The man who, just a few evenings before, had sat in a meeting and had called for a campaign of lies and perjury to 'destroy' Anvar Khan and cover up his own involvement in the sex industry had now transformed himself into Saint Thomas, the patron saint of happy families. For those who knew the truth, it was a chilling experience. If lying was an Olympic sport, Tommy would have accumulated more gold medals than Mark Spitz and Michael Phelps combined.

He told the *Scottish Mirror*, 'I'm doing it all for Gail . . . my priorities now are my wife and becoming a good father.' He roped in Gail herself, who told the *Evening Times*, 'I think what Tommy's doing now is dead brave and a big sacrifice and that shows his strength.' It was stomach-churning stuff. It was also highly implausible that a political dynamo like Tommy, at the top of his game, would want to stay at home changing nappies. Cherie Blair had given birth to her fourth child while her husband was Prime Minister. In the future, Gordon Brown would become Prime Minister, at a time when he and his wife Sarah had two pre-school children, including a one-year-old with cystic fibrosis. David Cameron was elected Prime Minister while his wife, Samantha, was five months pregnant.

In a bizarre aside, Tommy blurted out a confession that he had actually been involved in a relationship with Anvar Khan back in 1992, after she had interviewed him in Saughton Prison for the *Herald* newspaper. 'I was just twenty-eight and I was a naughty boy. I have never made it a secret to my wife that I was very sexually active and slept with lots of women.' When they read that in the *Scottish Mirror*, some of the journalists began to scratch their heads and wonder just what was going on. The Anvar Khan information had come from nowhere, unprompted. It was a revelation even to me, who had been close to Tommy throughout all these years since. But this was no casual slip-up – it was a pre-emptive strike. If Anvar Khan was to reveal any intimate knowledge of him – for example, of his body hair – he could explain it all away.

This was all becoming extremely messy and escalating of control. The SSP executive had reluctantly accepted that Tommy would deny the specific Cupids allegation if and when it was put to him. But this aggressive onslaught to mislead the public was never in the script. It amounted to rewriting the facts of the SSP executive a few nights before. Tommy and I had worked together on a carefully worded resignation statement, which had been deliberately vague and non-committal. It was a holding position that we could sustain, at least until we had a chance to meet again. We had agreed to stick strictly to that explanation. But within hours Tommy had reneged. Some of us were aghast. If Tommy had come to that executive meeting to hand in his resignation because Gail was pregnant, we would never have accepted it. No wonder some of our members were up in arms when they heard him on TV. Moreover, his fictitious version of events made a mockery of our unanimous decision to distance the party from his lies. If this was left unchallenged, then why wouldn't we support him in any legal challenge he chose to take? And why wouldn't we corroborate his story in court? I knew in my bones this wasn't just stupidity on Tommy's part – this was a calculated move, designed not only to dupe the media but also to lock the SSP into a lie. We were strapped in the back seat of a vehicle headed for the Court of Session, with Tommy in the driving seat. We had to find a way out.

Meanwhile, we were coming under heavy pressure from the media to confirm or deny Tommy's unconvincing explanation. Some journalists were already digging deeper. They included Paul Hutcheon of the *Sunday Herald*, who has since won a string of awards for exposing the shenanigans of Labour and Tory politicians, and the respected Tom Gordon of *The Herald*. Writing in the *Sunday Mirror*, the veteran political commentator, Tom Brown, who had been one of the first to notice this rising young star in the early days, was highly sceptical of Tommy's cover story:

> A tacky woman journalist has dropped heavy hints about a married MSP with very bad breath who liked to visit swingers clubs and enjoyed being spanked . . . Sorry Tommy, that's too much of a coincidence. Any politician who exposes himself in public with boak-making statements like 'I was always sexually active and slept with lots of women' is asking for it.

Others absurdly linked Tommy's resignation with his confession that he had had a fling with Anvar Khan in 1992. Iain Macwhirter, the normally incisive political commentator, wrote in the *Sunday Herald*, 'It seems Sheridan has resigned to spend more time with his family after being accused of sex before marriage (shock) and is apparently being disowned by his own party colleagues as a result.'

Much worse than this idle speculation was the whispering campaign suggesting that he had been ousted by a group of women MSPs, motivated by envy of his talent. Within three days of his resignation, *Scottish Mirror* columnist, Ron McKenna, brought the rumours out into the open:

> What went on that meeting? Answer: We don't really know.
>
> Let's look at the other rumours that have been flying around for ages.
>
> That Tommy's new colleagues, and particular [*sic*] the women in his group, don't think he is quite up to their standard. Laughable though that is.
>
> That Tommy has become more and more isolated from the strident and often hilariously inept MSPs he brought into the party he created.
>
> That they genuinely believe they would be better running the show themselves. And let's ask the question. Is that true? Did they bring him down? Did they seize their chance?

This was drivel without a shred of truth. Until the Cupids crisis broke, there was no trace of resentment towards Tommy from any MSPs or party workers. The only people in the party hostile to him were the two groups which would soon become his biggest allies – the Socialist Workers Party and the CWI. So where it had come from?

If Ron McKenna was some random, ill-informed scribbler, we could have brushed this aside. But he had been close to Tommy personally since the anti-Poll Tax days. A fellow columnist on the *Scottish Mirror*, he was also a trainee lawyer who would soon be helping Tommy arrange his no-win, no-fee defamation action against the *News of the World*. Coming from Ron McKenna, this speculation looked like confirmation of what some of us already suspected. Already, within a few days of his resignation, Tommy was planting seeds that would later grow into an Amazon jungle. Always a cunning and ruthless media operator, he was now targeting his own party. His motive? Partly to inflict damage upon those who had refused to cover up for him but mainly because he knew that his cuddly cover story was just too good to be true. Hard-bitten political journalists, accustomed to scheming and plotting, would find it easier to believe he had been forced out by jealous rivals desperate to seize his crown.

I suspected that Hugh Kerr was also up to his neck in this skulduggery and was in regular contact with Tommy from his two residences in Belgium and Denmark. Within a couple of days of the November 9th meeting, a story began to circulate that at the time made no sense to anyone, but in the weeks, months and years to come was repeated so frequently that it became accepted as Gospel truth. According to the story, three women MSPs had been jealous of Tommy's profile and had been out to get him since 2003. It was a cynical piece of misinformation without a scintilla of truth, and had Hugh Kerr's fingerprints all over it. For Tommy, any old smokescreen would do to obscure the real reason for his resignation.

I began to realise that Tommy was telling different stories to different people. To the wider public, he was presenting himself as a noble hero prepared to put family responsibilities above political ambition. To cynical journalists, he would hint that he had really been forced out by a coven of women MSPs. To the Socialist Workers Party, he would claim that the rest of the SSP executive wanted less emphasis on anti-war campaigning. The faction even sent out an internal bulletin to its members across the UK, saying, 'It is clear that some in the party were unhappy with the direction Tommy was taking the SSP. They didn't like the "Bring the Troops Home" campaign [actually called the 'Justice for Gordon Gentle' campaign] Tommy and Rose Gentle launched.' It was a travesty of the truth. The SSP had strongly supported the campaign from the start. Indeed, the two key people who had helped Rose Gentle set up the campaign in memory of her son who had been killed while serving in Iraq were George McNeilage, a close friend of the Gentle family, and Keith Baldassara.

On the evening of Friday 12 November – the day after Tommy's media binge – I got a call from our press officer, Eddie Truman, asking me to meet Paul Hutcheon, who was asking some awkward questions. It was the first time I had met the new political editor of the *Sunday Herald*. We were anxious to set at least a little part of the record straight and to knock on the head some of the malicious rumours that were now spreading like a virus. Yes, Tommy's story didn't stack up, we acknowledged but, no, there was no plot by jealous rivals to remove him. We told Hutcheon what we were already in the process of explaining to hundreds of our own members – that Tommy had been forced to resign over how he intended to handle allegations about his private life. That was as far as we were prepared to go. There was no way we would reveal the personal detail of the allegations. It would probably all come to light, perhaps even in that Sunday's edition of *News of the World*, but we would maintain an iron wall of silence.

The conversation with Paul Hutcheon was a damage limitation exercise designed to protect the party from the backlash that would erupt when Tommy's lies were exposed. It was also a warning to Tommy to halt his full-volume campaign of lies and misinformation. Unlike Tommy and Hugh Kerr, I had never before gone to the press with an off-the-record briefing. But these were exceptional times. This wasn't a game of croquet on the lawn. This was a rescue mission to save the party we had all built from destruction at the hands of a desperate man. Tommy traded on the fact that most SSP members and supporters had never had to deal seriously with the media and wouldn't fully understand what was going on. Eddie and I knew we were being dragged into dangerous waters and had to take whatever steps necessary to stop the entire party from going under. As future events would reveal, we weren't exaggerating the threat. Knowing what I know now, I have one regret about the interview. We were too subtle and cryptic. We should have come out all guns blazing and lashed into Tommy for wilfully misrepresenting the decision of the SSP executive. But we were anxious to avoid a public slanging match at a fragile time.

The following afternoon I got a call from the editor of the *Sunday Herald*, Richard Walker, asking me if I would sign a legal affidavit corroborating the quotes. Affidavits, which are signed under oath, are commonly requested by media lawyers as an insurance policy against legal action. If the facts they report are false or inaccurate, then an affidavit at least demonstrates that the information was obtained in good faith. The request seemed to me ultra-cautious – Tommy had other allegations to contend with that were much more damaging than this rather tame piece. However, I was due to pass through Glasgow city centre later that day and would be walking straight past the *Herald*'s solicitors' office so I agreed to drop in and sign the statement as requested. It was no big deal at the time but my spur-of-the-moment decision to sign the affidavit would come back to haunt us in the future.

The next day, Sunday 14 November, the Paul Hutcheon article appeared and barely caused a ripple within the party. That morning all attention was focused on two sensational new stories in the *News of the World* which would provide Tommy with the ingredients he needed to cook up a new and more plausible theory to explain his resignation. The SSP executive was due to meet again that day. We had half expected the newspaper to name Tommy as the mystery swinging MSP and, if that happened, we'd have to work out how to deal with it. But we were in for a surprise.

The paper did indeed splash Tommy across the front and inside pages. But, in a surreal twist, this was a different sex scandal, a brand-new story, which had nothing to do with Anvar Khan or swingers' clubs. Instead of rubber gloves and naked snooker, it was 'Whips, zips and handcuffs'.

And worse was to come. Spread over two pages inside were CCTV photographs of Duncan Rowan, our North-East Scotland organiser, talking to a reporter outside the *News of the World*'s Glasgow HQ, together with the transcript of an explosive conversation between him and the news editor of the *News of the World*, secretly recorded by the journalist. I began to wonder how much it would cost for a one-way ticket to a remote Pacific island without telephone, radio or Internet connections.

The tabloid reported that Tommy had had a four-year fling with a 'former escort girl' from Peterhead, a woman called Fiona McGuire, who was also a member of the SSP. An unnamed 'friend' of the woman was extensively quoted. This was a commonplace journalistic device which Tommy himself later used frequently during the police investigation. The friend was an invention. The person speaking was clearly Fiona McGuire herself. She claimed to have started a relationship with Tommy just months after his wedding and had regular three- and four-in-a-bed sex sessions with him and others in hotels in the Aberdeen area. Naturally, the *News of the World*, being the foremost scandal sheet on the planet, spared its readers none of the garish detail, which included the use of a whip, stiletto heels and ice cubes.

In a sidebar, the paper explained Tommy had resigned because 'activists were worried the party would be damaged by sex slurs and feared word of his romps with Fiona McGuire had leaked out'. This was theory number six and it was just as wide of the mark as the other five. Stripped bare of the exotic embellishments, the story appeared to be essentially about a run-of-the-mill affair, far less damaging than the Cupids club revelations. For Tommy, it was a gift from the gods. Whether or not there was any truth in the story, Fiona McGuire would be an easier foe to tackle than Anvar Khan. The *News of the World* columnist was a well-established and well-connected journalist and a member of the NUJ. As well as writing her weekly column for the *News of the World*, she had worked on *The Herald*, *The Sunday Times* and Radio Scotland. Fiona McGuire was, by all accounts, a former call girl with drugs problems and possibly mental health problems too. It was a perfect diversion – like the red herring in a Taggart plot. Tommy's public indignation reached a crescendo. 'I have never met the woman, I have never spoken to the woman. It is a set-up.'

One middle-aged woman watching the news bulletin in her Glasgow home knew for a fact that Tommy Sheridan was a liar and a hypocrite. Along with a friend, she had accidentally witnessed his behaviour with her own eyes. Moved to anger, she made an anonymous phone call, which was to be the first step on a long journey to the dark heart of Scotland's biggest-ever political and legal sex scandal.

But, at that point, we had more pressing problems, specifically the Duncan Rowan issue.

At the November the 9th executive meeting, we knew that Duncan Rowan was in bad shape but we couldn't have known what was about to happen the next day. That Wednesday morning, he had been in the SSP's HQ, from where, unbeknown to anyone, he had phoned the *News of the World*'s office and left a message. The news editor, Douglas Wight, called him back. They had a lengthy conversation and arranged to meet at lunchtime inside the *News of the World* HQ, just around the corner from where Duncan was talking. Duncan, who hailed originally from the small town of Portsoy on the Moray Firth, was less streetwise than he sometimes acted. He believed the conversation would be strictly confidential. At one point during the face-to-face meeting, he interrupted the reporter and asked, 'Is this off the record? No recording devices?' When the reporter assured him that his conversation was indeed off the record, Duncan, uneasy, asked the reporter to step outside the building. With a recording device running in his pocket, the journalist obliged and CCTV cameras captured the two deep in discussion outside the main gate of the Kinning Park fortress. Four days later, the footage and transcript would be plastered all over the *News of the World*, leaving Duncan Rowan in desperate turmoil.

The transcript of the recordings, read out in full in court during the libel case in 2006, conjures up a pitiful picture. Duncan tells the reporter that Fiona McGuire has taken an overdose and is in Aberdeen Royal Infirmary. He pleads with the newspaper to leave her in peace. 'She is terrified of things getting into the papers that her family don't know and her work don't know. Her marriage has broken up over this,' he says. That would have been fair enough but then Duncan offers to throw the reporter another name – 'Somebody else to work on. Somebody who can stand up to the pressure better than Fiona.' Grilled further, he tells the reporter, 'The name would be Katrine Trolle. She's a slender, attractive woman, late twenties, early thirties, short hair with a strong accent.' He tells the journalist, 'I'm doing this off my own back [*sic*]. If they find out I've done this, I'm finished.'

It was rash, reckless and naive. Worst of all, by naming Katrine Trolle, Duncan effectively condemned her to years of strife and humiliation. But the road to hell is paved with good intentions. Duncan had no grievance against Katrine Trolle. Under stress, he had acted impulsively, without even beginning to think through the potential consequences of his words. But his only motive was to protect a vulnerable woman whose life, he believed, was now in danger. Duncan went on to confirm to the news editor that Tommy was the unnamed MSP in the Cupids article: 'So, when I read about it, I knew exactly. She [Katrine Trolle] had mentioned that she had been down to Manchester with an Asian lassie. He was so stupid to shag a reporter but he has no brains.' He added, 'Sheridan's finished as far as I'm concerned. Think about it. There he is, standing up in front of a big crowd, waffling away as he does. There could be a hundred people but ninety-five to a hundred will be thinking about leather boots and spanking sessions.' He added that people in the party had been lining up to get Sheridan for years – a remark seized upon by Tommy as evidence of a plot against him. There were some people 'lining up to get Tommy' – but they were not the ones who had confronted him over the Cupids incident. Before the Anvar Khan story, the only people gunning for Tommy were the two London-based groups who believed that Tommy and the rest of the SSP leadership had sold out to nationalism.

I was also aware that there had been an undercurrent of resentment towards Tommy, Allan Green and me on the part of some of the

party's regional organisers, who felt that too much power was concentrated in Glasgow and the West of Scotland. Some of that tension
could be traced back to the 2002 conference decision to support
50–50 representation for women – a move that was bitterly opposed
by many party activists outside the Central Belt, especially in the
Highlands and Islands and the North East. Within the parliament,
there had been some minor friction but none of it involved Tommy.
The source of the tension had been Rosemary Byrne's resistance to a
proposal that the SSP's parliamentary staff be collectively employed
on standardised wages and conditions. Instead, Rosemary wanted to
employ her own staff personally. The dispute had dragged on for
months throughout 2004.

After the fall-out between Tommy and his closest allies, those who
had previously been most hostile towards him began to perform like
dolphins to gain his approval. Scenting that Tommy might now be
free from the influence of people like Keith Baldassara, Allan Green,
Frances Curran and me, the self-proclaimed revolutionaries of the
Socialist Workers and the CWI began to behave like love-struck
teenagers, competing for his affections. Desperate for allies who
would cheer him on during his long march towards the edge of the
cliff, Tommy manipulated them like marionettes. The people who
'had been lining up to get Sheridan for years' ended up joining forces
with Tommy to split the SSP.

But that was all in the future. As we filed into the SSP HQ that
Sunday morning for our second crisis meeting, we were focussed on
more immediate problems. And we had plenty of them, as was
underlined by the gauntlet of journalists, photographers and TV
cameras we had to run as we entered the meeting.

The SSP might not be Scotland's biggest political party but, for the
media, it was now the most exciting. Who wanted to hear John
Swinney explain the pitfalls of the Barnett Formula or Jim Wallace
drone on about the merits of the Single Transferable Vote, when the
SSP was starring in an X-rated movie with champagne-fuelled orgies,
Shakespearean skulduggery and more twists and turns than the final of
Strictly Come Dancing?

Late November 2004

Tower of Lies

Tommy came out fighting at the meeting, buoyed up by the new revelations in the *News of the World*. Tactically astute as always, Tommy understood that he had been thrown a double lifeline.

The Fiona McGuire story was 'utter pish', he said – a point he was to repeat in exactly the same words in a series of newspaper interviews over the next couple of days. Most people at the meeting believed his vehement denials. He was totally convincing, but then he had been totally convincing when he had denied the story about Anvar Khan and Cupids in front of the TV cameras a few days before.

Understandably, there was no show from Duncan Rowan, who had offered his resignation via Steve Arnott, the Highlands organiser. In his absence, Tommy ripped into him mercilessly. Duncan had been 'stitched up like a kipper', he said. Naming Katrine Trolle had been 'unforgiveable'. Listening to his self-righteous tirade against Duncan Rowan, it was easy to forget that it was Tommy who had plunged us all into this debacle in the first place. His behaviour and his refusal to take responsibility for his actions were now wreaking havoc not just on the party but on people's lives. Watching Tommy in action, I was torn between grudging admiration for his sheer nerve and contempt for his cynical triumphalism over Duncan's tragic blunder.

Jo Harvie, the editor of the *Scottish Socialist Voice*, injected a bit of humanity into the proceedings, highlighting Duncan's agitated state of mind and suggesting that he had acted foolishly rather than maliciously. The meeting agreed to suspend Duncan on full pay until we had a chance to hear his explanation first-hand. But, within a few weeks, he had fled south to a secret location in England, claiming he had received death threats. We never saw him again.

Tommy also initially challenged our interpretation of the decisions of the November the 9th meeting, until it was pointed out that he had left the meeting before the decisions were made. Even at that stage, five days on, he was already dabbling with the idea of rewriting history. After a five-hour discussion, we finally made a few concrete decisions, including the wording of a public statement which was agreed unanimously. It said, 'The SSP executive completely dismisses the rumours that have circulated in the press that Tommy's resignation was provoked by a leadership challenge, a factional power struggle or any other form of internal in-fighting.' It also acknowledged that 'recent allegations in a Murdoch newspaper may be the subject of a future libel action by Tommy Sheridan and consequently the Scottish Socialist Party does not wish to comment on matters concerning the allegation'.

The meeting took one other decision that we would soon live to regret. There had been some discussion over press leaks, briefings and counter-briefings. Some people at the meeting suggested that I should handle all media inquiries but, after a bit of discussion, the meeting decided instead to hold a press conference, chaired by me, with all six MSPs in attendance. It seemed like a good idea at the time.

Two days later, on the afternoon of Tuesday 16 Novermber, we arrived in the spacious committee room of the Scottish Parliament to be greeted by a battery of TV crews, radio microphones, photographers and reporters. Not since the day we returned six MSPs to Holyrood in the 2003 election had we faced such a packed, electrified press conference. Everyone is intrigued by a mystery and, in Scotland at least, Tommy's resignation was like a real-life game of Cluedo without the corpses and candlesticks.

I opened the press conference with what *The Scotsman* report described as 'a lavish tribute' to Tommy. We then fended off a clamour of requests for more detail about Tommy's resignation, including the minutes of the meeting. I explained that they were confidential and that every organisation holds private meetings from time to time, from the governors of the BBC to the board of News International. Unless and until our members voted otherwise, the details of the November the ninth meeting would remain confidential and the minutes would remain under lock and key.

It was Bernard Ponsonby, the STV's political editor, razor sharp as ever, who landed the first serious blow. 'Will you be supporting Tommy Sheridan's legal action against [the] *News of the World*?' he asked us. I had known Bernard for a long time. He had been the candidate for the Liberal Democrats in the 1988 Govan by-election, which the SNP's Jim Sillars won in a sensational landslide. As a political reporter though, he was respected for his hard-line, no-nonsense style of interrogating politicians whether they were from the Right, Left or Centre. Bernard had probably assumed that the answer would be a straightforward 'Yes, of course.' But we had a problem. If we now publicly backed Tommy in his legal action, we would be locked in to supporting the kind of strategy which had led to the political crucifixion of Tory politicians like Jeffrey Archer, Jonathan Aitken and Neil Hamilton. Although none of us had any time for the *News of the World*, neither were we inclined to give Tommy any encouragement to pursue a kamikaze court case by stamping it with a public seal of approval. But we couldn't say that openly at a packed press conference. It would be tantamount to denouncing Tommy as a liar – which he was – and torpedoing his legal action. We were cornered.

As you do in these circumstances, I tried to prevaricate:

Tommy is now a backbench SSP MSP. In Tommy's court battle, individual members may be prepared to back him all the way. But it's not the business of us as a political party to investigate allegations that have been made and to make judgements on the truth or otherwise of these allegations.

It wasn't exactly a ringing endorsement – and the journalists knew it.

Carolyn Leckie went further, saying, 'There is no official party backing behind any legal challenge.'

Ponsonby went in for the kill. 'Are you telling us that a socialist party is refusing to back one of its own in a legal action against Rupert Murdoch? Isn't this extraordinary?'

Yes, if Tommy had been an innocent victim of a *News of the World* stitch-up, it would have been extraordinary. There was an obvious reason for our reluctance but most of the journalists were too busy looking for a more complicated explanation. Perhaps the idea that Tommy was preparing to follow in the doomed footsteps of Jeffrey Archer and Jonathan Aitken was just too far-fetched for them to get their heads around. We could only shrug our shoulders and insist that this was his personal battle – that it was none of our business.

Inevitably, we were slaughtered by the media – and by some of our own members who couldn't understand what was going on. Tommy now went into overdrive behind the scenes. He told members of his family that Catriona Grant and Carolyn Leckie had been behind the decision to remove him. He briefed some of his friends in the media along similar lines. It was a barefaced lie but it had a certain cunning logic behind it. Keith and I, who had originally brought the crisis to a head, were too close for comfort. Just a few months before, we had been the only two SSP members to attend the funeral of Tommy's grandmother. We were virtually part of his extended family, Keith especially.

It wasn't credible to blame us. Frances Curran was also problematic –
she was part of the Militant old guard who had been involved in the
close-knit organisation five years before Tommy became involved.

Carolyn in particular provided a perfect cover story that Tommy
could use to explain my stance. I had been manipulated by a scarlet
woman. And, in turn, I had used my influence over Keith and others
to isolate Tommy. It was pure fiction but it fed into existing prejudices, not the least of which was misogyny. Some people in and
around the SSP and the Scottish media swallowed the toxic concoction like trout gulping down a juicy sliver of bait. The myth of the
scheming blonde was too good a story for some middle-aged male
journalists to question. The *Scottish Mirror*, under the editorship of
Tommy's close friend, Mike Graham, led the charge. 'LOVERS
PLOTTED TO AXE TOMMY' screamed the front-page headline in the
paper a few days after the press conference, alongside large-scale
photos of Carolyn Leckie and me. That morning, I got a phone call
from a senior figure in the *Scottish Mirror* who arranged to meet me in
the Firebird cafe-bar in Kelvingrove.

He was profusely apologetic about the front page and described the
headline as 'actionable'. Off the record, he told me that, late the previous
night, Mike Graham had gone to the City Café, a short walk from the
Mirror's HQ, along with the paper's star columnist, Ron McKenna. He
told me that there had been phone calls back and forth between the pair
and Tommy and the upshot of it all was that a minor human-interest
story – which had already been typeset and tucked away in the inside
pages – was elevated into a front-page splash, accompanied by a sinister
headline. I didn't ask the *Mirror* man how he knew all this but I had
no reason to disbelieve him. In a private conversation with George
McNeilage a day or so before the article appeared, Tommy had
muttered something about the 'black arts', adding, 'I've slipped a few
stories myself.' When I challenged Tommy about his role in the *Mirror*
smear story, he lamely denied any involvement.

By now it was clear that Tommy was conducting the media
orchestra. The symphony reached a crescendo with Iain Macwhirter's
column in the *Sunday Herald*. Macwhirter, a respected political
analyst, had, just a few days before, spent a long time engrossed in
conversation with Tommy in the garden lobby of the Scottish Parliament. For years, even after the party's 2003 breakthrough, Iain had
managed to ignore the SSP, apart from the occasional sneering
dismissal of the 'rent-a-quote Trots' – whose class politics were 'so
twentieth century'. Now, in November 2004, along with a tribe of
other hostile columnists in papers like the *Daily Express* and the *Daily*

Mail, he suddenly developed a deep concern for the health of the SSP and an affinity with Scotland's most prominent class warrior. He slammed the SSP for refusing to knuckle under to Tommy:

> It's an old story. Small-minded people with big ideas about themselves allow personal jealousy and resentment to cloud their political judgement. No longer prepared to walk in Sheridan's shadow, and convinced his celebrity was somehow unsocialist, they subjected their leader to a kind of witch-hunt . . . Sheridan's success was the cause of his downfall. Those who stood in the shadow of his charisma ended up hating him for it, and unable to live with their own mediocrity, they opted to destroy him.

This was totally unfair. He didn't know us, he had never spoken to us, he was ignorant of the facts and was basing his observations on the morsels of fiction spoon-fed to him by Tommy and the gossip circulating in the Holyrood hothouse.

Those of us at the centre of events were incensed. It was close to being the final straw. Why should we protect Tommy's confidentiality when he was exploiting his network of media contacts to spread malevolent lies about the rest of us? We were fighting with two hands tied behind our backs against a ruthless egomaniac.

A group of us got together informally that morning in Frances Curran's flat in Partick. Angry at the way Tommy was manipulating the media, I said I'd be prepared to go personally to Gail and Alice Sheridan and explain the situation to them. That would then clear the way for us to issue a public statement setting the record straight. Others were even more impatient. Rosie Kane and Keith Baldassara both offered to go public with the facts, on a lone mission. All they needed was the nod. They'd have to resign of course but at least it would silence the shrieking choirs who were singing so wildly out of tune. People like Allan Green and Richie Venton pointed to the turmoil it would cause in the party. Maybe they were right. It could have led to an instant split. We cooled down and gritted our teeth as intelligent but ill-informed media commentators continued to dredge up from the depths of their vocabularies the most vicious insults they could muster. We were political pygmies, devious plotters, jealous mediocrities, savage imbeciles, intolerant fanatics. The three women MSPs, Frances, Rosie and Carolyn, were a gaggle of witches, out to cast an evil spell on a decent man.

Some people maintain that, if we had brought everything out into the open back in 2004, the party would have been spared the much greater trauma of the defamation trial and the police investigation. Who knows? Even with the benefit of hindsight, it's impossible to know how events might have unfolded. Our enforced silence certainly allowed Tommy to scheme like a demon for the next 18 months, inside and outside the party.

The injustice of it all was hard to handle, even for veterans of the socialist movement who have had to withstand political abuse for most of our lives. It was one thing for Tom Brown, for example, to mock our politics in the *Daily Record* or *Scotland on Sunday*: 'Weird, wacky and wonderfully idealistic, the modern equivalent of Denis Healey's "socialism wandering in cloud cuckoo land".' That's hard-hitting polemical rhetoric but at least we can argue about it. The abuse now pouring out like molten lava from some sections of the press was of a different order. It was personal, spiteful and false. It was an object lesson in how easily sections of the media could be manipulated by a skilful politician. Some of the news journalists would at least try to hear both sides of the story before rushing to conclusions. But some of the opinion columnists were so gullible they shouldn't have been allowed out on their own.

Inside the SSP, the crisis rumbled on. At a third meeting of the executive, on 24 November, the minutes of the November the 9th executive meeting were distributed and signed for by twenty-two people, excluding Tommy who had tendered his apologies. In the future, during the defamation case, some of these people would claim to have read an entirely different document. The minutes had been based on handwritten notes taken down by the minutes secretary, Barbara Scott, one of the party's most efficient administrators, who had vast secretarial experience outside politics. These notes had been kept under lock and key in the Glasgow HQ of the SSP until the official minutes were drafted on a computer jointly by Barbara and Allan Green, the national secretary. Only one person questioned the minutes – Charlotte Ahmed, a member of the Socialist Workers faction. When Barbara pointed out that Charlotte had not been at the original meeting, she withdrew her objection and the minutes were agreed unanimously.

In one dramatic incident at the same meeting, Allison Kane (no relation to Rosie), the party treasurer, broke down in tears. Allison had been close to Tommy and was torn between duty and friendship. Like quite a few others, she was in a pretty distressed state. She was articulate and came from an unusual background. Her father, a Communist stalwart, had been cast adrift from his wealthy family of industrialists who had once owned the legendary Dixon's Blazes,

which used to light up the skies over the Gorbals. She spoke confidently with a well-modulated middle-class accent she never attempted to hide.

Trusting Allison and recognising that she could be a plausible and
personable ally, Tommy had tried to enlist her as a partner in
subterfuge. Fighting back the tears, Allison told the meeting that
Tommy had asked her to lie and leak false information to the press.
But her loyalty to the party and the truth had outweighed her friendship with Tommy. By blowing the whistle, she acted with bravery and
integrity. It confirmed exactly the suspicions some of us already
harboured about Tommy's conduct and helped explain why we were
taking such a hammering in the press.

The same meeting later agreed to convene a special National
Council the following Saturday – three days later – to allow the
broader membership their say. The National Council meeting would
be strictly members-only, with a rigorous registration system in force.
No minutes would be circulated; no one, other than the minutes
secretary, would be allowed to take notes; and there would be no
references to Tommy's visits to swingers' clubs.

We were now paranoid about internal security. Eleven days earlier,
the night before the infamous press conference, I had spoken at a
meeting in Dundee, attended by our members from across the North-
East region, which stretched from the Moray Firth down to Tayside.
After the Duncan Rowan disaster, I had been invited up to discuss the
fallout in the region and to explain the background to the crisis,
including the reasons for Tommy's removal. Immediately before the
meeting, some of the activists in the region urged me to come clean on
the detail of Tommy's behaviour, rather than vaguely beating about
the bush. But my instincts told me to steer clear of this. It was the right
call.

Four day later, the headline 'Tower of Lies' was splashed across the
front page of the *News of the World* and one of the inside pages of the
Sunday Herald. It was a straight quote from a phrase I had used at the
Dundee meeting – 'we have no intention of helping Tommy build a
tower of lies'. I had spoken without notes and had only a sketchy
recollection of using the phrase but someone present in the small
meeting of around twenty-five people had either secretly recorded my
speech or discreetly taken notes and passed the information on to the
two newspapers. I never found out who it was and was never sure
whether the intention was to undermine me or to damage Tommy – or
a bit of both.

The following Saturday, 28 November, we arrived at Glasgow

Caledonian University for the National Council meeting with the now customary throng of TV crews, reporters and photographers milling around the front entrance. The day before, I had met Tommy and Colin Fox in Edinburgh to try to thrash out a way forward that would protect his confidentiality, while maintaining the integrity and unity of the party. We had a frank but reasonably friendly discussion. On both sides, we had concerns. Tommy wanted reassurance that the minutes of the November the ninth SSP executive meeting wouldn't be distributed to the wider party. Colin and I wanted to draw a line under the events, close down all further discussion after the National Council meeting and then move on. As that could only be achieved with Tommy's cooperation I put three proposals to him.

The first was that he should draw up a press statement dissociating himself from the media attacks on the SSP and specifically refuting the false allegation that he had been the victim of some kind of coup or plot. We had to bury that myth in concrete otherwise the murmured calls for the minutes to be released to the wider party would grow into a deafening clamour. Tommy readily agreed to issue a statement backing the SSP executive's decision.

I further asked him to stop speaking to the press about his personal life. I pointed out that his lies and denials were wearing thin and were bound to come back to haunt him. They were also angering some of our own members who knew the facts. It was now time to shut up. He agreed unconditionally – though he later reneged on his promise.

Finally I requested that he drop his legal action. If he failed to do so, the party would inevitably be put under pressure to back him, as we had discovered during the ill-fated press conference of the previous week. While the legal case remained live, it would be impossible to move on and recapture the glory days of the previous year.

Tommy agreed to this too but asked for thirty days' grace. He insisted that the *News of the World* would back down within that timescale. The newspaper, he predicted with certitude, would issue an apology and a correction – and pay him compensation. I was highly sceptical but agreed that it would be reasonable to wait thirty days, just in case he was right. However, only the three of us knew about this because, if it leaked out to the media, there would be no chance of the *News of the World* backing off.

Naively, as it turned out, I took Tommy at his word. If Tommy had stuck to that part of the agreement, the Scottish Socialist Party would, I believe, have fully recovered during 2005 and gone on to hold the balance of power in the new Scottish Parliament elected in 2007. But there was no climb-down by the paper and Tommy went back on his word. For the next eighteen months, right up until the morning of the trial, he kept telling anyone who would listen that the *News of the World* was about to cave in. The ongoing defamation case debilitated the party for years on end.

Carolyn Leckie chaired the National Council meeting, with 105 delegates and scores of visitors packed into the lecture theatre, which rose up from the front table like a football stand. As with the earlier executive meetings, details of what was said have been preserved in the form of contemporaneous handwritten notes. Because Barbara Scott was unable to attend the meeting, the notes were taken by the co-chair of the party, Catriona Grant.

Allan Green began by painstakingly recounting the tumultuous chain of events of the previous few weeks in his usual low-key but devastatingly effective manner. He dealt with every twist and turn, while managing to skilfully sidestep the more delicate details of Tommy's behaviour. He spelled out, with stark clarity, the dilemma we faced and reminded the meeting of the fate of Jeffrey Archer and Jonathan Aitken. Allan acknowledged that we had all made mistakes but, in defence of the executive, we were dealing with an extraordinary set of circumstances and had acted at all times in the best interests of the party.

In an emotional speech, during which he wiped tears from his eyes, Tommy endorsed Allan Green's report. 'We remain resolute, united and committed to a vision of a socialist society that eradicates poverty, inequality and war,' he told the meeting. 'Much more unites us than divides us.' I had never seen Tommy shed a tear before.

The meeting was overwhelmingly supportive of the stance the executive had taken, though there was the usual cacophony of noise from the self-defined revolutionary vanguard, under instructions as always from London. The Socialist Workers faction, in particular, was deplorable, bleating on about Martin Luther King and Oscar Wilde. 'How can you mention Jeffrey Archer and Tommy Sheridan in the same breath?' one of them asked indignantly. 'Tommy Sheridan is not Jeffrey Archer. Tommy is a socialist who has fought against the war.' It was like watching a class of nursery school children trying to make sense of a Quentin Tarantino movie. I could just picture the judge at a future perjury trial, sitting there with his wig, Che Guevara T-shirt and CND badge, benevolently telling the defendant, 'If you were a Tory, Tommy, you'd be in big trouble. But since you're a socialist I'm going to dismiss all charges against you and commend you for standing up against the might of the Murdoch empire.' These were educated people – professors, lecturers, social workers. Did they seriously believe that an upper-class judge would treat Tommy Sheridan more indulgently than he would treat such pillars of the Tory establishment as Jeffrey Archer and Jonathan Aitken?

One of the smallest factions in the party, the Republican Communist Network, opposed us from the opposite angle. Always principled when it came to matters of democracy, accountability and transparency, they called for everything to be brought out in the open in front of the entire party membership, including the minutes. With the benefit of hindsight, it seems like a better idea now than it did it at the time. We resisted the proposal, fearing that the documentation would inevitably reach the media, with serious consequences for the marriage of Tommy and Gail. It seemed heartless and unnecessary – though a few days before, in the fire of the moment, some of us would cheerfully have taken out a full-page advert in the *Sunday Mail* explaining the facts. But, when push came to shove, we put our human concern for Tommy and his family above the political interests of the party.

Although we were under fire externally, a resounding majority inside the party backed our stance. The National Council voted by eighty-five to twenty, with no abstentions, to 'support the unanimous decisions of the executive concerning the convenor's position'. By an even bigger margin – ninety-three to ten – the meeting voted to accept Tommy's resignation and to 'completely dismiss the rumours that have circulated in the press that Tommy's resignation was provoked by a leadership challenge, a factional power struggle or any other form of internal in-fighting'. The ten dissidents were members of the Socialist Workers Platform who had been pre-programmed to vote against the executive, whatever the arguments they might hear at the meeting.

Tommy himself endorsed the decision and, as agreed the previous day, issued a handwritten statement which we distributed to those journalists still waiting outside the hall at the end of the marathon meeting. It stated:

The Scottish Socialist Party has today showed great maturity in reaching a unified position on the way forward. I would like to take this opportunity to confirm that my resignation as party convenor has nothing at all to do with internal power struggles. There is not and never has been any internal squabbles or backbiting about a leadership challenge. We are a party of principle and action. We have drawn a line under these internal deliberations. I will now work alongside the other party MSPs and the wider party membership to campaign for justice, equality, peace and socialism.

There was one faint, almost inaudible whisper of doubt which was to grow louder in the coming months and eventually become a deafening roar. Tommy had asked the National Council for the right to take libel action: 'If I am wrong, I am wrong. If I find myself in a more difficult situation, then I will accept that. It will be a personal libel action. If I get hung out to dry, then it is my problem.'

I responded by describing the problems the libel action had already caused us:

> Bernard Ponsonby of Scottish Television asked us at the press con-ference, 'Will you back Tommy Sheridan's libel action?' It was like the old question: 'Have you stopped beating your wife?' No matter what we answered we would be slaughtered, if not sooner, then later. By all means take libel action against the *News of the World* – but only if you're as clean as a whistle. Remember, they will have the power to subpoena members of the executive, and our minutes.

The legal terminology was wrong – I had obviously watched too many American courtroom dramas – but the fears I expressed then were to be borne out by later events. Our executive members and minutes were indeed cited – to use the proper expression – by the *News of the World* in 2006.

Yet, back in November 2004, the idea of a court action seemed far away and unreal. I had rather naively assumed that Tommy's gung-ho comments about his defamation action were purely for show. But doubts lingered. On the face of it, it made no sense. It was totally insane, the political and legal equivalent of a suicide bombing. No one thought it was a good idea, apart from the Socialist Workers group. But then, they were the type of people George Orwell was describing when he said, 'They played with fire – and they didn't even know fire was hot.'

Tommy was a different beast. Unlike most of his new fans, he had, in the past, tangled with the courts and the law. But as the months went by, there was no sign of retreat. As I began to learn more and more about the real Tommy Sheridan and the secret life he was living, I realised there was, indeed, a logical explanation for his kamikaze mission.

It could be summed up in one word – suppression.

Late 2004 Onwards

The Discovery of the Evil Empire

During the first five years of the Scottish Parliament, when it was based in temporary headquarters near the top of the Royal Mile, the favourite hang-out of politicians and journalists was a bar called Deacon Brodie's Tavern. The pub was named after a famous Edinburgh dignitary of the 18th century who had led a bizarre double life. By day, he was a respectable businessman, an influential local politician and a pillar of the Edinburgh establishment, but during the night, he would carry out daring burglaries to support his string of mistresses, his five illegitimate children and his gambling addiction. Eventually hanged at the Tolbooth, Deacon Brodie became the inspiration for Robert Louis Stevenson's psychological novella, *The Strange Case of Doctor Jekyll and Mr Hyde*, which explores the psychopathology of split personality or dissociative identity disorder, as it's now called.

After November 2004, I began to suspect that Tommy Sheridan might be our very own Deacon Brodie. During the crisis, I had clung to the belief that Tommy was basically a good guy who had gone off the rails under pressure. His conduct had been reckless. His response to the Anvar Khan revelations had been cowardly. If he had any sense of honour or decency, he would take responsibility for his own actions rather than try to drag his party colleagues into a dangerous cover-up. This was not the Tommy Sheridan of old, I thought. Somewhere along the line, fame and glory must have changed him.

Then, after November 2004, I began to hear about incidents and behaviour that made my skin crawl. This wasn't just Tam the Lad – a flawed individual who had succumbed to temptation from time to time, as people do. Behind that mask of polite charm lurked an abusive, exploitative, self-centred personality. Tommy, I began to discover, was addicted to voyeuristic and exhibitionist sex and he was prepared to go to any lengths to feed that addiction, no matter what the political cost might be or what impact his behaviour might have on the lives of others.

He would operate alongside other male companions and they would regularly book a room for group sex sessions – usually involving two males and one female – in the Central Hotel, adjoining Glasgow's main railway station – the same hotel that was later to be the venue for the launch of Tommy's breakaway party, Solidarity. Tommy and his accomplices also had regular arrangements with at least two women, who weren't involved in politics, in their homes in the Drumchapel and Pollok housing schemes. Other women were put under heavy psychological pressure to participate. One told me that Tommy always insisted that he wasn't gay or bisexual but 'just liked to watch'. He confessed to her that he was obsessed with sex and thought about it all the time. As a Glasgow councillor, he used his secluded office on the top floor of the City Chambers as a secret playground.

I began to hear of other visits to Cupids and to another swingers' club, Le Chambre, in Sheffield. Later, rumours began to circulate that Tommy had a long-term cocaine habit. Whether or not they were true, I had no way of knowing but, either way, Tommy still had enough skeletons in his cupboard to fit out a ghost train running from John o'Groats to Land's End.

During the previous couple of years, he had begun to exhibit a near-paranoid fear of media criticism. In 2001, he had been desperate to sue the *Daily Record* whose editor, Peter Cox, had worked himself into a lather over the SSP's drugs policy, which had been developed by Kevin Williamson who was well known in literary circles as the founder of the magazine *Rebel Inc* and the publishing imprint of the same name. The policy eventually proved far-sighted – our call for clean heroin to be provided free on prescription to registered addicts is now supported by numerous senior police officers as a common-sense measure to reduce drugs deaths and break the power of the criminal drugs gangs. But, in 2001, it was pretty radical – far too radical for the *Daily Record*. Tommy, as the party's public figurehead, was subjected to the Trinity Mirror phrasebook of insults, all of them pretty infantile and predictable.

We responded in kind, through the *Scottish Socialist Voice*, press statements and all the usual rough and tumble. But Tommy was desperate to go much further and began to explore the possibility of legal action. One evening, he took me to meet George Galloway, the king of the libel courts, in a Chinese restaurant round the corner from the SSP's office in Glasgow City Centre. George expressed his disapproval of our liberal drugs policy and told Tommy he'd be crazy to sue on the basis of the material which had appeared in the *Daily Record*. Galloway had just won a sizeable settlement from a local newspaper in the Isle of Man which had run a front-page article accusing the flamboyant MP of hypocrisy a decade earlier by encouraging Poll Tax non-payment while willingly paying his own Poll Tax. It had been patently untrue and could be proven to be so. He contrasted this with the bile and abuse of the *Record* which, although offensive and distasteful, would be impossible to challenge legally.

I had also spoken to the late Paul Foot, the acclaimed investigative journalist who was then working for *Private Eye*. Although Paul was a member of the Socialist Workers Party, he was not a man to submit to the mindless regimentation the party's Central Committee had managed to impose on most of its members. He implored us to desist from legal action. 'They'll crawl all over his private life – and not many people are a hundred per cent squeaky clean. I presume even Tommy has one or two skeletons in his cupboard?' he speculated, in what proved to be piece of inspired understatement. Paul said that he'd be prepared to fly to Glasgow right away to dissuade Tommy from a disastrous libel action. A few years later, when members of the SWP in Scotland were screaming support for Tommy's defamation case, I wished the veteran journalist was still around to knock some sense into their empty heads.

On another occasion, during the 2003 Scottish election, Tommy had a bitter fall-out with the *Sunday Mail*'s political editor, Lindsay McGarvie, over an article that reported Tommy saying he would not back British troops in Iraq. He was quoted as saying:

> We want them back home safe and don't want them involved in a conflict that doesn't involve us and that is an attack on a country which is a slaughter, pure and simple. We found out at Nuremburg that German officers said they were only following orders. I don't want our troops to have that excuse. For many folk, it might be treason to not support our troops in conflict. But anyone who doesn't stand by their convictions at a time like this is being dishonest.

Predictably, Labour, Tory and SNP politicians rushed to condemn Tommy's comments but, instead of standing firm and arguing his case, Tommy turned on the journalist, accusing him of making up the quotes. A few days later, he used his *Mirror* column to launch an extraordinary attack on the *Sunday Mail* reporter:

> I welcomed the journalist, Lindsay McGarvie, into my home and chatted to him in a friendly fashion. The following day, I was appalled to read fabricated statements attributed to me . . . I only hope he is thoroughly ashamed of himself.

Now, by the end of 2004, Tommy had a bigger and more hated foe to fight. Always a clever tactician, he skilfully portrayed his legal confrontation with the *News of the World* as a heroic political stand against the 'evil Murdoch empire'. In philosophy, this kind of rhetorical ploy is termed a 'false dilemma'. Historically, it is a familiar technique used by politicians and especially demagogues to pressurise people into going along with a flawed course of action against their better judgement. It involves reducing complex decision-making to a simplistic choice between two stark and opposing alternatives when, in reality, more than two options exist. George Bush and Tony Blair presented the public with a false dilemma to bolster support for their catastrophic invasions of Afghanistan and Iraq – either you're with the War on Terror or you're with the Taliban and Saddam Hussein. Stalin used it in the 1930s to silence dissent – either you're with the Soviet Union or you're with fascism. Israel uses it today to justify barbaric atrocities against the Palestinian people – either you're with us or you're with the terrorists who are trying to destroy Israel. Compared to the horrors of war, terrorism and tyranny, Tommy's conflict with the *News of the World* was a trivial affair. Yet he used the same insidious political blackmail to justify his actions and silence his critics – either you're with Tommy Sheridan or you're with Rupert Murdoch.

Since the 1980s, Rupert Murdoch had rarely appeared on Tommy's political radar – until November 2004. Margaret Thatcher, John Major, Neil Kinnock, Tony Blair, George Bush and a host of Scottish politicians had all been targets of Tommy's invective over the years but his only connection with Rupert Murdoch was via the media tycoon's local newspapers in Scotland – and Tommy's relationship varied between neutrality and cosiness. Back in 1999, weeks after he was sworn in to the Scottish Parliament, Tommy had even been offered a column by the *Scottish Sun*. In private discussions, he argued strongly in favour of accepting the offer. I was uneasy because of what the newspaper symbolised. The *Scottish Sun* and the *News of the World* had adapted to the more left-of-centre political climate in Scotland. Yet, among some older trade unionists who remembered the picket line battles at Wapping and Kinning Park, the Murdoch press was still associated with anti-trade unionism – even though unions were now recognised within the titles and every other newspaper owner had since followed Murdoch in replacing skilled labour with computer software. The *Sun* was also blatantly sexist in its portrayal of women. Tommy persisted. He told me he had discussed the offer with a senior official of the printers union in Scotland – the Graphical, Paper and Media Union (GPMU). According to Tommy, the official had told him that the unions at the time were having more problems with the *Daily Record* and Trinity Mirror than with Murdoch's News International. For Tommy, this was the green light. He believed it would allow him to get a socialist message across to the paper's predominantly young and working-class readership.

He had a point. Jim Sillars, the left-wing nationalist, had a column in the *Sun* at the time. I had no problem with us writing the occasional unpaid opinion piece whenever we were offered it but to join the *Scottish Sun* as a regular columnist would be seen by many of our stalwarts as a step too far. Jimmy Reid, the hero of the UCS work-in, had been denounced by much of the socialist Left when he accepted a column for the *Sun* in the late 1980s, not long after Murdoch had crushed the print trade unions.

I suggested that, instead, he should go and see Martin Clarke, the editor of the *Daily Record*, and ask him to match the offer of £300 a week for a column. The papers were bitter rivals and I guessed that Clarke would grab the opportunity to spike the guns of his enemy across the river. My calculation was correct. Clarke was a right-wing Tory from the south of England who had joined the *Record* from the *Daily Mail*. He also had a reputation as a tyrannical boss. Yet, curiously, his partner was a Glaswegian who had been involved in the anti-Poll Tax movement, which may have diluted his natural political hostility to Tommy and the SSP. Whatever the reasons, Tommy was offered the column. If he had been turned down, it's likely that, in 1999, he would have joined the payroll of the evil 'Murdoch empire'.

The difference between the two rival media stables was more image than substance. The *Record* was not exactly a shining beacon of social progress. During the debate over Section 28 (which barred the promotion of homosexuality in schools), for example, the *Record* became the main mouthpiece of Brian Soutar's 'Keep the Clause' campaign and poured out torrents of homophobic bigotry on a daily basis. The moralising, narrow-minded crusade was spearheaded by the paper's political editor Ron McKenna – who was later to become a media ally and legal adviser to Tommy. I was writing Tommy's column for the *Record* at the time and, to be fair to the paper's right-wing editor, he never tried to interfere with or censor any of the articles we submitted, including those supporting the scrapping of Section 28. Nonetheless, given the *Record*'s central role in a campaign that was infested with bigotry, I was uneasy about our association with the paper during that time.

The *Record* is also one of the central pillars of British unionism in

Scotland, fanatical in its opposition to Scottish independence. In contrast, the *Scottish Sun* and the *News of the World* had wavered back and forth over the years. Back in the early 1990s, Bob Bird – the man at the helm of the Scottish edition of the *News of the World* during the 2006 libel battle with Tommy – had stunned the media world by suddenly deserting the Tories and converting the *Scottish Sun* into a pro-SNP fanzine in the run-up to the general election that year. 'RISE NOW AND BE A NATION AGAIN,' proclaimed the paper's front page on the day it announced its shock conversion to the independence cause. The rest of the paper read like an SNP manifesto. To accompany the paper's switch to nationalism, Bird hired Jim Sillars as the paper's star columnist. By all accounts, the paper's abandonment of the Tories brought Bob Bird into conflict with his bosses in London but the rising circulation figures soon silenced the critics. Bird, a Londoner, had no strong affinity with Scottish nationalism but he had spotted an opportunity to boost the paper's readership among young working-class Scots. The senior management of News International, it was reported, hated the Braveheart politics of the new-look *Scottish Sun* but they loved the circulation figures.

While retaining their trademark sexism, the Scottish editions of *The Sun* and the *News of the World* continued to reflect Scotland's left-of-centre environment. After 2000, when Tommy was fired as a columnist by the *Daily Record*'s new editor, Peter Cox, he never referred to the paper as anything other than the '*Daily Distort*' and had begun to look more favourably on its tabloid rivals, the *Scottish Sun* and the *News of the World*, which generally gave him fairer coverage.

Following the 2001 general election, the *Scottish Socialist Voice*, in its assessment of the mainstream media coverage of the SSP, acknowledged that the *News of the World* had been more even-handed than most of the Scottish media. 'What a condemnation of the likes of *Scotland on Sunday*, the *Sunday Herald*, *BBC TV* and the *Daily Record* that they are beaten by the *News of the World* – a paper not exactly famous for its in-depth political coverage,' we reported at the time.

After the 2003 election, an editorial in the Scottish *News of the World* had praised Tommy fulsomely:

The SSP leader Tommy Sheridan has already proved that he can make a difference. His bill to abolish warrant sales was a fine piece of legislation of which he can be proud. Firebrand he may be, but he has learned to work within the system. His new colleagues across the smaller parties would do well to learn from his example.

Even just a few months before the Anvar Khan–Fiona McGuire scandal broke, the newspaper's political editor, Euan McColm, had commended Tommy as 'the straight-talking voice of Scottish politics, a champion of the nursery nurses, who in the Parly on Thursday showed a passion all too rare in Holyrood'. During 2004, McColm had commissioned one-off columns from Colin Fox and Tommy Sheridan. Colin's article had been printed but Tommy's had been squeezed out at the last minute by a major breaking-news story. During the 2003 election, the *Scottish Sun*'s election campaign diarist, 'Sergei Platt' – almost certainly Andy Nicoll, the paper's highly literate political editor – confessed, 'I voted for Tommy Sheridan last time, feeling he was a decent enough bloke who'd bring some zest to the proceedings.'

The allegations about Tommy's private life were certainly distasteful but the idea that he had been targeted by Rupert Murdoch in New York for political reasons was mind-blowingly absurd. Nowadays almost all major newspapers – with honourable exceptions such as the *Guardian*, the *Observer* and *The Irish Times* – are owned by giant corporations. *The Herald* and Glasgow *Evening Times*, for example, are owned by the Gannett Company Inc. which publishes 1000 titles in the USA, including eighty-five daily newspapers, and owns twenty-three TV stations. Whenever the SSP was criticised in the *Sunday Herald* or the *Evening Times*, no one would have dreamed of suggesting that it was orchestrated by the chief executive of Gannett Company Inc. in Washington DC. Even Tommy couldn't possibly be so deluded as to believe his own fairy tale. But there was no shortage of nodding dogs eager to believe anything other than the truth. And the sorry truth was that Tommy had simply been exposed by a local journalist because sex scandals sell tabloid newspapers.

Intrusion into people's private lives has long been a trademark of the British tabloid press. The *News of the World* is just as likely to target a right-wing Tory shadow cabinet minister, a millionaire businessman, a high-profile footballer or a member of the royal family as a left-wing socialist. Its scalps have included: Jeffrey Archer; Boris Johnson, the Tory Mayor of London; George Osborne, when Shadow Chancellor; and Sarah Ferguson, the Duchess of York. One of the newspaper's most recent court battles revolved around its report of sadomasochistic sex acts featuring Formula One boss, Max Mosley, the son of Oswald Mosley, a notorious far-right fascist leader.

Unfortunately, it's not only the Murdoch press that rummages through the private lives of celebrities in the hope of dredging up sleaze. The *Mirror* and *Sunday Mirror* were never any better or worse than the *Sun* and the *News of the World* when it came to exposing the most intimate details of the lives of footballers, supermodels, politicians, showbiz presenters, judges and actors, accompanied by lurid photographs and sleazy prose. Nor do the Trinity Mirror tabloids confine themselves to jet-setting A-list celebs. The *Daily Record*, for example, regularly exposes the personal shenanigans of football referees, police officers and local dignitaries. In April 2009, the *Daily Record*'s nomination for the Scottish Press Awards 'Scoop of the Year' was a story headlined, 'REFEREE REV'S ROMPS WITH A SUNDAY SCHOOL MISS'.

Complaining that tabloids intrude into people's personal lives is like complaining that boxers punch their opponents. That's what they do. Editors write headlines about 'Love Rats' while they themselves conduct extra-marital affairs. They do it not because they have a political, or even a moral, agenda but because it sells papers. The same people who are fascinated by the fairytale marriage of Tommy and Gail Sheridan or David and Victoria Beckham are even more fascinated when it all goes wrong. As Bob Dylan observes in his book, *Chronicles*, 'You can sell your privacy, but you can't buy it back. Once you've turned your life into a public art exhibition, it's hard to cordon off those galleries you don't want people to see.'

As public art exhibitions go, the personal life of Tommy Sheridan could have filled the Prado, the Louvre and the Tate Modern combined. He spilled the beans to journalists on everything from the colour of his bathroom wallpaper to his private little jokes with Gail. When his daughter was born, he itemised to journalists exactly how many cards and gifts he received. 'We had 350 cards and over 100 gifts, at least 30 from people we didn't even know,' he told the *Evening Times* months after the birth. Some people found it distasteful, but give credit where credit's due – Tommy knew exactly how to work the media and get the public onside. This was no prickly politician but a man prepared to share his life with the world at large, from the mundane details of his favourite food to the scan of his unborn child. All of which would have been fine and fair enough if it had been the whole story. But another part of him inhabited a seedy, twilight world – a world that was potentially more fascinating to the media than his twee stories of supermarket shopping with Gail or his sheepish confessions to voting in *Pop Idol*. The two lives of Tommy Sheridan were bound to collide at some stage.

The UK tabloids are the most shameless scavengers of scandal to be found anywhere. Yet, paradoxically, the libel laws in the UK are notorious worldwide for their power to protect public figures from media scrutiny. The first-ever libel laws were designed in medieval times to protect the English royal family from criticism and have been used ever since by the rich and famous to silence those who dare question their saintliness.

In 2008, a United Nations human rights committee condemned the libel laws in the UK – which are broadly the same in Scotland, Northern Ireland, England and Wales – as 'a violation of free speech'. In the USA in 1997, the Maryland State Appeals Court refused to recognise a libel action taken by a wealthy Saudi businessman against an American author and condemned the English libel laws as 'repugnant' to the ideal of free speech and a travesty of basic human rights.

The existence of a more open and free press in the United States can be traced back to a landmark ruling in the Supreme Court in 1964. This followed a successful defamation action by the Police Commissioner of Montgomery, Alabama, against *The New York Times*. The newspaper had published an advert by the civil rights movement alleging police brutality and the courts had awarded the Commissioner $500,000 in damages. But the Supreme Court overturned the decision, noting that, although there had been some erroneous statements made in the advert, these had not been made maliciously or recklessly. The press should, the court ruled, be given a 'breathing space' to allow for free expression. Up until that point, the authorities in the Deep South had successfully used the libel laws to intimidate local and national newspapers investigating civil rights abuses. But, after the *New York Times* v Sullivan case, the rules of the game changed. No longer is the burden of proof in the US entirely on the defendant. Public figures now have to prove that the writer or publisher of the defamatory statement either knew the statement to be false or at least recklessly disregarded the truth. In Britain, in a reversal of the norm, the defendant in a libel case is guilty until proven innocent. Only if they can prove that the defamatory statement is true will the court find in their favour, even if they have printed the story in good faith.

When I edited the *Scottish Socialist Voice*, we always sailed close to the wind, publishing numerous stories and comments which probably would have been difficult to prove in the libel courts, even though we knew they were true. The small-scale circulation of the *Scottish Socialist Voice* protected us – if we had been selling hundreds of thousands of copies, we would have had to either censor material or face the legal consequences which could have meant closure of the newspaper and bankruptcy for me as the editor. On a few occasions, we were threatened with legal action but nothing ever came of it.

Other small left-wing publications were less fortunate. In March 2000, legal action by ITN forced the magazine *Living Marxism* out of business when it successfully sued for hundreds of thousands of pounds in damages. The magazine had published an article by a German journalist suggesting that during the Bosnian War ITN had misrepresented its own footage by portraying a standard Serbian-run refugee camp as a Nazi-style extermination camp. *Living Marxism*'s article was substantially true but it was unable to prove that the ITN journalists had deliberately deceived the public. The case provoked international outrage, with internationally-acclaimed writers and journalists, including Doris Lessing, Harold Evans, Paul Theroux and Fay Weldon, condemning the ITN's 'deplorable attack on press freedom'.

There are strong arguments in favour of scrapping the libel laws. Spiked Online, which grew out of the bankrupted *Living Marxism*, argues that 'newspapers should have the right to publish abusive articles about politicians and celebrities, who, after all, are at the centre of public life, and who have recourse, more than anybody else, publicly to dispute unfair allegations made against them'. It suggests that 'as long as society is preoccupied with celebrities, whose private lives are – most often willingly – continually paraded before our eyes, we will have a media constantly searching for ever more salacious stories'. And with some justification, it argues that 'the way to deal with the dire state of public debate today is to fight for more free speech and debate, not less.'

Among the broadsheet-reading middle classes, the prevailing attitude towards tabloid muckraking is generally one of disdain. Yet there are strong progressive arguments in favour of press freedom. Gill Phillips, the director of editorial legal services for the *Guardian*, has condemned the growing trend towards the granting of judicial gagging orders to protect the private lives of celebrities which, she says, are designed to protect:

a rather sordid misogynistic world where Victorian value judgments prevail and where women seem to be treated as bits of property . . . They are not about privacy, they are about power and the abuse of power; they are about men's relationships with women and the abuse of those relationships; and they are about protecting reputation and commercial images.

Suppression of the truth does not change reality. When the newspaper tycoon, Robert Maxwell, drowned off the Canary Islands in November 1991, the British Prime Minister, John Major, and the

Labour leader of the Opposition, Neil Kinnock, paid lavish tributes to him. In Israel, he was given a state funeral on the Mount of Olives, where the country's President, Chaim Herzog, delivered the oration, saying, 'He scaled the heights. Kings and nobles came to his door.' It was no exaggeration. But then, just days after his burial, the world's media went on fire with stories about the tyrannical tycoon – his monstrous megalomania; his crooked wheeling and dealing; his sinister links with the Israeli secret services; his plunder of employees' pension funds to finance his lavish lifestyle; his monumental personal debt. During his lifetime, Maxwell's blanket use of the libel laws had gagged all criticism of his activities. He bombarded the media with so many writs that they eventually raised the white flag. But the dead can't sue for defamation and even the most powerful people on the planet cannot rewrite history.

Compared to Robert Maxwell, Tommy Sheridan was a small-time operator but his strategy of dealing with potential media scandal was broadly the same. He calculated that if he backed down from this confrontation now it could be open season. At the time, none of us had worked that out. From where we were standing, his defamation case made as much sense as jumping out of an aeroplane without a parachute to disprove the laws of gravity.

12

2005

A Game of Poker

When Colin Fox was elected to replace Tommy as the SSP convenor in February 2005, he told the cheering conference in Perth City Halls, 'The best days of the SSP lie ahead of us.' I'm sure his prediction will eventually come to pass but, by 2006, it felt like the most wildly optimistic forecast since Ally McLeod's promise that Scotland would bring the World Cup back from Argentina.

Colin had qualities I admired and respected. He could put strangers at their ease with his light touch and happy-go-lucky sense of humour. When Annabel Goldie, the rather stern and matronly Tory leader, was asked by a newspaper in 2004 who her favourite MSP was, she named Colin Fox. Naturally, we teased him about his popularity amongst the Tory blue-rinse brigade but it did show Colin's ability to break down barriers and confound the hot-headed, megaphone-waving, hard-Left stereotype. But – and, for me, it was a BUT with capital letters – I felt, at that point, we needed someone tougher up front to carry the party through the ongoing Sheridan crisis. I would have been happy with some of our women MSPs – Frances, Rosie or Carolyn – who had drawn clear conclusions about Tommy's character and would not have flinched from facing him down as and when necessary. But they had ruled themselves out. As the deadline for nominations drew close, I was finally persuaded to stand by some key figures in the party who thought I was better equipped to stand up to Tommy.

Colin presented himself as a unifier who could heal the wounds after Tommy's removal. I had championed the cause of socialist unity from the mid-1990s and knew the necessity of a single united party of socialism in Scotland. I also recognised the need to proceed by consensus, where possible. But I also knew that the Sheridan crisis wasn't going to just fade away.

On the face of it, he had little support within the party for his crusade to clear his name. Philip Stott of the CWI, for example, was adamant that it would be a disaster. So too was Steve Arnott, the regional organiser in the Highlands, Jock Penman, the regional organiser in Fife, Graeme McIver, the regional organiser in South Scotland, and Gordon Morgan, the assistant treasurer of the party. All of them went on to become key figures in Solidarity. The exception was the Socialist Workers Party. They were positively drooling at the prospect of Tommy taking on the hated Murdoch empire. Their support galvanised Tommy and their infantile enthusiasm fed his messianic complex. Instead of trying to close down a sordid sex scandal, Tommy, they seemed to believe, was now galloping on his white steed to the gates of the Murdoch castle.

Fired up by the adulation of a sizeable faction that he had previously despised – and by some even more surprising displays of hero-worship from elements of the media who had previously despised *him* – Tommy now became more emboldened. Scenting the possibility of bringing the party back into line, he embarked on a Mandelsonian-style smear campaign against those who had refused to support his doomed mission. His call for unity during the November National Council was now forgotten as he held a series of private face-to-face meetings with people he felt he could influence. Tommy had always been an expert at pushing the right buttons, scattering flattery like confetti and making people feel like they were ten feet tall. Sometimes he reminded me uncomfortably of General Trujillo, the degenerate former President of the Dominican Republic, as depicted in Mario Vargas Llosa's great novel, *The Feast of the Goat*, with his 'hypnotist's eyes, a master manipulator of innocents, fools and imbeciles, an astute exploiter of men's vanity, greed and stupidity'.

His charm was legendary – but not everyone succumbed. Davie Archibald was one of those on Tommy's hit list. He had known Tommy, Keith and me for decades but had been abroad during the November events. When he first heard about the crisis, he was fairly neutral, believing some compromise would have to be thrashed out. Tommy held his hands up to visiting the swingers' club, while insisting repeatedly that the executive had mishandled the problem. 'But you've put them in one hell of a position,' Davie told him. He left the meeting with one overpowering thought: 'This guy has a real issue about taking responsibility for his own actions.'

At that point, Tommy wouldn't have dared to openly make the accusations that he was later to trumpet at full volume in the Court of Session – especially not inside the party. The last thing he wanted was to open up a discussion about the real reasons for his resignation. Yet, behind the scenes, he fed the flames of suspicion. With the aid of his conspiratorial spin doctor, Hugh Kerr, he already planted the idea of a plot in the minds of some journalists who had not quite bought into his initial claim that he was standing down to spend more time with his family. This was a more conveniently obvious explanation of Tommy's resignation. And the fact that we were silent surely exposed our guilt, did it not? Like Iago, the manipulative villain in Shakespeare's *Othello*, Tommy was taking advantage of others' ignorance and misunderstanding to create an alternative reality. Ironically, he could only do this because we had stayed silent out of respect for his confidentiality. The seeds of a myth began to germinate.

Some of us understood what was going on and knew that there was serious trouble ahead but there was nothing we could do except wait. Some, who had initially supported the stand we took, had been flattered into submission by Tommy. Others were caught somewhere in the middle – including even Colin, which is the main reason I stood against him. During the contest, we engaged in a few bouts of shadow boxing on issues like independence. Colin, who was being backed by the anti-independence factions within the party, said that he believed socialism was more important than independence. My view was – and is – that we could never begin to move seriously towards socialism in Scotland without first gaining full national independence.

But we had a more immediate dilemma on our hands – how to prevent Tommy from dragging the party into a poisonous swamp. I felt we had to face Tommy down to prevent further damage. Colin was more pragmatic. In an interview during the convenorship election, Colin told the *Sunday Herald* that he felt, with hindsight, that Tommy 'probably should have been treated a bit more respectfully'. He suggested that three of our MSPs – Frances, Rosie and Carolyn – 'do seem to have a problem with Tommy, but they'll have to get over it'. Their response was characteristically blunt: 'You're damned right we've got a problem with Tommy.'

Tommy, in turn, enthusiastically supported Colin and helped him pull together an unstoppable coalition which included the SWP and CWI factions and all but one of the seven influential regional organisers, as well as Tommy's own hard-core fan club. Many of us were convinced that Tommy saw Colin as someone to be discarded when the time was right – a temporary vehicle he could use to transport himself back into the leadership. Our suspicions were eventually confirmed in the period preceding and following the 2006 defamation case.

I understood why people were beginning to waver. We were under fire from the media and the atmosphere within the party was feverish. I could also understand the desire for unity. But I knew Tommy better than most and knew how ruthlessly he would exploit any sign of weakness. His game plan was clear to me – force the *News of the World* to back down and then, basking in adulation, make his move to reclaim his crown. But what if the *News of the World* refused to back down? Some of us had already calculated that the consequences of a court case could be catastrophic. And even if he succeeded in forcing the newspaper to retreat, where would that leave the SSP? It would be an illusory, temporary victory based on lies and fraud. Those who knew the score would be forced to remain silent while the party re-installed a leader who was a walking, talking time bomb.

At the 2005 SSP conference in Perth City Halls, Colin was elected as expected. As a non-MSP, I had taken a credible 40 per cent of the vote. This was despite the bloc vote of around 20 per cent controlled by the SWP and CWI platforms who were out for revenge against me for my role in the wars of independence within the party. Tommy, too, was relieved that Colin had won. He was photographed on the steps outside the conference holding Colin's hand aloft. He praised Colin's victory in the *Scottish Daily Mirror*, while the newspaper's leader told its readers: 'If Fox had lost the leadership to Alan McCombes, it would have been curtains for the party.' It was reassuring that Mike Graham, the right-wing unionist who edited the *Scottish Mirror*, was so concerned for the health of Scotland's left-wing, anti-capitalist pro-independence party.

Colin, though, wasn't gloating. He knew he had to work with me to unify the SSP. And I knew that if Colin faltered it would be disastrous for the party. We vowed to work together to help put the party back on track. When the result was announced, Colin made his victory speech and I joined him on stage, to a rousing ovation from the 500-strong conference. A sense of relief resonated around the packed hall. The SSP was now united once again and could move forward to repair the damage of the previous three months. Or that's how it looked on the surface.

It soon became clear that Tommy's support for Colin had been a charade. He was playing the cynical politician's game of diplomatic skulduggery. To borrow the colourful phrase coined by Lenin, he was supporting Colin like the rope supports the hanging man. He now openly broke his promise not to speak to the press about his private life, telling the *Evening Times*, in a full-on personal interview, that he would never forgive the *News of the World* for 'threatening not only my child's life, but my wife's life'. This was melodramatic stuff – women give birth everyday in the war zones of Afghanistan, Palestine and Iraq and in disease-ridden shanty towns across Africa – but worse was to come.

> I'll never forgive it for that and I'll never forgive anyone who believed its lies either to be honest. If there was anyone who considered themselves close to me I'll never forgive them for effectively siding with what I would call the forces of darkness.

This was a thinly veiled public attack on the decision that we had taken back in November. It was also dishonest – no one believed the 'lies' of the *News of the World*. What we did believe were the facts, admitted by Tommy with his own tongue. That was what we based our decision upon – and Tommy knew it. He was now lying about his comrades in the SSP leadership not just to his close family circle or even privately to journalists through a third party but openly to the people of Glasgow through the evening newspaper. He knew we were effectively gagged and could not reply.

The extent of our secrecy was underlined by the political editor of *The Times*, Angus MacLeod, on STV's *Politics Today* programme. MacLeod, the most senior political journalist in Holyrood, was always disparaging of 'the Trots' as he invariably referred to the SSP and, in a studio discussion in the summer of 2005, remarked how incredible it was that the reason for Tommy Sheridan's resignation had remained such a closely guarded secret: 'You've got to hand it the Trots when it comes to iron discipline.'

In retrospect, the only way the catastrophe of 2006 and 2007 could have been avoided was if we had forced him to call off his court action by threatening to remove the party whip if he persisted and then issuing an explicit public statement explaining why we had done so. But, if you make a threat, you have to be prepared to carry it through. Effectively, it would have meant expelling Tommy from the party and the SSP had never before expelled anyone – let alone its most high-profile figure who, in many people's eyes, personified the party. It would also have meant publicly exploding the hand grenade of the Cupids story, with incalculable repercussions. All of that would have been a step too far and would never have got the support of the wider party. We were caught in a trap.

Far from being disrespectful to Tommy, we were gentle – too gentle by far. Yet we continued to be portrayed in the media as a gang of ruthless, backstabbing executioners. The irreverent and entertaining Tom Shields at least sugar-coated his pillorying of the SSP with a spoonful of humour when he ridiculed Colin in the *Sunday Herald* for dressing up as Robin Hood for a photocall.

> The SSP, once revered as a party of principle are now exposed, after the coup against Tommy Sheridan, as just like any other party when it comes to internal power struggles . . . When asked to vote SSP, left-wingers who value loyalty and integrity may find the phrase 'Away and take a Friar Tuck tae yerself' springs to mind.

Others in the media just spat venom. We had broken the rules of the political game. How dare a two-bit political party try to exercise control over the most charismatic political leader in Scotland? The message boomed out loud and clear – without Tommy Sheridan, the rest of us were nothing. We should have left well alone. We began to feel like Richie Roberts, the New York cop played by Russell Crowe in the Hollywood film *American Gangster*. On one operation in the 1960s, he had found $1 million – and handed it over. It was the end of his police career. He had behaved too ethically. In the then corrupt NYPD, no one ever trusted him again.

During the summer and autumn of 2005, the baiting of the SSP continued. Ten months after the decision, we were still unable to move on. In late August 2005, Peter Mullan, the acclaimed film director and actor, went on TV to denounce the ousting of Tommy Sheridan as 'disgraceful'. He continued, 'I was enraged. Still am. Most of us are. Most of the guys I know were sickened by it.' Peter was a member of the SSP at the time but had never participated in any of the discussions within the party over Tommy's behaviour and ongoing legal action. I was personally disappointed that he hadn't spoken to me, at least to hear what I had to say. Peter and I went back a long way – to back before either of us knew Tommy. George Galloway joined in, criticising us at the Edinburgh International Book Festival for 'a terrible blunder'. Colin tried to meet George and Peter separately, face-to-face, to explain our side of the story. George agreed and met Colin just before going on stage for his one-man show at the Citizens Theatre in Glasgow. He listened respectfully to the full story and agreed not to interfere.

Within a year, though, George seemed to have forgotten everything he had been told. On the eve of the libel case, he appeared on the BBC's *Politics Show* to support Tommy's imminent court action and to accuse us of a 'political assassination'. The Respect leader, normally a savvy, streetwise politician, told Glen Campbell, the presenter, 'I've spoken to Tommy and he's denied having an affair – and I believe him.' Also on the programme was Rosie Kane. In the same patronising tone with which he had previously lectured some of the young contestants in *Big Brother*, George told her, 'I was in politics before you were born.' This apparently was the clinching proof that Tommy was right and we were wrong. By Rosie's calculation, George must have become involved in politics when he was in Primary 2 – either that or she had just been paid an unintended compliment.

Peter Mullan, on the other hand, pulled out of the meeting with Colin at the last minute and was reluctant to arrange any further discussions. He had made up his mind. It was a pity. I respected Peter and some of the other actors and directors who had made a big contribution to the SSP since our formation. I especially liked Peter's sidekick, Davy McKay, a warm-hearted, friendly guy who was actually better known than Peter in Glasgow – by sight, if not by name – because of his appearances in *Rab C. Nesbitt* and other popular TV shows. I also liked the writer Martin McCardie, a talented scriptwriter, who has written for the 7:84 Theatre Group, *River City* and *Taggart*, as well as for SSP election broadcasts.

During the 2005 election, I spoke to Martin repeatedly to try to get the team of actors and writers together to produce our election broadcast. But, in contrast to previous elections, their response was lukewarm. Eventually, after repeated attempts to get a meeting together, it became clear we were flogging a dead horse. I hastily cobbled together a script myself and got the MSPs together in Shettleston Halls with a couple of lesser-known actors and a sympathetic cameraman. The short film was never going to win an award at Cannes but at least we had something. Tommy was fully cooperative, making his points on film with his customary eloquence and power. But I was convinced that, behind the scenes, he had subtly encouraged Peter Mullan and others to boycott the broadcast.

When we finished filming, some of us went over to the Òran Mór bar in the West End of Glasgow for a couple of beers. There I bumped into Davy McKay and Martin McCardie. Martin was apologetic about the broadcast. He explained that Peter had all the key contacts but he had been obstructive because of the way he thought we had treated Tommy. 'He shouldn't be taking sides in this. It would be like you taking sides if Peter and Davy were ever to fall out,' said Martin. It was a fair point – except that the next time I heard of Martin, he was up to his neck aiding and abetting Tommy in the run-up to his court case. Tommy had ensnared another decent, well-intentioned individual in his web of deceit.

The last meeting I ever had with Tommy took place in the Beanscene coffee shop, behind the Holyrood parliament, on a cold grey December

morning in 2005. Colin Fox and Allan Green were there too. They had
set up the meeting partly to try to repair relations between us. 'The party
wants to see you two working together,' Colin told Tommy and me.

Our friendship was long since dead and buried. At both a political
and a personal level, I deemed his behaviour intolerable but I had
always been willing to work with him. People have to put aside their
feelings to work with colleagues all the time. Even Tony Blair and
Gordon Brown at the time were working as a team. The first part of
the meeting was amicable enough. We both agreed we would meet
regularly and try to pull together politically for the sake of the party.
But then we moved on to discuss Tommy's reselection as top of the
Glasgow list in the 2007 Holyrood election, eighteen months in the
future. Tommy was resentful that the SSP's Glasgow regional council
had voted to delay the selection conference until after his court case.
I wasn't a member of the Glasgow regional council and hadn't been
involved in the decision but Tommy seemed to believe that I was
pulling strings behind the scenes. I wasn't, but if I had been at the
meeting, I would have voted with the majority to delay the selection –
and I told him so. There was no rush. In 2003, most of our regional
lists were selected barely six months before polling day. It seemed to
me that Tommy was trying to railroad his selection process early to
remove any leverage we might have over his looming court action.

'So what you're saying is that, if I lose the court case, I'm not good
enough but, if I win, that's OK?' he asked me belligerently. Allan
Green and I both waded into Tommy, with Colin in the role of
peacemaker. We explained that, if he took this all the way to the Court
of Session and lost, he would have big problems standing. In the first
place, he'd be bankrupted – which meant he'd be automatically
banned from standing for public office. And, if he won, he would
have even bigger problems because he could only win it by committing perjury. We appealed to him again to call off the case. The
Glasgow regional council would then green-light the selection meeting
– and Tommy would be guaranteed the number-one spot.

I had always been a reasonably easy-going, non-judgemental person, someone tolerant of other people's flaws and weaknesses, but
what I had discovered about Tommy over the previous twelve months
had destroyed any respect I had for him. Yet I was also pragmatic.
Only a few people, a handful at most, were truly in the picture. Most
party members – even those who were exasperated by his apparent
stupidity over the *News of the World* crisis – still saw Tommy as a
formidable political asset. And, in the eyes of our wider support base,
he remained a hero.

Tommy refused to budge. He insisted that the *News of the World* were ready to back down, saying, 'It's a game of poker.' Maybe but the stakes were slightly higher than for the games of poker I used to play in building-site bothies.

And what if they refused to blink?

'Gordon Morgan has looked into this. He's found out that they can't call Anvar Khan as a witness. This is only about Fiona McGuire, and they're not allowed to bring unrelated information into the case. So they've no evidence.'

Gordon – an IT consultant who had worked as a parliamentary researcher for the SSP group for a while – was a nice-enough guy and he had possibly watched a couple of episodes of *Rumpole of the Bailey*, but he wasn't the type of person you'd hire as a legal advisor if you were in trouble. In a defamation case like this, the character of the pursuer would be on trial. It was elementary stuff. This wasn't a criminal case where the defence lawyer can conceal from the jury the fact that his honest, upright client, who has been scurrilously accused of shoplifting, has masterminded a few bank robberies in his time. It was a civil case, brought by Tommy – and nothing about his personal life would be off limits. If Tommy admitted to visiting Cupids with a *News of the World* columnist and a gang of friends behind his wife's back, it would take no great leap of the imagination for the jury to accept that he might also be capable of having an extra-marital fling. And, if he denied it, then he was entering shark-infested waters – and possibly dragging the whole of the SSP in with him. As for his insistence that the *News of the World* would back down . . . If Tommy was as pure as the driven snow, then his confidence might be justified but this was the newspaper that had bugged the royal family and accessed David Beckham's private text messages. Who knows what ammunition they had already assembled? Maybe a few blanks. Or maybe a stash of gelignite.

Before the meeting ended, Tommy raised a more pertinent point. He had already run up around £10,000 in legal fees. Because it was a 'no-win, no-fee', arrangement, this would eventually be written off but only if he went through with the action. If he called it off now, he would have to cough up. 'OK,' we told him, 'we'll launch an appeal to raise the money among our members and supporters. We'll get the money.' It was a generous offer. Ten grand was a hefty price to pay to hoist him out of the trench he had dug himself into against our advice. Inevitably some party members would object and refuse to contribute but we had 3000 members and tens of thousands of supporters. Tommy refused to accept financial help. He no doubt calculated that it would mean a loss of face and would vindicate those of us who had challenged him. People like Tommy never admit to mistakes. Humble pie is never on the menu. He would rather bankrupt himself.

It was deadlock. And it was starting to look as though the future of the socialist movement in Scotland might end up being decided by a High Court judge, a handful of lawyers and a dozen random men and women who hadn't yet been selected.

13

Mid-May 2006

The Minutes Tick Away

Tommy was subdued, his attention far away, as he met with Allan Green and Morag Balfour. The day before, on Sunday 7 May, an SSP National Council Meeting in Edinburgh had been buoyant and optimistic. Opinion polls were showing the party in recovery mode and almost back to pre-crisis levels of support. Morale was rising and the gloom that had suffocated the party for six months had begun to lift. A few months earlier, Tommy had been elected unopposed to the post of co-chair of the party and was now meeting his other co-chair, Morag, and the National Secretary, Allan Green, to review the decisions of the day before.

By the Thursday, the reason for his detachment had become clear. Out of the blue, two sheriff officers appeared at the door of the SSP's HQ in Kinning Park brandishing a court citation. James Nesbitt, the Scottish Socialist Youth Organiser, phoned me on my mobile right away. 'We've just had a visit from the Sheriff Officers and you, Foxy, Frances and Eddie Truman have been cited to appear in the Court of Session. It's about Tommy's libel case.' He read me the citation. It ordered us to attend a hearing at the Court of Session the following Tuesday afternoon, before a Commissioner of the Court. It instructed us to bring 'all minutes, records, notes or other documents recording or bearing to record discussions at/or decisions of the meeting held on or about 9 November 2004', plus the same material concerning 'a meeting of members of the Scottish Socialist Party in Dundee on 15 or 16 November 2004.' This was the infamous 'Tower of Lies' meeting that had been leaked to the press.

No wonder Tommy had seemed preoccupied. At that very moment, his legal team were battling it out in an Edinburgh courtroom to stop the *News of the World*'s submission to cite our internal documents. But we knew nothing about it. Tommy had kept us in the dark. The tussle had raged on for three days, before the judge ruled in favour of the *News of the World*. By the time we discovered what was going on, our internal minutes had legally become the property of the court. By that stage, any attempt to change or destroy these minutes would almost certainly have led to serious criminal charges. Among his other convictions, Jeffrey Archer had received a four-year jail sentence for perverting the course of justice by altering an entry in his own diary to assist his libel case. Even if it had been politically acceptable to rewrite our own history by falsifying these minutes, redacting them, editing them or destroying them, Tommy's secrecy had made this impossible.

The *News of the World*'s citation of these minutes had been a speculative venture as the paper had no idea what they might contain. But we did. The document consisted of a summary of a statement by Tommy, followed by a similarly condensed version of my response. Then there was a list of those who had contributed to the discussion and an explanation of the decisions agreed by the meeting. In total, the document ran to just two pages but the 1500 words it contained were explosive. The minutes reported that:

> Tommy responded to a recent article in the News of the World which alleged that a married MSP had visited a swingers/sex club in Manchester in the company of a female journalist who had now written a book about her lifestyle. Tommy admitted to the meeting that he had in fact visited the club on two occasions in 2006 and 2002 with close friends. He acknowledged this had been reckless behaviour and with hindsight had been a mistake. He reported that he had met with Keith B and Alan Mc and asked them for the opportunity to fight this on his own and for other party members, if questioned about it, to either give no comment or refer all questions to himself. He said he was confident there was no proof in existence that he had visited the club. Tommy said he was not prepared to resign as convenor unless proof was revealed to exist. His strategy was to deny the allegations and in this regard he had already taken advice from NUJ solicitors.

Next came my response:

> Alan felt that the public would forgive sexual misconduct but not the convenor of the party telling lies about this and refusing to face up to the consequences. Alan had asked Tommy to manage the issue in the media as soon as he is named as the MSP involved in the story, apologise and resign as convenor, citing the reason that he wanted to spend more time with his family. However, Tommy had refused to do this, instead wanting Alan and Keith to participate in a cover-up. Alan voiced his concern about the NUJ being involved in this, as their help

had been enlisted with false information. He cited the Bill Clinton/ Monica Lewinsky affair and pointed out that the most damaging part of that to Bill Clinton was the public denial. He felt it would be political suicide to deny these allegations in the press.

The minutes continued:

Without exception, all contributors disagreed with the strategy of denying the allegations. All felt that this would be the most damaging strategy for the party. The general feeling was that this was a bad situation, and the 'least worst' option must be found. All agreed it would be better if Tommy changed his mind about denying the allegations.

The document concluded by listing the various votes taken at the end of the meeting. No matter how you read it, the release of these minutes would expose Tommy as a liar and blow his legal action out of the water. At the first sight of this document, the editor of the *News of the World* would be dancing a samba with his legal team.

When I heard about the citation I spoke informally to some other executive members. We agreed it was now vital to ramp up the pressure on Tommy to call off his action. Tactically, we thought it would be wise if I stayed out of these discussions. Nor would Frances, Carolyn or Rosie cut much ice with Tommy. At that point, he would be more open to persuasion by Allan Green and Colin Fox.

The three of them arranged to meet the following afternoon, a Friday, at Lenzie train station, on the northern outskirts of Glasgow. From there, they went to the beer garden of the Golden Pheasant, a pub in the village of Auchinloch. Allan and Colin adopted a friendly, reasonable tone but one that was intended to put Tommy straight. 'All along you've said that the party would be kept out of this. Now we've been dragged in against our will. You have to kill it now,' said Allan Green. 'If you don't, you're going to put people in an intolerable position.'

Tommy refused to consider backing off. 'I'm in too deep financially,' he insisted.

Colin repeated the suggestion we'd made to him before. 'We'll find ways and means of raising the money. We'll launch an appeal. I'll do whatever I can to raise the cash to get you out of this.'

Tommy was dismissive. 'Who's going to throw money into a bucket to defend somebody who's been labelled a love rat by the tabloids?' The laundering of his reputation seemed more important to Tommy than anything else, including the prospect of party members being locked up in jail. 'Anyway, the *News of the World* case is on the verge of collapse. That's why they've issued these citations – because they've nothing else. This is their last throw of the dice.' He claimed to have a mole inside the *News of the World*'s legal team, who had told him that Anvar Khan was coming under pressure from the *News of the World* to give evidence – but she didn't want to and was now seeking advice from her union, the NUJ. As it later transpired, there was some truth in this, though the source of the information was not the *News of the World* lawyers. Tommy also insisted that Fiona McGuire wouldn't give evidence either – though he didn't explain how he had obtained such information about a woman he claimed never to have set eyes upon.

Allan pointed out that, even if Tommy's intelligence was accurate, both women would ultimately be forced to give evidence under citation, just as SSP members were now being cited to produce the minutes. Whether or not they were reluctant was neither here nor there.

'Yes,' said Tommy, 'but who would have most credibility in front of a jury? Me – or a reluctant Anvar Khan and Fiona McGuire?'

Allan changed tack. 'So what are we supposed to do? Allow people to go to jail to rescue your court case?'

Tommy nodded. 'I'm saying we should hold our nerve. This is the last throw of the dice for the *News of the World*. They've got nothing except the SSP's minutes. If you hand them over, it'll be the SSP, my own party, that's destroyed my court case against these people. There's a tradition on the Left of defiance of the courts. The party shouldn't cooperate with this. We should be challenging them and defying them.'

The discussion wasn't going anywhere. Allan had brought a copy of the minutes for Tommy to look at. Colin excused himself at that point as he had been cited and didn't want to compromise himself by handling the minutes until the legal process had been exhausted. Tommy studied the minutes intently. He wasn't just reading them to get the general gist – he was totally engrossed. He made only one comment: 'I don't remember making that remark about a gift horse.' It was incidental. The full phrase as worded in the minutes was: 'He stated his belief that to stand down immediately would be a gift horse to the enemies of the party.'

Later, as he dropped Tommy off at Lenzie Station, Allan continued to press the issue. 'I'm not happy about what you're doing here, Tommy. It's intolerable. Personally, I'm now in favour of making

these minutes open to the party membership, then handing them over
to the court. Wouldn't it be better for you if you just handed them over
yourself? At least you'd come out of it with a bit of credibility.'

Tommy shrugged his shoulders. He then told Allan he had been
discussing the minutes with his lawyers. 'They're saying maybe it
wouldn't be fatal to my case.' It was a strange point to make, especially
given that he had just read his own explicit admissions as recorded in
those very minutes. And it contradicted his vehement arguments of
half an hour before.

That night, Allan Green phoned to tell me about the meeting with
Tommy. Up until that meeting, both Allan and Colin had been a bit
more sympathetic to Tommy than some of the rest of us on the executive
but now they were running out of patience. Allan had been chilled to the
bone by his attitude. He told me that it was now clear that Tommy was
oblivious to anything and everything except his own reputation. He
would watch people go to jail if he felt it would help him. He would coldly
lie in court to protect his image, whatever the damage it caused to others.
He summed up Tommy's attitude with a play on the title of an old Lesley
Gore song, 'It's my Party (and I'll lie if I want to)'.

Allan and Colin were both now convinced that we should just agree
to bring the minutes to the court the following Tuesday. Any other
way of dealing with it would be impossible to sustain. Defiance could
mean imprisonment for the four people cited. The two MSPs on the
list, Colin Fox and Frances Curran, would be forced to resign their
seats. There was no option but to comply.

I understood and accepted their point of view but I disagreed.
Handing over the minutes would torpedo Tommy's defamation
action and he would go on the political rampage. I could almost hear
his booming indignation as he lambasted the SSP executive as a
spineless collection of cowards who had caved in to the *News of the
World* and the judiciary without a whimper of resistance. I could also
imagine the sycophantic stamping, clapping and cheering of a big
swathe of his audience.

In the courts, we could justify our defiance by arguing the right to
confidentiality. Even BBC Scotland had refused to hand over the
tapes of the Holyrood documentary, *The Gathering Storm*, to a public
inquiry into the spiralling costs of the new building. We could also
argue that this court case should not involve the SSP because it was a
private dispute between Tommy Sheridan and the *News of the World*.

Allan Green excelled in getting right down to the logical core of any
argument. Based on reason alone, his arguments for handing over the
minutes were unanswerable but we weren't dealing with reasonable or

logical people. As events were later to show, there was no shortage of SSP members – some of them highly educated professionals – who were as susceptible to manipulation by a demagogic orator as the crowd at a Nuremburg rally. I knew in my heart that compliance would provoke an ugly political backlash.

By the following morning, I had a plan which I talked through with a group of people in Frances Curran's flat in Partick, the day before the executive meeting on the Sunday. I would take sole custody of the minutes – and refuse to hand them over to the court. I lived in a rented flat and the most valuable thing in it was an old guitar worth a couple of hundred quid at the most. I was not an elected MSP and had no parliamentary ambitions so I couldn't care less if I was banned from standing for public office. On the other hand, I had no romantic notions about life behind bars. I was now over fifty with three teenage daughters. Prison was a daunting prospect but the alternative was to capitulate to the courts – and see the work that I and other people had put in over decades reduced to ashes in the inevitable civil war that would erupt within the party. It was defiance or destruction.

The executive that Sunday afternoon were tense, though one familiar face was missing. Tommy had failed to show. Nor did he appear at any of the other crisis meetings over the next turbulent two weeks while the SSP was under siege in the courts. He submitted apologies to Allan Green using the lame excuse that he had been given legal advice to stay away from party meetings in the run-up to his own court action. The advice, however, didn't prevent him coming to a National Council meeting after I was locked up and publishing a defamatory and paranoid open letter in the press.

Because the latest crisis focussed on the minutes of the November 2004 executive meeting, it was agreed copies of the relevant minutes should first be circulated to everyone at the meeting who wished to read them, in order to refresh their memories. Colin, because he was cited, refused to take a copy. Jock Penman also refused to take a copy. Allan then explained the full background. Although he was still not convinced that we should defy the citation, he presented the various options fairly. We could comply, lie or defy. I put my position strongly, backed by Carolyn, Frances, Keith and others.

Eventually, the meeting voted on a series of resolutions. The first stated: 'As Tommy Sheridan's court action has negatively impacted on the party, its MSPs and office bearers, the executive committee calls on Tommy Sheridan to withdraw from the court action.' It was agreed with one person voting against – Donnie Nicholson, the party's youth organiser, who made it clear that his only objection was that it should have 'instructed' rather than 'requested' Tommy to end his action.

Those supporting the resolution included Jock Penman, who was later charged with perjury arising from his testimony in the defamation case, and Sinead Daly of the CWI group. Within a few months, the CWI group became instrumental in splitting the SSP and forming Solidarity, on the grounds that the SSP had failed to back Tommy's court action. Consistency had never been their strong point.

The other resolutions concerned the tactics over the minutes. One proposal – 'to allow these minutes to be destroyed' – was voted down unanimously. Eventually, the meeting voted for a resolution stating, 'Alan McCombes has custody of these minutes and should argue that the SSP NC has previously decided that these minutes are confidential, therefore they cannot be handed to the court.' This position was agreed, with just one vote against and one abstention. The vote against had been cast by the chair of the meeting, Morag Balfour, a strong pacifist and Quaker, who argued on humanitarian grounds that no one should have to go to jail to protect Tommy Sheridan. Allan was reluctant to vote for a resolution he knew would almost inevitably send me to jail so he abstained.

A few days later, on the late afternoon of Tuesday 16 May, the four cited SSP officials were called up to face a commissioner – an advocate lawyer appointed specifically to recover evidence sought by one of the parties in a legal case. Ranged across the front benches sat the two teams of lawyers representing the *News of the World* and Tommy Sheridan. Behind them, a few dozen SSP members packed into the tiny courtroom.

First up, in alphabetical order was Frances Curran. Courageous and dedicated to the socialist cause, Frances would readily have defied the courts on behalf of the party. But the rest of us were clear – Frances was a single parent with a seven-year-old son and we were not prepared to put her in the firing line. She faced the panel of interrogators.

'Were you at the meeting of the executive of the Scottish Socialist Party on November 9, 2004?'

'Yes.'

'Were minutes taken of that meeting?'

'Yes.'

'Have you ever seen these minutes?'

'Yes.'

'Are you in possession of these minutes?'

'No.'

'Do you know who has possession of these minutes?'

'Yes.'

'Who?'

'Alan McCombes.'

Next up was Colin Fox, who was asked the same questions and gave the same answers. Both felt uncomfortable about naming me but that's what they had to do – they were implementing the decision we had taken.

Then it was my turn. I admitted that I had sole custody of the minutes but they were not in my possession at that moment. Pressed further, I explained that these minutes were internal, confidential party documents and I would not be handing them over to the court. The commissioner moved on to the Dundee 'Tower of Lies' meeting. I explained that I had addressed the meeting without notes and had no documentation. He returned to the minutes and repeatedly asked me if I understood the gravity of the stance I was taking and the potential consequences of defying a court order.

'Yes, I understand that,' I explained. 'But this is a matter of principle.'

The commissioner then informed me of the standard legal procedure when a dispute arises over confidentiality of evidence. The document should be lodged to the court in a sealed envelope. A hearing would then be held to decide the rights and wrongs of the arguments. After listening to both sides, the judge would then view the sealed document and make a decision.

'And what if the judge decides that the document should be released?' I asked.

The commissioner explained that, if the judge found in my favour, the document would be returned to me in a sealed envelope and the contents would remain forever confidential. But, if the verdict went in the opposite direction, the document would then be handed over to the *News of the World*'s legal team.

'In that case I can't comply.'

We had reached a stalemate. The perplexed commissioner told me that he would now have to send a report to the judge dealing with the case. I could expect a citation soon asking me to appear at a full hearing of the Court of Session to face contempt of court charges.

Outside the courtroom, our members were supportive but sombre. The die was cast. The party was now on a collision course with the Scottish legal establishment. It was difficult to see how the grave consequences hinted at by the commissioner could be avoided unless one or other parties to the libel case backed down. But neither Tommy nor the *News of the World* was prepared to blink first. My liberty was never going to be part of the *News of the World*'s calculations and it didn't a matter a jot to Tommy either.

A few days later Colin took me to meet Fred Tyler, a top media solicitor who had been recommended to us by some pro-SSP lawyers in Edinburgh. In his office near Princes Street, Fred explained honestly that he thought we were on a hiding to nothing. His advice was to hand over the minutes in a sealed envelope and go through the normal legal process, though he accepted that we were not prepared to do that. You need a QC, Fred told us – and that could cost £4000 upwards.

He strongly advised us to hire Paul Cullen QC, the most experienced and outstanding practitioner in this specialised area of the law. The only problem might be that Paul was a Tory activist from the opposite end of the political spectrum. In fact he had been Solicitor-General – second in command of Scotland's legal system – under the John Major government between 1995 and 1997. We told Fred that we weren't looking for an ideological soul mate but for the lawyer who could most effectively argue our case for confidentiality. Because of the costs involved, we would first have to get the agreement of the party.

That Sunday, 21 May 2006, the SSP executive met in a committee room in Glasgow City Chambers to decide our next move. It was another no-show from Tommy. His sister Lynn Sheridan was there along with three members of the Socialist Workers Party who had failed to appear at the previous week's executive. Sinead Daly from the CWI was also present, plus some others who were to help Tommy engineer the split in the party a few months further down the road. In total, out of twenty-two people, seven would go on to help launch Solidarity. But not one vote was cast against the main resolution to be presented to a special full National Council meeting of the party the following week. It read:

> This NC notes and confirms the decision of the NC in November 2004 that the minutes of the November EC meeting should be kept confidential. It believes that we should have the right to keep our records confidential if we choose to. We resolve to: 1) Maintain the confidentiality of the 9 November 2004 EC minutes by keeping the sole copy of these minutes with Alan McCombes; and 2) Support the stance of Alan McCombes in keeping these minutes confidential.

The meeting further agreed that I should employ a QC at a cost of between £4000 and £5000 and the costs would be borne by the party.

We now had unity on dealing with the crisis. Over the next few days, we held two large all-members meetings in Glasgow and Edinburgh. Although no votes were taken at these meetings, the mood was overwhelmingly in support of the strategy we proposed. The only note of dissent came from a small knot of diehard Tommy loyalists from his own local branch in Cardonald. Outside the Glasgow meeting, in Renfield St Stephen's Church near Charing Cross, they had handed out copies of a resolution attacking the executive that had been passed at the Cardonald branch. It concluded: 'This branch demands that any such record or minutes involving comrade Sheridan and his private life, if such a record does indeed exist, should be immediately destroyed.' The tone and language of the resolution indicated to me that it had probably been drafted by Tommy himself, who was well aware that 'such a record does indeed exist'.

Otherwise, the meetings were solidly behind our stand. As usual, the SWP people went over the top. At the Glasgow meeting one woman, a university lecturer, waxed lyrical about the joys of resistance. 'This should be our motto,' she said, 'defy, defy without blinking an eye!' It was toe-curling. When I spoke, I told the meeting I would be prepared to defy all right 'but don't ask me not to blink my eye. This isn't a children's game we're playing.'

A few days later, I was chatting in the early evening sunshine with a couple of acquaintances outside the Counting House pub in George Square when Colin Fox phoned me from Edinburgh. 'I've had a strange phone call from Fred Tyler,' he told me. 'He says the *News of the World* have been given a copy of our minutes – the November the ninth minutes. Their lawyers have emailed a copy over to Fred asking him if he can get us to verify whether they're accurate.' I was stunned. By that time, I had the only copy of these minutes under lock and key in a box stashed in my flat in the Yorkhill area of Glasgow. This was impossible. How could the *News of the World* have a copy of this document, when there was only one in existence in the whole wide world? Colin hadn't yet seen the document but there was a copy waiting for him in his email inbox. He would send me it as soon as he could.

If this was a genuine copy of the minutes, we would be slaughtered within the party. You can't go through the turmoil we'd gone though, promising defiance and psyching up the party for the battle to come, and then furtively surrender. Our credibility – mine especially – would be shot to pieces. It would be worse than a jail sentence.

I called Allan Green right away – the only person, apart from me, to have had possession of the minutes. The notes upon which the minutes had been based had been taken by Barbara Scott, our minutes secretary. Allan kept the only copy still in existence. I couldn't believe he would have made a copy and sent it to the *News of the World* to keep me out of jail. What about Debbie, Allan's partner – out of misguided concern, perhaps? Definitely not, Allan assured me.

He was convinced this must be a fake. Copies of the minutes had been distributed to meetings of the executive on two occasions, in November 2004, then again in May 2006 when we were discussing the citation. But they had all been numbered and recalled, with the copies subsequently destroyed. The only way these minutes could have been leaked to the *News of the World* would be if somebody at one of those two meetings had secretly photographed the document with a mobile phone camera, then downloaded the image to a computer and made an electronic replica of the original minutes. It just didn't seem credible. There had only been fifteen to twenty people present at each of those meetings and any furtive behaviour would have been as conspicuous as a plain-clothes detective wearing a homburg and a lapel sticker bearing the words 'Private Eye'.

I began to wonder if my flat had been burgled. As I walked home, Colin phoned me. 'This looks like a forgery to me.' Although Colin hadn't read the disputed minutes since November 2004, he was sure this was a fake. When I opened the email attachment, I knew he was right. I also grasped that this wasn't just a crude hoax sent to the *News of the World* from someone outside the party. It was clever and sophisticated – and could only have been created by someone who had recent access to the authentic minutes. It followed the same format as the real minutes – a statement by Tommy Sheridan, then a statement from me followed an open discussion and finally a series of votes. But, in this new version, instead of admitting his visits to the Cupids swingers' club in Manchester, Tommy denies it. He asks the meeting to back his legal action to clear his name. I then ask him to desist from his legal action not because it's based on lies but because it could embroil the party in a costly financial venture. Finally, the matter is resolved when Tommy agrees to temporarily stand down as convenor to allow him to fight his legal battle against the 'lies of the Murdoch empire'. It was a complete fabrication. If the meeting had proceeded according to the account set out in these fake minutes, the SSP executive would have deserved the derision and hostility that was heaped on our heads from all sides back in late 2004.

Some telltale mistakes were made in the drafting of the forged minutes. The attendance list was wrong on two counts. First, it used initials rather than full names. That had been the standard format of

SSP executive minutes up until early 2004, when the previous minutes secretary, Felicity Garvie, had stood down from the position. Like me, Fiz had come from the somewhat conspiratorial Militant tradition and old habits die hard. Barbara Scott, who replaced Fiz and took the minutes of 9 November 2004 meeting, always used full names. Plus, the names of three people who had attended the meeting were missing: Fiz herself; Steve Nimmo, the Lothians regional organiser; and Kevin McVey, the Central Scotland organiser. Whoever had falsified the minutes had slipped up. Interestingly, these were the only three people present who were not cited by the *News of the World*'s lawyers to appear as witnesses in the libel case. The forger had provided a vital clue, in the form of initials, to the identities of sixteen key witnesses. The newspaper was then able to match the initials to the names of prominent SSP members – and serve them with citations.

During the later police investigation, we were to discover that the fake minutes had arrived at the *News of the World*'s HQ accompanied by an unsigned note written in block capitals on bright yellow paper. I never did see the note but I understand it appealed to the paper to drop its case and stop me from going to jail. It also portrayed me in an apparently flattering light and contained some uncomplimentary remarks about Tommy Sheridan. It was clearly designed to appear to have been written either by me or by someone sympathetic to me.

Who was responsible for the fake minutes and what was their purpose? Clearly, whoever fabricated the document hoped, in the first instance, to persuade the *News of the World* to back down but that was always going to be a long shot. The paper's lawyers would obviously seek to authenticate the document. But there was a Plan B. During the libel case in July, Tommy's legal team presented the forgery as part of their overall strategy to suggest that the minutes I had gone to jail for had been, in Tommy's words, 'concocted'. This had to be the work of someone who had recently familiarised themselves with the real minutes which had been distributed to the executive only a few days earlier. Only three of Tommy's supporters were present at the meeting – and two of these, Jock Penman and Leah Ganley, a young member from Inverness, had refused to read them. That left only Sinead Daly. For all my political differences with Sinead, I couldn't believe she'd be involved in this.

But there was one other person who had recently read the November 2004 minutes. Someone who had studied them like a crossword puzzle in the beer garden of the Golden Pheasant pub in Auchinloch. It wouldn't have needed Inspector Rebus to pinpoint the prime suspect.

Before the court proceedings had begun, Allan Green had brought a locked box containing the minutes to my flat, where I had kept them hidden under a bed settee. On the day I was due to appear before Lady Smith, Carolyn drove me through to Edinburgh, along with the locked box. I was pretty much resigned to a spell in jail and we guessed that the judge might issue a warrant to search my flat while I was locked up. Carolyn dropped me off near Waverley Station and I deposited the box in the left-luggage office. Later that night, after the first day in court, she retrieved it and took it to her home in East Kilbride.

For two days in the Court of Session, Paul Cullen QC turned in an awesome performance – a real tour de force. The Tory activist and former candidate had proved to be a decent, personable bloke – despite his dodgy politics – and a real heavyweight performer in the courtroom. We knew that our case, though morally justified, was legally threadbare. Paul made a brilliant case, pointing out that, if confidential records of private meetings could be cited by the courts, a culture of secrecy could take root. He produced example after example of instances where public and private bodies had successfully pleaded the case for confidentiality of materials. He cited the European Court of Human Rights in support of our arguments. He forced the judge to repeatedly consult her hefty legal tomes. For a time, against all the odds, it actually looked like touch and go.

But Lady Smith didn't look like the kind of judge who might risk a creative interpretation of the law.

'Your client is flouting the law,' she told my QC. 'It is difficult to resist drawing the conclusion he puts his loyalty to the Scottish Socialist Party above his duty to this court.' Like an old-time school-teacher, bespectacled and stern, she ordered me to stand up. 'Where are these minutes?' she demanded to know.

I told her they were somewhere in the West of Scotland but I wasn't prepared to be more specific than that.

The judge looked at her watch. 'It's now midday and I'm going to adjourn the court until 2.30 p.m.' She ordered me to hand the documents over before the court reassembled.

By this time, the court drama had become a major news story, with throngs of journalists, photographers, TV camera crews and radio reporters outside the court waiting for the result of the stand-off. I knew I was going to jail and I told them so. Inside the courtroom, there was a big team of SSP members supporting me. There was also a posse of reporters who seemed generally sympathetic to the stand I was taking. But one person was transparently unimpressed. Unfortunately for me, it was the most powerful person in the courtroom.

'What's the likely damage?' I asked Paul Cullen during the break.

He told me that it was pretty certain I'd be jailed for contempt – and the sentence could be anything from six months to two years.

We filed back into the rows of benches and Lady Smith called the court to order. 'You are flouting an order of court. No one is entitled to do that.' She ordered that I be imprisoned for a period of twelve days, before returning for a further appearance. If the minutes were not surrendered with that deadline, I could expect a hefty jail sentence. She also demanded that I hand in the names of all those who had attended the Cardonald SSP branch meeting that had passed a resolution calling for the minutes to be destroyed. In the eyes of the legal establishment, this resolution amounted to a demand that the SSP be involved in conspiring to pervert the course of justice – a deadly serious crime, in contrast to my relatively humdrum contempt of court, which was classified as a civil offence.

Voicing her concern over this threat to get rid of a vital piece of evidence, Lady Smith issued a general search warrant, covering all premises where the minutes might be held. Her orders were to be immediately implemented. Realising the wide scope of the search warrant, Carolyn sped across the M8 to East Kilbride in case her own home was raided. She grabbed the sealed box from under her bed and hurried away to a non-political friend's house in another part of town. Just to be sure, they hid the box away in the loft. Before the day was out, two teams of sheriff officers armed with search warrants had arrived on the doorsteps of our national HQ in Glasgow and our regional HQ in the centre of Edinburgh. They also contacted Carolyn, asking for access my flat so they wouldn't have to break down the door.

They were meticulous but polite. Back in the anti-Poll Tax days, we used to dub the sheriff officers 'Rottweilers in suits' because of their intimidating manner when dealing with non-payers. These were more like Labradors in suits. They explored cupboards and drawers methodically, opened books to check whether there was anything hidden between the pages and searched the hard drive of my computer. But it was a wild goose chase.

Back in Edinburgh, I waited in the deserted holding cells of the Court of Session until the paperwork was completed. Because I was a civil prisoner, I was transported across Edinburgh by sheriff officers rather than by police officers. One of the sheriff officers recognised me straight away. Sixteen years before, I had been involved in the first-ever occupation of a sheriff office in protest against Poll Tax warrant sales and he had been one of the young sheriff officers who had stood gaping in shock as we seized control of his company's Glasgow HQ. It had all been a long time ago and both of us were older and greyer, so we were able to joke about it. I reminded him that we had won a victory that day – the first of many.

But my thoughts were more preoccupied with the immediate future than the distant past. I had been locked up before, more times than I could remember, during the anti-Poll Tax campaign, at blockades of the Faslane nuclear submarine base and other political protests. I'd spent many a dreary night counting the tiles in a dingy prison cell. On one occasion in my early twenties, after leaving my house in Pollok to buy a packet of cigarettes at a nearby shop, I had been arrested and charged with driving a getaway car during an armed robbery 40 miles away. It was a case of mistaken identity and I eventually received an apology and financial compensation – but only after spending days locked up in a holding cell in Ayr.

Now I felt equally powerless. The die was cast. My liberty was in the hands of others – Tommy Sheridan and a Sunday tabloid. Surely one of these two combatants would back down?

14

Late May 2006

Open Letter Bomb

The streets were throbbing with life and the bars were crackling with laughter as the May holiday weekend kicked off but, inside Saughton Prison, it was just another Friday night, only worse. Roars of savage anger reverberated through the corridors and menace hung in the muggy air.

I'd just been taken to a grimy cell on the top floor of Glenesk Hall, the untried prisoners' block, and was fighting the rush of claustrophobia that threatens to overwhelm every new prisoner in the first few hours of incarceration. I hardly had time to work out how to switch on the tiny TV set in the corner when the cell door was thrown open and in charged a warder.

'Grab the stuff you need. Right away! It's an emergency.'

Bewildered, I was dragged across the corridor and bundled into a cell with a young guy in his late twenties, who told me his name was James. His Celtic posters and tattoos were reassuring – at least we support the same football team, I thought. James had been on remand since Hogmanay on an attempted murder charge. We discovered we had once lived in the same street in Magdalene, an Edinburgh housing scheme, and I vaguely knew a few of his relatives.

Outside, the sirens were screaming. Inside, it sounded like some kind of satanic symphony was being performed, the repetitive wail of the prison's riot alarm clashing in angry discord with a cacophony of banging and howling. Above the din, James managed to pick up some bits and pieces of information from the cells around and below us. The communication system in jail might be lo-tech but it's pretty efficient. A group of prisoners had taken a warder hostage, stripped him naked, stolen his keys and locked him up. They'd also taken a nurse captive and commandeered the medical supplies cell, flooding the hall with methadone and a cocktail of other drugs.

In the midst of the mayhem, James switched on the Scottish news to see if there was anything about the riot. Instead, the main item was a report from outside the Court of Session earlier that day. James did a double take and, right enough, the guy being bundled into a car by a couple of heavies is definitely the same bloke sitting there right beside him. Now the BBC man is asking me whether I expect to go to jail. 'Well, I don't think Lady Smith looks like she's in the mood for a fifty quid fine,' I reply. James burst into a round of applause, slapping me on the back. He then spread the word around the hall.

'Did you see the news? The guy's here in ma cell. He's brand new!' he yelled through the bars of the tiny back window.

Towards the end of the bulletin, there's a fleeting mention of 'an incident' now underway in Saughton Prison.

Now the riot was escalating. Through chinks in the cell doorway, we could see the corridor outside swarming with officers in full riot gear. Then, without a word of warning, our cell door flew open and I was dragged into the corridor. They ordered me to lie out on the floor, arms and legs spread-eagled. Only a few hours before, I'd been treated like a VIP at the front desk, where they told me I was the first civil prisoner in Saughton since Tommy Sheridan himself, fourteen years earlier. But these guys were in a state of panic. They didn't know me from the Yorkshire Ripper. They searched every orifice of my body, looking for something. Drugs, maybe. Or weapons. And why me? An absurd thought flitted through my brain: surely they're not looking for the minutes?

Eventually, I was dragged back into the cell and I decided, on balance, that this might not be the best moment to ask for a mattress and blanket. Soon afterwards, the Robocops brought out the teargas and stun guns. And I thought Glasgow city centre was wild on a Friday night.

By morning, order was restored and I was back in my own cell – or 'peter' as the inmates call it – reading a circular that had been pushed under the door. Headed 'Disruption to Regime', it told us we'd be locked down in our cells all weekend 'due to an overnight incident of concerted indiscipline in Glenesk'. By then, seven prisoners were in intensive care, smashed out of their heads on God knows how many different drugs. One had almost died, laid out on the floor just a few yards away from our cell. Later, three guys, identified as the ring-leaders, were hauled up to the High Court and hammered with an extra fifteen years in jail between them.

The mayhem inside Saughton, though, was nothing compared to the madness that was to devour the SSP. As the party gathered for an emergency National Council meeting on the Sunday afternoon, Tommy was preparing a political bloodbath. He had avoided all the crisis meetings 'on the basis of legal advice'. But in the murky netherworld of the party, he had been in overdrive, flattering the conceited and tantalising his former enemies with the hint of a promise that he might now be in their camp. Earlier that week, he had held a secret meeting in Glasgow with his old enemy Peter Taaffe, who had never forgiven Frances Curran and me. In his eyes, we had been the ringleaders of the rebellion that had freed the Scottish Left from London control. Now Tommy was offering himself up to Peter as an instrument of revenge. Peter grabbed his chance.

Tommy then brought the Socialist Workers Party into line. It wasn't difficult. Since November 2004, they had fawned over him like the directors of a failing bank courting a wealthy investor.

Following the citation of the SSP minutes, they had backed our strategy of defiance of the courts with the zeal of the crowd at a boxing match cheering on the fighters from the safety of their ringside seats. But after Tommy met their leaders on the eve of the National Council meeting, they switched abruptly. And, like a marching regiment ordered by the sergeant major to about-turn, SWP members instantly complied. Theirs not to reason why. When their own leaders are issuing orders, SWP members are as rebellious as Boy Scouts.

Outside the meeting, people had been dishing out two separate statements. One was a signed letter from a group of academics in the SSP pleading for the party to give Tommy unconditional support in his libel case. 'Without Tommy Sheridan, the SSP is finished,' it warned. The logic was alarming: because of Tommy's fame, he should be supported mindlessly, right or wrong.

The other statement – 'Open Letter to SSP Members from Tommy Sheridan' – was sensational. Turgidly written and replete with grammatical and punctuation errors, it nonetheless packed the destructive power of a political atomic bomb. He attacked an 'unsavoury cabal of comrades at the core of the leadership' who were 'attempting to implicate me as the culprit for the current *News of the World* and bourgeois court led attempts to destroy us'. He asked, 'Who is responsible for the mess we are in?' It was like Billy Bunter demanding to know who had eaten all the cakes. 'Who decided that our party should examine and discuss the private lives of comrades at meetings?' As a matter of fact, the 9 November executive meeting in 2004, which he was referring to, had not discussed Tommy's 'private life' – it had discussed how to protect the party from the very public consequences of Tommy's 'private life'.

Who decided that such confidential meetings should be recorded? Who decided to keep secret copies of such private and confidential meetings? Who decided to deliberately leak to the press and media that such a document existed? Who decided to appear in court and admit the existence of such a secret document?

To describe these rhetorical questions as misleading would be like describing the Pacific Ocean as a puddle. With his penchant for harmless little lies that made him look good, Tommy had always had a streak of the Pinocchio about him. By the time the crisis broke in 2004, he had already moved up a few levels, lying outrageously in front of the TV cameras while sounding as plausible as Trevor MacDonald reading the news from an autocue. But now he was rewriting history.

The decision to take minutes at the November the ninth 2004 meeting had been agreed by everyone present. It was normal practice, in line with the party's constitution which requires that minutes are taken at all executive meetings. The presence of Barbara Scott hadn't been challenged either. She was not, at that time, an elected member of the executive but attended the meeting specifically for the purpose of recording the minutes. According to the official handwritten notes of the executive meeting of 21 November, it was Rosemary Byrne – later co-leader with Tommy of Solidarity – who proposed that, for reasons of confidentiality, we should keep a single copy of the minutes, to be held by Allan Green. This arrangement was reported to a special 140-strong National Council meeting the following Saturday. Allan Green had asked this meeting to make an exception to the normal procedure of circulating the minutes because of their sensitive content. His plea had been backed by none other than Tommy Sheridan, who had also asked the meeting to keep the minutes confidential. That's why they were 'secret'. Not one person at that National Council meeting or any other meeting of the SSP had ever suggested that these minutes should be destroyed. Nor had anyone 'leaked' the existence of the minutes to the media. Their existence was a matter of public record. At the ill-fated press conference in the Scottish Parliament following Tommy's resignation, I had been asked repeatedly when we intended to publish them. I replied by pointing out that many organisations – 'including no doubt the BBC and the News of the World' held confidential minutes of board meetings which, because of their sensitive content, were never made available to the public. While this dialogue took place with the TV cameras rolling, Tommy had sat beside me and uttered not a word of dissent.

Only in the build-up to the libel trial did the existence of these minutes suddenly become contentious. In January 2006, Tommy gave a lengthy personal interview to Peter Ross, then a feature writer on the

Sunday Herald magazine. In an aside, the journalist asked Tommy about these minutes. His reply was peculiar. Instead of restating that these were confidential minutes and the party had voted not to publish them, he denied their existence. This should have set alarm bells ringing within the party. The newspaper's Scottish political editor, Paul Hutcheon, was onto the inconsistency like a cat pouncing on a mouse. He had read the interview before the paper went to press and phoned Eddie Truman right away.

'Is it accurate to say that the SSP normally keeps minutes of its meetings?' he asked.

Eddie confirmed that, yes, of course we do.

'And are there minutes of the November 9th 2004 meeting where Tommy resigned?'

Eddie thought nothing of the question. We had no reason to conceal their existence.

It wasn't until the next morning that Eddie discovered Tommy had given the opposite answer to the same question. A story in the newspaper quoted 'an SSP spokesperson' contradicting Tommy Sheridan over the existence of the minutes. Eddie, the press officer of the party, hadn't even known of Tommy's interview, never mind his inexplicable denial of a fact that we had always acknowledged.

Tommy and others later criticised Eddie for his honesty. Our press officer had plenty of talents but psychic power wasn't one of them. They also began to criticise the decision to take minutes in the first place – although, at the time they had been taken and reported to the membership, not one person had uttered a word of complaint. In a party like the SSP, there can be no question that key decisions have to be recorded along with an explanation for these decisions. The November the 9th minutes avoided salacious detail but they did provide an accurate and authoritative explanation for an extraordinary decision with historic significance.

As a former member of the clandestine Central Committee of the old Militant Tendency in its 1980s heyday, I can vouch for the fact that every single word spoken at these leadership meetings was recorded and stashed away in the vaults of the organisation's East London HQ, unedited and uncensored. It was a matter of preserving important historical records. Before the Provisional IRA disbanded, even this illegal underground army scrupulously recorded their discussions. In his book, *A Secret History of the IRA*, the journalist Ed Moloney describes how the IRA Army Council used to co-opt a couple of additional trusted people to attend its monthly secret meetings. One was a quartermaster and the other a minutes secretary.

The monthly minutes were, according to Moloney, 'possibly the most delicate and secret documents in the IRA's archive, and great care would be taken in storing and hiding it'. On one occasion, in the late 1980s, a dispute had erupted on the Army Council over whether it had the constitutional authority to call a Christmas ceasefire. To resolve the disagreement, one of its members was dispatched to unearth the minutes from a secret documents dump. And here we had people in Scotland – not just Tommy but many of his supporters – arguing that a highly public political party, with six MSPs, thousands of members and tens of thousands of voters, should have desisted from taking minutes explaining the most momentous decision we had ever had to take.

Written records are neither subject to memory lapse and nor can they be falsified without being physically destroyed or rewritten. They preserve the truth and ensure accountability. Even in the best of circumstances, unrecorded decisions can become subject to conflicting interpretations. In the worst of circumstances, the absence of written records can open the door to the deliberate rewriting of history by those with a political interest in manufacturing misinformation. In November 2004, within days of Tommy's resignation, the SWP had claimed in a bulletin to their membership across Britain and internationally that Tommy Sheridan was removed because of his support for the Rose Gentle Bring Our Troops Home from Iraq campaign.

Parts of Tommy Sheridan's 'Open Letter' appeared to be something of a receptacle for people with long-standing grudges to offload their grievances. One paragraph specifically expressed opposition to the party's progressive equality policies, complaining, 'We are a class-based socialist party. Not a gender-obsessed discussion group. Our socialist principals [sic] and class identity defines [sic] us first. Not our gender or sexual orientation.' Where did that come from? Tommy had never before expressed a hint of opposition to any of the party's policies on gender. During a controversial debate within the party over gender equality in 2002, he had supported – albeit passively – the proposal from the Women's Network to introduce a system of 50–50 representation for men and women in our candidates' lists for Holyrood.

Among the many spelling mistakes and grammatical errors, one in particular leapt out at me. Spelling 'Pollock' with a superfluous letter 'c' was a common mistake but not for Glaswegians. Few would insert an extra 'c' into Pollok and certainly not someone who had been born and brought up there.

The phrase 'gender-obsessed discussion group' gave the game away. I suspected that Tommy Sheridan's 'Open Letter' had actually been drafted by Steve Arnott, the SSP organiser in Inverness. Steve had crusaded like a man possessed against the 50–50 gender proposal in 2002. Unlike others who had shrugged their shoulders and moved on, Steve remained obsessive about what he called 'an outrage against democracy'.

In the most dramatic passages in the 'Open Letter', Tommy and his ghostwriter alleged that people in the leadership of the SSP had accused him of 'heinous crimes' including drug-dealing, human trafficking and frequenting prostitutes. And, further, that they wanted him out of the party and deselected as an MSP. The journos could hardly believe what they were reading. The statement had been sent to the media – including the Murdoch press – while the delegates to the National Council were still filing in. The 95 per cent of SSP members who were not delegates on the National Council only found out about it on the news or in the following morning's newspapers. But the initial reaction of political editors was to phone Eddie Truman to ask if this was some kind of wind-up.

Most SSP members, including those under attack, were similarly bamboozled. Over the previous two years, many in the party had felt betrayed by Tommy. His squeaky-clean image had been exposed as a hoax. His reckless pursuit of self-gratification had amounted to gambling with the future of the SSP. On top of that, he had revealed himself as a brazen liar. As a result, he no longer commanded the widespread respect within the party that he could once have taken for granted yet no one ever suggested that he should be expelled from the SSP or even deselected as top of the list for Glasgow. As far as I could see, even his most entrenched opponents were prepared to vote for him – albeit on condition that he first abandon his crazy court case. And who in the SSP would ever have accused him of drug dealing? Whatever his other vices, we believed that Tommy was teetotal and drug-free. At the time, I had never heard anyone suggest otherwise. Condemning him for dealing drugs would be like accusing Bill Gates of selling pirated computer software from a stall in the Barras.

To claim that he had been accused of involvement in the sex-trafficking trade was a classic case of tearing a fragment of conversation out of its context, then distorting it into something outlandish. It derived from a private conversation where one of our MSPs was asked why the SSP was so hostile to swingers' clubs. As part of her reply, she pointed out that much of the commercial sex industry is steeped in prostitution, which in turn has links with the sex-trafficking trade. If someone criticises me for wearing a pair of trainers made in China, I don't interpret that as an accusation that I've been involved in torturing pro-Tibet protesters.

Most SSP members were mystified about the accusations they were supposed to have been making against Tommy. But I recognised some of the allegations – not from anything I had heard within the SSP, but from a document my lawyers had been given to help them prepare our legal challenge against the citation of the minutes. Dated 21 April 2006, the '*Closed Record* (as amended) in the cause Thomas Sheridan MSP against News Group Newspapers Limited' was swathed in the usual fog of archaic legal jargon – 'Condescendence for Pursuer and answers thereto for Defenders' and suchlike – but the contents were incendiary.

The document revealed that Tommy's defamation case was not based solely on the Fiona McGuire story, as he had always maintained. It included a claim for reparation against 'articles [which] communicated the false idea that the pursuer had visited a "Swingers Club" with Anvar Khan, a *News of the World* Columnist'. I was startled when I read that. He had admitted this trip to Cupids with Anvar Khan to a formal, minuted meeting of over twenty people and to dozens, maybe even scores, of others privately. In addition, he was suing the *News of the World* for alleging – not in the newspaper but in its legal submissions – that he had cavorted naked in Glasgow's Moat House Hotel with two other people, one female and one male. This was exactly in line with the tales that Keith had heard from Tommy's friends several years before and it was being confirmed by two female witnesses. On top of that, Fiona McGuire had provided a witness statement that, among other things, claimed that Tommy had participated in group sex with her and three prostitutes, male and female. She also alleged that Tommy was a snorter of cocaine.

There was method, it seemed, in the apparent madness behind the publication of the 'Open Letter'. Tommy's bombastic denunciation of the accusations against him looked suspiciously like an attempt to pre-empt allegations which he knew were about to come out in court. He was creating a narrative that could justify his self-portrayal as the victim of a plot driven by the Murdoch empire, backed up by some mercenary witnesses who had been paid by the newspaper and bolstered by a gang of frenzied political enemies within the SSP. And it seemed to be working. Allan Massie, the right-wing journalist and author – and no Tommy Sheridan sympathiser – summed up the reaction of many:

Either Mr Sheridan is suffering from galloping paranoia or his idealistic comrades are as nasty a bunch of liars and slanderers as you could imagine. The latter seems to me more probable assuming, as I do, that there is not a scintilla of truth in the stories they are said to have spread.

That's exactly how journalists and the wider public were supposed to react. This wasn't an open letter to the membership of the SSP. It was an open letter to the jury in the looming libel case. It was designed to whip up an atmosphere of rampant hysteria in and around the SSP in advance of the court case, paving the way for Tommy to portray himself in court as the victim of a monstrous frame-up by this 'nasty bunch of liars and slanderers'.

Not one of these grievances had ever been previously aired by Tommy, either formally or informally within the party – not a word. For most people, they came like a snowstorm in the Sahara. In a political party – or in any organisation for that matter – most people would raise their complaints first with the people concerned, preferably face to face. If that wasn't satisfactory, they'd then make a more formal complaint. Within the SSP there existed clear grievance procedures to resolve perceived injustices. Even if there had been any hint of truth in this vitriol-saturated document, it would have been cowardly and irresponsible to raise these points for the first time in a press release masquerading as an open letter to SSP members. But these were not genuine grievances. The 'Open Letter' was a mud-slinging exercise designed to win Tommy public sympathy, and to smear in advance those who may be called upon to give evidence in the looming defamation case.

But one point in the 'Open Letter' baffled everyone. Buried in the tangled undergrowth of poisonous rhetoric and paranoid abuse was a passage demanding that the minutes be handed over to the court:

> I believe that Alan and a core group of seven or eight leading comrades have misled the party into their current quandary, but I salute his courage and determination to resist the undemocratic power of un-elected judges to interfere in the internal affairs of democratic political parties . . . Now a comrade is in jail and our resistance to the disgraceful and undemocratic interference of unelected judges has been displayed. He must languish in jail no longer . . . Further resistance at the expense of a comrade's personal freedom is unacceptable.

Tommy's use of the word 'comrade' and his praise for my supposed 'courage and determination' were like spoonfuls of honey in a barrel of toxic waste. It was mealy-mouthed diplomacy, designed to win over those who had voted for defiance. But what was more mysterious was his call for surrender.

What had changed his mind – and why was he now ready to hand his enemy a silver bullet?

28 May 2006

Mayhem and Misogyny

In his classic 1906 work, *An Enemy of the People*, the Norwegian playwright Henrik Ibsen tells the story of Dr Stockmann who, along with his brother the Mayor, brings prosperity to their small seaside town by developing a vast medicinal spa complex.

Overnight, the humdrum backwater is transformed into a prosperous tourist magnet, where visitors flock to luxuriate in the healthy waters. But then Dr Stockmann discovers the baths are contaminated, endangering public health. He proposes a solution. But some of the local dignitaries, including his brother and the editor of the local newspaper, fear his remedy will be financially ruinous. Instead, they organise a cover-up. Dr Stockmann refuses to go along with this madness. Desperate to protect their precious spa waters, the Mayor and the editor denounce the doctor as a liar and a fantasist and whip up the rest of townspeople into a frenzy of loathing for this 'enemy of the people'. In one memorable scene, Dr Stockmann calls a public meeting to explain the facts. He argues against 'building the town's prosperity on a quagmire of falsehood and deceit'. But the voice of reason is drowned out by the shrill rhetoric of self-deception, amplified by mass hysteria. The doctor is howled down and the scene closes with the mob chanting, 'Enemy of the people! Enemy of the people!'

I was still locked up in a prison cell fifty miles away when the SSP National Council assembled in the main lecture theatre of Glasgow Caledonian University to debate the Tommy Sheridan defamation crisis. According to those who were there, I was lucky. By all accounts, the atmosphere made the average Old Firm football clash look like a hippy festival of love and peace.

That Sunday morning Colin Fox had made a special arrangement to visit me via a prison official he knew through the Edinburgh People's Festival. For me, it was a welcome 30-minute break after being locked down in a suffocating cell all weekend. As I was escorted down the stairs from Glenesk Hall and through the passageways connecting the various buildings in the Saughton compound, the

warder filled me in about the riot. I was amazed when he told me he
was an SSP voter, as were several of his colleagues. It was difficult to
get my head around the idea that at least some of the guys who had
been charging around in rubber suits and steel helmets, armed with
batons, stun guns and tear gas canisters, were socialist voters in
civilian life.

Colin wanted to make sure I was still strong and committed to
defying the court order. He also wanted to chat with me about the
speech he intended to make at the National Council meeting. He
brought along a copy of the *Sunday Herald.* On its front page was a
rehashed version of the Paul Hutcheon story that had appeared on the
Sunday after Tommy's resignation. The article had scarcely raised a
murmur within the SSP at the time. It had simply reported what
hundreds of SSP members already knew – that Tommy had been put
under pressure to resign. The regurgitated version was spiced up to
give the impression that the paper had detailed knowledge of the
minutes of the November the 9th meeting. It also provided the
additional point of information that the original story had been backed
by a legal affidavit from a senior party official. It was guaranteed to
cause ructions at the National Council. The SSP wasn't exactly
teeming with senior officials so I expected to be easily identified as
the signatory, but I decided that this wasn't the time to burden Colin
with that knowledge.

I told Colin that I remained more convinced than ever that we had
to fight this all the way. Contrary to the impression sometimes
conveyed by the tabloid press, prison life doesn't quite compare with
the luxury of a five-star hotel suite on the Costa del Sol. I would have
gladly foregone the pleasures of Glenesk Hall to breathe the early
summer air again. But there was no turning back.

It was on the TV news that night that I heard the party had
capitulated before the courts. I couldn't believe my ears. Naturally
I felt some personal relief that my prison ordeal would probably now
be over but that was outweighed by political disappointment and a
sense that I had been betrayed rather than liberated. Why had so many
people changed their minds? Once we had set out down the road of
defiance, we should have seen it through to the end. This wasn't
serious politics.

The TV news that night showed Tommy arriving at the Glasgow
Caledonian University, like a latter-day Christ flanked by a posse of
apostles. This was the first time Tommy had shown his face in the
party since the citation of our minutes. He hadn't bothered to contact
me – not so much as a text message – while I was facing down the

courts to protect his confidentiality. Even though he was still a co-chair of the party, he had avoided every meeting in the run-up to my court case. Now that I was locked up in jail, he suddenly broke cover. As he entered the lecture hall – slightly late as always – a sycophantic roar of stamping and cheering welled up for the man who had single-handedly dragged the SSP to the verge of the precipice.

Before the meeting even started, Steve Arnott was up on his feet ranting against 'traitors in our midst' and demanding the right to put to the meeting an emergency resolution from Inverness branch about the article in the *Sunday Herald*. Apparently, the resolution had been drafted that morning in a petrol station on the A9 and it stated:

> This meeting expresses anger and astonishment that, at a time when Alan McCombes is in prison for refusing to make confidential SSP minutes available to the state or the *News of the World*, one or more leading members of the party were aware that the contents of the minutes were already in [the] possession of the bourgeois press as a result of their actions . . . The NC calls for disciplinary action to be considered against all those who were involved in and/or aware of this situation.

The screaming demands for disciplinary action would set the tone for the rest of the day. Even worse, the resolution was based on an incompetent misreading of the *Sunday Herald* article. The headline above the *Sunday Herald* article – 'Revealed: secret record of meeting that felled Sheridan and led to imprisonment of SSP Official' – had been misleading. Nowhere in the text did the newspaper claim to have ever been in possession of the content of the minutes. If the newspaper had had this detail since 2004 – backed up, moreover, by a legal affidavit – it would have been sitting on the scoop of the decade. For the past 18 months, the minutes of our November 2004 executive meeting had been the Holy Grail of Scotland's political journalists but what was contained in those minutes had been protected by an iron curtain of silence. This new story had been skilfully packaged for maximum impact but its essence was a simple restating of the basic facts of the sketchy report that the paper had published in November 2004. The following week, the editor of the *Sunday Herald*, in response to a request for clarification from the SSP, wrote back saying, 'I am happy to confirm that at no time was the *Sunday Herald* passed a copy of the minutes of the November 9th 2004 meeting of the Executive of the SSP, nor were we given any details of a personal nature.'

Yet the panic provoked by the *Sunday Herald* was enough to sway some delegates into abandoning their support for defiance and voting for surrender. The National Council's response to the provocation had been naive to say the least. The newspaper report had provoked understandable alarm, but this was the biggest crisis the SSP had ever faced and it should have been a time for clear heads and cool calculations. Instead, some people panicked over a rehashed newspaper article that no one seemed to have even read properly.

But there was more to it than that. Some people were already planning a walkout from the SSP and seized upon the article as an excuse to crank up the decibel level. Three women – Carol Hainey from Falkirk, Cathy Pedersen from East Kilbride and Pam Currie from Paisley – did courageously intervene to try to bring the meeting back down to earth but sections of the meeting were in no mood for reason or common sense. The A9 resolution was railroaded through.

Colin Fox kicked off the meeting proper with a methodical, blow-by-blow account of the sequence of events that had led to my imprisonment. He spelled out the fact that Tommy's case was not based solely on the Fiona McGuire story, which he had denied, but also on the Anvar Khan story which he had acknowledged was true. Up until then, some people had backed Tommy under the assumption that he was challenging a false story and that the swingers' club revelation would never be brought out in court because it was irrelevant. Their judgement had been naive on several levels but now Colin was laying it on the line. The Cupids trip was a key part of Tommy's defamation action. He was planning to deny in the Court of Session, in front of the entire Scottish media, something he had admitted to the party and to dozens of other people. Unless they were sitting with their fingers in their ears, not one of the 150 people present could have left that meeting in any doubt that Tommy planned to win his defamation action by committing blatant perjury and by falsifying the history of the party.

It should have instantly united the meeting against Tommy's court action. But it didn't. When Colin began to draw the obvious conclusion from the report and called for Tommy to abandon his defamation case, the barracking began. Several people leapt to their feet, interrupting manically and screaming him down.

Up until that day, the atmosphere within the SSP had always been tolerant and respectful of political differences. Just a few months before, at our annual conference, one senior broadsheet journalist had told me privately that he was genuinely impressed by the party's ability to accommodate entrenched differences of outlook – for example, on

Scottish independence – without ever descending into the vicious factionalism of some of the mainstream parties. Naturally, robust political argument was always part of the culture of the SSP but rarely did political debate boil over into personal abuse. But, with the court case looming and the future of the party in peril, personal abuse was now the order of the day. The SWP delegates had successfully moved that Tommy should have three times longer to speak from the floor than anyone else. Then, instead of engaging in a serious dialogue about our strategy, Tommy acted, in the words of one delegate, 'like Ian Paisley on cocaine'. Whatever might have been fuelling his paranoia, the speech he delivered was an incitement to hatred against those who had refused to back his court action.

Much of the content of his speech was a repetition, almost by rote, of the 'Open Letter' but words on a page can be transformed into something more menacing when roared at deafening volume by an accomplished actor. He threw in a few emotional thunderbolts designed to inflame the atmosphere further. Concentrating his fire on some of the women in the leadership of the party, he said that Catriona Grant had 'almost been responsible for the death of my wife and my unborn baby'. This alluded to Tommy's cockeyed interpretation of an email Catriona had just posted suggesting that maybe all the facts should have been brought into the open back in November 2004. This was emotional abuse at its most tasteless and shocking but the members of Tommy's fan club were whooping with delight. By juxtaposing the image of a vulnerable pregnant wife with a group of politically hardened female activists, Tommy was also tapping into the world's oldest prejudice. A vein of misogyny runs deep through society and even affects some of the most progressive institutions. By the end of that meeting, the vein running through the SSP had been slashed and the blood was flowing freely.

As a graduate of the old school of left-wing politics, the sociology of gender had never been my specialist subject. Like most men of my generation and working-class background, I couldn't claim to be a paragon of enlightenment when it came to sexist attitudes. But I had, as early as the mid 1990s, fought to commit Scottish Militant Labour to 50–50 male-female representation in the future Scottish Parliament. My support for the measure was motivated by a basic sense of fairness and justice rather than any profound insight into women's oppression. Politics at every level in Scotland, from local councils upwards, was overrun by middle-aged and elderly men in suits. This wasn't representative of the population as a whole. Support for equal representation for women in politics and especially within the socialist movement just seemed like straightforward common sense. But when, in 2002, a serious attempt was made to put this abstract ideal into practice by introducing a mechanism within the SSP, the backlash had been blood-curdling. At the time, eight regional SSP organisers were men, as were the national secretary, the national convenor, the trade union coordinator and the editor of the *Scottish Socialist Voice* – in other words, all of the key officials. Some people opposed the change for genuine political reasons. For others, privileges and personal ambitions were at stake. And the whole debate became tainted with the ugly tinge of misogyny.

By 2003, the position of women within the SSP had begun to improve. Because we had implemented the 50–50 policy, the SSP became the only party in any parliament in the UK with a majority of women representatives. Outside Holyrood, a group of talented women, including Kath Kyle, Jo Harvie, Roz Paterson and Pam Currie, were now producing much of the written material of the party including the *Scottish Socialist Voice*. Yet, in every walk of life including politics, women are confronted by prejudice and discrimination at every turn. Some of this is conscious and systematic; some of it is embedded in the culture and power structures of society.

In *A Time To Rage*, Tommy's co-author Joan McAlpine wrote eloquently of the Pollok witch-hunts in 1677, when five women were strangled and burned. She describes how men called witch-prickers earned their living by travelling around Scotland accusing women of witchcraft and then torturing them. They would pierce various parts of the woman's body with a long brass pin until she slipped into shock then stopped screaming. Triumphantly the witch-pricker would claim to have pinpointed the 'Devil's mark' – a spot insensitive to pain.

Centuries later, in some of the more backward corners of the world, institutional brutality against women, including organised witch burning, is still an everyday occurrence. In the liberal West, things are different. Women are no longer executed for witchcraft. Nor are they stoned to death for adultery as they are in Saudi Arabia and other states. But the fact that there has been progress doesn't mean oppression has ended. Black people in America no longer live in fear of lynching. One has even been elected to the White House. But racism hasn't been banished. And neither has misogyny.

At the extreme edge, women are battered, murdered and raped daily somewhere in the UK. At a more mainstream level, they are taunted, belittled, patronised, mauled, leered at, scorned, ridiculed and graded like dogs at Crufts on the basis of their appearance.

Strong, articulate women don't escape misogyny – if anything, those who stand up for themselves or for a cause they believe in are even more forcibly denigrated. As Joan McAlpine wrote of 17th-century Scotland, 'Witches were usually singled out because they did not knuckle under to authority.'

Anti-Irish bigotry, anti-Scottish bigotry and anti-English bigotry are all frowned upon in mainstream society. Yet there are hordes of male journalists and politicians in Scotland and across the UK, not all of them on the Right, who routinely engage in anti-female bigotry – perhaps because it makes them feel more like real men.

Ironically, Tommy Sheridan himself had condemned what he called 'Britain's sexist underbelly' in a piece he wrote in his *Mirror* column in 2004. 'It's always the women who get the blame', he commented prophetically, in response to a poll showing that most blamed David Beckham's wife Victoria and his alleged mistress for the couple's marital problems. Now it was Tommy who was blaming the women for every slight he had ever suffered, mainly those conjured up by his own imagination.

Tommy's removal as convenor back in 2004 hadn't been driven by Catriona Grant or Carolyn Leckie or Frances Curran or Felicity Garvie or Rosie Kane or Jo Harvie or any of the other women on the SSP executive. The two people who had precipitated the crisis in the party, first by confronting Tommy and then taking the problem to the executive, were Keith Baldassara and me. Yet, at that stage, Tommy was unwilling to attack either of us with anything like the ferocious hostility he levelled against the women. It was cowardly misogyny based on loathing and fear of women who had refused to knuckle under.

It was also expedient. Keith had been his right-hand man in Pollok for eighteen years and, for the previous seven years, his caseworker in Glasgow. The two had also been close friends, going to the gym together and socialising together with their partners. Keith had also been best man at Tommy's wedding. I was also closely identified with Tommy. It just wasn't credible for Tommy to claim that Keith and I had plotted his downfall. It was easier to sell the lie by scapegoating women.

Frances Curran, an MSP who had sat on the Labour's National Executive Committee during the infamous political bloodletting between Left and Right in the 1980s, was, for the first time at a political meeting, frightened by the atmosphere of aggression bordering on violence. One hysterical male delegate had screamed obscenities in her face. 'You fucking evil, lying bitch!' he roared, while some of his future comrades in Solidarity looked on impassively. When Carolyn Leckie spoke to try to redress the balance after Tommy's ten-minute tirade, her words were drowned out in a cacophony of bigoted abuse. One delegate, who later became a prominent member of Tommy's future breakaway party, stood in front of her as she spoke, shouting, 'Liar! Liar! Liar!' while making repeated stabbing gestures towards her.'

These were not teenage delinquents from the housing schemes. Many were educated people who had been brought up in comfortable middle-class homes, had attended good middle-class schools and had degrees and PhDs coming out of their ears. I missed these scenes but plenty of people assured me that I had it easy that weekend – I was only locked up in Saughton.

To be fair, most delegates didn't participate in this baying for blood. Some of Tommy's supporters looked visibly uncomfortable but not one of them stood up to appeal for calm and common sense to prevail.

Despite the deranged atmosphere, there were powerful speeches from some of the SSP executive members including Keith Baldassara, Frances Curran, Richie Venton and Carolyn Leckie. They could barely be heard above the howling jeers from the rent-a-mob brigade. Some of the younger activists, still in their teens and early twenties, such as James Nesbitt, Andy McPake and Lynsey MacGregor, also braved the howling mob to appeal for a bit of elementary common sense. The parade of speakers who supported Tommy had almost all opposed the SSP in its early days, only jumping on the bandwagon after it had begun to roll. Some of them were decent-enough people in private but, after decades of defeats for the Left, they had become burned out and in need of a messiah.

The executive resolution, which called for continued defiance of the courts, was defeated by 82 votes to 67. Those who had endured weeks of intricate and traumatic discussion about how to protect the party from the imminent hurricane had now been turned over. They were sickened. People who had – in some cases without a second thought – voted to send me to jail had now flipped upside down because Tommy had told them to. When I heard the news, I felt like a boxer on the verge of victory whose trainer had just thrown in the towel.

The decision was to prove the most catastrophic ever made by the SSP. If just eight people had voted the other way, I would have stayed in Saughton Prison for as long as necessary. The pressure upon both sides to back down – or at least come to some kind of agreement – would have become almost irresistible. The calamity of the 2006 defamation case, the full-scale perjury investigation that followed and the tearing apart of the most successful socialist project in Europe would never have happened. But from the moment those minutes were handed over to the *News of the World*'s legal team, there was zero chance of the newspaper backing down. Why would they when they now had documented evidence of Tommy's admission that he visited Cupids with Anvar Khan and others?

But surely the reverse logic also applied? Surely Tommy Sheridan would now understand that his case was doomed? That was certainly the belief of a number of delegates at the National Council meeting who voted in good faith to hand over the minutes. Tommy's call for my release had sounded brave and magnanimous. He was prepared to accept damage to his own defamation case for the greater good of the party. It seemed like an act of heroism. But it was a hoax – a cruel, devious and manipulative swindle. His call to release the minutes had not been honest, heroic or brave. His undeclared new strategy had already been plotted out. He would go into court to denounce the minutes as a forgery and impugn the integrity of the national secretary, Allan Green, the minutes secretary, Barbara Scott, and any other cited EC member who dared to defend the legitimacy of those minutes.

Up until that National Council meeting, even some of Tommy's staunchest supporters were unaware of his game plan. A few days earlier, Allan Green had warned Rosemary Byrne that he feared Tommy was on course to wreak destruction on the party by lying about the November 2004 events. That would mean denouncing members of his own party as liars and plotters. Rosemary was having none of it. 'Tommy would never do such a thing,' she insisted. But Tommy did do such a thing – and so too did Rosemary. By the time of the court case, she and others had been sucked into the quicksand – broken men and women, ready to publicly debase themselves and their party because they were too weak to resist the will of a more powerful personality.

As the National Council meeting dissolved, a further resolution from one of the Aberdeen branches, instigated by the Socialist Workers Party, was railroaded onto the agenda. It stated:

As a matter of socialist principle, this meeting fully supports Tommy's right to defend himself against the *News of the World* and the Murdoch press. Whilst Tommy is pursuing his libel case as an individual, we offer him our full political support in his battle against one of the most vicious and anti-working-class organs of the ruling class.

Those pompous words, 'a matter of socialist principle', were intended to impress. It revealed a common conceit of many people in politics, of all shades and hues, who confuse opinions with principles. This was not a socialist principle any more than it would have been a conservative principle for the Tory Party to support Jonathan Aitken's and Neil Hamilton's legal actions against the *Guardian*. The resolution was voted through without a word of discussion, not even a mover and a seconder, by 81 votes to 60. There was no hint in the resolution that 'full political support' should include perjury, conspiracy to pervert the course of justice and rewriting the history of the SSP, but that was how it was later interpreted by some people.

Initially, the CWI group around Philip Stott had expressly opposed Tommy's plan to take legal action against the *News of the World*. But sometime in the days leading up to the meeting, Tommy had managed to whip them into line. In an article for *The Socialist* – the newspaper of the CWI's organisation in England and Wales – Philip triumphantly reported the National Council's decision to back Tommy's defamation action. The article patronisingly commended me for a 'personally courageous stand' in defying the court, while condemning my action as 'completely wrong and frankly irresponsible'. Why? Because, explained Philip, 'the court had effectively unlimited powers to fine the SSP and bankrupt it, as well as imposing a jail sentence of up to a year on Alan McCombes'.

Half of this statement was inaccurate. The court had no power to fine or bankrupt the SSP. It could only take action against me as an individual. Philip had either wilfully misinformed his readers or had failed to understand the legal process. Either way, it was sloppy, misleading reporting. His claim that I could have been sentenced for up to a year wasn't quite accurate either – under Scots law, the maximum sentence for contempt of court is two years.

But given his support for Tommy's legal action, which he knew could only succeed through perjury, Philip's criticism of my stand was stunningly illogical. Open defiance of the courts on a matter of principle was 'completely wrong and frankly irresponsible' because it might lead to a one-year jail sentence. But voluntarily taking out a defamation case which could only be won by committing perjury, denouncing honest people as liars, and persuading others to commit perjury – that was a heroic crusade that should be encouraged and supported.

The stance of both the CWI and the SWP was based not on reason but on crude self-interest. By now, both organisations were in a wooing war over Tommy's hand in political marriage and it was a sorry sight to behold. Both groups were only in the SSP in the first place because there was nowhere else for them to go. Yet together they swung the vote, setting us on course for catastrophe. The party was now in danger, not from external enemies but from a rampaging egomaniac astride two wooden horses.

The following afternoon, after days locked down in my cell, I managed to make a brief call to Carolyn from the payphone in Glenesk Hall. She was still reluctant to hand over the minutes despite the decision of the National Council but there was nothing else for it. We had done everything in our power to protect the party. Now it had voted to hurtle towards the cliff-edge and we could only watch and wait.

Later that day, Colin Fox collected the minutes from Carolyn and handed them over to Lady Smith at the Court of Session. That evening, I was released. At the main gate, I was greeted by a throng of supporters, a few photographers and the *Herald* journalist, Tom Gordon. I sensed a bit of tension. Some of those there to greet me were SWP members, who effusively hugged me and shook my hands. I was still in the dark about the National Council meeting, when some of these same smiling wellwishers had been part of the lynch mob. No wonder people like Carolyn and Catriona were seething.

Tom Gordon took me into the cafe in the public reception area of the prison and grilled me about the 'Open Letter', which I still hadn't seen. He quoted parts of it out to me. The following day's *Herald* carried my reaction, under the headline, ' "Poisonous" Feud as Freed SSP Official Goes on Attack – Sheridan Accused Over Open Letter'. I expressed 'extreme disappointment that somebody who played a magnificent part in the past has been regurgitating such poison' and said, 'As far as I can tell, it consists of a series of abominable smears without a shred of foundation. It sounds like Tommy has thrown the mother of all tantrums.' By the time my reaction was printed, I had been given a full run-down of the National Council meeting and knew we were dealing with something much more serious than a childish outburst.

After leaving Saughton, I went to a bar near Waverley Station with Carolyn Leckie and Ken Ferguson and told them that I wanted to circulate a statement taking responsibility for the affidavit and ex- plaining the circumstances in which I had signed it. They were mortified. The National Council had been ugly and brutal. Half the party had turned into a lynch mob and were baying for blood. In this fevered atmosphere, I wouldn't even get the chance to explain the background, they reckoned. It would be instant expulsion. The party could be split down the middle. They implored me to stay silent and I took their advice.

I had to return to the Court of Session later that week to face Lady Smith one more time for my earlier contempt of court. I also made a final attempt to argue that the minutes, by now in the hands of the court in a sealed envelope, should not be released. We could no longer afford the services of Paul Cullen QC, though he did go out of his way to help me prepare the case, which I had to present myself. I put forward the obvious arguments – it was an infringement of a private organisation's right to confidentiality and it could affect all sorts of organisations, from the local bowling club to the Women's Institute – but I was battering my head against a brick wall. The fatal flaw in my argument was that the court case had been instigated by one of our own members – and not just any random member either but the one member of the SSP who was recognised by millions of people.

Lady Smith ordered the minutes to be handed over to the *News of the World*'s legal team. In recognition of the fact that I had already spent the best part of four days locked up, I was hit with a modest £500 fine but, on top of that, the *News of the World*'s costs were awarded against me, which meant I could be liable for thousands of pounds more. I wasn't too worried about that. As they used to say in Yorkshire when I worked there in the early 1980s, 'You can't get feathers off a cat.'

The judge dealt with one other piece of business that week. She had been livid about the Cardonald SSP branch resolution to destroy the minutes and demanded the names of those present at the meeting. I wasn't able or prepared to give her those names.

Tommy hadn't helped matters with his posturing before the media. When asked by *The Herald* if he would hand over the names, he ridiculed the judge, saying:

> She can ask me all she wants. I never took part in that decision, and if she asks me who was there, she can ask me till Timbuktu freezes over. Some people have obviously got ideas above their station and should remember we still live in a democracy.

A few days later, a sheepish delegation from Cardonald branch turned up at the Court of Session with an attendance list. They told the judge that they hadn't known they were acting in contempt of court, apologised profusely and begged forgiveness from her 'Ladyship'. It was clear to me they were acting under orders from Tommy who was, by now, worried about the consequences of his grandstanding bravado. And Timbuktu still hadn't frozen over.

With the defamation case scheduled to start on 4 July, the SSP descended into a state of torpor during the long June days. The party was now in the condemned cell, not because of politics or grand principles but because of a tawdry tabloid sex scandal. In the eighteenth century, a war broke out between Britain and Spain after a sea captain allegedly had his ear cut off by Spanish coastguards – the War of Jenkins' Ear, they called it. This was the War of Tommy's Halo.

Two further national meetings of the SSP took place before the court case began. In mid-June, the SSP executive met in the Calton Centre in Edinburgh, near Easter Road. By this time, those SSP members whose initials had been recorded on the falsified minutes sent to the *News of the World* had been cited to give evidence. Allan Green opened a discussion on how we should collectively respond.

The vote at the National Council meeting had ended our defiance strategy. Tommy and his allies had voted to hoist the white flag and capitulate to the *News of the World* by handing over our minutes. Most of us weren't happy about it but, once you've surrendered, you can't then un-surrender. Allan Green formulated a proposal, stating, 'In response to direct questions in court, those cited should not lie or commit contempt of court.' Seventeen people voted for the motion, including Sinead Daly of the CWI. Two – Lynn Sheridan, Tommy's sister, and Gill Hubbard, of the SWP – voted against, without explaining why. Another SWP member, Penny Howard, abstained.

Then we made a serious tactical mistake. We should have taken that resolution to the full National Council meeting of the party scheduled to take place in Linlithgow the following Sunday where we would have carried the vote hands down. It was one thing for people to argue abstractly that we should give Tommy 'political support' in his legal battle against the *News of the World* but only the most diehard supporters of Tommy – plus the SWP – would have been prepared to openly call for our members to lie in court and leave themselves open to future perjury charges and lengthy jail sentences. But Tommy made representations to Allan Green, asking for the resolution to be withheld from the National Council. The issues were sub judice, he said. He wouldn't be able to participate. In any case, it was unnecessary to discuss it. It would only cause division and now it was time to draw back from the bloodletting. We were too obliging. After the previous National Council meeting, no one had the stomach for a rerun. For the sake of unity, we agreed to Tommy's request for a truce. That meant no discussion at the National Council meeting of the court case. We believed that the overwhelming decision of the executive – that we should refuse to lie or defy – was sufficient. Even the CWI, who had been partly responsible for the shambles of the previous National Council meeting, had voted to tell the truth in court.

Outside Linlithgow Burgh Halls, delegates chatted nervously in huddles in the blazing sunshine as they waited for the meeting to kick off. Alice Sheridan, Tommy's mother, spoke to me for the first time since the 2004 crisis – or, rather, she shouted and bawled at me. We had been old friends. She had lived near me in Govan and she sometimes looked after my daughters when they were young.

'I used to love you like a member of my own family,' she yelled in front of dozens of uncomfortable delegates. 'But, for four years, you've been out to get Tommy.'

Where that came from, I had no idea. Tommy and I had worked together like brothers right up until November 2004, eighteen long months earlier. I guessed this reference to four years was something to do with my relationship with Carolyn. Tommy had no doubt spun her the Lady Macbeth version of events that Carolyn had come along, poisoned my mind and turned me against Tommy. I didn't blame Alice – Tommy was her son and she adored him.

'You don't know the full facts, Alice,' I muttered uncomfortably.

'I know the facts,' she snarled. 'You politically assassinated Tommy.'

Inside, the meeting went through the motions, literally and meta-phorically. We discussed our campaign on free school meals and our parliamentary bill to bring ScotRail back into public ownership.

It felt as though we were discussing which colour of wallpaper would look best in the front room while, outside, a bulldozer was about to start demolishing the building.

July 2006*

The Titanic *Sets Sail*

A fierce sun scorched the ancient cobblestones of the Royal Mile and the air crackled with the jangle of jukeboxes and car stereos. Edinburgh's Old Town had cast off its grey cloak and dressed itself up in psychedelic colours.

Out of sight of the tourist throngs, behind St Giles Cathedral, the media circus had commandeered Parliament Square. This small corner of Edinburgh's Old Town had been the scene of some of the most dramatic events in Scottish history. The cathedral had been the birthplace and stronghold of Scottish Presbyterianism. Under the paved square, once the kirkyard of St Giles, beneath parking space number 23, lies the grave of John Knox. Across the square, facing the cathedral, stands the equally sombre Supreme Courts of Scotland – once the home of the Scottish Parliament before it voted to dissolve itself in 1707.

Now the curtain was ready to rise on a political–legal drama of a different order. The 'Libel Trial of the Decade', as it was billed in the press, might lack the historical magnitude of the Reformation or the Act of Union but, for the next five sweltering weeks, Scotland's media would be transfixed by the daily torrent of scandal gushing out of the cramped courtroom that was so small it could only accommodate eighteen members of the public. By the final week, the show could have filled the Scottish Exhibition and Conference Centre.

At the centre of this saga was one man's single-minded crusade to turn fact into fiction and fiction into fact. Back in November 2004, Tommy Sheridan MSP, then one of the most popular politicians Scotland had ever produced, had privately pledged to destroy one woman – Anvar Khan. By the summer of 2006, he had evolved into

---

* Because of the availability of witnesses and other considerations, the defamation trial involved a certain amount of leaping back and forward from one subject to another. Some SSP witnesses, for example, were called in the first week of the trial, while others were called in the fourth week. For the sake of clarity, I have grouped the chapters on the defamation trial by theme rather than by chronology.

Tommy the Terminator, prepared to destroy everything and anyone who stood in his way.

In the weeks leading up to the court case, his supporters in the SSP had launched an online petition backing him in his 'titanic battle against the Murdoch empire'. The analogy was supposed to refer to the Greek gods rather than the doomed ship. Some of us feared that Tommy was navigating the socialist movement straight into a giant iceberg.

Allison Kane was first in the firing line. She was witness number 22 on the defender's list, but as she had previously booked a holiday, she was brought forward to give evidence on the first day, right after the jury had been selected and the other formalities dealt with. Allison had been the SSP treasurer, a member of the executive and a close friend of Tommy right up until the events of November 2004. Now she was in the witness stand, facing across to the jury, with the judge diagonally to her left and Mike Jones, QC for the *News of the World*, just a few feet away on the front bench. Tommy's legal team sat on the far side of the bench, over towards the jury.

Jones, a former RAF pilot, was renowned as a meticulous operator and a master of detail. In 1998, he had successfully defended the suspended Labour MP Muhammad Sarwar against bribery charges during a marathon nine-week trial in the High Court in Edinburgh. Now he was Scotland's highest-earning lawyer.

Having gone through the ritual formalities, the QC directed Allison to view a computer monitor displaying an onscreen version of the front-page *News of the World* splash that had triggered the crisis, headlined, 'Married MSP Is Spanking Swinger'. After questioning her about the *News of the World* article and other productions, Jones then directed her to the minutes of the November the 9th 2004 meeting. In a process he was to repeat over and over again in the next few weeks, he worked his way through the content of the document paragraph by paragraph. At each point, Allison confirmed the detail set out in the document. 'Yes, that's an accurate record of what happened,' she'd say. She provided no elaboration – just a straightforward, factual response to each of the questions. For Allison, the ordeal was soul-destroying – one of the most painful experiences of her life.

The press gallery listened to her evidence with incredulity. For the previous 18 months, Tommy had spun and woven an assortment of fairy tales to explain his resignation. Most of the Scottish media had lapped up his version of events like enthralled children. The rest of us had kept a steely silence, even in the face of extreme provocation.

'Champagne Tommy, a Club Called Cupids and a Hotel Three-

some' screamed the headline in the *Daily Record* the morning after
Allison Kane had given her low-key, matter-of-fact evidence. 'Chief
Whip' taunted the headline in the *Sun*. Compared to what was to
come, though, reports of Day One were like extracts from the *People's
Friend*. Tommy's bid to use the courts to clean up his reputation was
already beginning to resemble the actions of the man who amputated
his own leg to relieve a sore toe. Over the next few weeks, Mike Jones
QC and his backroom team built up their evidence like a scaffold. We
already had a sketchy picture of Tommy's secret behaviour but it was
like an incomplete join-the-dots children's puzzle. Over the next few
weeks, more and more connections would be made and a clearer
picture would begin to emerge.

On the second day of the trial, Allan Caldwell, a freelance investigative journalist, was called to the witness stand. This was not
someone who could easily be dismissed as a puppet of the Murdoch
empire. Caldwell was a respected journalist with over 30 years'
experience under his belt. Until a few years before, he had been
Father of the Chapel – the newspaper equivalent of the trade union
convener – for the National Union of Journalists in the Glasgow
Evening Times. It was while he was still working there that he received
a late-night call from a reliable contact he had cultivated over several
years. In his evidence, the journalist drew a clear distinction between a
contact and a source. A source might provide a specific piece of
information that may or may not be reliable. A contact would be
'solid', he explained. 'These are people you build up a wealth of
experience with over the years. You know them personally and they
are generally 100 per cent reliable.'

This particular contact was a businessman who habitually frequented Cupids and other swingers' clubs in the north of England.
Late one Friday or Saturday night, the contact had phoned Caldwell,
gurgling with laughter, and said, 'You'll never guess where I am and
who I've just been speaking to?' He wasn't looking for money or trying
to sell a story. He was just gobsmacked and had phoned Caldwell to
pass on a juicy piece of gossip about Scotland's most clean-cut
politician. Tommy had told the stranger that he had called in on
his way up from London and that Cupids was one of several swingers'
clubs that he frequented.

The deputy editor of the *Evening Times* instructed the reporter not
to bother pursuing the matter any further so Caldwell then passed
the information to Bob Bird, the editor of the *News of the World* as a
'tip-off' – a commonplace practice in the newspaper industry when a
journalist comes across a story which his own paper is unable or

unwilling to follow up. His testimony fitted into place with what we already knew. In November 2001, I had warned Tommy that there was a story floating around the *Evening Times*. He had denied it but then, a year later, he acknowledged he had spoken to a Scottish guy in Cupids.

Allan Caldwell provided one additional intriguing piece of information. His contact had been in touch with him again around February or March 2006, just months earlier. He had been in another swingers' club, La Chambre in Sheffield, with a girlfriend. Both of them had seen and recognised Tommy Sheridan in the club. On the face of it, the story sounded far-fetched.

In his cross-examination, Tommy's QC asked Caldwell, 'Do you imagine anyone in the position of Mr Sheridan would go to a swingers' club in March 2006 on the eve of a defamation trial against the *News of the World* unless he was a complete idiot?'

'I am passing on a conversation from a contact I trust one hundred per cent,' responded the journalist.

'This would be extraordinary, would it not?' asked the QC.

'I don't know because I don't indulge in that sort of habit and I don't know whether it's an addiction,' replied Caldwell. His tentative explanation sounded feeble at the time but, as the evidence of Tommy's recklessly repetitive behaviour began to mount up, the suggestion that Tommy had an addictive personality and was prepared to take outlandish risks to feed his craving began to look like a possible clinical diagnosis.

Anvar Khan and Katrine Trolle went on to corroborate the Cupids story separately. Their testimony should have nailed it beyond any reasonable doubt, even without the additional support of the SSP evidence.

In early 2004, just after his resignation, Tommy had told the press, out of the blue, that he had been involved briefly with Anvar Khan back in 1992, following his release from jail. It had been a strange admission to make. I had been close to Tommy and, until 2004, had never known of any connection between him and Anvar Khan, who was a reasonably well-known journalist. Moreover, she had never actually named Tommy as the Cupids MSP. Nor had she suggested they had previously been in any kind of relationship. This was no unguarded throwaway remark. Nor was it a candid confession. It was a calculated cover story. Their relationship had begun not in 1992 but in 1994. And it had continued, sporadically, until late 2002. So why he had he felt it necessary to mention it at all?

In November 2004, Tommy was convinced, mistakenly, that he

was about to be publicly named by Anvar Khan as the swinging MSP and was already planning ahead. If he pre-emptively outed their past relationship on his own terms, he could deal with any awkward, intimate information she might provide to back up her story. But to maintain his spotless image, he had to pretend that it was all over by 1992, before he was in an established relationship with Gail.

He would live to regret his decision to slyly feed the tabloids this sanitised, falsified titbit and his accompanying threat to sue Anvar Khan. Although she had privately identified the mystery MSP to a *Scotland on Sunday* journalist during an interview to promote *Pretty Wild* and to Bob Bird of the *News of the World*, she had refused to consent to his name being used. In the first few days of November 2004, she had also refused an offer of £30,000 from the *Daily Mail* for the exclusive story of her trip to Cupids with Tommy Sheridan.

In her evidence, Anvar described how she had changed her mind after witnessing Tommy's hypocritical media crusade to convince the world of his saintliness. His kiss-and-tell performance had clinched it. Five days later, she signed a sworn affidavit naming Tommy Sheridan as the MSP who had been with her and others that night at Cupids. The *News of the World* now had the legal corroboration it needed to name him publicly. But, by that time, Tommy had already initiated legal proceedings over the Fiona McGuire story, effectively closing down any further reporting of his private activities.

In the witness box, the *News of the World* columnist repeatedly offered to produce her telephone records stretching back to the 1990s to back up her evidence. She described her book *Pretty Wild* as an X-rated *Bridget Jones Diary*, which included a mixture of fact and imagination. 'But I didn't write the book under oath,' she said.

As well as identifying Tommy Sheridan as the MSP who had been in the Cupids expedition, she provided additional detail about the trip and this was separately corroborated by Katrine Trolle. She also identified Katrine from a photograph – before the Danish woman had given evidence – and was able to point out in the courtroom Andy McFarlane, Tommy's brother-in-law who had been part of the 'Cupids Five'.

She confidently faced down questioning by Graeme Henderson, the advocate who had temporarily stood in for Tommy's original QC, Richard Keen, who had been called to London to deal with a House of Lords appeal. Henderson's cross-examination included a peculiar line of questioning about her religious background and beliefs and some heavy hints that she had been involved in a sexual relationship with Bob Bird, her editor. Tommy himself had put this story around in the run-up to the trial. Six months earlier, he had told Allan Green, Colin Fox and me that this was one of the reasons the *News of the World* would back down. Anvar Khan laughed off the suggestion, saying, 'No, no, no!'

Because of the sensationalism of her column in the *News of the World* and the notoriety of her book, Anvar Khan had something of a reputation as a sex-obsessed ladette. That was certainly the impression I had from the Cupids revelations back in 2004. Yet she is a committed trade unionist and, according to those who know her, a strong, intelligent, articulate woman. In recent years, even the tone and content of her *News of the World* column changed markedly. While retaining her brash and breezy style, her writings became less salacious and more overtly political and feminist. Her testimony in court had been powerful.

Katrine Trolle's evidence was even more lethal. She described how she had been on a work placement as a trainee occupational therapist in Glasgow during a double by-election in Anniesland in November 2000. She had turned up to the SSP HQ to help out in the campaign. Tommy had been there and offered to take her out canvassing, to show her the ropes. He invited her to come to his house a few weeks later while Gail was working away from home. Katrine's evidence about what happened next understandably caused Gail great distress, provoking a passionate outburst from her in the witness box towards the end of the trial about this 'vile lie'. Katrine had not come forward willingly. For a long time, she had refused to confirm her involvement with Tommy when door-stepped and phoned by the *News of the World*. She was effectively dragged before the Court of Session as a result of the actions of other people. Duncan Rowan had named her to the *News of the World* back in 2004 as the unidentified woman involved in the Cupids trip. By ploughing ahead with his legal action, regardless of the personal consequences to others, Tommy had guaranteed that she would have to take the witness stand.

In June 2006, she received a citation from both sides in the forthcoming legal battle. She phoned back Tommy's lawyers, Bannatyne Kirkwood France & Co, and told them, 'I don't think that's a good idea because, if I were to be called up to court, I would be telling the truth.' The lawyer at the other end asked her for a brief account of her involvement and she told him, 'Yes, I had a sexual affair with Tommy Sheridan.' The line went silent. The lawyer at the other end seemed genuinely shocked at what he had just heard. That, in turn, triggered a whole series of phone calls from Tommy to Katrine, which she refused to answer. Instead, she called Bannatyne Kirkwood France again to ask them to instruct their client to stop phoning her. It worked. But the *News of the World* citation still stood and she would be forced into the witness stand to reveal every detail of her intimate involvement with Tommy under threat of contempt of court and perjury.

Under questioning, she explained how, on one occasion, she travelled down from Aberdeen to meet Tommy and was invited to go to Andy McFarlane's home to participate in a threesome. Tommy had repeatedly and approvingly referred to liberal Scandinavian attitudes towards sexuality. Katrine – an articulate and intelligent young woman with a professional career – felt under psychological pressure to prove herself. She told the court that Tommy had, on several occasions, tried to persuade her to visit Cupids. Each time, she found an excuse to avoid the trip to Manchester. Eventually, however, she agreed and went to a flat near Ibrox Stadium one Friday evening, where she met Tommy, Andy McFarlane and two other people she had never met before or since. One of them was Anvar Khan. The other, a man she knew only as Gary, appeared quite nervous and uncomfortable about the trip. She sat in the front passenger seat on the three-hour journey, with Tommy driving and the others in the back.

Tommy had described the club as a classy, upmarket kind of place with a Jacuzzi, sauna and gymnasium. 'I had thought it was going to be this really smart, fancy, nice place but instead it was more like a pub from the 1970s with Formica everywhere. It was a dump.' Katrine said that Tommy had given her what he had called a 'wonder drug to give [her] energy and make [her] amorous. Maybe it was Viagra.' Or maybe it was something else.

Her testimony closely matched that of Anvar Khan, except on one important point. The *News of the World* columnist had been sure the trip to Cupids had taken place in November 2002. She had told the court that it was difficult to recall the minutiae of dates and times from four or five years earlier but she knew she was living in London when she took a call from a Tommy to arrange a trip to Cupids. Katrine's memory was different. She thought that the episode had occurred in November 2001, when she doing a fieldwork placement.

As the trial progressed, Tommy skilfully exploited this divergence between the testimonies of Anvar Khan and Katrine Trolle. Yet all other details of their evidence tallied exactly, even though there was never any suggestion that the two women had met since the Manchester trip four or five years earlier. In the course of the trial, the *News of the World*'s lawyers produced telephone records which could have pointed to either of two possible dates. On Friday 23 November 2001, Tommy's phone records revealed that he had called his contact number for Katrine Trolle at 4.37 p.m., then at 7.02 p.m. and then again at 7.03 p.m. Later that night, at 11.40 p.m., he made a phone call to Cupids. But on Thursday 26 September 2002, he had phoned not just Katrine Trolle but also the rest of the team who had visited Cupids – Anvar Khan, Andy McFarlane and the man Katrine knew as Gary – some of whom he phoned on several occasions.

Mike Jones for the *News of the World* suggested that, on the second occasion, Tommy had been trying to round up the group for a return visit to Cupids. In doing so, he was accepting that Katrine Trolle's recollection was accurate and, by implication, that Anvar Khan was mistaken about the date. Presumably, the lawyers felt that, because they had specific evidence of a phone call from Tommy to Cupids late at night on 23 November 2001, then that must, indeed, have been the date of the visit. But there is an alternative and more likely explanation. In the period spanning November 2001 to September 2002, Tommy visited Cupids not once but twice – or more. There is no doubt in my mind that he was in Cupids on the weekend beginning Friday 23 November 2001 – one week before I was first alerted to the rumour circulating in media circles that Tommy been in a Manchester sex club. His earlier phone calls that day to Katrine Trolle may well have been for the purpose of inviting her to go with him. In her testimony, Katrine recounted that, several times before the visit, Tommy had invited her by phone to 'this club in Manchester where people would go and have sex. On a few occasions I was almost persuaded to say yes but better judgement got the better of me and I said no or told him I was too busy.'

Tommy himself had admitted to the SSP executive making two visits to Cupids – one in 1996, the other in 2002. An additional factor – not brought out during the court case – was the fact that Tommy's phone calls to the four other people who ended up in Cupids took place on the Thursday night immediately before the local Glasgow autumn holiday weekend. The September Weekend, as it's called in Glasgow, would be an ideal time to get people together.

After the Cupids visit, Tommy had asked Katrine on several further occasions to return to the club but she refused. In 2003, she introduced him to two friends in Dundee, where she had moved for work. She was sharing a house at the time with a couple, Ruth Adamson and Ralph Barnett. On one occasion, Tommy had spent the night there with Katrine, while the other couple slept in another room. Both were cited as witnesses and backed up Katrine's story.

In November 2004, straight after Katrine had been named by Duncan Rowan in the *News of the World*, Tommy had phoned her. He had called Duncan a 'rat' – a word he was later to direct at many other SSP members – and sought assurances from her that she wouldn't speak to the press about the Cupids incident or their other encounters. 'He was agitated,' she told the court. 'Not speaking nicely about other SSP members.' He had later texted her to say, 'Chin up. It will be fine. They don't have a story. Everything's OK.' He followed this up with another four or five phone calls seeking reassurance.

Duncan Rowan had also phoned Katrine on the eve of the publication of the *News of the World* article where he named her. He apologised profusely and admitted that, in his desperation to protect Fiona McGuire, he had made a terrible mistake. When Katrine was then door-stepped by the newspaper, she denied everything. 'But I never imagined it would ever come to court,' she explained.

For Katrine, the whole experience was purgatory. She was plastered over the front page of every tabloid in the land. 'Danish Blue' ran the headline in *The Sun*. Other reports described her as 'a flame-haired Scandinavian sex bomb'. Tommy Sheridan – who by then was conducting his own defence – had publicly labelled her a liar and perjurer while personally questioning her on the intimate details of their physical relationship. After the trial, her boyfriend broke up with her and she left Scotland to return to her native Denmark, broken and humiliated by her ordeal.

July 2006

Tabloids in Paradise

Back in November 2004, Tommy had convinced almost everyone that the Fiona McGuire scandal was a baseless fiction invented by a demented woman. The Anvar Khan revelations had left him reeling inside the party. But far from being a knockout blow, the new revelations had galvanised him.

With relish, he had lambasted the woman from Peterhead. She was a crazed fantasist, he told the world. Most people outside the party accepted the word of Honest Tommy, Scotland's icon of integrity, against this unknown woman. And just for good measure, he drip-fed the press information pointing to the fact that she was a former escort girl with alcohol and drugs problems. The MSP had clearly been fitted up.

Even among the circle of SSP members who knew some of the details of Tommy's adventures in Swingerland, most fell for his forceful repudiation of the Fiona McGuire claims – but not everyone. A few of us sensed that something was not quite right here. We had no specific evidence linking him to Fiona McGuire. We did, however, know a few things that the press and the public were unaware of. We knew that he was the mystery MSP who had visited Cupids with Anvar Khan. And we knew of a previous pattern of behaviour that tallied with some elements of the Fiona McGuire story. But why would he bother denying this story to the SSP executive, when he had already owned up to the more damaging allegations about Cupids? Surely this demonstrated that the story was false? Maybe . . . or maybe not.

Within days, possibly even hours, of the November the 9th 2004 SSP executive meeting, Tommy was already regretting his candour. But he also knew that his options at that meeting had been limited. He had already owned up to the sex club visits to Keith Baldassara and me. How could he then tell the SSP executive a different story without accusing the two of us of trying to frame him? If he had suddenly announced back in November 2004, out of the blue, that his two closest political associates had fabricated an elaborate story for the purpose of forcing him to resign, he would have been laughed out of the meeting. Instead he used the 'boiling frog' technique, where the temperature is increased gradually, without the creature noticing until it's too late. Over time, bit by bit, he would lay the groundwork for what was to evolve into a full-blown conspiracy theory.

But he hadn't admitted the Fiona McGuire affair to Keith or me or anyone else, which meant he could safely denounce the story as a pack of lies. It was what he believed he *should* have done from the start with the Cupids allegations – deny them to me, deny them to Keith, deny them to the SSP executive. Then he might have been able bring everyone on board his legal crusade.

The great advantage of the Fiona McGuire story in his eyes, whether true or false, was that he now had a clean weapon with which to silence the *News of the World*. If he could persuade his party that this allegation really was false, then he could get support, or at least acquiescence, for legal action to gag the *News of the World* and suppress all further comment on his behaviour. It would buy him time until the day of reckoning somewhere in the mists of time when it came to court. By then, he suspected, the *News of the World* would already have backed down. Problem solved.

Most people in the media and within the SSP accepted it. The word of an ex-prostitute against that of a celebrity politician? No contest.

In 2006 Fiona McGuire's evidence was widely ridiculed. At the time it was only sketchily reported in the media, which predictably concentrated on the most lurid details. But the full verbatim notes of her evidence paint a picture which appeared to me raw and authentic. She told the court she had first met Tommy in late 2000 in Duncan Rowan's flat in Aberdeen. At the time, she was friendly with Duncan, moving in the same social scene. When Tommy spotted her, he asked Duncan, 'Who's your little friend?' There was bit of light-hearted banter and Fiona McGuire gave Tommy her phone number. Within a few days, he called her and asked if she was 'up for a bit of fun'. He also asked if she had any friends who she might be able to bring along.

The story that had appeared in the *News of the World* had painted a picture of a romantic first date. That was one of the reasons it seemed implausible – candlelit meals, champagne and strawberries were not Tommy's style. Often, the tabloids spice up their scandals to sell more papers but, in this instance, the real story had been sanitised. Under oath, Fiona McGuire described an encounter that had Tommy's trademark stamped all over it. She told of a group sex session, involving Tommy, her and three other people – two male and one female – in a small room in the Treetops Hotel on the western outskirts of Aberdeen. She also insisted that all five people present had taken cocaine.

At the time Fiona McGuire was working with an Aberdeen escort agency. By her own admission, she was messed up with drugs and drink – exactly the type of woman that Tommy, as I now knew, would have no scruples about homing in on. She made no claim that Tommy had paid for any services. But he had asked her in his first phone call if she had any friends she could bring along. She testified that she had invited three other people – two women and a man – she knew through the escort agency. Whether they were colleagues or clients wasn't made clear. The tabloids, naturally, were in paradise. Tommy had graduated from threesomes to fivesomes – and they weren't talking Scottish country dancing. A cocaine-fuelled five-in-a-bed orgy was the perfect follow-up to the Cupids revelations. It was so lurid that many people started to wonder whether it was all just a torrent of fiction. But this was the kind of stuff you just couldn't make up. For those who knew something of the secret life of Tommy Sheridan, it sounded drearily familiar.

Fiona McGuire told the court that she had fudged the details of her first sexual encounter in order to salvage some glimmer of self-respect. By 2004, she had left the sex industry far behind, and had begun to carve out a promising career with a company which sold educational support materials to parents of children with learning difficulties. Her job took her all over Scotland, meeting head teachers, parents, children and education authorities. She explained to the court that she had prettified the story of her first date with Tommy to make it look as though she had been desired for her looks or her personality. Now she was telling it straight.

In one exchange with Tommy's advocate, Graeme Henderson, she was asked about photographic or documentary evidence. 'I don't know about any photographs. As for documentation, if you're shagging someone, what documents do you need? Please sign here so you can't sue me if you pick up an STD?'

She stood by another part of her story, which took place in Newcastle, where she was attending a work-related conference. She had met Tommy there and gone with him to the lap-dancing club, For Your Eyes Only. It was familiar name. Back in late 2001, I had stood in as a substitute for Tommy at a rally in Newcastle to launch the Tyneside Socialist Alliance. At the end of the meeting a member of the Socialist Workers Party had made a request for volunteers to picket a new lap-dancing club had just opened in the city on the grounds that it involved commercial sexual exploitation of women. They might well have got a shock at the identity of one of the customers trying to cross the picket line. In the club, according to Fiona McGuire, they met another couple and went back with them to their hotel room. It turned into a familiar story – a triangular sex session, this time involving Tommy, Fiona McGuire and the male stranger, whose female companion had refused to participate and walked out.

The court had earlier heard hours of transcripts of taped conversations – some of them secretly recorded – between Fiona McGuire and Douglas Wight, news editor of the *News of the World*. It revealed a woman who knew some fairly obscure detail about Tommy's habits, such as which sunbed salons he used and his role as a local councillor prior to 2003. None of this was cast-iron evidence of a relationship but it did ring true. The tapes also suggested that she had been much more involved with the SSP than any of us had previously been aware.

Since 2004, Tommy had claimed that Fiona McGuire had never been a member of the SSP. This was important to Tommy's case as it was on public record that he had visited Peterhead on a series of occasions between 2000 and 2004, campaigning against the threatened closure of Peterhead Prison and in support of the fishing industry in the UK's leading white-fish port. In a small town where the SSP membership could be counted on two hands, it would have been unlikely that he could have visited Peterhead on political business without encountering Fiona McGuire at least once.

Duncan Rowan could have clarified the issue but he was out of the picture and incommunicado. No one else on the SSP executive had much knowledge of the SSP in deepest Aberdeenshire. In court, Tommy produced a single witness to refute Fiona McGuire's claim of SSP membership. Andy Cumbers, a lecturer at the University of Glasgow who had previously been an SSP member in Aberdeen, testified that he had never met her. His evidence was honest but worthless. It was hardly surprising their paths had never crossed. Fiona McGuire, according to her own evidence, had only joined the SSP when a branch was founded in Peterhead in July 2001. Andy Cumbers had moved to Glasgow five months before, in January 2001. After that, by his own reckoning, he had only returned to the area a couple of times, when he stood as an SSP candidate in the 2003 election in Aberdeen Central – thirty miles from Peterhead. Why didn't Tommy bring in an SSP member who actually lived in Peterhead? Perhaps he had been unable to persuade any SSP members from Aberdeenshire to commit perjury. Later, the *News of the World* lawyer produced minutes of the local branch meeting showing that it had actually held meetings at the home address of Fiona McGuire.

The court case did clarify the background to the *News of the World* story. Fiona McGuire had a link with a local freelance journalist, Ken Adams, who did some occasional work for the *News of the World* and other papers. She had fed him various stories, at least half a dozen of which had been published, on issues such as staff cuts at Peterhead Prison and child abuse. On one occasion, she mentioned that she was meeting Tommy Sheridan and, in her own words, became 'a bit giggly' when the reporter pressed her further about why she was meeting Tommy. It had been a boastful, throwaway remark by a woman lacking self-esteem and eager to impress. She had under-estimated the enormity of her story in the eyes of a tabloid journalist and quickly became inundated with texts and phone calls pleading for more information.

Soon, Douglas Wight, the seasoned Scottish news editor of the *News of the World*, was on the case. At that level, tabloid reporters will use every trick in the book – and some that are never written down anywhere – to scoop their rivals and get the sensational front-page exclusive. In his own testimony, Wight more or less admitted that he had deceived and manipulated Fiona McGuire. For the *News of the World*, this was a huge story – and it was corroborated by other information the newspaper was beginning to gather from other sources, including the Cupids tip-offs. Fiona began to get the message that the paper was going to run a story about her and Tommy Sheridan anyway. It would be in her best interests to cooperate, she was told, because then she would have control over how the story was presented. And she could pick up a cheque for £20,000.

According to her evidence and the earlier testimony of Douglas Wight, Fiona eventually agreed to set up a sting. She attended a weekend rally of the SSP in Glasgow, booking in at the Radisson Hotel near Central Station. She had made an arrangement to go to the Cottier Theatre in the West End on the Saturday night for an SSP benefit gig performed by comedian and author, Mark Steel. Tommy would be there. They would leave the event discreetly and she would smuggle him back into her hotel room. On the way in, she would be photographed by the *News of the World*. The plan fell through because Tommy turned up with Gail whose suspicions had perhaps been aroused. One Glasgow SSP member noticed Gail glowering murder-ously at a woman he later recognised from newspaper photographs as Fiona McGuire. Gail's suspicions, it seemed, had saved Tommy from being caught bang to rights. Afterwards, Fiona McGuire returned to the hotel with Duncan Rowan – 'though not in a sexual context' she told the court. From her room, she phoned the *News of the World* to explain why the sting had failed, while Duncan drank his way through the mini-bar, paid for by the newspaper. After that weekend, Fiona McGuire turned cool towards the *News of the World* – perhaps because Duncan had persuaded her to withdraw cooperation.

It might have been left at that but for the Cupids front-page story on Halloween. Although Tommy wasn't named, Anvar Khan had privately confirmed his identity to the editor, Bob Bird. And the story she told him was not only extraordinary – it was also remarkably similar to the story told by Fiona McGuire. Douglas Wight phoned Fiona McGuire right away and she agreed to meet him in Aberdeen on Wednesday 3 November 2004.

The news editor told the court, 'I felt there might be a chance that each story would corroborate the other because it was almost as though each woman was giving a genuine account of a sexual relationship with one man.' That day, Fiona McGuire signed a contract worth £20,000. According to Wight, there was no haggling involved. 'She never actually asked for any money. It was almost like a shrug – "OK if you want to pay money for your story, fine." She certainly wasn't looking for it.' Fiona herself told the court that she had given away £19,000 of the cash to friends and charities.

The newspaper's lawyers were now convinced that the story was watertight. However, the journalists intended to spend more time backing it up with photographic and documentary evidence. But then, a week after Fiona McGuire signed her contract, the SSP dropped its bombshell – Tommy Sheridan was no longer the party convener. Events then accelerated. The MSP himself, following the Cupids story, had gone on a public lying spree, lashing out at 'baseless rumours' and staking his claim to be the most spotless celebrity since Snow White. Instead of killing off media interest, his protests had roused the curiosity of some of the more inquisitive journalists, who began to scent a scandal. A *Sunday Mail* journalist was now on Fiona McGuire's case. The *Daily Mail* was pursuing Anvar Khan. The tabloids were now in a race to find the ammunition and fire the first bullet. On Sunday 14 November, more hastily than they would have preferred, the *News of the World* pulled the trigger.

For the next eighteen months, Fiona McGuire was to become trapped in the crossfire of the ensuing feud between Tommy Sheridan and the *News of the World*. The tabloid press in Britain is notorious worldwide for its ruthlessness and cynicism. But the self-righteous socialist politician showed he could teach the most hardened tabloid hacks a thing or two. In the run-up to the defamation case, he had even cited Fiona McGuire's medical records, presumably to prove that she was mentally unstable. As it happened, his legal team never did produce the document as evidence – possibly because it failed to provide the information Tommy had expected to find. His readiness to use the judicial system to gain access to a witness's confidential medical history was disturbing. To make matters worse, he was invading this woman's privacy at the very time that the SSP itself was battling with the courts to protect *his* privacy.

Tommy had also orchestrated a series of tabloid smear stories to besmirch Fiona McGuire's reputation. Back in November 2004, the day after the story broke, the Scottish *Daily Mirror* had run an exclusive under the headline, 'FORMER HUBBY BRANDS FIONA A LIAR'. The story reported that Fiona McGuire's ex-husband, Michael Cavadias, had branded her a 'fantasist' and a 'compulsive liar'. It was an extraordinarily speedy response to the *News of the World* story, suggesting the *Mirror* story had been prepared in advance. As it happened, Tommy had been in touch with Michael Cavadias and offered him assistance in a custody dispute with Fiona McGuire over access to their child.

In a follow-up attack on Fiona McGuire in August 2006, just two days after the close of the defamation trial – again, quite obviously prepared in advance – the *Sunday Mirror* ran a similar 'exclusive' under the headline, 'TOMMY CASE HOOKER LIED THAT SHE WAS DYING FROM CANCER, SO I MARRIED HER'. Now Michael Cavadias was claiming that Fiona had duped him into marrying her by falsely claiming she had terminal cancer. He continued:

> I know she is a money-grabbing fantasist. And when I read this stuff about her and Tommy Sheridan I knew right away it was rubbish. I felt sorry for Mr Sheridan because it was obviously a complete fabrication and I am so pleased he has won his case.

Part three of the Michael Cavadias story, however, was never reported in the *Mirror*. It was carried only in the Aberdeen *Press and Journal*, on 5 January 2008 under the headline, 'SHERIDAN SAGA HUSBAND ADMITS: I LIED'. By this time, Tommy had been charged with perjury. Michael Cavadias now confessed that he had fabricated the smears against his ex-wife and that he now wanted to come clean and clear her name. 'She never said these things. I was just speaking out of anger. I'm not proud of what I said at all. In fact, I'm very embarrassed.'

'At the time,' he added, 'there was a lot of fighting between me and Fiona and there were other people who were really stirring things up.' He didn't specify who had been 'stirring things up' or explain why they had done so. He didn't have to. That missing piece of information had the name of an MSP printed all over it.

The Fiona McGuire story would remain a mystery. Unlike Anvar Khan and Katrine Trolle, whose allegations would be strongly corroborated by witnesses and telephone records, there was no supporting evidence to confirm her testimony. For whatever reason, she refused to provide the names of people she knew in the escort business who might have been able to back up her claim of a group sex session in the Treetops Hotel. She told the court that she paid for the room in cash. Nor did anyone ever uncover any telephone records demonstrating a link between her and Tommy. She told the Court of Session that she had lived a chaotic lifestyle and had gone through at least fourteen different mobile phones during that period.

Had her story been fantasy from start to finish? Was it pure coincidence that some of the details she provided closely matched a consistent pattern of behaviour by Tommy Sheridan? Or had her script been written for her by journalists and she was just an actress reciting her lines? Maybe, but there is another, slightly less far-fetched explanation – that she did actually have a loose arrangement with Tommy Sheridan which involved casual sex on a handful of occasions over four years. The absence of concrete evidence didn't necessarily mean that her story was fictitious.

For his part, Tommy has always denied any connection with Fiona McGuire. Maybe, for once, his denials are authentic. Or maybe, as the call-girl Mandy Rice-Davies replied when told that Lord Astor had denied having an affair with her: 'Well he would, wouldn't he?'

July 2006

The Moat's Murky Waters

When 52-year-old shopkeeper Anne Colvin picked up her mobile phone to make an anonymous call to the *News of the World* on that grey Monday morning back in 2004, she never dreamed that it would lead her all the way to highest law court in the land.

It was the day after the Fiona McGuire story had been splashed across the front page of the *News of the World*. All day and into the next day, Tommy Sheridan had been on TV, radio and in the newspapers describing the allegations as 'utter pish' and lashing Fiona McGuire as 'a fantasist with psychological problems'. He told the media bluntly:

> I have never had an affair. It is a matter of public record that before 1992 I was a sexually active, young single man but, after 1992, there are no affairs. I will take anybody on who wants to allege otherwise.

He had vowed to sue the newspaper that printed the story.

Anne Colvin had never heard of Fiona McGuire but she *had* heard of Tommy Sheridan. She had even met him – under the most bizarre circumstances imaginable. And she knew for a fact that he was a liar.

One Friday night back in June 2002, she had been cajoled into attending 'a VIP party', with her childhood friend, Helen Allison, by another woman, Jackie Whyte. The party was to be in the Moat House Hotel, a sixteen-storey smoked-glass landmark on the banks of the Clyde. It was an expensive hotel – the favoured accommodation of international superstars playing concerts in the adjacent Scottish Exhibition and Conference Centre. Bob Dylan, Mick Jagger and Dolly Parton had all stayed there. It has since been renamed the Crowne Plaza and today faces straight across to the gleaming glass headquarters of BBC Scotland on the other side of the river.

Anne and Helen both led a quiet life. They were none too enthusiastic about the event but Jackie had been persuasive. There would be a famous footballer there and other celebrities, she told them. At about 10.30 p.m. on the night of Friday 14 June, they arrived

outside the hotel by taxi, where they met a man called Matt McColl, a
friend of Jackie, in the hotel lobby. They expected to be taken into a
large function suite but, after several drinks and much hanging about
in the hotel bar, were taken instead to one of the hotel suites. On the
way up in the lift, they had asked who was going to be there. 'Shh!
Keep it quiet but Tommy Sheridan will be there,' said Matt. Not
exactly Tom Jones but maybe there would be other celebrities.

But when they reached the suite, they were puzzled. There were
only two rooms, plus a bathroom. One door was closed. They were
ushered through the other door into a sitting room where another man
sat alone. There was no food, no drinks and no music. It was all
beginning to look pretty strange. They chatted for a while to a man
named Jaz, who told them he was from Maryhill but now lived in
Jersey.

After half an hour or so of small talk, the two women began to
wonder just what was going on. When they first arrived in the suite,
they thought they were just waiting there for someone and then they'd
be taken on to another part of the hotel. But nothing seemed to be
happening. Anne decided to have a snoop around. She wandered
across the sitting room in the suite and opened the door to the other
room to have a quick look inside, to check out the decor, the bedding
and the curtains. She had no idea anyone was inside.

'I got the shock of my life at the scene I witnessed,' she told the jury
in the Court of Session. 'There were three people engaged in sexual
activity, none of which I understood. I was mortified, horrified.' She
drew back, closed the door and called for her friend Helen 'to show her
what a seedy predicament we were in'.

Helen opened the door and stepped into the room. There she saw
'Tommy Sheridan having sex with a female on the bed, and another
man sitting at the side of the bed putting a condom on'. She
recognised Tommy immediately. 'He smiled at me. I was absolutely
devastated. Angry. Very upset. I just about-turned and left the room.'

The two women returned to the sitting room, distressed by what
they had seen. When they switched on the TV to try and hide a private
conversation to work out what to do next, they could find only porn
channels. They felt unsafe. With four men and four women in the
company, they feared they had been lured into something beyond
their experience and were trying to work out how to extricate themselves. The man who had been with Tommy Sheridan came into the
room and began to dance and gyrate, wearing just a skimpy towel,
which he let fall to the floor. Unsurprisingly, Helen and Anne failed to
recognise the 'famous' footballer. He played for a small Junior League

team, in front of crowds of a few hundred. It was his stag night and, the following day, he was due to wed Gail Sheridan's sister and become Tommy Sheridan's brother-in-law.

Then the woman, now dressed in jeans and a top, came into the sitting room. She told Helen and Anne that she was involved in prostitution and had been flown up to Glasgow from Birmingham by Tommy Sheridan. 'Tommy phones me when he wants me,' she explained. Minutes later, Tommy himself appeared wrapped in a white hotel bathrobe. He threw himself heavily onto the sofa and lay silently, looking 'spaced out'.

'Up until then I had admired him a lot for his politics,' Anne Colvin told the jury. 'But my estimation of him was now shattered.' She told Tommy he should be ashamed of himself and that he was risking everything he had.

'Why are you here?' she asked.

Tommy leered back at the silver-haired grandmother. 'I'm here because I knew you were coming.' Anne was angry at the sarcasm and double entendre, but it was the excuse she needed.

Anne picked up her bag and stormed out, along with Helen, and Jackie followed close behind. Anne and Helen were furious with her, though Jackie denied setting them up.

It was now 1 a.m.; they had been in the hotel suite for no more than an hour, mainly chatting with Jaz. When Anne Colvin arrived she immediately phoned her elderly aunt and uncle in East Kilbride and told them: 'You'll never believe this! I don't know whether I've attended my first gang-bang or my first orgy.' Before leaving the Moat House, she had already made a complaint about the incident to two members of the hotel staff, naming Tommy Sheridan as one of the participants. Over the next few months, the two women told up to a hundred people of the incident – family, friends, people at the hairdressers. But they did not go to the press. As they say now: 'If we had wanted to sell this story for money, we would've done it while the bed was still piping hot.'

However, that all changed in November 2004, when Anne made her spur-of-the-moment phone call. She gave her name as Margaret and said she wanted no cash. But she was livid at Tommy Sheridan's hypocrisy and felt compassion for the woman he was attacking, Fiona McGuire. 'This woman could be telling the truth,' she told the reporter on the other of the line. 'Just because she is a prostitute doesn't mean she isn't telling the truth. I am a decent woman but unfortunately I've witnessed Tommy Sheridan's behaviour.'

The reporter skilfully drew her into a much longer conversation than she had ever intended. But she insisted she didn't want to meet him. A few days later, she got the second shock of her life. According to her testimony in court, she had 'almost died to find Douglas Wight [the news editor of the *News of the World*] on my doorstep. I hadn't given him a name, I hadn't given him a phone number, I hadn't given him an address. I had been secretive about the whole thing.'

Douglas Wight would later claim that he had simply Googled her phone number and discovered it was one of several contact numbers for a Glasgow-based business, which had only one female director – Anne Colvin. He then used the information to track down her address.

She told the journalist that she wanted nothing to do with it. 'It's behind us. It was three years ago. If we'd wanted to speak out, we'd have done it then. I just wanted to offer support to the woman he was attacking.'

But the *News of the World* wasn't giving up so easily – not when Tommy Sheridan had just begun a high-profile defamation action against them. They turned up the heat. Anne brought in a lawyer she knew, Martha Rafferty, 'to protect our good name and character'. She was worried that her presence and that of Helen Allison in the Moat House hotel suite with Tommy Sheridan and the others might be misconstrued by the newspaper. The three women arranged to meet Bob Bird and Douglas Wight in the Pond Hotel on Glasgow's Great Western Road, where the *News of the World* had booked a suite. But Helen and Anne had had enough of hotel suites and insisted that the meeting go ahead in the public restaurant. Later, in the lawyer's office, they were shown numerous photographs of footballers to help them identify the mystery man in the towel. But there was no-one they recognised. Just as they were about to give up, someone produced a photograph taken at Tommy and Gail's wedding. They gasped in unison, recognising Andy McFarlane as one of the kilted men in the photo. They were incredulous when they were told this was Tommy Sheridan's brother-in-law. Eventually, after signing affidavits, the women were given £10,000 each 'towards expenses', with the promise of a further £5,000 if they agreed to have their photographs taken outside the Moat House hotel. They refused and never received the money.

Their account confirms the story that Keith Baldassara had been told by friends at Andy McFarlane's wedding the day after the Moat House escapade. At the SSP executive meeting where Tommy had been forced to resign, Keith had even mentioned the specific detail that a woman had been flown up from Birmingham to take part in an orgy. His comments are recorded in handwritten notes of Barbara Scott, the minutes secretary.

Tommy had already initiated his legal action by the time these two ghosts from his past reappeared. He received the ominous news on Tuesday 4 January 2005 while most of Scotland was still on holiday. That afternoon at two o'clock Jackie's friend Matt McColl, the organiser of the unusual stag party in the Moat House, had been accosted outside his home by the ubiquitous Douglas Wight. They had then gone for a drive to the countryside in Matt McColl's car. Wight was wired up and the transcripts of their conversation were presented in court. The businessman was clearly shaken but denied everything. Immediately after the conversation, he got on the phone to Tommy, whose own phone records showed that he, in turn, made eight separate phone calls and sent three text messages that afternoon and evening to Andy McFarlane.

I was startled to learn that Tommy had included the Moat House allegations in his defamation action. The story had not yet been published and was totally unknown to the general public. But these allegations had been printed in closed legal submissions, which allowed Tommy to add the Moat House case to his defamation actions over the Fiona McGuire and the Cupids stories. Now he was fighting three separate accusations – even though two of them, at least, were substantially true.

Faced with this growing mountain of evidence, most normal human beings would have thrown in the towel but Tommy had conditioned himself not to think like a normal human being and his iron determination to carry on regardless did possess a certain remorseless logic. If he backed down, not only would he be named and shamed over Cupids – he would also be hung out to dry over his participation in a threesome with his brother-in-law and a mysterious woman in a hotel room. In his view, the appearance of these two women made it even more imperative that he fight and win the case.

The *News of the World* attempted to cite Matt McColl but he had just moved house and there was some doubt over whether he received the citation. In the meantime, he went to ground in a caravan in Argyll for the duration of the court case.

Helen Allison was the first of the two Moat House women to give evidence, on day six of the trial. The softly spoken fifty-two-year-old nervously described the sequence of events that had led her into court. Helen was able to describe details of the hotel suite – the shape of the couch, where the TV was, the sideboard running along the wall, a cupboard with drawers. She admitted receiving a payment of £1000 from the *News of the World*, negotiated by Martha Rafferty. Few people who heard her evidence had any doubts that this was the honest testimony of a woman who had been in the wrong place at the wrong time.

She told the court that, after losing touch for a couple of years, her old friend Jackie Whyte had contacted her again in January 2005, just after Matt McColl had been door-stepped by the *News of the World*. Jackie had been angry and told Helen, 'You don't know what you're dealing with. Tommy Sheridan has got someone up from England to pull out someone's tongue.' Then Matt McColl had phoned and told her, 'If it's money you're wanting I can help you.' This was the first hint that something more sinister was lurking in the undergrowth.

Although it wasn't Helen who had made that anonymous call to the *News of the World* in November 2004, she was to suffer years of torment as a result of being dragged into the fray. She gave the court a harrowing account of how she and her fourteen-year-old daughter had suffered repeated harassment and constant intimidation from friends or associates of Tommy Sheridan. Her windows had been pelted with eggs and both she and her daughter had been subjected to verbal abuse and obscene gestures in the street. On one occasion, her daughter had to physically run away from a beating. Eventually, they sold up and moved home. Now she had been press-ganged into giving distasteful evidence in a celebrity court battle in front of a drooling national media. And things she did not fully understand were happening behind the scenes.

During his cross-examination of her, Graeme Henderson, advocate for Tommy Sheridan, read extracts from a statement provided by a man called John Lynn to her. According to his statement, he had, by chance, met a woman called Helen Allison, who was wearing dark glasses because she was in hiding from the *News of the World* who wanted her to appear in court. The statement continued, 'Helen Allison told me that a friend called Jackie had taken her to a hotel party where there would be VIP guests, but when she got there she realised there was no party and left.' She then told John Lynn that, when the Fiona McGuire story surfaced, she had received a phone call from her friend Anne who suggested they concoct a story about Tommy Sheridan having been at the party. 'She said it had started off as a joke and an easy way to make money but things started to get out of hand when the *News of the World* began demanding more information.' Given the content of his statement, it was surprising that John Lynn was never called as a witness for Tommy Sheridan. But not so surprising in the light of information that was unknown at the time to either of the two legal teams. In the meantime, Helen Allison in the witness stand was completely baffled by the statement and told the court a different story.

Four weeks before, as a favour, she had driven a friend, Tom, who had been banned from driving, to a business meeting with a man called John Lynn in the Angels Hotel in Uddingston, a small town on the south-eastern fringes of Glasgow. She had never met John Lynn before and the court case was never mentioned. A few weeks later, on the Saturday immediately before she took the witness stand, she had driven her friend back to what she believed was a follow-up meeting at in the Bothwell Bridge Hotel in the upmarket village of Bothwell, the haunt of top Scottish footballers, lottery winners and well-heeled entrepreneurs.

Instead of talking business, John Lynn immediately turned to Helen and told her he would 'come straight to the point'. He told her a garbled story. He had a son in jail in Ireland, he said, who had recently stabbed a warder and had been moved to a prison hospital. He wanted his son transferred to a Scottish jail and he had met a man who said he might be able to help. He then went through to the bar area from the lounge and returned with this man. In a strong Irish brogue, Dennis Reilly introduced himself as 'a candidate for Tommy Sheridan's Party' and a retired member of the Garda, the police force of the Republic of Ireland.

By this time Helen was wondering what was going on. Who were these two men and what did they want from her? Shockingly, it became clear that they knew she was due to be called as a witness that coming week in the Sheridan versus the *News of the World* defamation case. They gently suggested to her that she had, perhaps, been put under pressure by the *News of the World* to lie in court. John Lynn suggested that he could get her 'between £200,000 and £300,000' if she went to a rival newspaper and told them that she had been pressurised into lying.

But she hadn't been pressurised into lying – she had been pressurised into telling the truth. Dennis Reilly told Helen that he idolised Tommy Sheridan and couldn't believe he had done these things he was accused of by the *News of the World*. When Helen then told him what she had seen in the Moat House Hotel that night back in 2002, Dennis 'was very quiet'.

He said, 'You brought me to my knees telling me this story. Tommy has never said anything to me about this.'

'Why would he tell you?' was Helen's logical response.

As she drove home, she was unhappy with her passenger friend. 'It really sunk into me that I had been set up,' she told the court. The two men in the Bothwell Bridge Hotel bar had been polite enough. 'I liked John Lynn. He was a very nice man,' she said and she described Dennis Reilly as 'a very pleasant man'.

Dennis Reilly is indeed a very pleasant man – friendly, open and avuncular. A retired Garda officer, he had stood in several elections as a candidate for the SSP. He had also won awards for fostering scores of children. John Lynn, in contrast, had a rather less respectable background. In 1989, he had been sent to Frankland Prison in County Durham on an attempted murder and firearms conviction after shooting a barman in Blackpool during a drunken argument.

According to one crime reporter, John Lynn had been 'a well-known figure in Glasgow's sex industry' in the 1990s, with financial interests in two city-centre saunas – the Carlton and the Oasis – believed to be fronts for prostitution. In early 2001, he was arrested in Dublin after a £2-million heroin seizure along with a number of other men, including his son, John Lynn Jr and Thomas Mulvey, who was described in court as a 'criminal Godfather from Liverpool'. The trial had been a bit of a mess – two separate juries had taken six attempts to reach a verdict. John Lynn walked free but his son and the Merseyside crime boss were hammered with twelve-year jail sentences.

When she returned from the Bothwell Bridge Hotel, Helen Allison was worried and confused. The men had asked to meet her and Anne Colvin on the Monday morning – the day they were due in court. She spoke to her friend Anne Colvin, who 'phoned John Lynn and gave him short shrift'. Before Helen Allison left the witness stand, she was asked a few final questions by Mike Jones QC. Did she know a man called Keith Baldassara? Had she ever heard of a man called Keith Baldassara? She answered no to both questions. What she didn't know was that Keith had given separate evidence which totally corroborated her testimony.

In her evidence, Anne Colvin said she had been 'mortified' and 'horrified' by Tommy's behaviour and his leering attitude towards her at the Moat House. But she had left it at that, disillusioned and disgusted by her fleeting encounter with Scotland's working-class hero. Two and half years later, she made an anonymous call to the News of the World, who then tracked her down.

Graeme Henderson then rose to conduct his cross-examination. After a couple of warm-up questions, he moved in for the kill. 'You talk about character. Are you a person of good character?'

'I like to think so,' she replied.

He then asked Anne if she had any previous convictions.

'None.'

'You've never served a jail sentence for an offence?' asked the lawyer.

Anne Colvin was puzzled. She mentioned she had once been stopped by traffic police and breathalysed but she'd never been to jail.

'You don't remember receiving an eighteen-month sentence?'

Now she was starting to get angry. 'I have never had an eighteen-month sentence. This is ridiculous and I would ask you to prove the accusation you have just made. Please, Your Honour, I want to clear my name. This has never happened to me.'

The judge then directed Tommy's advocate to formulate the question more clearly – to state the nature of the offence that Anne Colvin had supposedly committed, the date of the conviction and other specific details.

'The offence was some form of cheque card fraud and the sentence was eighteen months,' Henderson told the witness, who was by now open-mouthed with disbelief.

Again she insisted that this accusation was false and 'absolutely ridiculous' and she demanded the right to clear her name. Again, Lord Turnbull asked the lawyer to provide more concrete information – for example, when was this supposed to have taken place? Henderson explained that the information had come from 'a trusted and reliable source'. But he refused to reveal his trusted and reliable source. Nor was he able to produce any documentary evidence to back up this sensational accusation. In fact, it was totally false. Anne Colvin had never been convicted of fraud or served a jail sentence.

As he adjourned the court for the day, Lord Turnbull slapped reporting restrictions on the media under the Contempt of Court Act to prevent press coverage of the unproven accusation. What he had to say to Graeme Henderson in private could only be imagined.

Before the trial recommenced the next day, events took an even more sensational twist. Graeme Henderson approached the bench to inform Lord Turnbull that his client, Tommy Sheridan, had dispensed with his lawyers. He had sacked the lot of them, including the firm of solicitors who had taken on his 'no-win, no-fee' case, plus his QC, Richard Keen, and, of course, Graeme Henderson. Tommy would now carry on the battle himself, backed by a makeshift amateur legal team.

Publicly, Tommy expressed anger at the botched cross-examination of Anne Colvin, heaping the blame on his lawyers, particularly Graeme Henderson. While the advocate had clearly failed to take the necessary steps to verify the information and back it up with doc-

Tommy Sheridan in Lanarkshire during the anti-Poll Tax campaign. In the background are Davie Archibald (with *Militant* newspaper) and Ian McDonald (beside the car).

Anti-Poll Tax activists gather to stop Glasgow's first attempted Poll Tax poinding outside the home of Jeanette McGinn, the widow of legendary folk-singer Matt McGinn.

The Battle of Turnbull Street, 1 October 1991, for which Sheridan would eventually be sent to jail.

The making of a folk hero: Glasgow children with a Sheridan poster during an election campaign in Pollok.

Sheridan in October 1992 with candidate Alan McCombes, during a regional by-election in Govan-Drumoyne.

Mattie Smith and George McNeilage carry Sheridan shoulder-high from Queen Street Station to Glasgow City Chambers after his release from Saughton Prison.

Speaking at a Scottish Militant Labour election campaign meeting, 1992.

Media launch of the 1999 SSP manifesto that saw Sheridan elected to the Scottish Parliament.

Sheridan, looking conspicuous in his politician's uniform, with Rosie Kane at the Calton Hill Rally for a Scottish Republic, a few weeks before his resignation.

Former Labour MP and MSP John McAllion with Sheridan in October 2004. McAllion later joined the SSP and remains a member.

Looking distracted at an anti-war press conference with Rose Gentle, George McNeilage and Rosie Kane on 28 October 2004, a few days before the *News of the World* broke the Cupids story.

The 6 SSP MSPs with RMT General Secretary Bob Crow on the far left, February 2005.

The first-ever SSP election broadcast, filmed at Tinto Park in Govan (home of Benburb FC) in March 1999.

Gail and Tommy, 1999.

Five SSP MSPs publicising Workers Memorial Day, April 2004, to commemorate those killed at work (left to right: Colin Fox, Tommy Sheridan, Rosie Kane, Rosemary Byrne, Carolyn Leckie).

Sheridan using his charm on striking nursery nurses, 2004.

April 2005, the launch of the SSP's general election manifesto in Glasgow.

At a lobby of the Scottish
Parliament, 2006.

Colin Fox, SSP joint national spokesperson. (Photo by Eddie Truman)

March 2006, Dunfermline by-election, just prior to the defamation case. Sheridan campaigns for SSP candidate John McAllion.

Richie Venton, the SSP's trade union organiser (right), with Len McCluskey, the General Secretary of Unite.

Kevin McVey, now the SSP National Secretary, who became active in socialist politics during the 1984 miners' strike, around the same time as Sheridan.

Former MSP Frances Curran, joint National Spokesperson of the SSP, who served on Labour's National Executive Committee from 1984 to 1985 alongside Tony Benn, Denis Healey and Neil Kinnock.

Catriona Grant, former co-chair of the SSP and a witness in both trials.

Jo Harvie, the former editor of the *Scottish Socialist Voice*, was the first witness to be cross-examined by Sheridan after he sacked his legal team during the perjury trial.

26 May 2006: Alan McCombes outside the Court of Session prior to his jailing for refusing to hand over the minutes of the SSP's Executive meeting of 9 November 2004.

Katrine Trolle. (Photo by Allan Milligan)

Rosie Kane, Keith Baldassara and Barbara Scott at the SSP's Unity Integrity Socialism Rally in Glasgow, 2 September 2006. (Photo by Alan Milligan)

Allan Green, SSP National Secretary from its foundation in 1998 until 2006.

Felicity Garvie, Sheridan's PA from 1999 until the split in the SSP in 2006. (Photo by Eddie Truman)

Eddie Truman, SSP press officer 2003–2006, and Ken Ferguson, SSP press officer 2006–present.

Tommy Sheridan with Gail after the verdict, 23 December 2010. (Scotsman Publications)

umentary evidence, Tommy's own role in the affair remained murky. He later told the court that 'the question was not prompted by myself'. It was a less than convincing abdication of responsibility.

After the trial, Anne Colvin complained to the Law Society about the incident. The society investigated and reported its findings to Campbell Deane, the solicitor instructing Graeme Henderson. The results were also conveyed to Tommy. But Anne Colvin was denied access to the results of the investigation she had requested on the grounds she was not Campbell Deane's client. She then asked Tommy to waive confidentiality – as was his right – to let her see the paperwork. He refused. Anne told *The Herald*, 'I would ask Mr Sheridan to reconsider. It would also clear his name. If he did not suggest the question to Mr Henderson then he has nothing to worry about.' (*The Herald*, 4 January 2007) Tommy remained tight-lipped. To this day, Anne Colvin is convinced that her 'conviction for fraud' was a deliberate invention by Tommy designed to set up Graeme Henderson. It certainly provided the perfect pretext for the MSP to fire his advocate and take over the case himself at a time when everything was going badly wrong.

A further mystery surrounded the sacking of his legal team. He could have singled out Graeme Henderson. His original QC, Richard Keen, had been temporarily diverted to deal with a case in the House of Lords. A top-flight specialist in litigation and media law, he was – and is – one of the most sought-after QCs in the country. Tommy had been fortunate to secure his services in the first place. And Keen was due to return to the Court of Session on the next working day. Tommy was in illustrious company, though. Slobodan Milosevic, the Serbian war leader, Ted Bundy, the charming American mass murderer, Peter Manuel, the serial killer who was the last man to be hanged in Scotland, and Saddam Hussein had all sacked their legal teams and conducted their own defence.

It was gripping stuff and, for those fortunate enough not to be personally embroiled in this jaw-dropping cavalcade, hugely entertaining. Top prize for the pithiest summing-up of the latest twist had to go to the anonymous *Daily Record* sub-editor who coined the following morning's headline, 'Tommy Drops His Briefs'.

Tommy's budding new career didn't get off to a flying start. Lord Turnbull had adjourned the court from Friday morning through to the following Tuesday to allow Tommy time for preparation. His first task was to conclude the cross-examination of Anne Colvin. She wasn't a woman to be pushed around. She had stood her ground valiantly against a proper lawyer and wasn't going to crumple before the pompous interrogation of an amateur – not when she was telling the truth and knew for a fact that her accuser was a brazen liar.

Tommy began by apologising profusely to Anne Colvin. Those of us who knew him recognised this as diplomacy, designed not to soothe Anne Colvin but to impress the jury. He then went on the attack. The essence of his case was that she and her friend had concocted the story for money. They had 'fabricated a story, memorised a script and rehearsed the lines perfectly'. It was nonsense but Tommy could make fairy tales sound like hard-nosed science.

'How much were you paid by the *News of the World*?' he demanded straight up.

When she acknowledged that she had received £1,000, he then slipped the ball into his own net by asking if she remembered how she had spent the cash.

'Yes, certainly I remember. I gave it all away. Every penny.'

Tommy pushed her further about the financial arrangements with the newspaper, and the £6000 her lawyer had provisionally negotiated.

She explained why they hadn't received the balance of the money. 'We were asked to have our photographs taken outside the Moat House Hotel. I would never have agreed to such an arrangement. I don't want to see this situation glamorised in any way.' This wasn't quite the image he was trying to invoke of two scheming women driven by greed.

Tommy then laboured over the date of the incident, which he tried to nail down to Friday 7 June 2002. Like Helen Allison during her earlier cross-examination, Anne Colvin knew for sure it had been on a Friday night – either the seventh or the fourteenth of June – but, three years on, neither of the two women could be any more precise than that.

An edge of desperation crept into Tommy's line of questioning. 'Surely you wouldn't have waited a full twelve days before you returned from holiday to go and tell your friend all about it?'

The bemused witness simply repeated that she couldn't be sure – maybe it was twelve days, maybe it wasn't. At the time, she didn't know that Tommy's alibi hinged on one specific date. In the *News of the World*'s initial submission to the court, they had identified 7 June 2002 as the date of the Moat House shenanigans. But that night, Tommy had been in the Himalayan restaurant near his home and in an adjacent bar until midnight with large group of family and friends to celebrate the forthcoming wedding of Andy McFarlane and Gillian Healy, Gail Sheridan's sister. The group in the restaurant had included Keith Baldassara, whose evidence had specifically stated that the Moat House incident had occurred the following Friday, June the fourteenth, the night before the wedding. Tommy had no alibi for that night – at least not yet, not without dragging members of his family into the twilight zone of perjury.

Throughout the cross-examination, Anne Colvin maintained her composure – even when Tommy moved into the murky terrain of the actual incident in the hotel bedroom. With the detached air of an academic inquiring about a philosophical conundrum, he asked questions such as 'Did this mystery man dance naked in front of you with an erect penis?' By now, Tommy was looking like a man intent on humiliating and degrading his accusers.

Win or lose his legal battle, he would destroy the lives of others in the process. They had committed the cardinal crime, in his book, of refusing to bend to his will.

19

July 2006

Losing the Plot

From the surreal high drama of cocaine-fuelled orgies, sleazy sex clubs and illicit rendezvous, the courtroom conflict gradually descended into the drearier, more plausible world of backroom committee meetings, obscure points of procedure and political factionalism.

This strand of the trial, focussing on an obscure SSP meeting that had taken place twenty months earlier, wasn't about what people had seen and done. It was about what they had said and what they had heard other people saying. For the average juror, trying to make sense of what might have been said at a Scottish Socialist Party Executive meeting over a year and a half earlier was like trying to decipher the footnotes in *Das Kapital*. But, for those thousands of people in Scotland who had been activists in the socialist movement, this dimension of Tommy's case was more shocking by far than the salacious revelations that had the tabloids drooling. Here was the most famous politician in the country accusing his own closest colleagues of the socialist equivalent of high treason. It was as though the Queen had appeared on TV to indict the rest of the royal family for plotting a republican coup.

We had a glimpse of what lay in store on the first day of the trial when Tommy's QC, Richard Keen, cross-examined Allison Kane, the SSP treasurer. He had produced as evidence the fake minutes that had been sent to the *News of the World* on the eve of my court appearance back in May. The QC had then asked Allison about the 'various factions within the party out to knife Tommy Sheridan'. One of these factions, he suggested 'wanted to stab him in the back and they were prepared to use the *News of the World* to further their aims'.

In the days and weeks to come, even those of us who had begun to understand the extent of Tommy's damaged psyche recoiled in horror. From a legal standpoint, his attempt to frame his oldest comrades was logical. How else could he fight his case and hope to win? But, from the standpoint of morality, humanity and integrity, it was gross – particularly from someone who publicly preached equality, compassion and solidarity.

On the Friday of the first week, I became the second SSP witness to be called. For almost an entire day I was grilled in the witness box, while members of the jury fidgeted and yawned. One woman smiled sweetly throughout my evidence, while a middle-aged man stared me in the eye like a Wild West gambler trying to figure out whether his opponent is bluffing.

After affirming, I told the court:

Can I say that I am here under the strongest possible protest? Your client, the *News of the World*, symbolises everything that, as a socialist, I have always stood against through my whole adult life. I have no wish to take sides in this dispute which I regard as a squalid little squabble which should have been settled by one or both of the parties.

I ended by denouncing the case as 'a bizarre pantomime'.

'Oh, no, it's not!' interjected Lord Turnbull, though not necessarily in those words. The trial judge didn't quite conform to my natural prejudices or assumptions. For a start, he wasn't ancient. They say that you know you're getting old when the police start to look young. You know you're really getting on a bit when High Court judges start to look young. If it wasn't for the wig, gown and grand title, Alan Turnbull would have looked like a regular middle-aged bloke, possibly with a couple of teenage kids and an interest in football and rock music. He gently but firmly reminded me that this was not a public meeting but a courtroom and my role was not to make speeches but to answer questions. After three or four other SSP witnesses had taken the stand and made similar points, Lord Turnbull started to clamp down on these verbal protests. Other judges might well have snapped and sent at least one of us down to the cells *pour encourager les autres*. But, whether or not they had a chance to state their dissent, every SSP witness had been press-ganged into the courtroom and would rather have pulled out their own teeth than give evidence.

Just after rising to cross-examine me, Richard Keen QC produced the *Scottish Daily Mirror* front page of 18 November 2004, with photographs of Carolyn Leckie and me, accompanied by the banner headline, 'LOVERS PLOT TO AXE TOMMY'. I had always suspected that Tommy, then a columnist with the paper and a close friend of the editor, had had a hand in the headline. At the time, I had put it down to a petty act of revenge because I had refused to go along with his strategy of denial. But, after it was dragged up repeatedly as evidence of a plot, I began to suspect Tommy's motive had been altogether more sinister. Now my suspicions were borne out as Keen harangued me with the false assertion that 'rumours had been circulating for some time during 2004' that Carolyn Leckie and I were hatching a plot against Tommy.

'There were no rumours before October the 31st 2004,' I assured him. 'And I guarantee you won't be able to provide any evidence to back up your accusation, because it's not true.'

The testimony of Keith Baldassara, the next witness, was devastating in its detail and its clarity. He had been confronting Tommy about these issues for years. Reading verbatim notes of the exchanges that took place made me wonder what must have been going through the minds of Tommy's lawyers. Before the court case began, they had only spoken to Tommy himself. We had refused to give statements – known as *precognition* under Scots law – to either side. As far as we were concerned, we were independent witnesses beholden to no one. Now Graeme Henderson and his back-up team were beginning to discover that maybe there was more to this case than met even the highly trained legal eye.

By the time the next witness, Allan Green, took the stand, Tommy had sacked his legal team and was conducting his own case. Tommy accused Allan of 'concocting' a document that was as 'dodgy as ten-bob note'. It was a curious simile, given that the old ten-shilling notes were legitimate legal tender. Possibly drawing from the old advertising maxim that nothing beats repetition, Tommy reiterated his slur over and over again.

Eventually the normally placid schoolteacher turned on Tommy with quiet ferocity:

I've always given you what I considered to be the best advice I could. I tried to talk you out of an action that would be highly risky for you. And now you turn round and accuse me of a monstrous frame-up. It's appalling. I can hardly believe you are doing this. Like yourself, I have devoted my entire adult life to building the socialist movement. I have carried out to the best of my abilities the tasks I have been asked to do by the party. And now you think I'm dispensable, and now you think you can lie and make such accusations. It is shameful, Tommy, shameful.

Tommy swiftly changed the subject but not before making a nasty aside to the jury about 'histrionics in the witness box' and 'a lot of rehearsing of lines'. In the future, evidence would be uncovered that would reveal that one person had indeed been rehearsing their lines – but it wasn't Allan Green.

A further parade of SSP witnesses faced Tommy down.

Richie Venton told him, 'I am sorry to say, Tommy, but you did admit to visiting the Manchester club concerned and, for me, far more to the point, argued that, if you were named, you would deny it.'

Just before he was called to the stand, Colin Fox received a text from Tommy Sheridan. It was a forwarded message from Bob Crow, the leader of the RMT, which was then affiliated to the SSP. It read, 'Never mind these scabs, Tommy, we're right behind you.' Right up until the last minute, he was trying to pile on the psychological pressure.

When Tommy suggested that Colin's recollections of the SSP executive meeting were mistaken, Colin replied 'I am not mistaken. I am absolutely, categorically clear on what took place in the meeting'.

Carolyn Leckie told Tommy, 'I'm not surprised you can't look me in the eye when you're saying that, because it's absolute rubbish.' When Tommy mumbled something about having to read his notes, she hit back straight away, saying, 'You wouldn't need notes if you were telling the truth.'

By the time Tommy had cross-examined Catriona Grant, Jo Harvie and Rosie Kane, he looked as though he was ready to hoist the white flag. He was trying to smash solid rock with a feather duster and seemed desperate to get them out of the courtroom as quickly as possible.

Perhaps the most poignant testimony of the entire trial was provided by Barbara Scott, who had taken the minutes of the meeting, by hand, in an A4 notebook. She had a well-deserved reputation for being conscientious and meticulous and had taken minutes at the highest level within private and public sector organisations. Now Tommy was accusing her, in front of the whole nation, of behaviour that would have her blacklisted by every employer in the country for the rest of her life. 'Miss Scott, I would put it that you have colluded to undermine me by concocting this dodgy minute?'

Barbara, who had once lived in the Western Isles, responded with Old Testament fire and brimstone. 'I am absolutely incandescent with rage that you would say these minutes are concocted because you know as well as I do they are the truth.'

Lord Turnbull, it seemed, could hardly believe what he was hearing. Something was seriously amiss. He repeated the accusation back to Barbara, asking her if she realised that Tommy was accusing her of perjury.

'I refute it,' said Barbara. 'It is complete nonsense. It is absolute lies and Tommy knows it's lies.'

Mike Jones QC then brought out the full implication of Tommy's cross-examination. 'Just to be clear – do you realise that Mr Sheridan has just accused you and others of conspiring to pervert the course of justice – a very serious allegation?' Barbara nodded agreement and he continued, 'Do you understand that, if people come to court having conspired to pervert the course of justice, they would face many years in prison? And you are also accused of perjury. If you have committed perjury, you can also expect a prison sentence.'

Outside the court, within the socialist movement in Scotland – and even more so in England – there was no shortage of armchair perjurers ready to condemn those who, in a real courtroom, in front of a real judge and facing a real jail sentence, were not prepared to offer themselves as martyrs. But even then, they missed the point. The stand taken by the majority of SSP witnesses was not driven by fear of the courts and even less was it driven by jealousy of Tommy's status. This was about ethics and morality. To corroborate Tommy's version of events, it was necessary to brand those who told the truth as liars and perjurers. We were acting in solidarity – with each other and with women such as Katrine Trolle who were also being falsely accused of perjury.

Tommy himself had no qualms on that score. When Jones questioned him, he ran through a list of SSP witnesses and asked Tommy if they had lied in court. Allison Kane? 'Yes.' Alan McCombes? 'Yes.' Keith Baldassara? 'Yes.' And so on up to the eleventh witness, Rosie Kane. 'Each and every one of them gave perjured evidence,' Tommy insisted. 'We are in the midst of a political civil war and, in pursuit of that strategy, they have been willing to commit perjury.' We were indeed in the midst of a political civil war – one that had been declared by Tommy against the rest of us. And why? Because we had *refused* to commit perjury.

Lord Turnbull told him, 'It is very serious for a witness to be accused of perjury. And it is all the more serious if the person making that allegation is a public figure. If a Member of Parliament is accusing someone of perjury, that is very serious, is it not?'

Tommy agreed, 'Yes, I think anyone accusing anyone of perjury is serious but, yes, it is more serious if it's a Member of Parliament.'

In case there was any misunderstanding, he repeated his accusations again and again. Some of those who had given evidence against him were motivated by money, others by politics, but all were perjurers.

The handful of SSP witnesses who buckled under the pressure to give false evidence on behalf of Tommy were, to be fair, more half-hearted in their accusations. None of them had the stomach to go quite so far as their hero. As a result, they were scattered like ninepins during their cross-examinations. The first two, Rosemary Byrne and Pat Smith, escaped relatively lightly. Rosemary falsely claimed that Tommy had denied everything to the meeting but she shrunk from accusing the rest of us of perjury. We must have been mistaken, she suggested.

At this point, Tommy tried to reintroduce the fake minutes as evidence. The mysterious document had never been heard of since the opening day of the trial, when Richard Keen QC presented them to Allison Kane. It was now the fourteenth day and suddenly the document was resurrected. During the intervening thirteen days, another ten SSP witnesses had been cross-examined by Tommy and his lawyers. These included Barbara Scott, the minutes secretary, and Allan Green, the national secretary, who had written up the real minutes.

Lord Turnbull, naturally, was perplexed. 'To my surprise, this document has not featured again until today. It was not put to any other SSP witnesses after Allison Kane.' He asked Tommy if he was trying to suggest that this was the authentic minute. Tommy prevaricated. 'But who could have created this document but the minutes secretary?' asked the judge. 'And why didn't you ask Barbara Scott about it?' She had explained exactly how the real minutes were created – when they were written, where they were typed up and how they were subsequently presented for endorsement. At no point in his cross-examination had Tommy asked her about this entirely different version of events, purporting to be the official minutes of the exact same meeting.

'I forgot about it,' Tommy muttered implausibly. 'In retrospect, I should have raised it.'

If he had done so, the jury would have been left in no doubt that his version was a forgery. And flowing from that, the inevitable questions would be posed: Who forged it? Why did they forge it? Whose interests did it serve?

Tommy was forced to withdraw the document. Instead, he asked Rosemary, 'Do you think a sensible person would visit a swingers' club with a *News of the World* journalist and then tell a meeting that there was no possibility that it would get out publicly?' If Tommy had been a fictional character in a movie, it might even have been possible to admire his brass neck. Now he was trading on the outlandishness of his own behaviour, exploiting his own downright recklessness, knowing that, sometimes, things can sound too crazy to be true.

Next on the stand was Pat Smith from Edinburgh. Tommy had choreographed his witnesses carefully. Rosemary and Pat were both respectable, well-spoken women around sixty years of age. One was an MSP and former secondary school head of department and the other a children's nanny.

Pat Smith was a member of the Socialist Worker Party. A former drama teacher, she was confident and polished in the witness box but her version was subtly different from Tommy's. She repeated the lie that Tommy had denied allegations that he had visited a swingers' club but she acknowledged that the meeting had been 'acrimonious' and that 'some people present, but not all, believed that he was the unnamed MSP at the centre of the Cupids allegations . . . Some people were very entrenched in their position.'

Graeme McIver, who later became the national secretary of Tommy's breakaway Solidarity party, then took the witness stand. A father of four from Galashiels, Graeme had always struck me as a decent and personable bloke. He had solidly backed the decision to remove Tommy as convener back in 2004, expressing his shock and betrayal at Tommy's behaviour in no uncertain terms. Now, for whatever reason, he had decided to give evidence backing Tommy's version of events.

In the witness box, he was torn to shreds. Mike Jones had given Rosemary Byrne and Pat Smith a relatively easy ride but, with Graeme, he removed the gloves. In contrast to Tommy, Graeme had a conscience and was not prepared to accuse his colleagues of a frame-up. Instead, he insisted that we had been mistaken. Line by line, Graeme denied the legitimacy of the minutes. None of this had ever been said, he insisted. If Graeme was telling the truth, then the rest of us surely had committed perjury – that conclusion was inescapable – but, when put under the cosh, Graeme backed away.

'You know the consequences of perjury are very serious indeed,' said Mike Jones. 'Alan McCombes has testified that he said these things to the meeting. You say he didn't. If you are right, he has committed perjury. Do you understand that?'

'Yes,' said Graeme.

'It's a serious crime he's being accused of?'

'Yes.'

'And he could be prosecuted for perjury?'

'Yes.'

'And sent to jail?'

'Yes.'

'For a long time?'

'Yes.'

'So did he say that to the meeting or not?'

'I honestly can't remember,' replied Graeme.

Pushed further, he eventually admitted, 'Well, if Alan says he did say that, then he did. I just can't remember him saying it.'

Lord Turnbull then intervened and dismissed the jury. Behind closed doors, he no doubt issued stern warnings about the seriousness of perjury. When the full court reconvened, Graeme's position shifted even further.

'You are not challenging Mr McCombes evidence?' asked the QC.

'No.'

'So what he said to the jury is true?'

'If he said it, then it's true, yes.'

The QC then returned to the minutes of the meeting, which Graeme had rejected line by line as inaccurate. 'Are you seriously suggesting to the jury that all of these inaccuracies are just mistakes that Barbara Scott made?'

'Yes,' said Graeme.

'And Allan Green?'

'Yes.'

By all accounts, Graeme was squirming like a schoolboy who had just been caught shoplifting. It was a painful sight to behold. And it provided a glimpse into the absurdity of the argument that we should all have gone into the witness box and lost our memories. One by one, we would have proceeded into the witness box, the leadership of a major political party with six MSPs and 150,000 voters, to tell the court and the assembled national media, 'Er . . . um . . . eh . . . Your Honour, it was all just a big misunderstanding, as result of which we sacked the most charismatic party leader in Scotland . . . er . . . by mistake.'

Tommy's next witness, Mike Gonzalez, fared almost as badly as Graeme. A professor at the University of Glasgow, Mike was known as one of the more reasonable and intelligent members of the Socialist Workers faction. Now he was being wheeled out to give an academic stamp of credibility to Tommy's fairytale.

'I take it, as a professor of Latin American studies and an intelligent individual, you would understand it is a crime to tell a lie from a box?' asked Tommy.

'Yes, I would hardly risk my professional reputation by telling a lie in court.'

Under cross-examination, he would insist, 'If people are called to court give evidence, they have no choice but to give evidence and tell the truth.' Indeed.

Mike then challenged the authenticity of our minutes. He had never seen minutes of a meeting like this, he claimed. 'Of the many, many minutes I have seen, they generally run to two or three lines which describe the decisions made, sometimes with the initials of those present.' Had he bothered to check his email inbox, the absent-minded professor would have discovered that, during the three years he had been on the SSP executive, he had received a monthly set of minutes usually running not to two or three lines but to two or three pages. The SSP minutes always contained the full names of those present, a digest of the points made during the discussions and a full explanation for any decisions, especially those of a controversial nature. Mike's definition was strangely restrictive. As one of the top theoreticians internationally of the self-proclaimed 'Leninists' of the Socialist Workers Party, Mike would probably have on his own bookshelves such tomes as the *Minutes of the 1903 Congress of the Russian Social Democratic Labour Party*, which runs to over 500 pages of verbatim reports of every word uttered.

Under cross-examination, Mike floundered like a cabinet minister being grilled by Jeremy Paxman over the latest government U-turn – except that victims of the *Newsnight* presenter only have to filibuster for five minutes while Mike's interrogation dragged on for an hour or more.

Jock Penman, an affable Fifer in his mid-fifties, was next up. Possibly chastened by the frying and grilling of Graeme McIver and Mike Gonzalez – and by the warnings of a perjury investigation to come – Jock's version of events inched closer to the truth. He did not deny the existence of the minutes, and verified the accuracy of most of the content of the document. His recollection of my remarks to the November 2004 meeting was pretty much in line with what was recorded. Yes, agreed Jock, Alan McCombes had reported a con-versation in which Tommy had admitted he was the unnamed MSP who had gone to Cupids with Anvar Khan. Like Mike Gonzalez, Jock admitted he was shocked not just by the allegations but by where they were coming from. He certainly hadn't heard any rumours of a plot. He told Tommy, 'It was like a family fall-out because the people who were most vociferous were those who had known you the longest and were closest to you in your work and your private life too. I had thought that group were good friends of yours.'

On one crucial detail, Jock backed up Tommy's fictionalised ver-sion of the meeting. He insisted that Tommy had denied rather than admitted to the meeting that he had gone to Cupids. But, like Graeme McIver, Jock couldn't bring himself to accuse the rest of us of perjury.

'I don't believe they would deliberately come to court to lie,' he said.

So how could he explain the startling contrast between his recollection and ours? It wasn't like an argument over whether or not a disputed goal was offside. It was more like a debate over whether the match had been played at Ibrox or Old Trafford.

'That's what they thought they heard – it was a case of the emperor's new clothes,' he explained, with all the conviction of a newsreader announcing the latest UFO sighting.

Steve Arnott, originally from Fife and now the Highlands regional organiser of the SSP, was a close friend of Jock and he expanded on this interesting new theory that we were mad rather than bad. Although he was a member of the executive, Steve hadn't actually been present at the November the 9th 2004 meeting and I had phoned him straight after the meeting to fill him on the details. He had unconditionally supported our ultimatum to Tommy to come clean, keep quiet or resign. Steve told the court that, when I had phoned, he had indulged in a few glasses of wine. He was certainly talkative – I had stood in the doorway of the Stanley Bar in Kinning Park for over an hour listening to him while, inside, the shell-shocked remnants of the SSP executive sank a couple of beers along with the staff of the *Scottish Socialist Voice* who had been working late. Duncan Rowan was there too, lashing the bottle and looking pretty traumatised.

Steve had given me a lengthy psychology lesson, insisting that Tommy was the victim of a dissociative personality disorder. 'There are two Tommy Sheridans. One exists in his own imagination in bold capital letters – a superhero who is playing out a role 24 hours a day. Then there's the real Tommy Sheridan who is weak and vulnerable but whose identity has been subsumed by the persona of the invented superhero.' That was why Tommy had behaved in such a crazy, reckless fashion, he suggested. And it was why he was now in denial of the facts. Twenty months on and it appeared that Steve had dusted down his old undergraduate dissertation on cognitive psychology.

Presented with the minutes – the same document he had signed for, read and voted to endorse – he replied, 'I would never have agreed to this document. It would have met with a strong objection from me.'

'So this document is a fake?' asked Mike Jones QC.

'Yes, I have to conclude it's a fake.'

'So Allan Green and others were guilty of lies and forgery?'

'The possibility is that Mr Green might have been mistaken. He may even be deluded. He may even be subconsciously lying to himself.'

The QC was curious to know whether his diagnosis extended to Colin Fox and all the other SSP witnesses who had confirmed the authenticity of the minutes.

'I have no way of telling whether they are mistaken, whether they are deluding themselves or whether they are lying.'

If this wasn't so serious, it would have been comical.

Steve's testimony did reveal one interesting piece of information about Duncan Rowan's infamous stitch-up by the *News of the World*. Before Duncan had visited the *News of the World* to plead with them to leave Fiona McGuire in peace, he had discussed his plan with Steve Arnott. Since 2004, we had always been under the impression that Duncan had acted spontaneously, off his own bat. Duncan had tendered his resignation as a full-time official for the SSP via Steve Arnott but Steve himself had never told us that he had known in advance of Duncan's intentions.

Now he told the court, 'I still feel guilty that I did not try to prevent him from doing that. I don't know what was on my mind.'

Steve never made it clear whether the idea to name Katrine Trolle to the *News of the World* as a decoy had been discussed between the two of them. But what was now emerging was that Duncan hadn't acted on a sudden crazed impulse but had been implementing a premeditated plan he had discussed with Steve Arnott. The naive initiative had then backfired, leaving Duncan Rowan as the fall guy.

By the time Tommy's loyalists had finished their evidence, the picture of what had happened in that improvised meeting room in the backstreets of Glasgow eighteen months earlier was becoming as convoluted as the plot of *The Da Vinci Code*, the blockbuster movie in the cinemas that summer.

It didn't matter too much that Tommy's own witnesses were blatantly contradicting one another. What was more important was that the jurors were now becoming seriously bamboozled – which was good news for Tommy.

20

Early August 2006

Tears and Triumph

In his summing up of Jeffrey Archer's famous libel trial in 1987, the presiding judge, Sir Bernard Caulfield, made a speech so blatantly biased that it was to become the raw material for a thousand jokes, cartoons and comedy sketches in the years to come.

The millionaire novelist and Tory MP had initiated legal action against the *Daily Star* after it followed through a *News of the World* investigation into the relationship between Archer and a thirty-five-year-old call girl, Monica Coghlan. The woman had been reluctantly dragged into the Archer scandal after one of her clients spotted the golden boy of the Tory Party picking her up outside a London hotel and tipped off the Sunday tabloid. The newspaper then set out to ensnare Archer, secretly taping phone conversations between him and Ms Coghlan and photographing one of his associates handing her an envelope stuffed with thousands of pounds in cash on the concourse of Victoria Station.

Monica Coghlan had led a tragic life. She had become involved in prostitution at the age of seventeen after being sexually attacked and made homeless by an ex-partner. Over the years she had accumulated a string of convictions for prostitution, shoplifting and social security fraud. During the Archer libel case, she was branded a vicious liar out to destroy a successful, talented and popular national celebrity. Fourteen years later – and just a few weeks before Jeffrey Archer was due to face a criminal court charged with perjury and perverting the course of justice during the 1987 libel case – she was killed in a car crash.

In contrast to the vilification heaped upon Monica Coghlan, the politician's wife, Mary Archer, was treated with quasi-religious reverence in court and in the media. When she was called to the witness box and asked how old she was, the seemingly smitten Lord Justice Caulfield interrupted, saying, 'I'd suggest you should rephrase that question and ask how young she is?'

Later, in his summing-up to the jury, he reminded the court of her testimony:

Your vision of her will probably never disappear. Has she elegance? Has she fragrance? Would she have, without the strain of this trial, radiance? What is she like in physical features, in presentation, in appearance? How would she appeal? Has she had a happy married life? Has she been able to enjoy rather than endure her husband, Jeffrey? Is she right when she says to you – you may think with delicacy – 'Jeffrey and I lead a full life . . . Is he in need of unloving, rubber-insulated sex in a seedy hotel?'

By all accounts, Mary Archer had been the star witness. Her husband was awarded £500,000 plus costs against the *Daily Star* and his literary and political career soared to new heights, aided and abetted by Sir Bernard Caulfield. In contrast to the arrogant English judge, Lord Turnbull was scrupulously even-handed.

However, the Scottish media had discovered its very own Mary Archer. As a witness, Gail wasn't allowed in the courtroom until she was called to the stand. But day after day, she glided towards the Court of Session hand in hand with her husband, smiling at the scrum of photographers as they scrambled to zoom in on the stylish couple. As the trial progressed, Gail began to attract even more attention from the paparazzi than her famous husband. Chic and elegant, she was, the fashion commentators agreed, the embodiment of understated glamour. The message was none too subtle. With a wife like this, how could Tommy Sheridan possibly be into participating in sordid orgies in seedy sex clubs?

When she took the witness stand, Gail's gallus Glaswegian dialect, colourful imagery and flashes of angry humour blasted through the stuffy courtroom like a blowtorch. The drama of her testimony was heightened by the fact that she was being questioned in the witness box by her husband who, in quaint deference to archaic protocol, insisted on calling her Mrs Sheridan. Dutifully, Gail lashed into some of the women SSP members, saying, 'They all had it in for you – Allison Kane, Rosie Kane, Carolyn Leckie. I warned you, your mother warned you, people in the party warned you, people in the media warned you about them.'

Tommy used to grumble to me that his wife, his mother and his sister were always sniping at some of the women in the party. He was exasperated by what he believed was petty resentment based on unfounded jealousy and suspicion. But, after November 2004, he turned that one-sided friction to his own advantage. It made it easier to dupe Gail into believing that these women had concocted a feminist plot to overthrow him. She had been right about them all along, he would have told her.

Gail's outrage over the plot against Tommy was real and more convincing to the jury than the half-hearted, equivocal and contra-dictory testimonies of his SSP witnesses. Her angry insistence that, if she really believed these allegations were true, she would be in the dock herself for murder sounded authentic. In press interviews, she promised that she would have had Tommy tied to a concrete slab and thrown into the Clyde if she thought for one minute there was any truth in the allegations against him.

The most memorable and widely quoted part of Gail's testimony came when Tommy asked Mrs Sheridan, 'Is it your evidence that I have more than average body hair?'

Gail replied, 'You are like a monkey – you are covered from head to toe in hair.' She went on to refer to him as a gorilla and joked about how impossible it would have been to rub ice cubes along his body. 'You have more hair on your body than you have on your head and yet not a soul has mentioned that.'

From that moment onwards, the image of Tommy Sheridan as a kind of downsized King Kong became part of the folklore surrounding him – just like his perennial suntan. The tabloids loved it, as did the cartoonists and comedians. After the trial, Tommy stripped to the waist for the famous celebrity photographer, Harry Benson. The image was displayed for months on end in an exhibition in Glasgow's Kelvingrove Art Galleries and reproduced in a book of celebrity photographs. The *Daily Record* printed the photo on its front page – a bare-torsoed Tommy, wearing a Che Guevara pendant, being stroked lovingly by his doting wife with a wedding photo and other images of matrimonial harmony judiciously placed in the background.

In his closing speech to the jury, Tommy would play up the point for all it was worth. At one stage, he even offered to strip to the waist to display the body hair which had never been mentioned by any of the women who had admitted to an intimate relationship with him. It was widely reported as a killer blow to the female witnesses who had either been with Tommy or seen him unclothed. But why should anyone have mentioned Tommy's body hair? As Mike Jones QC explained in his summing-up: 'I did not ask any of the witnesses about Mr Sheridan's distinguishing features because I did not go into any details of his sexual encounters. There was no need to put the witnesses through the lurid, tiny, minute detail.' Nor had Tommy himself ever asked any of the other witnesses under cross-examination to describe his body. The questions 'Why ask only his wife?', 'Why not the other witnesses?' and 'Was he afraid of scoring an own goal?' could well have been asked.

More seriously, Gail's evidence was shown to be false on several key points. Asked by Tommy about Katrine Trolle, she replied, 'I know her very well, Katrine Trolle. I have socialised with her. I have canvassed with her. The last time I saw her was at the SSP conference, just after the Fiona McGuire stuff had been in the press. I was pregnant at the time and she hugged and kissed me and patted my tummy. She told me she had the *News of the World* at her door and they had offered her money to tell them she had an affair with Tommy.' Gail went on to specify that the conference had been in Perth early the previous year, 2005. This was explosive. It would have blown Katrine Trolle's evidence out of the water and exposed her as a perjurer – had it been true.

After Gail's testimony, Katrine Trolle was recalled as a witness. She told the court that she knew Gail but insisted that no such conversation had ever taken place. Moreover, she had not even been present at the SSP conference in Perth in 2005. Tommy cross-examined Katrine and repeatedly implied she was lying. The conflicting evidence had the jury scratching their heads. One of the two women had given false evidence. In fact, the records of the 2005 SSP conference back up Katrine Trolle's testimony. As with all mainstream party conferences, every delegate and visitor is required to register and pay a fee. Katrine Trolle's name is nowhere listed in the attendance register. Rather than lying, Gail – perhaps mistakenly rather than deliberately – had confused Katrine Trolle for another woman she had spoken to at the SSP conference.

By an intriguing coincidence, this woman – from an entirely different part of the country from Katrine – had also been involved in a long-term affair with Tommy. She probably *had* been approached by the *News of the World*. Tommy, apparently, had ended their affair in early October 2004, just weeks before the Cupids story went to press. I suspected that Tommy had a hand in Gail's confusion. The encounter between Gail and this other woman would have added to Gail's suspicions about her husband's behaviour. But not if Tommy misled her into believing that the woman was Katrine Trolle, who had already been linked with Tommy in the *News of the World*.

The other piece of false evidence given by Gail was to land her, along with her father Gus Healy, in serious trouble. There had been some confusion about the precise date of the Moat House Hotel incident. On one of the possible dates, Friday 7 June 2002, Tommy and his accomplice, Andy McFarlane, had been with a large group of family and friends in the Himalaya Indian restaurant near his home and in the nearby Quo Vadis pub. But the Moat House event had by now been pinned down to Friday 14 June – the eve of Andy's wedding.

Gail told the court that she and Tommy had visited her mother's house on the evening of 14 June sometime after 8 p.m. and left 'around ten-ish'. She claimed that they had then gone to Andy's home to check out his kilt for the wedding and to have a look at his speech notes. She also took the dog out for a walk. While Gail was doing all this, Tommy and Andy were quietly playing a game of scrabble.

'How long did all this take, Mrs Sheridan?' asked Tommy.

'A good few hours,' replied Gail.

'And what time do you remember leaving Andy's home?'

They left after midnight, according to Gail. She had then tidied up the house and the couple had gone to bed around 12.45 a.m. If her evidence was correct, then the Moat House incident was indeed a fiction and at least three more people had committed perjury – Anne Colvin, Helen Allison and Keith Baldassara.

Under cross-examination, Gail insisted that her cover story was true. 'That is a lie, Mrs Sheridan, and you know it,' fumed Mike Jones at one point.

'No, it is not a lie, Mr Jones, and you know it,' said Gail.

Her version of events was partly corroborated by her father Gus, who said that Tommy and Gail had come to his house between 8 p.m. and 10 p.m. that night. Under cross-examination, however, he did admit that they may have left a little bit earlier, perhaps 9.45 p.m. This did not necessarily contradict the evidence of Anne Colvin and Helen Allison. They had only gone into the hotel suite and encountered Tommy sometime around 11.30 p.m. In theory, Tommy could have left Gail's parents' home at 9.45 p.m. and been in the Moat House Hotel by 10.15 p.m.

According to most observers, Gail's testimony was Tommy's trump card, a turning point after eighteen dismal days in which his reputation had been pulverised. His own appearance in the witness box – ironically, he was called by the *News of the World* – had been less than compelling. Mike Jones QC had begun by drawing his attention to an official DVD produced by the Scottish Parliament, which included short personal interviews with each of the 129 Holyrood MSPs. Asked what his pet hate was, Tommy had replied, 'I think the pet hate I have got is dishonesty.'

Under examination, he was edgy and hostile, as the QC produced a series of damning telephone records. He had phoned Cupids swingers' club at 11.40 p.m. on Friday 23 November 2001 – just one week before the Socialism 2001 conference where I was first informed that he had been spotted in a sex club in Manchester. He explained away the late phone call by telling the court that he had only phoned to inquire if any journalists had been prowling around asking about him. His excuse for phoning Katrine Trolle eighty-three times in 2004 was even more far-fetched. With a straight face, he told the QC that he had been discussing the Danish minimum wage and its relevance for Scotland with her. The normally thorough Mike Jones QC failed to spot one glaring flaw in his explanation – Denmark has never introduced a minimum wage.

He had phoned Anvar Khan on a series of occasions in August and late September 2002. According to Tommy, this was to discuss a property dispute she had asked him to pursue. 'She sought my assistance with a long-running dispute she had with her landlord. I wrote letters on her behalf, I made calls to her.' But even Tommy's powers of invention were stretched beyond the limit when the records showed that he had phoned Anvar Khan, Katrine Trolle, Gary Clark and Andy McFarlane on a single Thursday night – 26 September 2002, at the start of the traditional Glasgow autumn holiday weekend.

'I don't know what these calls are about – I am very close to Andy and very close to Gary,' he replied lamely.

And the calls to the two women?

'The call to Anvar might have been about her property problem or it might have been a media inquiry.'

He also had difficulty explaining why he had made two phone calls to Gary and Katrine at 9.29 p.m. and 9.36 p.m. on the night of the November the 9th 2004 SSP executive meeting at which he had been presented with the resignation ultimatum. Neither of the two names had been mentioned at the meeting. After the most earth-shattering meeting in the history of the SSP, he had phoned Katrine Trolle 'to arrange a work-related trip to the Scottish Parliament', he told the jury by way of explanation.

Tommy's entire case consisted of seven essential points:

1. he had been targeted by the *News of the World* in revenge for his political views;
2. a woman in Peterhead with mental health problems, whom he had never met or heard of before, had invented a relationship with him to impress a journalist – and it had all escalated out of control;
3. around the same time, a *News of the World* columnist, Anvar Khan, who once had a brief fling with Tommy before his relationship with Gail, had written a fictional chapter in her memoirs about attending a swingers' club with an unnamed MSP – and had then been put under pressure by her editor to falsely identify Tommy Sheridan as the mystery politician;

4. in pursuit of an unexplained political vendetta, the entire leadership of his own party, including his closest friends and colleagues, took advantage of Anvar Khan's malicious accusation to remove him from his position – even though they knew her story to be false;

5. not content with ousting him, the SSP then forged documents incriminating him and also persuaded a grassroots member of the SSP in the north-east of Scotland to make up a fictitious account of a long-term affair with him;

6. that member then conscripted two of her non-political friends to corroborate her perjury;

7. two respectable middle-aged women read about a sex scandal involving Tommy Sheridan and decided to fabricate a story about an incident in a hotel room eighteen months earlier.

In terms of plausibility, this was *Doctor Who* meets *Snow White and the Seven Dwarfs*. But it was no laughing matter. Tommy was deadly serious. If his version of events was true, dozens of people with a range of political and financial motives had been involved in a grand conspiracy to pervert the course of justice and had committed systematic perjury to achieve their aims. When Mike Jones QC put it to him, once again, that his accusations could put a number of people in the frame for lengthy prison sentences, Tommy readily agreed, saying, 'I think they have been very foolish indeed.'

Concluding his evidence, he told the jury:

I am either a complete and utter idiot or I am someone who loves my wife deeply and would not betray her trust. I find it absolutely incredible . . . three-in-a-bed sex, five-in-a-bed sex . . . I am the mild-mannered Clark Kent of Scottish politics, Superman by night. The only difference is that Superman is made of steel – I am not made of steel, I am made of flesh and blood.

He later asked how he could possibly have found the time for the 'sexual Olympics' of which he had been accused.

His closing speech to the jury relied heavily on emotion. Several media commentators described it as the speech of his life. He delivered it with passion and panache. The rhetoric was scintillating, the timing deadly, the pacing powerful, the swoop and fall of his inflection awesome. It was partly designed to sow some doubts in the minds of the jurors but its main purpose was to tug at their heartstrings. As a seasoned orator, Tommy knew that one tear can be worth ten hard facts.

He begged for sympathy. For Mike Jones QC this was just another job. For the giant multinational corporation that owned the *News of the World*, the sums of money at stake amounted to a pittance but the verdict could ruin him financially and politically, destroy his family and trash his hard-won reputation. After weeping shamelessly, he asked the jury, 'Are these the tears of a man who is loving and faithful to his wife or are these the tears of a clown, the tears of a fool, the tears of a complete and utter idiot?' Again and again, he hid behind the mind-blowing outrageousness of his own behaviour.

I fancied a wee bit of swinging but I didn't want anybody to know about it. So I went to a club in Manchester, where no one knows me. And just to make sure no one found out, I invited the sex columnist of the *News of the World*. She writes about sex in the most salacious ways possible. According to her own admission, she is a media whore. So I thought, 'Why don't I invite Anvar Khan? That will keep it secret.' That doesn't just make me a swinger. If it's true, it makes me an idiot.

And just in case any of the jurors had still failed to grasp the point, he rammed it home:

If I am guilty of the things that I am accused of, I am not just an adulterer, I am not just a swinger, I am not just a participant in orgies – I am an idiot. And you know something? If I had partaken in these activities in the course of the last four years or whatever, then you would be right to brand me an idiot.

He talked lovingly of his wife and his baby daughter and the painful separation he had to endure from his one-year-old daughter as a consequence of this court case. He described himself as 'an innocent man' and 'the accused'. He talked of 'being convicted' and asked the jury to 'find him not guilty'. This was all nonsense. The only person who was in that courtroom by choice was Tommy Sheridan.

'It was his most clever rhetorical flourish,' observed the writer, Johnny Rodger, in the Scottish literary magazine, *The Drouth*, pointing out that Tommy could have been taking instructions from Cicero, the celebrated lawyer, statesmen and orator of ancient Rome, who advised, 'It is defending, above all, which creates glory and all the more so when the person defended seems harassed and threatened by the resources of a powerful man.'

His final address to the jury had been eloquent and passionate but it had lasted just 45 minutes and sidestepped much of the detailed evidence. The style of Mike Jones was starkly different. He spoke for three hours – four times longer than Tommy – and evaluated every piece of evidence with scientific precision. He laid bare every flaw, every contradiction and every inconsistency in Tommy's case. If it had been a boxing match, Tommy's trainer would have thrown in the towel after the first hour.

The QC mocked the notion that Tommy had been likened to some kind of sexual Olympian.

> On my calculations, we are talking about a few dozen sexual encoun-
> ters with three women at the centre of this case over four years. Out of
> 1460 days, that adds up to perhaps between twenty-four and thirty
> days. When he compares himself to Superman, Mr Sheridan is
> flattering himself.

He went on:

> Mr Sheridan has the right to defend his own reputation. But, in doing
> so, he has attempted the destruction of the reputation of no fewer than
> eighteen other people – and that doesn't include the journalists. Of
> those eighteen, not one has been a willing participant in the proceed-
> ings. Yet Mr Sheridan has accused them of perjury and the 'mother of
> all stitch-ups' . . .
> And think about these witnesses: they include Barbara Scott, who
> was so inspired by Mr Sheridan that she joined the SSP in the first
> place. There is Rosie Kane, upon whose reputation for honesty the
> liberty of asylum seekers depends. There is Carolyn Leckie, who has
> been vilified in public and her daughter reduced to tears because she
> has told the truth about Mr Sheridan.
> There is Keith Baldassara, a close friend, a close political ally, his
> best man, and a man whose livelihood depends on Mr Sheridan. There
> is Richie Venton, so striking as he spoke in the witness box, a man of
> real integrity, who has devoted his life to his conscience. There is Alan
> McCombes, who went to prison and would have stayed in prison as a
> matter of conscience, to preserve Mr Sheridan's confidentiality and is
> now accused of concocting a fabricated minute and of giving perjured
> evidence.
> There is Katrine Trolle whose life has been soured by the pain she
> has caused people close to her, by revealing her past. And Fiona
> McGuire, who has lost her husband and her job as result of this case.
> There is Ruth Adamson, who has been accused of a serious crime on
> the basis of no evidence except than Mr Sheridan's say-so. And Ralph

Barnett, again who faces an end to his career if, as Mr Sheridan says, he has come here to commit perjury. These are just a few of the people Mr Sheridan is asking you to brand as liars and perjurers.

He accused Tommy of having 'a monstrous ego', as illustrated by the politician's claim that eighteen witnesses unconnected to the *News of the World* would commit the serious crime of perjury in order to bring about his downfall. 'He is a man who is no different from many, many others who have been brought down by their own recklessness and by their own failure to take responsibility for their own actions.'

Before the jury retired to consider its verdict, the judge delivered his summing-up. Given the weight of evidence, Lord Turnbull was remarkably even-handed. Perhaps because Tommy had dispensed with his legal team and conducted his own case, the judge decided that it would be appropriate to bend over backwards to make allowances for Tommy's lack of professional expertise. He avoided steering the jury in either direction and was careful to use tentative, conditional language in evaluating the evidence. His speech was redolent with phrases such as: 'I can give you no assistance as to how to resolve these competing points of evidence. All I do is to leave them to your own good judgement.'

He left the court in no doubt, however, that, whatever the jury's verdict, there would be repercussions. He talked of the 'sorry state of affairs for the Scottish Socialist Party' and 'the particularly unsavoury sight of senior members of a mainstream political party giving evidence in direct contradiction to one another about a meeting at which they were all present'.

In a hint of what was to come, he told the jury:

> There is little room for any conclusion other than some of them, at least, must have lied in evidence. That is Mr Sheridan's position. He says that is exactly what has happened – there was a plot against him, and that the witnesses called by the defenders were engaged in a political war. But whichever way you look at it, you might well find it difficult to avoid the conclusion that some of these witnesses have lied. That is a very serious matter, especially when it involves five Members of the Scottish Parliament. It is the criminal offence of perjury – and it is punishable by imprisonment.

But for now, all power was in the hands of the jury. Few people would have wagered even a dodgy ten-bob note on Tommy's chances of success. Even he now seemed to have resigned himself to defeat. The 'titanic battle' had turned into a damage limitation exercise. His most wildly optimistic hope now was that the jury would take pity on him, find in his favour and award him a derisory token sum – a penny or a pound. It would be humiliation but he could spin that as an honourable draw.

Because of the length of the trial, one jury member had been given dispensation to go on holiday. At 12.54 p.m. that stifling Friday afternoon, the remaining seven men and four women trudged out of the courtroom to take a decision which would have political, personal and legal reverberations for years to come. At 3.45 p.m., they returned.

'How do you answer the issue, yes or no?' barked the Clerk of the Court.

'Yes,' replied the foreman of the jury, to stunned silence.

The majority, he told the court, had been seven to four. There was an even greater shock to come when the Clerk of Court asked the foreman for the jury's assessment of the damages.

'£200,000.'

Across Scotland, the phone lines went on fire.

Alone in my Glasgow tenement flat, I took a call from Ken Ferguson, our press officer.

'He's won,' he said. 'Two hundred grand.'

This was surely a wind-up. But Ken wasn't a man for silly pranks. After the evidence that had been presented in the Court of Session, this was truly incomprehensible.

From the day the trial kicked off, I knew there was no possible verdict that could have anything other than disastrous consequences for the SSP. The only outcome that would be more catastrophic than a defeat for Tommy Sheridan would be a victory for Tommy Sheridan because the price of that victory would be the annihilation of the SSP and the destruction of the reputation of dozens of honest men and women.

Colin Fox phoned to read me a press release he had drafted:

Tommy Sheridan's victory in his action against the *News of the World* is an extraordinary achievement against heavy odds. Every socialist will rejoice in the jury's rejection of the *News of the World*'s journalism which this verdict represents. We now have to turn our attentions to the difficult task of taking the SSP forward, healing the wounds opened up by the case and I expect the help of all members in the work.

There was no way I could agree with him on this. Within the SSP, Tommy would now sweep Colin aside and reinstall himself as leader of the party, which in turn would trigger a walk-out by a big section of the membership in the party's Glasgow heartland. And that would just be for starters.

If Tommy had lost, he would have been bankrupted and humiliated. He would have been forced to join the pantheon of disgraced politicians. But at least he might then be left in peace to wallow in his own ignominy. The verdict of the jury – reinforced by their decision to award him £200,000 in damages – would guarantee that this case would run and run and run. Already, within minutes of the verdict, the *News of the World*'s editor had slammed the jury's decision as 'perverse' and pledged to lodge an appeal. That wouldn't be the end of the matter, either. A full-scale criminal investigation wasn't just a possibility or even a probability – it was now an inevitability. As surely as the heatwave searing Scotland would sooner or later give way to clouds and rain, the SSP would be dragged into something much bigger and more serious than a civil defamation case.

Colin and I weren't going to agree over the press statement but, after the trauma of the past four weeks, we were anxious to avoid a row. I suggested that Colin should put out the statement in his own name while I consulted with the other two members of our press team, Eddie Truman and Ken Ferguson, and with the other three MSPs who had stood firm during the trial.

In the names of Frances Curran, Rosie Kane and Carolyn Leckie, we put out a statement with a different slant:

> We are angry that the Scottish Socialist Party has been dragged through the Court of Session for four long weeks and now faces another ordeal as the *News of the World* launches an appeal. This was a court case we didn't want to be involved in and one that Tommy Sheridan should never have initiated. Tommy has lied his way through this court case and we want no part in that. We have told the truth and we stand by the minutes of our party which record the truth about Tommy Sheridan's standing down as national convener in November 2004 and we will resist any attempt to revise the SSP's history.

The divergence between the two statements was stark but we didn't fall out over it. Colin, as the party convenor, felt under pressure to restore unity. But, after the public accusations and counter-accusations of the past four weeks, it was like trying to piece Humpty-Dumpty together again after his great fall.

August 2006

Tommymania

The mood in Parliament Square that sun-baked Friday afternoon was euphoric as Tommy, hand in hand with his fragrant wife, made his exit from the courtroom, surrounded by an excited posse of journalists and photographers.

Gail looked delirious with joy. Tommy was more restrained. Fleetingly, an expression that looked like fear haunted his eyes. It was as though, in this moment of jubilation, he had suddenly glimpsed the magnitude of the recriminations that might follow.

He began to address the crowd. He started low-key, thanking his two sisters and John Aberdein from Orkney 'for being the best legal team in the world'. He was soon in full flow:

> We have, over the last five weeks, taken on one of the biggest organisations on the planet . . . Well, brothers and sisters, what today's verdict proves is that working-class people, when they listen to the arguments, can differentiate the truth from the muck. They are liars – and we have proved them liars!

The decibel count intensified, his eyes shone with triumph and the hint of a smirk played around his lips as he warmed up for the grand finale:

> I want to finish, brothers and sisters, by saying one thing. Gretna have made it into Europe for the first time in their lives. But what we have done in the last five weeks – is the equivalent – of Gretna – taking on Real Madrid! – in the Bernabéu Stadium! – AND BEATING THEM ON PENALTIES!

As Davie Archibald pointed out later, a more apt sporting analogy would have been that of a boxer being knocked to the canvas a dozen times before staggering to his feet – and then being awarded a victory by the referee. Nonetheless, within a few years, the Gretna analogy

would start to look uncannily prophetic as the club which had reached
the Scottish Cup Final in 2006, backed by the cash of a multi-
millionaire businessman, crashed and burned out of existence.

The moment Tommy finished his speech, a gang of burly heavies
appeared from nowhere and bundled him and Gail into a waiting car.
It was like a scene from a James Cagney movie and had TV viewers
across the land scratching their heads. Who were these goons who had
whisked away the victorious MSP as though he were a gangland
godfather making a rapid exit?

A week later, a Tayside local newspaper, the *Perth Advertiser*,
cleared up the mystery. The front-page splash, headlined 'Our Boys
Done Good for Tommy', explained how the town's rugby club had
been hired by the *Daily Record* to put on a theatrical show outside the
court as Tommy's minders. The tabloid had signed an exclusive deal
with Tommy and Gail. For a fee of £20,000, they would be hidden
away for the next four days in a hotel suite, where they would pose
for cheesy photographs and regale the paper's journalists with their
innermost thoughts about the trial of the decade.

'They've probably gone to the Moat House,' suggested Ken
Ferguson.

In fact, their secret hideout was the luxury Mar Hall in Bishopton,
Renfrewshire where the couple racked up a £7,000 bill in four days.
The photographs were tacky and tasteless, even by the standards of
Tommy and Gail. One showed the celebrity couple posing like mature
mail-order catalogue models in matching white bathrobes. It was
enough to make strong men vomit.

But it was a great story. Rupert Murdoch, the international media
tycoon, had been out to crucify Tommy in revenge for his socialist
beliefs. The popular local hero had single-handedly slain the beast.
Against all the odds, truth and justice had prevailed. It was just a pity
none of it was true.

Nonetheless, for the time being, the Scottish media was in the grip
of Tommymania. Everyone loved to see David triumph over Goliath –
though, when Tommy used this well-worn Biblical analogy on a radio
show, he managed to expose his shaky grasp of the Old Testament.
'We were fighting a David and Goliath battle – but this time David
won.'

Newspaper columnists who had previously despised his politics
became overnight converts to the cult of the celebrity leader. 'You just
want to be on the side that's winning,' sang Bob Dylan, contemptuously, in 'Positively 4th Street'.

Even the far-right press joined in the celebrations. 'For Mr Sheridan, this is a tremendous victory on two counts. Primarily, of course, it has demonstrated that he is not a hypocrite and an adulterer, and has left him with his reputation intact,' said the *Daily Express*. Its Sunday sister title praised 'the maverick politician's inner strength' and went on:

> Politics aside, it is difficult not to have respect for Mr Sheridan after he stood in front of the jury and conducted a case which could, ultimately, have ruined his life as well as those of his wife and family.

Columnists in the hated Murdoch press joined in the chorus of hero worship. 'If he's not a millionaire with his own chat show by the end of the year I'll eat a judge's wig,' wrote Bill Leckie in the *Scottish Sun*. Tommy, he claimed, had 'proven himself more believable than the 18 – count 'em, 18 – witnesses swearing on the Bible that he's a coke-fuelled madman who's been in busier beds than the one where the little one said roll over.'

In the *London Review of Books* Ayrshire-born writer Andrew O'Hagan labelled Tommy 'a national hero' and, of Gail, gushingly said, 'Nobody who saw her stride into the Court of Session could imagine her to be concealing anything. The smile for the cameras, the starlet walk, the grip on her husband's hand.'

If that was the extent of the media commentary on the court case, we might have been able to laugh off their gullibility. But, for some, it wasn't sufficient to sanctify the glamorous couple. Fired up with prejudice and ignorance, they lashed into the rest of us political nonentities with loathing and venom. As socialists swimming against the political stream, we were used to harsh condemnation. In three decades of activity in the rough and tumble of leftist politics, I had acquired a pretty thick skin. But the abuse now being directed at those of us who had done the right thing was strong stuff. If I relied for my information on the mainstream press, I would have no reason to doubt that a talented and honourable man – a living legend, no less – had been brought down by a gang of jealous, vicious, lying dimwits.

With the predictability of the One O'Clock Gun, Tommy's old mate Ron McKenna launched his own mortar attack in the *Sunday Mirror*. He fumed about 'the cancer at the heart of the SSP, the factionalism, back-stabbing and nastiness'. And he left no one in any doubt who he was talking about – Carolyn Leckie, Rosie Kane and Frances Curran, naturally. 'In their comments in and out of court the trio showed the real heart of the SSP. Petty, self-obsessed individuals who put themselves first . . . a jury saw only underlying malevolence. And deemed them liars.' The fact that Frances Curran hadn't even been called to give evidence seemed to have escaped the notice of the eagle-eyed journalist who was also employed by the legal firm which had taken on Tommy's case on a no-win, no-fee basis.

Another *Sunday Mirror* columnist threw in her tuppence worth. Anna Smith couldn't conceal her contempt for the MSPs who had failed to commit perjury at their leader's behest. 'To say these MSPs were scrubbers at the stairheid is an insult to the intelligence and integrity of scrubbers at the stairheid.' She accused them of strutting around in designer clothes, while being unable to string a proper sentence together. 'Like the jury, I just didn't believe that ramshackle procession of SSP idiots who went to court to knife him in the back.' In 2009, Anna joined the *News of the World* as a columnist and was welcomed warmly by the editor Bob Bird as a 'tremendous boost for the paper'. When she eventually discovered the truth, she would turn on Tommy with a vengeance.

Against the magnitude of the crimes of which we were accused, those kinds of insults were petty. But they were spiteful and ridiculously wrong. None of these MSPs ever wore designer clothes. They lived on an average worker's wage, had children to support and – in the case of Rosie, Carolyn and Frances – had no other household income. The only SSP MSP who possessed a designer wardrobe was Tommy Sheridan.

In the *Sunday Herald*, under the headline 'Muppet Marxists who couldn't take the heat', Iain Macwhirter wrote, 'The affair has exposed the sordid reality of ultra-left politics: the vanity, self-delusion, paranoia. Ranting about integrity, honour, truth; accusing each other of lying, betrayal, sexual misconduct.' He continued:

It all stemmed from [Tommy's] willingness to play the game, become a real politician, use his media skills to get the party taken seriously. Sheridan accepted that, in a real parliament, you have to win arguments and conduct debates, play by the rules, do your homework on committees and generate initiatives and policies . . . The other SSP MSPs seemed more interested in staging student occupations and walkouts.

All of this was the opposite of the truth. In particular, Carolyn Leckie and Frances Curran had worked like Trojans within the parliament to ensure that the day-to-day business of the SSP group was dealt with, while Tommy more or less opted out from anything that didn't involve the media spotlight. Carolyn was the SSP representative on the Business Bureau and organised the SSP's voting and participation in the parliamentary bodies, while Frances was the SSP group secretary.

Before 2003, when Tommy had been the sole Scottish Socialist MSP, he had regularly come under fire for his poor attendance at key meetings. He had even been forced to stand down from the only committee on which he had sat, the important Equal Opportunities Committee, after attending just three meetings out of a possible twenty-three in 2000–2001 and failing to attend a single meeting of the committee the following year.

By 2004, however, under the influence of some of the new MSPs, the SSP was to come top of the league table for activity within Holyrood, as measured by speeches in the chamber, voting records, attendance at committees, questions raised and motions put down. Even the *Daily Record* had praised the SSP for the effectiveness of the party inside Holyrood. But now all of these inconvenient facts were forgotten in the unseemly scramble by Scotland's chattering classes to bask in Tommy's glory while smearing his SSP colleagues.

Underlying the torrent of abuse was the same naked misogyny which we had witnessed among those around Tommy in the SSP. Misogyny is not be confused with old-fashioned sexism. Some sophisticated professionals can be more vicious than any macho building-site worker when it comes to expressing contempt towards women.

Many of these attacks on women members of the SSP were also laced with class snobbery. Like Tommy, Rosie Kane, Carolyn Leckie and Frances Curran had been brought up in the deprived, peripheral housing schemes of Glasgow. But, unlike Tommy, none of them had had ever gone to university – not because they lacked the ability but because of the poverty in which they had been brought up in the 1970s. Carolyn and Frances had both watched their fathers die young, in their early forties, leaving behind low-income, one-parent households where university was never an option. The daughter of an Irish navvy, Rosie was brought up in a large family. She was a victim of the assembly-line, exam-obsessed education system and had dropped out of school at a young age. For middle-class journalists, they were just a bunch of uncouth working-class women who could never have dreamed of achieving high political office except on the coat-tails of a charismatic, university-educated man. The truth was, each of them, and Colin Fox too, was in a different league from Tommy when it came to culture, humour and broad knowledge of the world outside politics. When Word Power Books in Edinburgh published a book of witty stories and one-liners from SSP MSPs, compiled by Gregor

Gall, it was no accident that it was titled *Revolutionary Witticisms of Colin Fox, Rosie Kane and Carolyn Leckie*. Tommy had a talent for oratory and slick, quick-fire sound bites. He was a brilliant networker with a knack for charming journalists and flattering celebrities. But that was about it. Strip away these skills and there wasn't much left.

The Nobel prize-winning writer Doris Lessing once drew a distinction between myth and fiction. To paraphrase her, a myth is an exaggeration of reality based on a kernel of truth. Based on that definition, the Tommy Sheridan myth wasn't even a myth. It was a JK Rowling-style fantasy.

Some columnists – and more than a few reporters on the ground – refused to buy into that fantasy but were now heavily censored by nervous newspaper lawyers. The highly respected political writer, Ruth Wishart, wrote a restrained but perceptive piece on the dangers of large-as-life, charismatic politicians being carried away with their own fame. She ended with a prophetic warning: 'Keep checking your feet for clay, Tommy.'

The *Guardian* writer Julie Bindel attended part of the court case and bravely contradicted most of the British media – Left, Right and Centre – by challenging Tommy's status as a hero and by casting doubt on the outcome of the court case itself. She perceptively pointed out 'the irony that the women giving evidence in court to support the *News of The World* case were portrayed as those the paper is usually out to get – feminists, hookers, gold-diggers, witches and man-haters', and lamented the court's decision as a setback for the cause of women's equality and feminism.

Magnus Linklater, a respected former *Scotsman* editor, had always been a political opponent of socialism. In *Scotland on Sunday*, he acknowledged 'a famous victory, a triumph of soap-box oratory over the dull pedantry of the law'. But he pointed out that it came at a cost. Sheridan had 'traduced in court the loyal workers who gave evidence against him, and who, this weekend, find their reputation in tatters, each of them accused of conspiring to lie.' He went on:

All in all, in the course of Sheridan's pugnacious self-defence, some 18 witnesses have been branded by him as perverters of justice . . . Along with their shredded testimony, a left-wing movement has been exposed to ridicule and contempt . . . How can those MSPs who gave evidence against Sheridan command respect for their views when at any point their opponents can legitimately question both their credentials and their personal integrity . . . What happens to the manifesto for a socialist Scotland, dedicated to the common benefit of the people, when those who composed it are revealed as vicious back-stabbers, prepared to sacrifice their comrades in pursuit of their personal ambitions?

The veteran journalist was careful not to make any accusations but his tone implied scepticism at the verdict and incredulity at the notion that Tommy had been the victim of a plot.

Unfortunately, these voices of reason tended to be drowned out by a chorus of ill-informed quackery passing itself off as serious political analysis of what was then a significant political party representing hundreds of thousands of Scots. The SSP, which had won at least grudging respect up until 2004 from the Scottish media, was now Scotland's pariah party. If we had launched an armed struggle, we could hardly have expected more hostile treatment. We fought back in the media, as best we could. On the live radio programme *Good Morning Scotland*, Carolyn Leckie caused tremors of anxiety in the legal department of the BBC when she described Tommy as 'a cross between Goebbels, Walter Mitty and Benny Hill'. Colin Fox on *Newsnight Scotland* said that Tommy had uncovered so many plots he didn't know whether to blame MI5, MFI or IKEA.

The BBC also gave us a fair hearing in a hastily put-together but gripping documentary on the court case which was transmitted on the Tuesday night following the verdict. The producers were anxious to strike a balance so a number of us from both sides of the court battle were interviewed. Of all the participants, two people in particular – Katrine Trolle and Keith Baldassara – conveyed their feelings with compelling honesty and poignancy.

We knew we were fighting a rearguard action. But, even so, what the *Daily Record* printed on 7 August 2006, the Monday morning following the verdict, came as a brutal mugging.

From the most expensive suite in the Hilton Hotel, Tommy had for days been plying the newspaper's journalists with gushing rhapsodies to Gail, family life and fidelity, while denouncing the evil newspaper on the other side of the river. But, in his bellicose triumphalism, he was unable to restrain himself from also using his lucrative new platform to malign his own party colleagues. In the *Sunday Mail* – the *Record*'s sister paper – he now attacked Keith Baldassara and me for the first time. 'Undoubtedly, the performance of Keith Baldassara and Alan McCoombes [*sic*] hurt like a hot poker inserted into my heart. We had fallen out two years previously over the accusations and their own private lives.' This reference to falling out over 'their own private lives' was a malicious invention. We had only ever fallen out over his determination to lie. In crudely abusive language, he told the newspaper:

> Even if in some delusional way they believed what they were saying, they said it on behalf of the *News of the World* and that makes them scabs. Where I grew up, in Pollok, people who side with the establishment are regarded as rats.

At least the Sunday tabloid provided a bit of balance by carrying an alternative explanation of events by Rosie Kane in her regular column for the newspaper.

But the *Daily Record* was less scrupulous. Splashed across the front page was the hate-filled headline: 'I WILL DESTROY THE SCABS WHO TRIED TO RUIN ME'. And worse was to come. Spread across pages four and five was a quartet of large photographs of Colin Fox, Carolyn Leckie, Rosie Kane and Frances Curran. All were identified by name and emblazoned across each photo was the single word, 'SCAB'.

It was hard to imagine a more inflammatory or defamatory slur. As *The Herald*'s Anne Simpson put it to Tommy in an interview a week later, the term scab was 'an antique, but still venomous curse'. In the lexicon of the labour and trade union movement, the word, which is usually directed towards those who break strikes by crossing picket lines, remains a vile insult, reeking of dishonour and betrayal. In 1903 the American socialist writer, Jack London, wrote a famous essay in which he declared:

> After God had finished the rattlesnake, the toad, and the vampire, he had some awful substance left with which he made a scab. A scab is a two-legged animal with a corkscrew soul, a water brain, a combination backbone of jelly and glue.

The smear was contemptible. The four MSPs had never in their lives crossed a picket line or undermined a legitimate struggle of working people. The only person in the SSP who had betrayed the principles of solidarity out of naked self-interest was the *Daily Record*'s new pin-up boy. He had trashed his own party, tried to rewrite its history and attempted to frame his comrades on serious criminal charges – all for his own self-interest. Now he was being paid £20,000 – the equivalent at the time of two years' pay for a full-time worker on the adult minimum wage – for vilifying his victims. It was an incredible sight to behold. Whether out of ignorance or cynical one-upmanship,

Scotland's top-selling daily newspaper was colluding with a perjurer to destroy the reputation of four elected MSPs who were only guilty of telling the truth under oath.

This onslaught was more damaging than anything that had ever been published in the *News of the World* about the antics of Tommy Sheridan. The editorial treatment of the story, including the front-page headline and the rogues' gallery of photographs of 'scabs', seemed to be designed for the purpose of inciting hatred and contempt against our four MSPs. Ironically, the editor Bruce Waddell had been the editor of the *Scottish Sun* until a few years before, which, in Tommy's book, would have qualified him as the chief envoy of the Murdoch empire in Scotland.

Apart from Tommy, the only other SSP MSP who escaped unscathed from the media bombardment was Rosemary Byrne, who had backed Tommy's false account of events. Had the other four MSPs acted in the same way, Allan Green and Barbara Scott and anyone else who refused to go along with Tommy's crazy charade would have been ruined personally and professionally. With six MSPs lining up to denounce them as forgers and liars, few people would ever have trusted them again. At best, they'd have been branded with infamy for the rest of their lives. At worst, they could have faced serious criminal charges – perjury and conspiracy to pervert the course of justice. They might even have been prosecuted. And, if five MSPs had continued to stand firm with Tommy Sheridan all the way through a future criminal trial, honest people might even have gone to jail.

Far fetched? So too were the tales of the Birmingham Six and the Guildford Four. And of TC Campbell and Joe Steele. Far-fetched too was the story of Sally Clark, the qualified solicitor who spent three years in jail in the 1990s, convicted of the murder of two sons who were later found to have died from natural causes. Sally never recovered from her nightmare and died tragically at the age of forty-three. The list could fill an encyclopaedia.

Nor was it only SSP activists who were potentially in the firing line. Others with no political connection to Tommy Sheridan had been dragged into this court case under citation. They included women like Helen Allison, Anne Colvin, Katrine Trolle, Anvar Khan and Fiona McGuire. Their lives too had been poisoned by the lies and vitriol heaped on them by Scotland's new media idol.

What kind of socialist party would gang together to destroy the reputations of a group of women whose only mistake had been to cross Tommy Sheridan? If every last member of the SSP had lied through their teeth to prove that Tommy was a paragon of virtue and fidelity, these women would have been turned into objects of public ridicule and contempt. Until their dying days, they would have lived under a cloud of suspicion that they had lied in court to destroy a great and honourable man. Who knows – they too might have been investigated, charged and maybe even convicted of perjury. The SSP would have had a lot to be proud of.

For now, Holyrood's first couple were basking in the glory of the moment. There would be fashion spreads, celebrity photographs, profiles in glossy magazines, radio chat shows and TV appearances. Meanwhile, their political hangers-on were excitedly planning Tommy's restoration to the leadership of the SSP and revenge against those who had chosen the wrong side.

Back in 2004, I had warned that Tommy was intent on building a 'tower of lies'. It had been a flight of rhetoric – or so I thought at the time – but, over twenty months, the structure had shot up like a skyscraper. As the rest of Scotland gazed upwards in wonder, we could see only the precarious foundations. Sooner or later, this tower would come crashing to the ground.

August–September 2006

The Bollocks of Henry the Eighth

Just as the 'libel trial of the decade' was about to be begin, cinemas across the UK were screening *The Wind that Shakes the Barley*, the latest in series of powerful collaborations by director Ken Loach and Glaswegian screenwriter Paul Laverty. The duo – then and now, both strong supporters of the SSP – had previously made such urban classics as *My Name is Joe* and *Sweet Sixteen*. In contrast, this new drama, dark and powerful, centred around two brothers on opposite sides of the civil war in Ireland in the 1920s. It felt painfully close to home.

Family feuds can be the most vicious and unforgiving of all. The convulsions within the SSP involved no physical violence. Nor did it revolve around any profound principle. It was triggered by one man's selfishness. It was ugly and depressing. But we could identify with the passion and fury that, in more brutal circumstances, had driven close comrades to take up arms against one another. At every level of the SSP, lifelong friendships were broken forever and, in a number of cases, members of the same family found themselves on opposite sides of the verbal barricades.

Tommy's supporters ranged from the ultra-naive to the ultra-cynical. I had long understood the politics of tyranny – the social and economic conditions upon which people like Hitler, Mussolini, Stalin and a hundred lesser dictators rose to power. But now, for the first time, I was beginning to get an insight into the *psychology* of tyranny. Autocrats don't always bully their way to power. More often, they use charm, seduction and manipulation. Meanwhile, those they manipulate believe what they want to believe, ignoring all the evidence that doesn't fit in with their faith and seizing upon any fragment – fact or fiction – that fortifies their certitude. These were intelligent, educated people we were up against. At least some of them knew the facts. But facts can be manipulated or ignored at will, as any tabloid editor will confirm. Some people had edited the facts in their mind until their narrative bore no relation to reality.

Outside the courtroom, the TV cameras had caught a glimpse of John Aberdein, who had played a key backroom role in Tommy's court battle. I had always liked the big bearded writer. A former fisherman in his early sixties from a working-class Aberdonian background, he had gone to live on Orkney, where he taught English. By now, he was retired and, in 2005, published his first novel, *Amande's Bed*, to critical acclaim.

But from the distant Northern Isles, John's vision was blurred. I had already explained our dilemma to him and he had been fully supportive of our efforts to pressurise Tommy into abandoning his court case. 'Even if he wins, it'll be like the Dutch boy with his finger in the dyke. It'll all catch up with him eventually,' he said prophetically. But now, a year later, he had succumbed to the hysteria rampaging around the party – especially in rural Scotland. We had exchanged words outside the final National Council in Linlithgow before the court case. By then Tommy had convinced many people in the party that the *News of the World* was about to throw in the towel. Their case is about to collapse, John had insisted. Tommy has inside information. I had heard this nonsense so many times that I was rapidly running out of patience.

'John, you need to understand this. Tommy is a fantasist. He believes what he wants to believe. And he'll bring everybody down to save his own skin.'

The big man looked a bit shaken at my ferocity but he had already made up his mind. 'I don't want us to fall out over this,' he said. 'Whatever happens we should remain friends.'

In the Court of Session, after Tommy's lawyers were given the red card, John became the brain of the new amateur legal team. Ironically, his eloquent novel, set in 1956, had explored the moral dilemma that faced some of his own family members, Communist Party stalwarts, during the crushing of the Hungarian uprising by Soviet tanks. In one scene, his father is angry because he believes the party's newspaper, the *Daily Worker*, has lied to its readers in its coverage of the events. 'I'm sorry to have to say this to you, Billy, but bein' in the party doesna mean you put your brains oot wi' the empty milk bottles in the morning. Somebody said, was it Ruskin or Mill maybe? Truth is indivisible.'

In an interview published in the *Sunday Herald* two days after the verdict, John said he expected Tommy to be 'magnanimous to his accusers within the party and not seek revenge against them in the form of pushing for them to face perjury charges'. And, it got worse. 'As a former English teacher, it did occur to me that there was something of *The Crucible* about all this – with its mix of sex, lies, rumours, hysteria and persecution,' he said, referring to Arthur Miller's famous play about the Salem witchcraft trials in seventeenth-century colonial America.

> There were a lot of people out to get Tommy for many years. They felt they had no chance of ever being as effective as him. They never had the slightest chance. It's appalling they couldn't transcend that. I've no time for them. Their opportunism shows their ignorance.

I could scarcely believe that John Aberdein was capable of such drivel. He knew we had not committed perjury. The baying, hysterical mob reminiscent of *The Crucible* were those who had allowed themselves to be whipped into a lather by a pathological liar. How could someone who portrayed himself as a serious novelist, an artist, get things so wrong? Perhaps he had been seduced by the cult of the Great Leader? At the frenzied SSP National Council meeting while I was in Saughton Prison, John had implored those present to back Tommy in his legal battle not because he had right on his side but because he was 'the greatest socialist leader in a generation'. That was the crux of the divide in the SSP. For some, the great leader was so revered that his reputation had to be defended at all costs and, if that meant lies, fraud and character assassination, then so be it.

Another member of the SSP's artistic community, the film director, Peter Mullan, repeated the tired old lie that the whole thing had been driven by jealousy. 'There's no getting away from the fact that envy had a lot to do with it. I think some people within that party felt he was getting all the limelight.' Grotesquely, he went on to talk darkly of Nazi collaborators. 'If a Jewish man or woman is in front of the Gestapo, you don't say, "They're Jewish." and you don't expect them to say, "They're Jewish." because, within that context, so-called truth is obviously absurd.'

At another level, the analogy was interesting. Unlike Tommy and John Aberdein, Peter was criticising us not for lying but for refusing to lie. Instead of denouncing us as dishonest, he was condemning us for being too honest. At best, it was naive. You cannot falsify a major part of your own history – especially when hundreds of other people know the truth. Even if everyone present at the November the 9th 2004 meeting could have been persuaded or coerced into committing perjury, each of those 22 people would have been like climbers roped together across a sheer cliff face. One slip, or one jump by one person could have brought everyone else crashing down.

Even Jeffrey Archer had only involved a couple of people he was close to in his conspiracy to pervert the course of justice. One of them was Terence Baker who, over lunch, a few months after giving false evidence in court, confessed to his old friend Nick Elliott that he had provided Archer with a false alibi in court. The significance of that morsel of information did not immediately register with Elliott. Nor, apparently, did Terence Baker fully realise the gravity of his admission. Then, in December 1999, Elliott – by then the controller of drama at ITV – was listening to a radio programme about the Archer case. Terence Baker had long since died and Jeffrey Archer had been selected as the Tory candidate for London Mayor. That restaurant conversation from twelve years earlier came flooding back and Elliott went to the lawyers representing the *Daily Star*, the newspaper Archer had sued for £500,000. From then on, Archer's libel victory began to unravel. Another witness who had lied in court for Archer came forward and a police investigation was launched. The flamboyant novelist was expelled from the Tory Party in disgrace and, in July 2001, he was sentenced to four years' imprisonment for perjury and perverting the course of justice.

If the state was prepared to prosecute a pillar of the Tory establishment more than a decade after he had won a libel case by fraud, why wouldn't they be prepared to annihilate a left-wing, anti-establishment party like the SSP if any evidence ever came to light that its entire leadership had perjured themselves, conspired to pervert the course of justice and defrauded a newspaper out of hundreds of thousands of pounds?

Incongruously, the Peter Mullan interview was published in *The Sunday Times* – the flagship broadsheet of Rupert Murdoch's News Corporation. Unlike those he was criticising, Peter hadn't been forced to 'collaborate with the Murdoch press'. Yet Peter was actually one of the moderates in Tommy's camp and ended the interview by calling for an end to sectarian hostilities. 'They ain't my enemies,' he said, 'they're my comrades.' He never did get involved with Tommy's breakaway Solidarity.

George Galloway was less restrained. In his political memoirs, *I'm Not the Only One*, published less than six months before the original Tommygate crisis in 2004, George had managed to write at length about politics in Scotland, Britain and internationally without a single mention of the SSP or Tommy Sheridan. Nor did Tommy's name feature in the extensive list at the end of the book of almost one hundred names of friends that George had known over the years. Yet, the moment the crisis opened up in the SSP, George's interest was suddenly aroused. Naturally, he sided with the famous celebrity against the socialist nobodies, irrespective of the politics or the morality behind the dispute. Now, in the aftermath of the trial, he told the press, 'There will have to be changes in the SSP. Tommy will have to put to the sword and expel those involved in this conspiracy against him.' In his talkSPORT radio show a week after the verdict, George denounced Colin Fox as a 'Judas'.

Within the SSP too, Tommy's fan clubs were baying for blood. Hugh Kerr told the *Sunday Herald* that the 'scabs' and 'supergrasses' who had testified against Tommy should be expelled from the party. Ian Ferguson, the spokesman for the Socialist Workers faction, put out a statement saying, 'We call on these *News of the World* witnesses to do the honourable thing and resign from the Scottish Socialist Party.' Not to be outdone, their CWI rivals called for the suspension of all of those 'political scabs' who in court had carried out the decision taken by the SSP executive.

Some of the women SSP witnesses were even subjected to literary onslaught from the pen of Martin McCardie, a talented actor and dramatist, who was, at the time, a member of Tommy's local branch in Cardonald. In a vicious piece circulated on the Internet after the court case, he wrote:

> The Edinburgh sunshine bathed them in their own spotlight, and how they grabbed it, their fifteen minutes of infamy! All smiles and laughter, Hello boys, to the camera men, as if walking down a red carpet to the premiere of their dreams . . . skeletons in search of a cupboard, stones in need of a stoning, their smiles betrayed their happiness, their eyes ecstatic with false morality . . . Bad actors with an awful script, they truly tried their best, smothering a good man with their Judas kisses . . . Jealousy dripping from every mouth, from every eye, from every pore . . . You are now a shameful footnote to a party of broken dreams.

He had written the histrionic lines in response to a photograph in *The Herald* showing a group of female SSP witnesses laughing as they entered the Court of Session. Tommy had brandished the photo, during and after the court case, to demonstrate that they hadn't given evidence under duress but had relished the task. It demonstrated nothing, except Tommy's paranoia. A photographer had captured a momentary outbreak of laughter, a spontaneous release from the tension, in response to a quip by Rosie Kane. In the film *Orphans*, made by Martin's friend Peter Mullan, there are memorable scenes of hilarious laughter amidst the grief surrounding a mother's funeral. In real life too people seek out laughter even in times of darkness. Both Martin and Peter later distanced themselves from Tommy and, in private at least, criticised his actions. But the damage had already been done.

By this time, we felt like we had been battered over the head with a dictionary of insults. We had been called scrubbers and scabs, plotters and perjurers, supergrasses and Judases, Nazi collaborators and medieval witch-hunters. And we knew that this ghastly, shrieking, screeching orchestra of hate was all being conducted by a single deranged man. The complaints about our supposedly harsh treatment of Tommy Sheridan were laughable. Far from being intolerant fanatics, we had let him away with murder. No other political party would have put up with his behaviour during the spring and summer of 2006.

Back in May, following the publication of the slanderous open letter, one unidentified Labour MSP had told the *Scotsman* that he was amazed the SSP had taken no action against Tommy Sheridan.

> If this had happened in any other party, if an MSP had done what Tommy has done to his fellow MSPs, the whip would have been withdrawn, he would have been carpeted and possibly even chucked out of the parliamentary group.

The SNP had driven out respected MSPs, such as Margo MacDonald and Dorothy-Grace Elder, for dissent. One SNP MSP, Campbell Martin, had recently been expelled for suggesting that the leader John Swinney, wasn't up to the job. Yet Tommy had dragged almost the entire leadership of his party to court under citation and accused most of us of perjury, while belching out a daily torrent of lies. And now he had assembled a political and media lynch mob to scream for *our* expulsions from the party whose honour we had defended. And we were intolerant?

On the night of the verdict, a Friday, I attended my first meeting of the United Left platform, a large and diverse grouping within the party which had backed our stance during the court case though I never did join the organisation. Over a hundred people packed into the long and narrow back room of the Times Square bar, near the St Enoch Centre in Glasgow. Chairing the meeting was Pam Currie, who later became the National Secretary of the SSP. Pam was part of a new wave of rising leaders within the SSP. A feminist and a Quaker, Pam combined a powerful intellect with organisational dynamism and a strong moral sense of right and wrong. She couldn't be further removed from the stereotypical leftist apparatchik as portrayed in the media.

The mood of the meeting was grim. These people knew the score. If Tommy had won a legal battle against the *News of the World* fairly and squarely, they would have been jubilant. But he had lied and cheated, swindled and forged, deceived and betrayed his way to victory. We felt like football fans who were unable to celebrate their team's cup final victory because we knew it had been achieved only by bribery and intimidation. And now the once-proud club would be closed down in disgrace.

Some people had already torn up their SSP membership cards. Others wanted to walk out as a group and launch a new party. Still others believed we had to stay and fight on to the bitter end. It was a meeting for venting feelings rather than for passing resolutions. The atmosphere was too intense, the timing too early, the feelings too raw to take any big decisions.

We agreed to continue the discussion on the Tuesday evening, after pondering the situation over the weekend. The following day, I revised and completed a lengthy statement I had begun to work on during the final week of the trial, intended for circulation in the SSP members' bulletin. Allan Green arranged for a team of activists to come into the SSP HQ late on Saturday afternoon to begin the task of printing the statement and sending it out to our 3000 members across Scotland. Struggling with a fierce hangover, I wrote and wrote and wrote. By late that grey Saturday afternoon, which marked the end of the extended heatwave, the statement had burgeoned into a 12,000-word document, 'The Fight for the Truth':

Whatever the intentions of the Court of Session jury, these 11 people and others now stand condemned of a monstrous political crime. We are also accused – and in effect have been found guilty – of serious criminal offences which could lead to long term prison sentences. Those accused cannot remain silent, because to remain silent would be an admission of guilt. We now have no option but to fight to clear our name. And to clear our name, we need to bring out every relevant piece of information.

The document set out a blow-by-blow account of the conversations, discussions, debates and decisions that had taken place on this issue over 18 months. The bulletin also included the minutes of the November the 9th 2004 executive meeting. Up until now, most party members, depending upon which region of the country they lived in, had heard only bits and pieces of information. Now, for the first time, they had all the facts at their disposal. Already many members had thrown in the towel politically after being shocked to the core by the daily headlines during the trial.

As well as trying to set the record straight, 'The Fight for the Truth' challenged the disturbing cult of personality that had begun to escalate out of control. I acknowledged Tommy's 'charisma and talent' which had been so vital to establishing the SSP as a credible force. 'But there is a fatal dividing line between utilising charisma and descending into the cult of the Great Leader.' This was 'an elitist and politically corrupt philosophy'. There was now 'a deep divide in the socialist movement, transcending political programme and policy, between those who believe that socialist politics has to be based on ethics and morality and those who believe in the pursuit of electoral success by any means necessary'.

How much impact the document had was hard to gauge because of the scattered, disparate nature of the SSP membership outside the big cities. But no one tried to refute it. Factions who normally combed through SSP documents in search of political deviations – like the school nurse looking for nits – fell silent. The CWI, who would become the backbone of Solidarity, used to pore over every article I ever wrote on Scottish independence looking for telltale signs of 'petit-bourgeois nationalism'. They went through the book *Imagine* line by line and discovered heresies on every page. Yet, despite the fact that this new document was the polemical equivalent of Semtex, they just pretended it had never been written. 'The Fight for the Truth' had been the first political statement I had written for years that didn't provoke a flurry of criticism from the fundamentalist factions within the SSP. Tellingly, no one issued a legal writ, no one took out an interim interdict, no one sent a lawyer's letter.

The recalled United Left meeting had to decide whether to walk or stay. The organisation had played a critical role in supporting the party during its worst-ever crisis. This wasn't a close-knit sect like some groups in the party. It mirrored the diversity of the SSP itself and included people from all sorts of backgrounds and origins – Scottish Militant Labour, the Communist Party, the Green movement, the national movement, the Labour Left, CND and the trade unions. It also included most of the youth activists in the party. Nor was it an anti-Tommy Sheridan faction. In fact, it had initially taken shape as a counterweight against those regimented factions who were intent on turning the SSP into dogma-ridden replicas of themselves. The

United Left was simply a space where people who actually believed in the SSP project could meet and discuss the party's progress without being harangued by messianic zealots.

Some people believed that, after his court victory, the restoration of Tommy Sheridan as SSP convenor was unstoppable and, when he went down, the whole party would go down with him. So we should break with him without delay. It was an understandable and, in some ways, an attractive proposition. Many of us had been worn down by the intense factional warfare of the past months and could see no end in sight except a split. But some of us strongly believed we should stay and fight. Even if we were defeated, we were convinced that any defeat would only be temporary. And we were confident that, as the truth about the events in the Court of Session seeped deeper into the party, Tommy's support base would begin to disintegrate. That broad position was largely accepted by the United Left meeting, though some individuals had already resigned and would never rejoin the party while Tommy Sheridan was a member.

For the rest of that week, the two rival camps stared each other out. Tommy was first to blink. In the media, he began to float the possibility that he might give up politics to become a lawyer or a lecturer.

Then, on 16 August, he held a press conference where he declared that the SSP had 'reached its historical limits'. He went on, 'I have in mind a new movement that would continue the battle for the vision we all hold dear' and invited party members to attend a meeting where they would have 'a historic decision to make'. It was a classic Tommy tactic – go to the media first and present his underlings with a fait accompli. It was democracy turned upside down. Usually, in a crisis, a political party sacks its leader. Here, Tommy had sacked his party. And he knew he could get away with it. He wasn't just demanding loyalty – he was demanding fealty from his new political allies. They, in turn, were honoured that the overlord had anointed them as his vassals.

Even before the meeting took place, Tommy had already christened his new party 'Solidarity'. The name was tantamount to theft. It was reminiscent of those bloodthirsty Third World dictators who used to expropriate the title socialist to describe the corrupt, gangster-ridden prison camps they presided over. Solidarity was the tidal wave of financial and physical support for the miners during their epic last stand in 1984. Solidarity was the boycott of South African goods under apartheid. Solidarity, at its most heroic, was the great mobilisation of the International Brigades to fight alongside the Spanish people against Franco. This new party represented the opposite of solidarity. One of Tommy's favourite slogans around this time derived from the catchphrase of the character played by the socialist actor Ricky Tomlinson in the TV series, *The Royle Family*. Surely this was some new adaptation of the joke and Tommy would rise at the founding meeting of his new party to roar out, 'Solidarity . . . MY ARSE!'

Some people immediately dubbed the new party 'Squalidarity', while others devised a graphic in which four of the letters were highlighted in a different colour from the rest – LIAR. But, whatever its name, one point was clear. Tommy may have duped a jury and substantial sections of the Scottish media but he had lost the battle within his own party.

On Sunday, 20 August, the Scottish Socialist Party executive met to discuss the split and released a hard-hitting statement:

> This is nothing but a vehicle for the out-of control ego of one individual and is based on the fiction that Tommy Sheridan has been the victim of a conspiratorial frame-up by his own party. He has now lost comprehensively because the membership of the SSP were not prepared to sign up to Tommy Sheridan's fictitious rewriting of the party history, nor were they prepared to stomach Tommy's thuggish and insulting behaviour.

Solidarity was launched at a public rally in the Glasgow Central Hotel – a venue which Tommy had used frequently for less public activities. Tommy and his main backers – his once-despised enemies in the Socialist Worker Party and the CWI – had pulled out all the stops, mobilising every member and loose sympathiser to maximise the attendance. From the north-east, the Highlands and the south of Scotland, where the full-time SSP organisers had testified for Tommy, buses were hired to transport SSP members to Glasgow. Naturally, the event had also generated a commotion of advance media publicity. Even at the quietest of times, Tommy Sheridan was box office. After his famous court victory he was fast becoming a superstar. And now he was breaking from the party he had fronted from its inception to launch a new movement. It was fascinating stuff. The upstairs meeting room of the hotel, overlooking the concourse of Glasgow Central Station was packed to its 450 capacity.

The previous evening the SSP had held an alternative rally, which was slightly smaller. More low-key, its main aim had been to pull together the core of the existing membership in defiance of the split. Ominously for Tommy, the solid backbone of the party – the

Central Belt activists, most of the veterans of all the big political campaigns stretching back to the Poll Tax days, the Scottish Socialist Youth movement and the women – had overwhelmingly opted to attend the SSP rally. A large part of the Solidarity rally had been made up of curious members of the public who never stuck around afterwards.

The new party had no discernible differences with the SSP. In fact, Tommy, at the time, was probably closer politically to the SSP leadership than to most of his new activists. But this was not a party founded on principles, policies or programme. It reminded me of the rhyming taunt the Irish playwright, Brendan Behan, once directed at the Church of England: 'Trust not the alien vicar/ Nor his creed without reason or faith/ For the foundation stones of his temple/ Were the bollocks of Henry the Eighth.'

At the rally, he justified the breakaway by launching into his ritual tirade against his former comrades: 'Some socialists were tried in a time of adversity and sadly, they failed the test. They took the side of the boss class instead of the side of the socialists . . .' According to *The Herald* report, the rest of his sentence was drowned out in riotous applause.

Buoyed by the turnout, Tommy made some ambitious claims for the new party. Within six months, it would have 1500 members. Even more fanciful was his boast that the new party was on course to win power in Scotland. Rather than fighting for the 130,000 voters who had backed the SSP three years before, Solidarity would set out to emulate Venezuela and Bolivia where the socialist Left had won majorities.

Tommy's sense of confidence and power was now bordering on megalomania. The SSP had built the most successful socialist project to the Left of Labour in any part of the UK since the 1930s. But we were still in the foothills and, even without the catastrophic court case, would have struggled to hold on to our support base of around 5–7 per cent. But now, on the very day he had fatally ruptured this united socialist project, Tommy was projecting himself as the Hugo Chavez of Caledonia. The magic realism was most gloriously expressed by his mother, Alice Sheridan, at the end of the rally, when she took the platform uninvited and proceeded to belt out the song, 'The Impossible Dream', while gazing adoringly at her son. BBC TV News carried extracts of her performance, with Tommy looking like he was silently praying for the fire alarm to go off.

Most people dismissed the incident as another example of Alice's eccentricity. But during the few days following the court case, while he was hidden away in the Mar Hall hotel, Tommy had told the *Daily Record* that one of the inspirations that kept him strong was a favourite song his granny used to sing – 'The Impossible Dream'. It was a revealing insight into Tommy's self-image:

> That one man, scorned and covered with scars,
> Still strove, with his last ounce of courage,
> To reach the unreachable star.

Tommy was probably unaware that the song had been written for the 1965 musical, *Man of La Mancha*, based on the famous novel *Don Quixote* by Miguel de Cervantes. In the musical version, the song is the theme tune of Don Quixote – the delusional knight whose sense of reality has become so distorted that he believes every village inn is an enemy castle and every windmill is an evil giant that has to be slain.

Unfortunately for the rest of us, our 21st-century Don Quixote also had a mini-army of Sancho Panzas eager to play the role of the dutiful peasant who, blinded by loyalty and stupidity, buys into the insane fantasy world of his master.

August–October 2006

Sex, Lies and Videotape

In the league table of public affection, tabloid editors usually fall somewhere between serial sex offenders and Nazi war criminals. Their reputation, not wholly unjustified, is of barking bullies striking terror into the hearts of those who dare look at them the wrong way – and that's just when they're relaxing at home with the family.

In a world of Kelvin McKenzie clones, Bob Bird is regarded as rather a laid-back character. Tall and blond with a polite middle-class accent, he was once married to one of Scotland's media icons – the news presenter, Jackie Bird. After editing *The Scottish Sun*, he had returned to his native London for a spell to take up the post of deputy editor of the UK edition when it exposed the truth about Jeffrey Archer's fraudulent libel action. Now he was back in Glasgow, editing the Scottish edition of the *News of the World* – and it was beginning to look as though he had a glittering journalistic career behind him. The Sheridan defamation case had cost the paper up to £2 million. Its reputation – not exactly up there with the *Financial Times* and the *Wall Street Journal* to begin with – was now pretty much in tatters.

It was less than a week after the trial when he got the phone call. 'Is that Bob Bird?' growled the voice at the other end. 'I'll get straight to the point. I've something that might interest you. Something explosive connected with the Sheridan trial.' The caller refused to identify himself but suggested that Bird should jump in a taxi immediately and head for Mosspark Station, a few miles from the *News of the World* offices. 'And, by the way, don't bring any bags – just bring yourself. Somebody will meet you there and tell you where to go.'

At the station, a young guy with a baseball cap pulled over his eyes approached the conspicuous stranger. 'Right, Bob, hand over your mobile phone. You'll get it back later today. Walk across the railway bridge, then you'll come to an iron bridge over the river. Keep going until you come to the main road. Turn right there and just keep walking.'

By now, the die was cast. Bob Bird reluctantly handed over his mobile phone, resigned to the fact that he might never see it again, before trudging over the two footbridges that lead across to Linthaugh Road, the dual carriageway that skirts the edge of the Pollok housing scheme.

Five minutes later, a figure appeared from the clump of trees that marked a fork in the road half a mile on. He instructed the well-dressed stranger to turn left and walk towards Crookston Castle. Sure enough, there in the middle distance loomed the slightly surreal sight of a fifteenth-century castle rising above the prison-grey blocks of post-war council housing. It's a well-worn joke in Pollok – Whoever thought of building a medieval castle in the middle of a housing scheme? Before he reached the castle, there was another junction. Over on the right was a desolate row of shops splattered with graffiti. On the left, a narrow street was bordered along one side by dense woodland. And loitering on the corner stood another walking, talking signpost. 'Just turn into this street – somebody will get you at the other end.' After a few more directions, the newspaperman must have felt like he was walking round in circles but then he was startled by a piercing whistle from a nearby window where an arm appeared, gesturing him towards the door.

In the doorway, a six-foot tall, strongly built man in his early forties put his finger to his lips as he handed the newspaper editor a hand-written note saying, 'Go through the door on your right and strip down to your underwear. Put your things in the plastic bag and place the bag outside the back door.'

When Bob Bird reappeared, minus most of his clothing, the big man apologised. 'I've got to assume you're wired up – and I'm taking no chances. This is too big. Do you know who I am?'

Bob Bird confessed that he hadn't a clue, though he recognised his voice from the phone.

'George McNeilage. Been involved politically with Tommy for twenty years. Known him for thirty years. I'm going to give you a wee film show. See that tape on the table? That's the tape of a conversation between me and Tommy in November 2004, the week after he resigned as leader of the SSP.'

George had made the phone call after reading the 'scabs' article on the front page of the *Daily Record*. He was volcanic with rage. Over the years, he had gradually become more and more disenchanted with his old school friend and political comrade – his recklessness, his hypoc-risy, his grandiosity, his obsession with celebrities, his infatuation with the media. Tommy had used his Pollok background to lend himself street cred but in recent years he had rarely set foot in the scheme.

In court, Tommy's behaviour had been despicable but his outburst in the *Daily Record* had been the tipping point. Tommy was now beyond the pale. It was a question of destroy or be destroyed. George began to think the unthinkable. Within a few days he had made up his mind. He was ready to press the nuclear button.

The two men sat down to watch the tape, though there wasn't much to see – just a fleeting glimpse of the side of Tommy Sheridan's face as he sat down in George's front room, asking jokingly, 'Hope I'm no' being recorded, big man?' Now and then, his hands would appear, gesticulating to emphasise a point. But the lens stayed fixed on George McNeilage. This was the famous politician as the public had never heard him before. The voice was unmistakeable. The intonation, the dialect, the timing were all pure Sheridan, but gone was the smooth-talking charm. Out poured a deluge of foul-mouthed vitriol, directed mainly at his comrades on the SSP executive. For forty minutes he ranted without a trace of remorse for his own actions. His only regret was that he had 'owned up to these c**ts'. But it was not the crudity of the language that held Bob Bird spellbound. It was the content. After weeks of golden oratory in the courtroom which, against all the odds, had persuaded the jury that Tommy Sheridan's middle name was Fidelity, here he was confessing that the allegations were indeed true. Yes, he had visited a swingers' club in Manchester. Yes, Anvar Khan, the *News of the World* sex columnist, had been there too. And yes, so also had Katrine Trolle, with whom he had been having an affair. Just a week or so before, Katrine had been splashed over the front page of every newspaper in Scotland and denounced as a malevolent fantasist after being cross-examined in court by Sheridan. Now here was the same man, two years before, praising her. 'Katrine Trolle – she's a diamond. She'll never talk. Money? She's no' interested in money. She's solid.'

'What can I say? It's sensational! The smoking gun!' Bob Bird didn't try to hide his excitement. So how much was he looking for?

George launched into an impassioned diatribe against the tabloids in general and the Murdoch press in particular. The first picket line he had ever stood on was outside the News International building in Kinning Park. His own family had been treated despicably by *The Scottish Sun*, at a time when his brother lay fatally injured and his father was critically ill. 'It might surprise you that a guy like me, with my accent and my background never reads your newspaper – or any other tabloid for that matter. I only read serious newspapers.' He wasn't interested in helping the *News of the World* – only in exposing Tommy to clear the names of his friends and comrades who had been falsely branded as liars, plotters and perjurers. If he released the tape, the truth would be out. But who would be the main beneficiary? The newspaper that he despised. George knew that Bob Bird wanted this badly. His bosses would have to pay a heavy price.

'How much, George? Just give me a figure and we'll start talking,' said the editor.

George didn't beat about the bush. 'I'm looking for poetic justice. The same as Sheridan got from you.'

'You mean two hundred grand?!'

'That's exactly what I mean. Plus fifty grand for the local comminity centre. That is two hundred and fifty thousand pounds.'

There was a sharp intake of breath from the editor, while George turned up the heat. 'This is the only copy of this tape in existence. If you go through to the kitchen, you'll see a bucket of acid just by the sink. If you're not interested, then fair enough – I'll just put the tape of bucket and we'll forget all about it.'

'Leave it with me and I promise we'll be able to reach some agreement.' Bob Bird was convinced the tape was genuine but every newspaper editor lived in perpetual dread of falling prey to an elaborate sting.

In the 1980s, two of Europe's most prestigious publications had been humiliated in the Hitler diaries hoax. The German magazine, *Stern*, had paid $5 million for what it believed was the newly-discovered sixty-volume compilation of the Führer's innermost thoughts before and during World War Two. *The Sunday Times* had coughed up a further $400,000 for the English-language rights. Only after publication had the calamitous truth been exposed.

Naturally, the *News of the World*'s top executives in London were sceptical. Among them was Andy Coulson, then the paper's UK editor and now David Cameron's right-hand man. It all sounded too good to be true. One of Tommy's best men at his wedding had been a key witness in the defamation case and now, lo and behold, another best man had appeared from nowhere brandishing a taped confession. They would have to verify this tape. But there was a problem. No way was George McNeilage going to hand over the original tape to the *News of the World*. If the newspaper was nervous that this might be a set-up, George was even more suspicious of the *News of the World*. He knew he was dealing with some of the most devious operators in the world, with generations of expertise in skulduggery. Just a few weeks earlier, some of the newspaper's journalists had even been caught hacking into the voicemail messages of members of the royal household.

As a precaution, George contacted his lawyer. In the meantime, he made a copy of the tape for the *News of the World* and kept the original locked away in a safe in his lawyer's office. Andy Coulson and other senior executives of the newspaper travelled up to Glasgow to view the copy of the tape, inside the Kinning Park HQ of News International in Scotland. It certainly sounded authentic but, before a penny could be handed over, the original tape would need to be analysed and verified by audio and voice-recognition experts.

George's lawyer then travelled to York with the original tape. There he would meet representatives of the newspaper and draw up a contract. Together, they would then take the tape to the laboratory of Peter French, the President of the International Association for Forensic Phonetics and Acoustics, where it would be analysed. Professor French had been an independent witness during the war crimes trial of Serb leader Slobodan Milosevic. He had also worked for the defence team of Maxine Carr during the Soham murder trial, and of Colm Murphy, a suspect in the Omagh bombing. He had even given evidence authenticating the voice of Prince Harry when the third in line to the throne was accused of cheating in his A-level Art exam.

In York, the recording was transferred onto a computer hard drive and then sent electronically to another two experts for additional corroboration. One of these was Dr Dominic Watt, the Director of the Phonetics Laboratory at the University of Aberdeen, whose team specialise in analysing the entire range of Scottish dialects. The other was Tom Owen in New Jersey – one of just eight voice analysts in the US who is certified by the American Board of Recorded Evidence. Owen has worked for NBC, CBS, CNN, Chinese Television and a host of other international media organisations. In April 2003, he had authenticated the voice of Osama Bin Laden on the infamous videotape released by al-Qaeda.

The science of voice recognition is highly sophisticated. It involves microscopic analysis of pitch, intensity, frequency, pronunciation, stress, intonation, pacing, rhythm, and vocal vibrations. These are visually imaged on a machine called a spectrograph. The most common problem with voice analysis is obtaining an authentic recording of the voice that requires to be identified. In Tommy's case, however, there was a mass of recorded material already in the public domain. All of the experts confirmed that this was most definitely the voice of Thomas Sheridan MSP.

The newspaper editor and the community activist had two further meetings – in Bellahouston Park, Glasgow, and in the car park of a B&Q store off the M77 motorway. Two sets of lawyers were brought in for the final negotiations. Finally, the deal was done.

On 1 October 2006, almost two months after George McNeilage had first made contact with Bob Bird, the paper broke the story. This sensational new twist in the Tommy Sheridan soap opera was plastered across the front page, not just in Scotland but also across its UK editions. Inside, it printed page upon page of transcripts from the recordings. It was the media scoop of the year.

It was also legal and political dynamite. Here was Tommy Sheridan, from his own lips, blowing apart the foundations of his entire defamation case. His courtroom version of the November the 9th 2004 SSP executive meeting now stood exposed as a fraud.

> They want me to come to that meeting that night to explain myself and this is where I make the big mistake. A fucking huge mistake. Humungous fucking mistake. I go to the meeting. There's 19 people round a fucking circle, sitting on desks, sitting on chairs. The atmosphere you could have cut it with a fucking knife, man. I then make the biggest mistake of my life by confessing something in front of 19 fuckers . . . what am I doing confessing in front of these c★★ts?

Tommy then talks to George of his on-off fling with Anvar Khan. Already eighteen months in advance of the case, he is calculating how to dupe a future jury.

> In 1992 me and Billy were shagging her. Which in certain respects is my saving grace because if there's any story about what she knows about my personal habits, or if she knows I've got a hairy back or a hairy arse, of course she does because she fucking shagged me and I've admitted that. That's out in the open. That's a matter of public record.

He recounts his initial conversations with Keith Baldassara and me back in 2002 about the Cupids allegation.

> Right, obviously you've got a situation where, ehm, I was upset with Keith a couple of years ago because he told Alan about me going down to Manchester in 2002. And Alan pulled me up about it. And I said to him: 'Look, stupid, shouldnae have done it. Done it once before in '96 and went back in 2002. And cheap thrill, but it's been done and that's it. At the time it was a great idea. But I'm confident nothing will come back out of it.'

He then describes the late-night phone conversation between the two of us on the night the story broke in the *News of the World*:

Alan comes on the phone, saying: 'Is this you?' I said, 'Of course it is. I'll speak to you tomorrow.' So I meet with Keith and Alan in the City Chambers and Alan says to me, 'Listen, I've had a long think about this and I think you should own up.' I says, 'Well, wait a wee minute, Alan – first of all I'm no' even fucking accused of anything. Is this no' a wee bit harsh here?' The point is, Alan's suggestion to me is: 'Just own up, people will forgive a sexual liaison, but they'll no' forgive a liar.'

He then tells George:

So I say to Alan and Keith that what I want to do is to face it down. I think they've got fuck all on me. I think if they had anything on me they'd have used it long before now. George, I've put my hand up and said 'mistake', I've put my hand up and said 'recklessness', I've put my hand up and said 'you know, in the balance of things, I've made a mistake', right? I ask Alan and Keith to give me the opportunity to see it down and I say to them, 'I guarantee you if I am presented with incontrovertible evidence – videotapes, CCTV, something of that character – I'll put my hand up and say I'm sorry . . . and I'll walk away.'

The newspaper printed only part of the full transcript. The rest was held back until the following week, when Part 2 would appear. But already Part 1 had blown apart his testimony in court.

To pre-empt claims that the tape was a forgery, the newspaper printed a hotline number which readers could call to hear some extracts from the tape. The lines were jammed as tens of thousands of callers checked out the recording for themselves. For the next two days, extracts were played repeatedly on TV and radio news bulletins right across the UK. The voice on the other end of the line was one of the most instantly recognisable in Scotland. 'If that's not Tommy Sheridan, Rory Bremner's out of a job tomorrow morning,' I told one newspaper.

Naturally, the appearance of the tape caused some consternation in SSP circles. Most people could easily understand why George had brought the tape out into the public domain. If he had failed to use this evidence to expose the truth, he would have been complicit in a gross injustice. But some people were shocked that he had sold the tape to the *News of the World*. If the tape had been passed over to the SSP, we'd have probably booked the Glasgow Film Theatre and invited the whole of the media along to a special showing. George's defence was that the tape would instantly save the *News of the World* its £200,000 pay-off to Tommy and the legal costs of fighting the case. He had put himself and his family in the firing line to bring out the truth and was now seeking to extract as much compensation as possible. His attitude was: 'Why should I bail them out for free?' At the time, George also felt he couldn't trust the other main newspapers in Scotland. Tommy was a close friend of the editor of the *Scottish Mirror*, while the *Daily Record* and *Sunday Mail* had forked out £20,000 for Tommy's exclusive inside fairy tale. Since his court victory, the bulk of the Scottish media seemed to have fallen under Tommy's spell.

The reaction of most of us directly in the firing line was straight-forward relief. Our backs were to the wall. Almost every newspaper in the land was accusing us of trying to frame up Scotland's most popular political leader. In the eyes of the media and most of the general public, Tommy had successfully fought off a gang of good-for-nothing perjurers and forgers. Our reputations were in shreds. A full-scale police investigation was now underway and it felt like we were the chief suspects. Now, suddenly, everything had changed. This was surely the smoking gun that would clear our names. Of course, we'd rather the evidence had been brought out in the pages of the *Scottish Socialist Voice*, the *Morning Star* or the *Guardian*. But, when you're trapped in a building, you don't demand that your rescuer produces a Fire Brigades Union membership card.

Rumours raced around Scotland about the amount that George had received, fuelled by his enigmatic reference during a TV news inter-view to having received 'an ironic sum' from the newspaper. Some people guessed it was £30,000 – the figure Tommy was alleged to have received from the *Daily Record*. In fact, the *News of the World* paid George £200,000 for the tape. I personally wasn't going to condemn George for wheeling and dealing with the *News of the World* to get the truth out. But I also knew that any money he received would be coming from a tainted source. If the SSP had asked for a cut, George would have given the lot. By all accounts, he spread plenty of the cash around his local community. But neither the SSP nor any member of the SSP asked for or received a single penny.

Another question that baffled many people was why the tape had ever been made in the first place? Some SSP members – including those who had, by now, turned contemptuous of Tommy – couldn't fathom out why George had secretly recorded a private conversation. Those who had split from the SSP suggested that elements within the leadership had been involved in making the tape. The accusation was false. George had acted entirely on his own.

George insists that he hadn't made the tape with the intention of stitching Tommy up. He knew, more than anyone, about the real Tommy Sheridan and his murky secret life. But he had become increasingly distrustful of Tommy. Tensions had begun to surface as far back as 2001. In the first half of that year, there had been a spate of murders in the Pollok area. Most of the action revolved around a feud between two families. But then, in an unrelated incident, a young man was stabbed to death while walking home in the early hours of the morning. The local community had called a public meeting to get something done. Tommy – as an MSP, a local celebrity, and the councillor for the adjacent ward – was invited to speak at the 250-strong meeting, along with the local MP, the priest and local housing officials. He thundered his condemnation of the tragedy at full volume. But the mood of the meeting, just two days after the murders, was sombre. Tommy, apparently desperate to provoke a response, announced that it was time to 'name names'. He then identified a family who had neither been involved in the feud nor in the murder. Keith Baldassara and George McNeilage held their heads in their hands while Tommy ranted. This was tantamount to making a false public accusation. Unlike Tommy, who had moved out to a plush villa in the rather more upmarket Cardonald area, they lived in the scheme and knew they would have to mop up the mess. And these people were serious heavyweight gangsters. You don't declare war on them spontaneously at a public meeting without first consulting your people on the ground and taking all the necessary precautions.

Inevitably, there were recriminations. Tommy was denounced as a 'grass' by members and associates of the family he had named. Death threats were issued. Now that Tommy had created a problem, Keith and George wanted to tackle it head on by organising public meetings and mobilising the local community but Tommy had run for cover. From then on, he stayed well clear of Pollok.

Within five years, the two most prominent members of the family Tommy had named were dead. The danger had subsided but Tommy's reckless populism and subsequent cowardice had shaken the confidence of some of his two close friends. Their unease was to grow over the next few years, as Tommy distanced himself from his roots in the housing scheme and began to embed himself in Scotland's celebrity circuit. Keith Baldassara covered almost all his local surgeries. He repeatedly failed to attend the annual North Pollok Gala Day, an event organised by SSP members and the local community council and attended by thousands. On one occasion, he opted instead to play a charity football match for the celebrity team Dukla

Pumpherston FC, where he knew he'd be rubbing shoulders with showbiz stars, professional footballers and media people.

Then, in October 2004, Tommy returned from a visit to London and began to put pressure on George to organise a local march in Pollok in support of the Justice for Gordon Gentle campaign, Gentle being a local soldier killed in Iraq. He insisted that it should take place within the next fortnight, specifically on 30 October. George felt the whole event was being rushed and couldn't quite understand why. Nonetheless, he sorted out the leaflets, the placards, the publicity, the speakers and everything else. Tommy's behaviour had been strange and slightly suspicious. Even though he was desperate that the event went ahead on that date, Tommy played no part in its organisation, turning up only to speak and be quoted in the media.

That night, the Cupids story broke. George began to wonder if there was any connection between the two events. Had Tommy been using the Gordon Gentle campaign as publicity to deflect attention away from the *News of the World* article? And had he been cynically using the campaign to bring the large Socialist Workers faction onside? In the past, the group had been critical of Tommy for, as they put it, concentrating too much on bread-and-butter issues, rather than focusing single-mindedly on the Iraq war. All of these undercurrents were preying on George's mind when he met Tommy in his front room one week after the November the 9th SSP executive meeting. He wanted to be crystal clear about the dispute. He had already heard Keith's account and now he wanted to listen to Tommy's version of events and be able to scrutinise it.

He had intended to show the tape to some of the local activists in Pollok that Tommy had refused to meet. People like Tam Dymond, Colin McGregor, James McGregor, Brian Kidd and John Auld had always been there, through the good times and the bad times, since the 1980s and George felt they should be given an opportunity to hear what Tommy had to say. In the event, he only showed the tape to Willie Moore, a veteran trade union and community activist who at the time was helping George to decorate his house.

The content of the discussion had, in George's own words, 'broken [his] heart'. He quietly decided to store the tape away. It wasn't pretty but that's the way things were at that stage between the two old friends.

The tape lay undisturbed for the best part of two years. George had never really expected Tommy to go to court. Like most people, he had dismissed Tommy's repeated bluster about 'seeing the *News of the World* in court' as sabre-rattling. Even when the court case got underway, he hadn't quite known where it was all going. But, as the epic legal drama rolled on, it dawned on George that Tommy was prepared to smash all obstacles that stood in his road to victory, including the party that had united the socialist Left in Scotland. George decided to act. He dug out the tape and worked out his plan.

Two days after its release, Tommy came out fighting. He told a rally to launch his new Solidarity Party in Dundee, 'Just as Freddie Starr did not eat his hamster, this video has been concocted. The *News of the World* have produced a dodgy video from a dodgy geezer to tell lies against me.' The dodgy geezer, of course, was George McNeilage who had never hidden his criminal past, which he had put behind him decades earlier. Scotland's political journalists had turned out in force to the rally in the Queen's Hotel's Claverhouse Suite, named after the 17th-century royalist general who had crushed the rebellious Cove-nanters. Even Tommy's friends in the media were startled when he went on to allege that a range of 'sinister forces', including MI5, the CIA and Rupert Murdoch, were out to get him. 'When this history of this story is written, I think you'll find MI5 were certainly involved.'

He couldn't dispute that the voice on the tape was his. Instead, he claimed the tape was a 'concoction', created by 'splicing' extracts from his own voice with other voices.

> Sometimes you think that maybe sounds like me, and then you listen to the tape for a continuous period of six to eight minutes and you can now hear what sounds like water running, you can hear what's in the background and it becomes clear that what's happened is that someone else's voice has been used.

Tommy had listened to the *News of the World*'s copy of the recording, which did include some background interference. But what he didn't know was that George had recorded the conversation straight on to a digital master tape, which could not be altered without leaving forensic data behind.

Tommy suggested that the experts who had authenticated the tape were also involved in the grand conspiracy. The American voice recognition specialist was, he claimed, 'a friend of George Bush, a friend of the CIA'. This was dutifully repeated by others. But it wasn't true. The voice expert, far from being a friend of George Bush, had actually been hired by the *New York Times* in 2005 to authenticate a tape of the Republican President confessing that he had used mar-ijuana – a pretty damaging disclosure for the man whose political base was redneck, Bible-Belt America.

In the same diatribe, Tommy stated, without any foundation, 'Rupert Murdoch has said that he wants me, the two-bit Commie bastard, destroyed.' Nowhere was there any record of Rupert Murdoch making such a comment. Before the court case, Tommy Sheridan's name would never have appeared on the radar of the man who owned a global corporation of many hundreds of newspapers, magazines, TV channels, film studios and Internet companies across five continents. The £200,000 damages Tommy had been awarded in court amounted to around one hour's revenue for the media empire that owned the *News of the World*.

Tommy's claim that he had been singled out for special attention by Rupert Murdoch, backed by hints that George Bush himself may even have had a hand in it, was inspired not just by personal grandiosity. In that time of deep crisis, he knew he had to keep his own support base on board. You either believe me, was his message, or you're on the side of these people.

It was Little Red Riding Hood versus the Big Bad Wolf. But Tommy calculated – rightly, as it happened – that there would always be some people around ready to devour such simplistic fairy tales.

24

October 2006–May 2007

Enter the Police

The day after the videotape bombshell exploded, Lothian and Borders Police announced they would be launching a criminal investigation into whether perjury had been committed. Although the tape would become a key piece of evidence, the timing of the announcement was purely coincidental.

Back in mid August, the Crown Office – Scotland's national prosecution service – had instructed the local procurator fiscal in Edinburgh to scrutinise the circumstances surrounding the defamation case. For six weeks, Lesley Thomson, Edinburgh's chief procurator fiscal, had been poring over the court transcripts. She and her team had now concluded there was sufficient evidence to order a full-scale investigation.

At that stage, no one was quite clear who was being targeted as the chief suspects. In the weeks following the verdict, Tommy continued to point his finger accusingly at those who had challenged his version of events in court. Beyond the narrow circles of those who had been close to the trial, few people doubted the word of the smooth-talking media celebrity. The verdict of the jury had exposed the ragbag of backstabbing politicians, gold-diggers and damaged women who had testified against him as liars. That's how it looked from the outside. But cracks had begun to appear. For a start, the *News of the World* wasn't accepting the verdict. On the Sunday, the paper's UK-wide edition splashed its defiance of the jury's decision across its front page and printed a special eight-page pull-out on the trial, repeating the allegations which had landed it in court in the first place – and firing in a few extra for good measure. The headline above the editorial comment scarcely needed further elaboration: 'SEE YOU IN COURT AGAIN, TOMMY'. This wasn't the way newspapers were supposed to behave after losing a £200,000 libel action.

Barbara Scott, the SSP minutes secretary, was also on a mission. The trial had shattered her reputation. A month before, she had been a hard-working parliamentary secretary, respected for her efficiency and integrity. Now she was a suspected perjurer and forger. One way of clearing her name would be to track down the original handwritten notes of the November the 9th 2004 SSP executive meeting. Forensic analysis would prove the notes had been written some time ago – certainly long before the court case. They would also reveal more detail about what had been said at that now infamous meeting.

When she found the notes, she phoned a couple of SSP members to sound them out about how she should proceed. She photocopied the sheaf of notes and tipped off the *Herald* journalist, Tom Gordon. On Monday morning, she marched into the headquarters of Lothian and Borders Police to hand over this new piece of evidence. She told the journalist, 'I need to clear my name. I did not commit perjury and neither did the ten other SSP witnesses who told the truth, the whole truth and nothing but the truth.' The paper carried extracts from her notes, which included her spontaneous written exchange with Catriona, scribbled in the margins.

The following week, a group of six activists in Glasgow wrote a letter to the *Scottish Socialist Voice* stating that Tommy had admitted personally to each of them that he had visited Cupids with Anvar Khan. He also confirmed to these six people that he had indeed owned up to the visit at the November the 9th SSP executive meeting. These were not political novices but longstanding activists with more than a century of combined socialist struggle between them. Davy Archibald, Nicky McKerrell, Charlie McCarthy, Liam Young, Jim McVicar and Steve Hudson had all been involved in politics since the 1980s and four of them had been close friends of Tommy from long before the anti-Poll Tax campaign.

Tommy had met each of them separately in a series of meetings in a pub near Glasgow City Chambers on the eve of the SSP conference in February 2005. He had arranged the discussions to try to convince each of them to vote for Colin Fox instead of me as SSP convenor at that weekend's SSP conference in Perth. Tommy had held up his hands to the Cupids allegation, which was already well known in the SSP, and then insisted there was no 'silver bullet'. For that reason, he said the SSP executive had been wrong to force his resignation and, because I had been the ringleader, he advised them that they should vote for Colin.

Eighteen months later, after reading Tommy's 'scabs' rant in the *Daily Record*, the six met together and agreed that it was now time to put that information into the public domain. 'We cannot stand by and watch this grotesque, Orwellian situation continue,' they wrote. They urged Tommy to 'publicly retract the accusations he had made against the honest decent men and women he has slandered'. It was like urging Lady Thatcher to offer a public apology for the miners' strike, but for those of us who stood accused of perjury, plotting and perverting the justice, it was a welcome challenge to the widely accepted Hans Christian Andersen version of events.

Some newspapers, such as *The Observer*, the *Sunday Herald, Scotland on Sunday* and the *Sun*, ran the story but, after Tommy's defamation victory, many editors and media lawyers were terrified to touch it. The same editors and lawyers, however, were less hesitant to print hostile articles about those who had told the truth. The attitude of much of the media was summed up by Alistair Bonnington, the secretary of the Scottish Media Lawyers Society and the principal solicitor for BBC Scotland. In a Sunday newspaper two days after the verdict, he dismissed those who had given evidence refuting Tommy's version of events as a 'very unimpressive' parade of witnesses – 'prostitutes and ex-prostitutes and people who wanted money for their stories'. It was breathtakingly shallow. Eighteen witnesses unconnected to the *News of the World* had contradicted Tommy's evidence. None was a prostitute. One had been involved in prostitution many years before. Three had been paid for their original stories. Fifteen had neither received nor asked for payment.

Back in August, Lord Turnbull had explicitly stated in his closing remarks to the defamation jury: 'It seems to me pretty much inevitable there will have to be a criminal inquiry into the question of whether witnesses have committed perjury.' And it was Lord Turnbull who set the ball rolling – the judge whom Tommy had praised fulsomely for his 'fairness', his 'wisdom' and his 'lack of pomposity.'

The week after the verdict, the judge had ordered the Crown Office to begin an investigation into perjury. From that point onwards, the momentum was unstoppable. Neither the Crown Office nor the Area Procurator Fiscal for Edinburgh had any choice in the matter. They were legally obliged to examine the evidence and then bring in the police if they suspected a crime had been committed.

At the time the inquiry was announced, we expected it would all be wrapped up within six months – with any luck just in time for the 2007 Scottish elections. We were confident that the SSP would be vindicated and that we could then start to rebuild the party into a serious political force again. At the very least, we hoped to maintain a foothold of sorts in Holyrood after May 2007. But the police investigation turned into an epic. It wasn't so much an episode of Taggart, as the full seventeen-volume chronicles of Inspector Rebus. Murders were committed, investigated, solved and prosecuted while this inquiry trundled along with no apparent end in sight. After a while, it began to feel like the hunt for Osama Bin Laden.

Over the next two years, the investigation would cost up to £2 million and consume 40,000 hours of police time. It would stretch from Aberdeen to the Channel Islands, from Manchester to Copenhagen, from Birmingham to Florida. Along the way, the CID visited Cupids – fully dressed – the Moat House Hotel, the Treetops Hotel and other venues where Tommy's trysts had taken place. Hundreds of witnesses were interviewed, including business-men, politicians, actors, journalists, footballers, swingers, political activists, lawyers, hotel managers and underworld gangsters, some for days at a time. During the investigation, Lothian and Borders Police began to take some flak. They were accused of engaging in a personal vendetta against Tommy, wasting public money on a wild goose chase and deliberately prolonging the investigation out of malice. The claim was absurd.

Tommy had always taken time to cultivate good relations with the police at every level, from the friendly neighbourhood cop right up to the top brass. Even when he was being arrested on breach of the peace offences at Faslane and the like, he would indulge in friendly banter with the officers. He had even addressed the Scottish Police Federa-tion conference and was presented with a set of mounted and inscribed handcuffs that he displayed on the walls of his home. It would be fair to say that Tommy Sheridan had been held in relatively high esteem by many Scottish police officers. In the early days of the investigation, he retained that positive attitude, possibly believing that his charm could win them over.

Initial contact between Lothian and Borders CID and the SSP was strained. At the start of the investigation, the officers involved in the case were clearly treating the SSP witnesses as potential suspects. Only gradually did their attitude alter. Every day, they were learning a little bit more about the real Tommy Sheridan. Eventually, the CID officers let it be known that they no longer considered us suspects but victims.

There was a good reason for this investigation dragging on for weeks, then months, then years. This was no run-of-the mill crime of dishonesty. The police were dealing here with a master weaver who had spun an incredibly complex labyrinth of lies and deception, aided and abetted – in some cases wittingly, in other cases unwittingly – by a phalanx of helpers.

Just a month after the launch of the police investigation, Tommy acquired a new part-time job as a presenter with a local Edinburgh

radio station, Talk 107. He had been hired by his old friend, the station's programme director, Mike Graham, who had previously been editor of the *Scottish Daily Mirror*. Tommy was given the Sunday morning slot, from 10 a.m. to 1 p.m., to present his phone-in show *Sunday Morning with Citizen Tommy*. I never actually heard the programme but politically impartial listeners and reviewers generally found Tommy to be laborious, dull and repetitive. His formidable skills, both as an orator and a media spokesperson, couldn't quite translate to the more conversational medium of talk radio. The most entertaining part of the show, by all accounts, was the theme tune 'I Wanna Be Like You' and its opening line . . . 'Now I'm the King of the Swingers'.

Tommy did use his programme effectively, however, to build up his portfolio of celebrity friends and to provide a platform for his political allies. His guests even included, on separate mornings, Donald Findlay and Paul Ferris. Findlay had been Ferris's QC during a famous gangland murder trial in the 1990s and unexpectedly pulled off a not proven verdict. In the future, the eccentric and colourful Tory unionist would offer to defend Tommy free of charge.

In the early part of 2007, while the police investigation rumbled on in the shadowlands, we trudged nervously towards the Holyrood elections. After the initial crisis in late 2004, the SSP had taken a political battering. Then we had begun to recover. The annual conference in February 2005 had been the biggest in the party's history. By the spring of 2006, we had made a full recovery in the opinion polls. The SSP was back on track and could realistically expect to hold on to at least some of our MSPs. But over the summer of 2006, the party had been ravaged. Where there was once a single party of the Left, we now had two bitter rivals fighting for the same space. The number of socialist activists in Scotland had tumbled like the stock exchange in a slump. And the 150,000 people who had voted socialist just three years before were now deserting the cause like civilians fleeing a war zone.

On the road to May 2007, we were distracted along the way by some strange diversions. In late March, Tommy announced that a listening device had been found in his car – apparently buried deep in the back seat, under a foam covering. The Honda Civic had been in the car park in the basement of the Scottish Parliament when the equipment was discovered, late on a Thursday afternoon, just as MSPs were heading home at the close of the week's parliamentary business. Over the next few days, Lothian and Borders Police swept Tommy's home and his Holyrood and Glasgow offices, in case they too were bugged. Naturally, the Holyrood media pack was excited by this latest bizarre twist in the Sheridan saga. Could this be the CID, the *News of the World*, the SSP or even the shadowy secret intelligence services that Tommy had alluded to following the release of the videotape? What kind of device was it exactly? And who had found it? None of these questions was ever clearly answered.

The press reported that a member of Tommy's staff had 'stumbled across' the device – presumably while they were looking for sweeties down the back of the rear seat. By the following day, the tale had grown legs. Tommy told journalists he had been alerted to the possibility his car was bugged by an anonymous letter sent to his office in Holyrood. 'So we felt it was important enough to get it checked. I contacted a security analyst and I contacted the police. Both of them searched the vehicle and found a device.' Lothian and Borders Police, however, presented a slightly different sequence of events, insisting that the device had already been discovered before they were contacted.

The press and TV also reported – based on information supplied by Tommy or an associate – that the device was capable of transmitting audio and pictures and had been able to track the location of the vehicle. The letter – which was passed on to Lothian and Borders Police for forensic and DNA tests – had, according to Tommy, included details of trips that his car had made. The author of the letter was not sympathetic to his politics and had called him 'a conceited self-publicist' but had wanted to warn him his movements were being tracked. 'It was not day-by-day accounts,' Tommy told *The Sunday Times*, which he seemed to have forgotten was the flagship paper of the hated Murdoch empire.

> But it did indicate that I had been in a place a number of times when in actual fact I had not been in that place but my car had. Someone had a loan of my car and spent a couple of weekends at a place, but this information suggested that a different line of inquiry was being followed, that I might be having an affair with someone in this place.

Tommy's assistant, Hugh Kerr, added a little bit more detail to this rather vague story. The letter writer, he explained, had suggested that a newspaper was going to run a story about Tommy having an affair with a woman in Oban. Tommy's brother-in-law, Andy McFarlane, of Moat House and Cupids fame, had apparently borrowed the Honda and driven it to Oban.

A few days later, Tommy was at the centre of another security alert when he told journalists that someone had warned him that 'hostile forces' had been intercepting his mobile phone calls and messages. The clear implication was that the *News of the World* was involved. He told the *Mirror*, 'Everybody in Scotland knows I have been involved in a major battle with News International. I would not be surprised if they are brought into it, given their record of bugging people in the past.' This was a reference to the recent jailing of the *News of the World*'s royal correspondent for illicitly accessing voicemail messages of members of the royal household.

Later, in 2009, *The Guardian* would reveal that private investigators, working on behalf the *News of the World*, had attempted to intercept the voicemail messages of a number of celebrities and public figures around that time. Why wouldn't they have tried to plant a listening device in Tommy Sheridan's car in 2007? Actually, for a number of reasons. For one thing, Tommy's device was discovered *after* the royal scandal, which had forced the resignation of the UK editor of the paper, Andy Coulson. Secondly, *The Guardian* investigation suggested that the *News of the World*'s surveillance operation had been limited to attempts to access private voicemail messages – a simple procedure that involves making a speculative telephone call and entering the network provider's default pin code. But most important of all, the Scottish *News of the World* was cooperating closely with Lothian and Borders CID over the perjury investigation and was also involved in preparing its own legal appeal against the verdict. To carry out a criminal bugging operation in the Lothian and Borders police area against an elected MSP who had just defeated them in a court case would have been ridiculously stupid.

Lothian and Borders CID officers were privately sceptical of the whole story. The device they had been handed was a primitive piece of equipment with all the hi-tech sophistication of a wind-up alarm clock. It had no tracking capabilities and was about as powerful as a home baby alarm. One CID officer, referring to the recent poisoning of the Russian journalist Alexander Litvinenko, commented privately: 'The Russian Secret Service fly across Europe and inject their enemies with polonium. Rupert Murdoch plants a listening device that cost twenty quid from Argos with a range no further than the bottom of your garden.' During the investigation, one SSP witness asked a Lothian CID officer if he had any idea who had been behind those fake minutes which had been sent to the *News of the World* accompanied by an anonymous letter. 'The same person who bugged Sheridan's car,' he replied.

The bugging incident prompted the former leader of Strathclyde

Regional Council to write to the press recalling an incident during an anti-Poll Tax protest many years before at the council's HQ. Tommy had arranged with an independent radio producer to wear a hidden microphone while he negotiated with the council leader. In mid conversation, according to Charles Gray, 'a wee black microphone' popped out of Tommy's shirt. At the time, the press had denounced him for his deceit and stupidity.

A month after Hondagate, Solidarity's Holyrood election broadcast was screened. For five minutes, Tommy was shown driving his car through the streets while engaging in a taxi-driver style rant against poverty, inequality and war. The message was familiar but the usual polished, eloquent charm had been replaced with hostile belligerence. At the end of the diatribe, Tommy turned to the camera and whispered, 'And by the way . . . Ah don't care who's filming this.'

Election day turned into a catastrophe for the Left. At the time of the split, Tommy and his supporters had claimed that there was 'room for more than one socialist party in Scotland'. In the November issue of the *Scottish Left Review*, one Solidarity official had justified the split on the basis that it 'offered a choice' to voters on the Left. John McAllion, the ex-Labour MP and MSP who had joined the SSP at the end of 2005, had written a counter-article warning that 'progress has been put at risk by the setting up of a rival socialist party that can only divide the Scottish Left and return it to its pre-1999 political impotence and irrelevance'.

Tommy was invited to join the politicians from the big political parties on BBC's TV and radio election night specials. The SSP was ignored. It reflected the widespread expectation that Tommy would be the last man standing on the Left. These programmes start broadcasting just after the polls close, when there is no purpose in spin and politicians can afford to appraise their chances honestly. Tommy oozed confidence, assuring viewers and listeners that he would definitely hold his Glasgow seat. He predicted that Solidarity would become the biggest of the small parties and maybe even win another couple of seats outside Glasgow. He certainly had reasons to be cheerful. During the campaign, Tommy had the benefit of sympathetic coverage from sections of the press, especially around his campaign to ban airguns. In the housing schemes, the use of airguns was becoming a serious nuisance. In the Easterhouse area a few years earlier a toddler had been accidentally killed by the pellet from an airgun and his parents had begun to campaign for a ban on the weapons. Tommy, his populist antenna finely tuned, turned the idea of an airgun ban into Solidarity's flagship policy in the election.

Ironically, most of his Solidarity activists who had been around at the time of the Dunblane massacre had refused to support the Snowdrop petition, which had called for ban on real guns. As editor of the *Scottish Militant* newspaper in 1996, I had written an article calling for a ban on handguns which the CWI leaders in London had refused to print in the UK edition of the paper. Why? Because 'the workers will need arms to fight the revolution'. But, by 2007, groups like the SWP and the CWI would have supported Tommy if he had called for a ban on household cutlery.

Solidarity also had strong support from at least one daily newspaper, the *Scottish Mirror*. Although no longer a columnist, Tommy was close to the paper's political editor Mark Smith, whose partner was a Solidarity candidate on the Lothians regional list. One front-page splash in the newspaper, under the headline 'TOMMY POLL IS SEVEN HEAVEN', predicted that Solidarity was 'on track for a sensational showing according to a new poll . . . his party is tipped to win seven seats – one better than his record high of six with the SSP'. What the article failed to reveal was that the sensational poll had been commissioned personally by Tommy and the questions were heavily loaded. As the old saying goes, 'Ask the right questions and you'll get the right answers.'

Other newspapers were equally helpful. The Saturday before the election, the *Evening Times* ran a double-page soft-focus spread, 'The House of Sheridan', accompanied by full-colour photos of the man himself, his wife, his mother and his sister. Tommy had used his family shamelessly throughout the election. The front cover of the Solidarity manifesto had consisted of a large full-colour photo of Tommy and Gail on a protest march with their two-year-old daughter perched on his shoulders. In the *Evening Times* article, the star-struck journalist described the Sheridans as 'Glasgow's first family of politics' and gushed on for 1,500 toe-curling words about Tommy and his amazing relatives.

Inevitably, the battle between the SSP and Solidarity resulted in mutual annihilation. Where there had been six Scottish Socialist MSPs, there were now four Scottish Socialist ex-MSPs and two Solidarity ex-MSPS. From 130,000 regional votes in 2003 for the SSP, the combined vote for the two parties was now under 45,000. Part of the slump could be accounted for by the surge of the SNP under Alex Salmond, which would have eaten into the socialist vote whatever the circumstances. But, on top of that, tens upon tens of thousands of former SSP voters had delivered their electoral verdict on the court verdict. It was, in the Shakespearian phrase, a plague on both your houses. Of the hard core that stayed on board, a two to one majority were prepared to give Tommy the benefit of the doubt in his dispute with the SSP.

Tommy and Solidarity tried to draw some sustenance from the fact that the breakaway party had polled more than double the vote of the SSP. 'Solidarity has come from nowhere to become the biggest socialist party in Scotland,' proclaimed Scotland's most famous former MSP, over and over and over again. He was like a reckless driver, lying in his hospital bed after a smash, gloating that at least he was less seriously injured than the guy he had crashed into. Over the next few years, even that absurd consolation was gone, as the SSP started to recover while the condition of Solidarity grew increasingly critical. Notwithstanding the bravado, the 2007 Holyrood election was a shattering blow for Tommy Sheridan and Solidarity. At the start of the campaign, the bookies had offered 1/100 on Tommy holding his seat in the Scottish Parliament, which is the kind of odds you might get if you bet on rain falling on Glasgow within the next year. Tommy's failure to get re-elected in his own city was the shock result of the 2007 election.

The morning after polling day, I turned up at STV's sparkling new studios overlooking the Clyde to appear on an election results special in a slot alongside Patrick Harvie of the Greens and Tommy representing Solidarity. We would be interviewed in a tiny studio by the political editor, Bernard Ponsonby – and this would be the first time I had come face to face with Tommy since my appearance in the witness stand at the Court of Session almost a year earlier. But it was no-show from Tommy. The programme's producer, Stephen Townsend, told me that he had pulled out because he would feel uncomfortable in my presence. It was the first time I had ever known him to miss out on a TV appearance.

It was the end of an era. Tommy had been an elected full-time politician since that day back in 1992 when he had been released from Saughton Prison and carried triumphantly into Glasgow City Chambers. Now he was a political reject, deserted by his own people, in his own city. To paraphrase the poet Hugh MacDiarmid, he had soared like a rocket – then come down like a stick.

Mid–Late 2007

'You're under arrest.'

Back in the summer of 2006, just after the defamation verdict, the Scottish Socialist Party offices in Glasgow received an unusual request.

A woman with a cut-glass English accent had phoned up, looking for Tommy Sheridan. She explained that she wanted to invite him to 'Lunch With The Hamiltons'. This rather formal request, it transpired, was a reference to the show she and her husband were about to stage at the Edinburgh Festival Fringe. The caller's name was Christine; her husband's name was Neil.

Though from the opposite end of the political spectrum, Neil Hamilton had much in common with Tommy. In the 1980s, he had successfully sued the BBC over a Panorama programme, *Maggie's Militant Tendency*, which alleged that he and another Tory MP had links with the European neo-fascist Right. In the 1990s, he launched a further libel case, against *The Guardian*, after it accused him of corruption in the infamous cash-for-questions scandal. But this time he backed down on the eve of the trial – though he continued to protest his innocence. The voters refused to believe him and, in the 1997 general election, he was defeated by the former BBC journalist and anti-sleaze candidate, Martin Bell.

Like Tommy, Neil Hamilton was irrepressible – and addicted to the limelight. Just a week after losing his Westminster seat, he appeared with his wife, Christine, on the satirical current affairs quiz, *Have I Got News for You*. The sleaze allegations had boosted his fame; at the end of show, he was presented with his 'fee' in a brown envelope. The couple went on to appear in a string of TV game shows, including *The Weakest Link*, *Who Wants To Be A Millionaire?* and a celebrity edition of *Mastermind*. By 2006, they were showbiz veterans and launched their own comedy show at the Edinburgh Festival Fringe.

Exactly a year later, Tommy launched his own comedy career at the 2007 Fringe. Regular performers must have been green with envy at the advance publicity for this new kid on the comedy circuit. In the greatest arts and comedy festival in the world, based on the volume of advance media coverage, *The Tommy Sheridan Chat Show* was one of the biggest events in town. As the curtain opened in the Gilded Balloon theatre, the sound system blasted out his radio theme tune. The King of the Swingers himself sat on a throne, centre stage. 'Ladies and Gentlemen, put your keys in the ashtray . . .' Anyone expecting cutting-edge political satire would be leaving disappointed. The *Tommy Sheridan Chat Show* was more Bernard Manning than Mark Steel. 'The women in Edinburgh are very posh. You don't get crabs, you get lobsters. You don't get the clap, you get applause!' On the Glasgow airport bombing he asked, 'What about the suicide bombers' heavenly reward – but where would they find twenty-one virgins in Glasgow?' The comic Tam Cowan allegedly provided Tommy with the gags. Presumably he kept the best ones for himself.

'Lame jokes about blondes and Catholic priests delivered with all the panache of a man with 20 years experience in hectoring political oratory . . . on this evidence, Sheridan's next brush with the law may be for crimes against entertainment,' was the verdict of *The Guardian*. 'Truly horrible . . . the stuff people dream about in the moments before they wake up screaming uncontrollably. Nothing Sheridan says is funny, but it's funny he's saying it . . . a sad spectacle,' said *The Sunday Times*. 'Awkward and irrelevant,' said the *Sunday Herald*. 'Plodding . . . his interview technique consists almost exclusively of howling with desperately forced laughter while thumping the arm-rest of his throne,' said *The Times*. 'Oh dear. This Festival show was bland at best, embarrassing at worst,' said *Scotland on Sunday*. Unfazed, Tommy earnestly told journalists that his promoter expected the show to go on tour and maybe even on to TV.

By this time, the police inquiry was in full swing, so to speak. In May, Lothian CID officers had travelled to Manchester and a senior police source close to the investigation told the *Sunday Mail*:

> There are witnesses – staff and patrons – who claim to have seen Mr Sheridan in Cupids. They are people who have never been contacted in relation to this. They were not called as witnesses in the defamation trial – they were not even spoken to as both legal teams prepared their case.'

One member of staff at Cupids told the newspaper, 'To be honest, we've had it up to here with Tommy Sheridan. This club survived for 10 years because of discretion but all that is gone and it's really hurting us.' These were strange days indeed, when the once squeaky-clean politician was under fire for damaging the reputation of a sleazy backstreet sex club.

According to a report in the *Sunday Herald* the following week – again from inside the investigation – Cupids staff and management had told CID officers they had been offered cash bribes in exchange for refusing to cooperate with the investigation. The police apparently knew the identity of the 'third party' who had approached the staff with the offer they could, and did, refuse.

Lothian detectives confronted Matt McColl – the alleged organiser of the Moat House Hotel stag night – with receipts from the hotel for the night of 14 June 2002 and with airline tickets for a flight he had booked from Birmingham to Glasgow. The CID also obtained his phone records, then systematically tracked down and interviewed everyone whose number had registered on his mobile phone bills around mid-2002. Police also pored through Gail Sheridan's phone records for the same night – the eve of her sister's wedding – and traced people she had called. She had phoned her husband's number repeatedly and then phoned round others trying to find out his whereabouts. The evidence now being uncovered by the CID starkly contradicted the alibi Gail had provided during the defamation trial, when she claimed she had been with him all through that evening and night.

People who had not given evidence in the original trial were tracked down and interviewed. Martin McCardie, who had written quite a few *Taggart* scripts, found himself caught up in a real-life criminal investigation, though fortunately there were no 'deid boadies'. Martin was grilled about the motion that he had confessed to writing for his local Cardonald SSP branch in the run-up to the defamation case, which had called for the destruction of the November the 9th 2004 meeting minutes.

The investigation extended deep into England. Police traced Duncan Rowan, who had disappeared after his unfortunate tangle with the *News of the World*, to a coastal town in the south of England. Another witness, who had been in the Moat House Hotel suite with Tommy and the others, was interviewed on the island of Jersey. Lothian CID also tracked down a woman in Birmingham, who admitted she had been present that night in the Moat House Hotel. They interviewed the ex-gunman John Lynn and the ex-Garda officer Dennis Reilly about their conversation with Helen Allison in a Lanarkshire hotel bar during the defamation trial. They travelled to Copenhagen to speak to Katrine Trolle.

The SSP element of the police investigation was straightforward enough. They focused mainly on the meetings that had taken place in late 2004. Our computer hard drives were removed in order that key documents, such as the minutes, could be forensically analysed. If it could be proven that the disputed minutes – the 'dodgy document', as Tommy had repeatedly described it in court – had been typed up in November 2004, as Allan Green and Barbara Scott had testified, then it would corroborate our evidence. Scores of SSP members were interviewed – some of us twice over. My first interview stretched over three days although this length of time is deceptive. While an interview with a journalist is conducted at normal talking speed, with the conversation recorded either on tape or taken down in shorthand, these interviews were written out, word for word, in longhand. Most of what I had to say was already in the public domain. I was merely repeating what I had said previously in court and written in the 12,000-word document we had circulated to SSP members following the defamation verdict.

The investigation also scrutinised the logistics of the November the 9th 2004 executive meeting. A police team arrived at our HQ to measure and photograph the compact, rectangular office where the confrontation had taken place and to reconstruct the exact seating arrangements. Their purpose was to establish whether it was possible for anyone to mishear what was being said. In a case like this, where the geography and layout of a physical location might have a bearing on the outcome, it would be routine practice to bring in the jury to inspect the venue at first hand. But, by then, we had sold the building to a veterinary practice. As an alternative, police set about creating an interactive computerised reconstruction of the meeting room. The judge, the QCs and the members of the jury would then be able click on someone's name – Tommy Sheridan, say, or Rosie Kane – and see and hear exactly what they would have seen and heard at the meeting from where they had been seated.

Tommy continued to accuse others of the crime he had committed. 'I will never get over the betrayal, over the fact that former friends and colleagues lied in court,' he told the *Sunday Express*. 'It's unforgivable and that is that.' In an interview with the Murdoch-owned London *Times*, he resurrected his courtroom claim that the SSP had 'fabricated these minutes' as part of a plot. 'I hope that the police can prove that these people lied,' he continued, before adding – with a tinge of hope, it appears, in retrospect – 'But I don't think they will, because it's very difficult to prove somebody has lied. Very, very difficult.'

By late 2007, the noose was tightening. On 26 November 2007, Lothian and Borders Police handed over seven volumes of evidence to the procurator fiscal's office in Edinburgh. Two weeks later, in the early afternoon of Sunday 9 December, two detectives drove to South Gyle, a business park on the western edge of Edinburgh. There, they staked out the studio of the Talk 107 radio station and timed Tommy Sheridan as he left the building to walk to his car after his weekly chat show.

The following Sunday, three officers sat in an unmarked white Mercedes round the corner from Talk 107 listening to Tommy's show on the car radio. The main topic of the day was 'Should Scots vote for Leon Jackson to win *X Factor* just because of his nationality?'. There had also been a discussion about the current dispute over police pay– with Tommy arguing strongly for the right of the police to take industrial action. Minutes later, they did indeed strike – but not in the way he had intended. At 1.10 p.m., as he walked out the front door of the building, the Mercedes screeched in front of him, blocking his path. Two detectives jumped out and confronted him, while the driver remained behind the wheel. Tommy then stepped into the back of the police vehicle and, after few minutes' conversation, was whisked away to Gayfield Police Station, near the top of Leith Walk.

Senior executives at the radio station had watched the incident through the windows, but hadn't been quite sure what was happening. Mike Graham, Tommy's friend and boss, thought it might even be possible that he had been kidnapped. But one of the station's Sunday presenters, Ramsay Jones, knew better. As the press officer of the Scottish Tory Party, he swiftly realised what was going on and phoned round his multitude of media contacts. But Talk 107 had the scoop. 'Huge news,' announced the station's deputy news editor at 1.40 p.m., interrupting its *Sunday Kickabout* football programme. 'Tommy Sheridan has been arrested outside Talk 107.'

Other cops had also been listening to Tommy's robust defence of their right to strike. They were driving westbound along the M8 at the time, headed towards Glasgow. Just after Tommy was arrested, two officers, one male and one female, knocked on the front door of his home on Paisley Road West, the busy thoroughfare that cuts a swathe through the south west of Glasgow. Another three uniformed officers sat in an unmarked Ford saloon, parked outside on the main road.

Inside Gayfield, Tommy was interviewed for eight and half hours, including breaks. According to police officers present, it was all very civil, with Tommy engaging in friendly chitchat in between the interview sessions and detectives returning the banter. At 9.05 p.m., he appeared on the steps of the police station accompanied by his lawyer, Aamer Anwar, to face the media. His demeanour changed abruptly. Righteous indignation poured out like cask-strength whisky.

'I believe I am the victim of a political witch hunt,' he roared.

I believe this whole farcical inquiry has usurped an incredible amount of police resources. It has been orchestrated and influenced by the powerful reach of the Murdoch empire and I believe I am the victim of a witch-hunt from the Murdoch empire.'

He continued:

I will prove my innocence in the fullness of time and I wish to thank all those who have tried to get messages to the police station today. I look forward to getting back and hugging my wife and two-year-old child who's had to go through the very, very, frightening experience of having nine police officers invade her home. She should have been at a Christmas party today but instead has had to suffer that ignominy. That is all I can say at the moment. This battle goes on – however long it takes to clear my name.

As a sharp political operator, he knew that attack was often the best form of defence. The next day, he held an impromptu press conference on the doorstep of his home. He told reporters:

It's nine days before Christmas. My house has been ransacked, my wife has been traumatised and my two-and-a-half-year-old child has been reduced to tears by the presence of nine police officers. So, when you ask me how I feel, I am furious, I am disgusted, I am shocked and shattered – but I'm determined to fight on.

I watched his performance impassively on TV. After twenty years, I was bored by Tommy's fake anger. He could recite the telephone directory and sound like a Free Presbyterian minister fulminating against fornication.

The police made no public response but privately the detectives involved in the house search were seething at Tommy's performance. They insisted that the raid had been low-key and sensitive. Gail, they claimed, far from being traumatised, had been friendly and made them tea and biscuits. They dismissed as fiction the suggestion that the couple's young daughter had been reduced to tears by their presence and insisted that she had only been in the house for a short time before being taken away by Tommy's sister Lynn and sister-in-law Gillian. After the search, Gail had even thanked the police for causing minimal disturbance and tidying up behind them. Some people suspected that Tommy's real concern wasn't the behaviour of the police but the fact that they had landed a sucker punch by unexpectedly removing highly sensitive material from his home. In total, they removed nine bag-loads, including Tommy's personal computer, piles of documents and even bedding. Most of the stuff was later returned but a significant quantity was retained as evidence.

Among the files, detectives discovered incriminating notes in Tommy's own handwriting that he had not even bothered to destroy. One of these was a statement specifically addressed to 'Colin and Richie' – Colin Fox and Richie Venton – asking them to testify that he had denied going to Cupids but, because the SSP was close to bankruptcy, it couldn't support his legal action. This was, to adapt Tommy's oft-repeated assertion, the mother of all self-stitch-ups. It was up there on a par with the armed robber who handed the bank cashier a note scrawled on the back of an envelope – with his own name and address neatly typed on the other side.

And it got worse. He had also written out in longhand a list of questions – together with anticipated replies and follow-up questions – to ensure that his lawyers would be on the ball. After my cross-examination, I had already suspected that the line of questioning put to me by Richard Keen QC had been devised by Tommy himself. Now the police search had unearthed confirmation that the lawyers had simply been firing ammunition manufactured by their client. In itself, that was no crime. What was most intriguing was the script he had written for the cross-examination of Keith Baldassara. It went along the lines of: 'Did you, Keith Baldassara, appear at Mr Sheridan's door two months before November 9 2004 when you knew he was not at home? Did you speak to Gail Sheridan? Did you tell her you were passionately in love her? Did you beg her to leave her husband?' It was a desperate ruse but could have provided some kind of logical, albeit twisted and dishonest, explanation for the fact that Tommy's closest friend and right-hand man had turned on him. However, in court, Tommy, Gail and his lawyers never so much as hinted that such an incident had ever taken place – presumably because Tommy had failed to persuade his wife to go along with it.

It was to be a bleak midwinter for Tommy and Solidarity. In the May 2007 elections, Ruth Black had become the first and only Solidarity councillor elected in Tommy's home patch of Cardonald. She had worked closely with Tommy's sister Lynn in the Scottish gay and lesbian rights movement. In the run-up to the defamation case, she had been one of his staunchest supporters and had been involved in the Cardonald branch discussions about the destruction of the SSP minutes.

By December 2007, the new Solidarity councillor had become disillusioned with Tommy Sheridan and Solidarity – possibly because she was starting to discover the truth about the defamation case. She held a series of secret meetings with Labour council leader, Stephen Purcell, who persuaded her to defect to Labour. According to some insiders, Purcell – who would later be destroyed in a separate political scandal over drugs and gangland links – still anxious about her past links with Tommy, sent in Brian Lironi, the former *Sunday Mail* political editor who was now his chief press aide, to grill her for two days. She told him everything she knew. The Labour council leader insisted that she spill the beans to Lothian and Borders CID before they could accept her membership of the Labour group. On 20 December 2007, she announced her defection to Labour. A few years later, Ruth Black and Stephen Purcell would both be expelled from the Labour Party as a result of two separate political scandals.

The next day, the largest grouping in Solidarity, the Socialist Workers Party, published a lengthy and damning critique of the failures and weaknesses of the breakaway movement they had helped to create. It concluded by effectively writing Solidarity off: 'There is no other electoral alternative to Labour and the SNP in Scotland, and it is important that there should be one. We had hoped Solidarity could be that alternative.'

The Herald's chief Scottish political correspondent, Robbie Dinwoodie, described the crisis in Solidarity as 'close to meltdown'. To all intents and purposes, the party was over. But Tommy knew he had to keep it on a life-support machine for the purpose of maintaining his political hold over those who had helped him build his tower of lies. The SWP retained formal membership of Solidarity but, from then on, effectively ignored its existence.

Tommy must have been glad to see the back of 2007. The year had been a litany of failures. In May, after fifteen years representing the people of Glasgow, he had been given his P45 by the city's voters. In June, he had made his comeback on the charity boxing circuit and was battered black-and-blue by Irish-born football coach, Roddy Collins. In August, his comedy career had crash-landed straight after take-off. In December, his only elected representative had defected and his biggest bloc of supporters had turned lukewarm. But, worst of all, his glorious court triumph of the previous year was starting to unravel. Tommy's supporters had labelled his defamation action a 'titanic struggle'. There was nothing titanic about it, other than the fact it was ultimately doomed. It had been a petty scrap over a nineteen-month-old fish-and-chip wrapper that would have been long forgotten if he had taken our advice back in 2004.

Now his supporters were stunned. SSP members were expecting arrests – indeed, given what we knew, we'd have been shocked if there had been no charges. Tommy, though, had convinced those around him and his contacts in the media and celebrity-land that the police investigation was going nowhere. They have no evidence, he told those who knew the truth. There *is* no evidence, he told the rest. The Crown Office would never proceed, he insisted. It wasn't in the public interest. It would be too costly to bring it to trial. And they couldn't afford the humiliation of losing such a high-profile court case. It was what his supporters wanted to hear. More importantly, it was what they needed to hear to keep them on board. They were like hapless punters repeatedly backing the same clapped-out racehorse because the jockey had once won the Grand National.

Soon, a Defend Tommy Sheridan Campaign was in full swing – although most of the names on its lists of supporter seemed to be members of the CWI-affiliated Socialist Party in England. Glaringly absent were the names of some of the celebrity actors, film-makers and academics who had supported him during and immediately after the libel case. For some people at least, it seemed that the penny had dropped.

2008

Friends and Enemies in High Places

In February 2008, the net widened when another six witnesses were charged with perjury.

The first batch of arrests involved four former members of the SSP executive, all of whom had given evidence backing Tommy's falsified version of the meeting back in November 2004. This time, there were no surprise swoops or house searches. The four were politely requested to call in at a Lothian and Borders police station at a time of their convenience.

Of the four, the best known was Rosemary Byrne, who had been an MSP between 2003 and 2007. At the time of her arrest, Rosemary, from Irvine in Ayrshire, was 59 years old and a grandmother. The other three were unknown to the wider public. Apart from the brief flurry of press attention they had received during the defamation trial, they were anonymous backroom figures, first in the SSP, then in Solidarity. Jock Penman, then 58 years old, lived alone in the old mining village of Kelty and had been the SSP Fife regional organiser before joining Solidarity. Graeme McIver was younger, just under 40, with four school-age children. From Galashiels in the Borders, he had been the SSP South of Scotland regional organiser until the split, when he became the national secretary of Solidarity. Pat Smith was 60 years old and a private nanny to the children of the acclaimed Edinburgh-based architect, Malcolm Fraser. This wasn't exactly the Cosa Nostra. Their actions hadn't been motivated by self-interest. They had nothing to gain other than a pat on the back from Tommy. They were guilty of gullibility, low self-esteem and misplaced loyalty to an individual they wrongly believed was more special than themselves. Despite everything, I felt pangs of pity when I heard the news of their arrests.

Four days later, on 19 February 2008, Gail Sheridan was also charged with perjury. It was no surprise – one week before Christmas, news of her imminent arrest had been broken by the *Daily Record* in a sympathetic front-page exclusive. Tommy had tipped off the newspaper, ensuring that his friends, family and supporters would have time to get used to the idea that Gail would be arrested and charged. It was a typical Tommy pre-emptive strike, suitably dressed up to generate maximum sympathy. The *Record* report had quoted a 'source close to the family' – in other words, Tommy, either directly or through an intermediary.

They are concerned police may carry out a dawn raid in the run-up to the festive season, and that could mean Gail being left in the cells until after Christmas. They want some sort of understanding that will not happen and they are left with some dignity and spared a dramatic dawn raid with cameras and police vans present.

This was emotive stuff, designed to heighten the sense of persecution Tommy had nurtured. In the future, he would start to refer to the 'dawn raid' that had taken place on his home, even though it had been one o'clock in the afternoon. One east coaster suggested that the sun must rise pretty late over in Glasgow in December.

In the same front-page exclusive, the *Record* had suggested that 'a journalist in the case may also face charges'. This snippet of mis-information, scripted clearly in Tommy's invisible handwriting, was intended to create the impression that Lothian and Borders Police were still unsure who had told the truth and who had committed perjury. No journalist, from the *News of the World* or any other newspaper, was ever charged. But there was one surprise arrest. Gus Healy, Gail's 71-year-old father, was also asked to come to Gayfield Square Police Station in Edinburgh to be interviewed along with his daughter. To shelter them from the ordeal of running a media gauntlet, Lothian and Borders Police offered Gail and Gus the option of driving straight into the private car park and entering the offices via a side door but, to the despair of their lawyer, they pulled up outside the front entrance in a Honda Jeep, accompanied by Tommy, who then took Gail's arm and ushered the pair straight through the throng of reporters and camera crew. Gail's giant sunglasses couldn't mask the tension etched on her face as she walked into the building to face what would be a six-hour interview. But Tommy looked to be in his element.

When Gail and Gus reappeared at 7.15 p.m., he was at the front door to greet them and once again launched into a diatribe on the steps of the police station, as the cameras flashed and the reporters scribbled.

> I am dismayed, disenchanted and disgusted by the behaviour of Lothian and Borders Police. They have detained a 44-year-old mother-of-one, who has never been in trouble in her life, for six hours and charged her with perjury. The streets of Lothian must be crime free if the police can devote time to harassing a family.

At that point, he held back one significant piece of information. Gail had been charged not just with perjury but also with theft of a quantity of miniature bottles of spirits from her employer, British Airways. A few days later, after British Airways received a report from Lothian and Borders Police, she was suspended from her job, pending further inquiries. The news of her suspension was again broken by the *Daily Record*. The front page had, once again, clearly been planted by Tommy and included a quote from the now familiar 'source close to the family' who told the reporter, 'If Gail didn't think there was a witch-hunt against her before, she certainly does now. It's fair to say she's gone off her trolley. She's absolutely livid.'

As it happened, the decision to arrest and report Gail over the miniatures turned into a PR debacle for Lothian and Borders Police. The action appeared draconian and unconnected with the perjury investigation. Writing in *The Scotsman* on the threat to civil liberties of a national DNA database, the formidable writer and radio broadcaster, Lesley Riddoch, suggested that 'the case for a compulsory national DNA database had been hurt by the over-zealous search of the Sheridan home'. She went on:

> The police search of the Sheridan home was initiated for the legitimate purpose of gathering evidence for the perjury charges Gail and Tommy Sheridan face. Once inside the house, though, the search appears to have gone beyond that initial purpose to discover miniature bottles of alcohol and perfume – not connected to the perjury case and not in itself a discovery that screamed aloud that a crime had been committed.

It was a fair point. As Lesley asked rhetorically, why not check that the Sheridan's TV licence had been paid or seize any overdue library books they might find? But what wasn't widely known at the time was that Lothian and Borders Police were specifically looking for miniatures as part of the perjury investigation. Their interest in the seemingly irrelevant hoard of small bottles of spirits and perfumes derived from their earlier interrogation of one of the witnesses in the defamation trail, Anvar Khan. The information she supplied to detectives included the detail that Tommy had turned up to her flat a few years earlier, with ten miniature British Airways bottles of red and white wine, from a large stash kept by Gail.

During the defamation case, Tommy had claimed that he had a brief fling with Anvar Khan in 1992 – before his relationship with Gail had begun. Anvar Khan had insisted that her affair with Tommy hadn't started until 1994 and that it had continued intermittently for a decade. The discovery of the hoard of miniatures provided additional corroboration that Anvar Khan's testimony had been honest. Lothian and Borders CID could have ignored the miniatures – in which case this evidence would not be available in any future perjury trial. Alternatively, they could confiscate the miniatures but that would then require them, by law, to report a suspected theft to both British Airways and the procurator fiscal.

The attitude of many people, including those now hostile to Tommy, was that, whatever the origins of the miniatures, they were a perk of the job, like tax-free tips for bartenders or inflated expense claims by politicians and journalists. By March, when Tommy, Gail and Gus Healy appeared in court on petition to formally face charges, the theft charge against Gail had been quietly dropped. And, after a short appeal, British Airways lifted her suspension. The problem for the police was that they were fighting a legal battle while Tommy was fighting a PR battle. He knew that, for the general public, details and nuances are like the small print on an insurance policy that nobody bothers to read. It was headlines that mattered. His indignation over what he termed a 'police vendetta' now appeared to have at least a grain of justification.

From start to finish, one of the curious features of the Tommy Sheridan saga was that the controversy cut across all the usual ideological divisions. The broad political Left in Scotland was divided but, from the Centre and the Right too, people jumped in head first to take sides – often without checking to make sure there was water in the pool.

Allan Cochrane, the Scottish political editor of the right-wing *Daily Telegraph*, waded into the controversy. The staunch Tory unionist, suggested that the treatment of Gail reflected a wider malaise in Scotland's separate legal system:

Senior members of Scotland's legal fraternity, including some with the closest of links to the Scottish Executive, are beginning to share my view that the Sheridan case is beginning to show this country's legal system in a very poor light . . . Scottish justice is getting a very bad name from the Sheridan case. It may not have the trappings of a show trial, but Mr Sheridan's treatment thus far is beginning to look like cruel and unnatural punishment.

Meanwhile, the *Daily Telegraph*'s old enemy, George Galloway, leapt into the fray, sword flashing defiantly, to gallantly defend his sometime friend. 'I would Defend Tommy Sheridan Even If I Thought He Was Guilty', ran the headline in his *Daily Record* column. The small print of the disclaimer, 'Which I Don't', sounded less than convincing. He went on to compare the search of Tommy's home by Lothian and Borders Police to an anti-terrorist operation and then suggested that this could become 'Scotland's Dreyfus Affair'. This was absurdly over-the-top, even for George. The Dreyfus Affair, which shook France to its foundations for the best part of a decade in the late 19th and early 20th centuries, had involved trumped-up treason charges against a young captain in the French Army. After spending five years on Devil's Island, the notorious prison colony, Alfred Dreyfus had been exonerated – a Jewish victim of an anti-Semitic conspiracy. The scandal exposed widespread corruption at the heart of the French political and judicial system. The only similarity between the Dreyfus Affair and the Tommy Sheridan Show was the mysterious appearance of forged documents. In Tommy's case, though, the forgery had been for the purpose not of incriminating *him* but of framing his political opponents.

Naturally, comments such as these were seized upon by Tommy to bolster his claim that he was the victim of a vendetta. The Defend Tommy Sheridan website claimed that 'the possibility now of a perjury trial is a continuation of this witch-hunt by the Murdoch empire'. Others suggested Tommy had been targeted because he was a political threat to the state. Peter Taaffe's CWI group claimed it was an act of revenge for the defeat of the Poll Tax 16 years before.

Deciding which of these conspiracy theories to believe was like to trying to work out whether JFK had been assassinated by Che Guevara or exterminated by the Daleks. By the time Tommy was charged, he was an exploded shell, rejected by 96 per cent of voters in his own city and reduced to telling blonde bimbo jokes at a third-rate comedy show. His major achievement in the previous two years had been to split and weaken one of the most successful socialist parties in Europe. Global capitalism wasn't quaking in its boots at the thought that Tommy Sheridan was still on the loose.

If anything, allegations that the state were targeting Tommy for the Poll Tax only served to highlight the Anglocentricity of sections of the British Left who often talk about 'the state' without even realising that

Scotland has an entirely separate and fully autonomous legal system. The British state operates in Scotland mainly through institutions such as Ministry of Defence, the Armed Forces and MI5 rather than through the legal system, which is accountable to Holyrood not to Westminster.

The SNP, which currently runs the Scottish Government, was elected in 2007 and controls the justice system and the Crown Office. The party supported the anti-Poll Tax campaign. Alex Salmond, now the First Minister of Scotland, spoke alongside Tommy at anti-Poll Tax rallies, as did the Justice Minister Kenny MacAskill who, at the time, was one of the most combative SNP advocates of mass non-payment.

The idea of the 'legal establishment' conjures up images of octogenarian, private-school-educated judges still living in the 19th century. In the past, that caricature could sometimes rub shoulders with reality, including in Scotland. But since devolution the picture has become more complex. Even the judge who ordered the police investigation after the defamation case, Allan Turnbull, was still in his forties and was educated at a state comprehensive in Fife before studying law at the University of Dundee. Despite her aristocratic and masculine formal title, the Lord Advocate (Scotland's equivalent of the Director of Public Prosecutions in England and Wales) is even further removed from the stereotypical crusty, old, reactionary male. Also still in her forties, Elish Angiolini was brought up in the backstreets of working-class Govan and attended the same Catholic comprehensive state secondary school as Tommy Sheridan and Rosie Kane, at around the same time. Her number two, the Solicitor General Frank Mulholland, was brought up in Coatbridge, the son of a taxi driver and a telephonist. He too was educated at a state comprehensive. He rose to prominence after successfully prosecuting the gas corporation, Transco, for gross negligence in the deaths of a Lanarkshire family. During the six-month trial, which resulted in a record £15 million fine for the company, he repeatedly lambasted Transco for 'putting profits before safety'.

Unusually, the two most senior figures in the Crown Office, responsible for prosecuting crime, had previously been solicitors, which meant that they had not been part of the elite Faculty of Advocates. As public servants, the annual salaries of these two pinnacles of 'the Scottish legal establishment' amounted to less than a sixth of the earnings of Richard Keen, the QC employed by Tommy at the start of his libel case. Neither Angiolini nor Mulholland could easily be dismissed as Rupert's poodles or Maggie's avengers.

That it is not to idealise the Scottish legal system, which still locks up too many people, especially women, for petty crime. All legal systems reflect, to one degree or another, the prejudices of the society they operate within. But by late 2007 there was no reason, no motive and no purpose for the Crown Office to single out Tommy Sheridan for special treatment. Nor did Lothian and Borders Police ever display any special prejudice against Tommy Sheridan before the investigation began. Over the years, many police forces across the UK – notably the Met – have been infested with racism. Yet since 2006 the strongest criticisms of Lothian and Borders Police have come not from the Left but from a right-wing consortium of newspapers and Tory politicians for supposedly prioritising minorities over fighting crime. In early 2008, the force became the first Scottish organisation ever to feature in Stonewall's top twenty employers for lesbians, gays and bisexuals. After flying the rainbow flag in celebration of gay history month in February 2008, the force came under attack from Tory Justice Spokesperson Bill Aitken, who said:

> Flags flying from public buildings should be the national flag, either the Union flag or the Saltire. This simply makes Lothian and Borders Police look just a little bit silly, and I'm extremely surprised that they have gone down this route.

Sometimes there is no need to chase shadows because the obvious explanation is the right explanation. The unprecedented investigation had been prompted by unprecedented circumstances. No one in Scottish legal history had ever before fought a civil defamation case on such a blatantly fraudulent basis.

Perjury may well be committed every day in Scottish courtrooms but not by high-profile members of the national parliament. Nor do everyday perjurers notify several hundred people in advance of their intention to commit the crime. Nor do they try to persuade or coerce dozens of others to commit perjury on their behalf. Most perjurers would be sufficiently circumspect to confine their crime to perhaps one or two lies that would be difficult or impossible to prove. They certainly wouldn't normally leave a trail of evidence as long and wide as the M8. And only in their daydreams would most perjurers imagine walking away £200,000 the richer as a result of their crime. This was definitely not an everyday tale of everyday folk.

Perjury prosecutions are far less commonplace than prosecutions for breach of the peace or theft but this is not because the courts regard perjury as a trivial matter, like dropping litter in the street. Perjury strikes at the heart of the legal system. It is one of the most serious crimes in the book but, in common with rape – which also has extremely low prosecution and conviction rates – it is notoriously difficult to prove. In court, people often give conflicting evidence, based on different recollections or varying interpretations of a single incident. Psychologists say that no two people experience the same event in exactly the same way. Perceptions differ. In some cases, witnesses do tell blatant lies but, even then, it can be almost impossible to establish the truth – for example, when it's one person's word against another's or someone has provided an alibi for someone else, without any corroborating witnesses. These are grey, murky areas, where truth and lies merge into one amorphous mist. Trying to separate fact from fiction can be like trying to separate different paint colours after they have been stirred in the same pot.

Moreover, perjury investigations may be rare but not unheard of. In the period of a year or so before and after Tommy's libel case, a number of people were jailed for perjury in Scotland. They included Gordon Woods, a 19-year-old with learning difficulties from Airdrie, who lied under oath 'out of fear and confusion', according to his lawyer. The teenager had been persuaded to make a false statement during the trial of a 22-year-old man accused of having unlawful sex with a 15-year-old girl. Gordon Woods wasn't an accomplished politician with an honours degree and a multitude of connections in high places – he could barely read or write. But he was jailed for nine months for perjury. Then there was Kai Sedgwick from Aberdeen, who tried to take the rap for his accused friend after a stabbing incident. He got three years. And Glasgow-based lawyer, Shahid Pervez, was sentenced to five years – later reduced on appeal to 32 months – after pleading guilty to having provided a false alibi for a man accused of abduction and extortion. His lawyer said he was terrorised into committing perjury after death threats to himself and his family. The list goes on and on.

Tommy's perjury charges hadn't arisen from a criminal trial, argued his supporters. His was a civil defamation case. But so too had been the libel action taken out against *The Guardian* in 1998 by Jonathan Aitken, a Tory MP and former Cabinet Minister, who had vowed to 'cut out the cancer of bent and twisted journalism in our country with the simple sword of truth and the trusty shield of British fair play'. His trial collapsed when the newspaper provided evidence that he had lied about who paid his hotel bill for the Ritz in Paris five years earlier. For his relatively small-scale deception – certainly in comparison to Tommy's extravaganza – this pillar of the British establishment was sentenced to 18 months' imprisonment.

Jonathan Aitken had pled guilty and was suitably contrite, but not so his fellow Conservative high-flyer, Jeffrey Archer, who was sentenced to four years imprisonment for trying to rig his own libel trial.

When these giants of the Tory Party were toppled by their own arrogant disregard for the rules governing everyone else, only the most diehard right-wing media commentators offered any sympathy. The rest went to town. The *Mirror*, even before Archer had been charged with perjury, ran the editorial headline, 'JAIL HIM!' The *Daily Record* plastered its own verdict on Jeffrey Archer across its front page in screaming capitals, 'LIAR, LIAR – THE SLEAZY ARROGANT SCHEMING CHEATING THIEVING LYING RAT'.

In the wake of the Archer conviction, Iain Macwhirter had even called for the libel laws to be put in the dock. In the *Sunday Herald*, he wrote:

> To protect Archer's honour, the law let him lie, cheat, steal and deceive with impunity . . . So long as powerful individuals can use the threat of defamation to furnish them with protection from public scrutiny, then we remain a glorified banana republic, a diseased democracy . . . Everyone – politicians and press – is saying how they knew all along about Archer. So why did nobody publish and be damned?

It was strong stuff from Macwhirter and spot on. A few years later, it could equally have applied to Tommy Sheridan. Unfortunately, when the SSP did stand up and challenge Tommy's lies and fraud, first inside the party and then in the Court on Session, the columnist turned his invective on us. Then, on 17 December 2007, the day after Tommy was arrested and charged with perjury, Macwhirter wrote in *The Guardian*:

> It has surprised a number of people in the legal profession that this investigation took place at all, let alone led to Sheridan actually being charged. Perjury actions are rare in Scots law even in criminal cases, and in civil actions they are practically unheard of.

That same evening, Alistair Bonnington, BBC Scotland's top lawyer, appeared on *Newsnight Scotland* and made similar points:

> Perjury is committed if you think about it logically in almost every criminal court in Scotland every single day and nothing happens . . . accused persons put up alibis – what happens about that? Nothing at all. For Scotland this sets a precedent.

From a legal standpoint, such arguments were illogical. With much of the British media circulating and broadcasting on both sides of the border, failure to act against Tommy Sheridan would have given a green light to any would-be Jeffrey Archers to sue in Scottish courts, unhindered by inconvenient details such as perjury laws. And, if some of the more unscrupulous Scottish-based tabloids knew that they too could line up a parade of paid witnesses to lie in court, safely protected from any legal consequences, they could publish whatever they wanted about anyone, true or false.

Buoyed by the idle speculation of middle-class media pundits, the Defend Tommy Sheridan Campaign held a 200-strong rally in June 2008, in Glasgow's Langside Halls. Kenny Ross, then the Scottish Secretary of the Fire Brigades Union, angrily denounced the SSP witnesses who had given evidence at the defamation trial. 'They had a choice and sided against the movement. It's a sordid story of disgrace and dishonour – they are class traitors.' This was shocking stuff designed to win cheap applause. These 'class traitors' had raised money, built support and stood on the picket lines alongside the FBU when the union was under siege from most of the media during the firefighters' strikes a few years earlier; indeed, some of us had been on FBU picket lines back in 1977, when Kenny Ross was still a schoolboy. His outburst was also dishonest. We had a choice all right – we could give truthful evidence, commit perjury or refuse to give evidence and go straight to jail. Faced with the same choice, would the blustering trade union official have laid down his own liberty to protect the reputation of his friend?

The rally was also addressed by two people who knew what the inside of a jail looked like. Paddy Hill of the Birmingham Six had been a stalwart of the Miscarriages of Justice Organisation (MOJO) in Scotland and he was joined on the platform by Gerry Conlon of the Guildford Four. Gerry had clearly been persuaded to attend under false pretences. On the Defend Tommy Sheridan website, he left this message: 'The press play a huge role in the conviction of innocent people, our only strength is to stick together, solidarity for Tommy.' Like many people, he truly believed Tommy was innocent.

Presumably, so too did Paddy Hill and the other organisers of MOJO. People who have been wrongfully imprisoned have a natural and understandable distrust of the police. But most wrongful imprisonments result from lies and perjury. Why would an organisation, whose declared mission is to fight for justice, defend perjury unless they were ignorant of the facts? The Birmingham Six had been convicted precisely because police officers had perjured themselves.

They were charged but never prosecuted – which itself amounted to a further miscarriage of justice.

An injustice had certainly been committed during the defamation case but Tommy Sheridan was the perpetrator not the victim. This hadn't been some harmless prank. These were real people he had trashed in court and was still trashing two years on, aided and abetted by trade union, showbiz and media hangers-on. Many months after the court case, some of us were still being assailed in the street by total strangers demanding to know why we had concocted such vile lies about Tommy Sheridan. Nor were his victims only those directly in the firing line. All of us who had been branded perjurers, conspirators, forgers, scabs, rats, liars, backstabbers – and a whole lot more besides – had families. While the media was transfixed by the Tommy and Gail show, dozens of other families were suffering pain and humiliation. It isn't easy to pick up a newspaper or watch the TV news and have your daughter, your son, your mother, your father, your partner vilified and denigrated when you know they have acted with conscience and honour.

In the months following the court case, Rosie Kane had lost both her mother and her father. Her mother, May McGarvey, had written letters of solidarity to Tommy when he was in Saughton Prison and had been proud to call him a friend of the family. She went to her grave with his triumphant ranting against her daughter still pounding in her ears. Carolyn Leckie's mother was diagnosed with terminal cancer in the midst of the turmoil around the court case. She spent the last precious months of her life devastated by the public demonisation of her daughter.

Despite everything, if Tommy had put his hands in the air, admitted his guilt and apologised to those he had falsely accused, I would have been the first to call for leniency. Personally, I believe that society should develop punishments other than imprisonment for non-violent criminals who are not a danger to the public. But the bottom line was that, if Tommy was allowed to walk away untouched by justice, he would be unstoppable. History would be rewritten to his script and the reputations of honourable people would be forever stained. In the eyes of the general public, the judicial system carries a lot of weight. Only after the Birmingham Six and the Guildford Four were exonerated in a court of law did their status change from convicted terrorists to innocent victims. TC Campbell and Joe Steele would have been released from prison many years earlier if they had falsely admitted their guilt in the Ice-Cream Wars murders. They refused to do so and forfeited parole because they knew it was important to clear their names through the legal process.

Our problem was on a different scale but the same principles applied. As things stood, Tommy was an honest man and we were liars, perjurers and fraudsters. That false perception had even subverted democracy in the 2007 Scottish election, when tens of thousands of SSP voters deserted the party, believing or at least suspecting that we had committed systematic perjury to destroy our former leader. In that election, Solidarity polled twice as many votes as the SSP.

After the arrests, the tide began to turn. The first big political test came during the Glasgow East Westminster by-election. The constituency had, in the past, been fertile terrain for the SSP. It included some of the most deprived communities in Western Europe. The headlines naturally concentrated on the struggle between Labour and the SNP but there was a secondary contest – 'the Battle of the Left', as it was dubbed in the press. The SSP candidate was Frances Curran, now the national co-convenor of the party alongside Colin Fox. She and her Solidarity rival, Patricia McLeish, had attended St Andrews Secondary at the same time.

Just as the election kicked off, Tommy provided yet another entertaining diversion when he made a guest appearance on the BBC Radio Scotland comedy programme *The Ellis and Clarke Show*. He was billed as 'Tommy What a Whopper Sheridan' and hammed it up in a sketch called 'Carry on Swinging' which was replete, as the title implied, with old-fashioned innuendo. Tommy had the lines, 'My enemies are everywhere. Last week I spent nestled in Sister Elaine's huge Victorian chest.' To which his co-star replied, 'Oh, I thought I saw something popping out when I bent down to take out my big jugs.' Once again Tommy was trading on his notoriety. But he was still protesting his innocence.

The socialist vote was squeezed, as everyone knew it would be, in a first-past-the-post by-election fought out between two giants with much at stake. Frances Curran had taken fifth place, ahead of Solidarity, the Greens and two independents. More significantly, the combined SSP and Solidarity vote was higher than the vote for the Liberal Democrats and five times greater than the vote for the Greens. It offered a poignant glimpse into what might have been.

Now approaching 45, Tommy's career took a new turn. The previous year, after his ejection from Holyrood, he had tried to break into showbiz and comedy, aided by a galaxy of existing comedians and entertainers he had cultivated over the years. But he was completely out of his depth – his talent no match for his ambition. Then, in the autumn, he began studying for a Masters research degree in social sciences with the vague aim of becoming a lecturer. But, ever since his success in court, he had started to nurture the idea of becoming a lawyer – no doubt a swashbuckling QC jousting with the giants of the legal system in the highest courts in the land. In October 2008, he began a law degree at the University of Strathclyde. It was an audacious move, demonstrating to the world at large that he had no fear of a perjury prosecution since a convicted perjurer would never be allowed to practise law. It looked like he was confident of seeing off Lothian and Borders Police and the Crown Office. And maybe, if the worst came to the worst, it would be useful to have a bit of detailed legal knowledge inside prison. As a veteran politician, Tommy understood the power that flowed from being able to provide people with concrete advice and assistance. Or perhaps he was just getting some expertise under his belt in preparation for conducting his own defence in a future perjury trial.

In the meantime, Tommy still had a few tricks up his sleeve. News of his latest escapade was broken in the *News of the World* a few weeks before Christmas 2008, in a scoop by the paper's Scottish political editor, Euan McColm. 'SHERIDAN'S IN THE BB HOUSE!' shouted the front-page headline. For the newspaper's readers, the initials were enough. And no one would misinterpret the reference. Tommy hadn't visited the headquarters of the Boys' Brigade or booked into a guest house offering bed and breakfast. He had signed up for the forthcoming round of *Celebrity Big Brother*, the notorious reality TV show.

It was no mean feat that he had managed to inveigle his way on to the show and even get paid for it. In England, he was pretty much unknown outside the circles of activists in left-wing politics. And, in Scotland, his celebrity star was fading. He had been spurned by the voters in May 2007. His new showbiz career had nosedived at the Edinburgh Festival Fringe. His attempt to relaunch himself at the Glasgow Magners Comedy Festival in March 2008 had crashed, when his promoters scaled down his show from a week to two nights. And, in April 2008, his radio programme had been axed.

The new station director of Talk 107 had pointedly explained that 'we want presenters who are well-informed, have a sense of humour and a good rapport with listeners'. It should have been a warning to anyone who expected Tommy to set the *Big Brother* house on fire with his wit and wisdom.

2009–2010

From Big Brother *to Big Bother*

Most of Scotland was either recovering from the New Year or still drunk when Tommy made his grand entrance into the *Big Brother* house late on Friday the second of January.

As he walked up the gangway the crowd booed. Not that they knew much about him – the fact that he was introduced as a socialist politician was enough to provoke their irritation. The mainly teenage *Big Brother* fans who congregate outside Elstree Studios in the East End of London aren't the most politically aware section of society. To keep abreast, so to speak, of current affairs, they would definitely prefer the *Daily Star* to the *Morning Star*. They might storm the barricades but only if the Page 3 girl removed her top on the steps of the *Big Brother* house.

Channel 4 had certainly succeeded in delivering the usual mix of stereotypes to keep its viewers enthralled: Coolio, a big, bad, black gangsta rapper who called women hoes and bitches; Verne, a cute dwarf who could be dressed up as a teddy bear; Ben, a heartthrob boy-band singer; Tina, a coarse and garrulous actress with a thick Scouse accent; Ulrika, a former weather girl whose colourful love life had sold tabloids galore; La Toya, an unworldly member of the legendary Jackson clan; Terry, a fast-talking Mancunian DJ; Tommy, a fire-brand politician with a hint of scandal surrounding him; and Michelle, Mutya and Lucy for the boys to ogle.

The producers clearly hoped Tommy would stir things up. According to some press reports, the *Big Brother* company had approached Lembit Öpik, the geekish Lib Dem MP, best known for dating one of the Cheeky Girls pop duo, but were unable to entice him on to the show. Nor could they tempt David Irving, the infamous holocaust-denier. But a left-wing extremist would be a reasonable substitute.

Outside, Tommy's disciples were mortified. In his entertaining book, *What's Going On?*, the comedian Mark Steel, an activist of George Galloway's Respect Party, described his horror when he discovered that the anti-war campaigner had joined the 2006 series of *Celebrity Big Brother*. 'I felt like I was back in school and my dad had suddenly wandered into the assembly stark naked next to the head-master with a banana up his arse.' Now some of Tommy's party members were beginning to feel the same way.

The day the show opened, the CWI faction of Solidarity – by now Tommy's closest political allies – rushed out a statement.

> The appearance of Tommy Sheridan in Celebrity Big Brother will have disappointed many people who know of his role as an uncompromising fighter for the rights of the working class over the past 25 years. We share this disappointment. We believe that Tommy's decision to take part in CBB is a mistake that will damage his standing . . . this programme is widely criticised for its format which seeks to denigrate and humiliate those who take part.

They could also have asked what the scourge of international right-wing media moguls was doing appearing on a show produced by an international right-wing media mogul. In 2007, Silvio Berlusconi – the billionaire Prime Minister of Italy who made Rupert Murdoch look like a bleeding heart liberal – had led a buy-out of Endemol, the *Big Brother* production company. But still, there was something not quite right with this criticism from the CWI. They had no problem with Tommy cavorting around swingers' clubs while using his wife as a political accessory. They had no problem with him patronising commercial sex clubs while legislating in Parliament on lap dancing and prostitution. Then they cheered him like excited schoolchildren when he took out a high-profile court case to deny his behaviour. They applauded his skills as a liar and condemned those who refused to join in the game. They raised not a murmur of dissent when he falsely denounced his own party leadership as scabs, perjurers, forgers and plotters. They aided and abetted him when he split the most successful socialist unity project in Europe. But now he really had damaged the socialist movement . . .

While some of his staunchest supporters were squirming with embarrassment, others were warming to the now insipid rebel. Radio Clyde sent paid campaigners on a tour bus around the West of Scotland armed with 'Vote Tommy' leaflets. The *Daily Record* signed up Gail as a columnist for the duration of the show and struck a deal with Tommy to get his exclusive insight into life in the *Big Brother* house following his eviction. Tommy had become a tame court jester – even if not a very funny one – whose politics could be indulged as a spot of harmless eccentricity. Notwithstanding the intervention of

Radio Clyde and the *Daily Record,* the normally formidable Scottish block vote, which in the past had delivered victories for Michelle McManus on *Pop Idol* and Leon Jackson on *X Factor,* was only able to spare Tommy the ignominy of being the first contestant to be voted out by the public. That honour was bestowed on La Toya Jackson. But Tommy was next for the chop.

At the start of the show, 'a friend' had told the *Daily Record,* 'Tommy's in it to win.' The bookies were equally confident that he had no chance, offering odds of 25/1 against him emerging victorious. By the final week, they were offering 200/1. To put that in perspective, the same bookies were offering odds of just 20/1 against aliens landing on Arthur's Seat in the centre of Edinburgh. It wasn't that he had become a hate figure like some *Big Brother* contestants in the past. It was just that he lacked any entertainment value.

Yet he was always mesmerised by celebrity culture and hungered to be part of it. He collected celebrity acquaintances like other people collect books or CDs and networked relentlessly with journalists, actors, artists, entertainers, sports stars, comedians, writers, trade union leaders, academics and even businessmen.

He had once cut a rap record, 'Daddy Dog', with an Aberdeen-based band, Jasmine Minks, though Eminem could relax. He had dabbled in acting and had launched two failed careers in radio and comedy. He had also tried his hand at celebrity boxing, fighting TV football pundit and ex-Rangers star, Gordon Smith. Although his opponent was ten years older, Tommy lost the fight on points though he was still complaining about the verdict four years later: 'I think I deserved to win and only with Stevie Wonder judging could you think otherwise.'

His main achievement in *Big Brother* was to befriend Coolio, whose Neanderthal attitude towards women would have had him drummed out of the Taliban as an extremist. 'Them bitches should never have had the vote' was one of his more moderate opinions. Anti-bullying charities condemned his lewd behaviour and offensive language towards some of the women on the show. But Tommy never could resist the lure of gangster chic and sought to impress the millionaire from South Central LA with sexual bragging and tales of violence. 'Golf is a game is a game for pussies,' Tommy told him. 'Eighteen holes and not a hair on any of them.' He boasted how, in his twenties, he would set a target of how many women he could sleep with in a single day. At times, he gave the impression that he was itching to tell Coolio of his more recent sexual adventures – but this was live TV.

He talked proudly of his friendship with Paul Ferris – 'maybe the top or second-top gangster in Glasgow'. When Coolio described how he had been shot at ten times, Tommy claimed that he and his pals used to 'bully people, take their money off them and that sort of thing. I was fit so people used to think I was a good fighter. I used to challenge people and they would back down.' Then there was the scar on his head which he'd acquired when a bottle was smashed over his head in a gang fight. Those who grew up with Tommy ridiculed his confession of teenage thuggery as a fantasy designed to ingratiate himself with the alpha male of the house. Strangely, in a conversation with Terry Christian, a one-time member of Militant, he also claimed to be a Celtic fan. I had known Tommy for twenty-five years and this was a revelation. It was like hearing Margaret Thatcher describe herself as a socialist. When he was an MSP, Tommy had told the *Sunday Times*: 'I have not been a Celtic fan since the early 1980s, when Mark Walters of Rangers was subjected to horrendous racial abuse at Celtic Park.' The black Birmingham-born winger had suffered some racist abuse from a small section of the crowd when he made his debut at an old Firm match – but that was in 1988, many years after Tommy had switched his allegiance to Rangers. He later described himself as a Motherwell supporter, and told Rosie Kane, when he was elected as an MSP, to stop supporting Celtic because it would alienate half of Glasgow.

The *Big Brother* debacle was just the latest and, for many people, the most visible episode in the long, slow degeneration of a political icon who had once signified something that mattered in Scotland. *The Scotsman* billboards on the final day of the show summed it up succinctly: 'From Class War To Crass Bore'. Serious voices in the media, including some who had respected Tommy in the past, expressed their dismay at the whole dismal affair. Ruth Wishart in *The Herald* put it most poignantly in an article that started and ended with the same words: 'Oh dear, Tommy. Oh dear, oh dear.' She suggested that 'perhaps the common thread that binds a certain breed of people blessed with fine minds and poor judgement is an insatiable appetite for personal publicity.'

When he got out, Tommy went on the offensive against those who had dared question his judgement. In an article in the *Big Issue*, he railed against the 'puffed-up columnists who have criticised me'. He also gave the *Daily Record* his exclusive inside story of life in the *Big Brother* house under the inaccurate headline, 'BAR-L HELPED ME SURVIVE BB'. Tommy had never been in Barlinnie Prison – on the day they ran the front-page headline, 'DOWNFALL OF A DODGER', the newspaper had obviously forgotten that the jail Tommy had been carted off to in 1992 was

Saughton Prison in Edinburgh. Alongside a cheesy, full-colour photo of Tommy and Gail and a birthday cake, and a vaguely exhibitionist image of the former MSP in a reclining pose, three quarters naked, he offered his thoughts on the other contestants. 'Michelle was too thick to have a game plan for winning the show,' he sneered. 'Ulrika must have been desperate for cash to leave behind her seven-month-old baby,' he moralised. 'Coolio was head and shoulders above everyone else,' he drooled. 'I thought it was surreal, a wee boy fae Pollok having a work-out with this rap superstar.'

A few days later, on the morning of Tuesday 24 January, Tommy's lawyer, Aamer Anwar, sent out a press release announcing there would be a lunchtime press conference outside his office in Glasgow city centre. Some journalists wondered whether the perjury case had indeed collapsed, in line with Tommy's repeated predictions. But there was one clue that gave the game away. Tommy Sheridan would be present, said the notice – but he would not be able to speak or answer questions. Everyone knew that, if this was to be a victory announcement, Tommy would be roaring it from the rooftops.

Aamer looked even more sombre than usual. He read out a prepared statement:

> I can confirm that an indictment was served today for charges of perjury against Thomas and Gail Sheridan. A preliminary hearing is fixed for 26 February 2009 at the High Court in Edinburgh and a trial will then be fixed for later on in the year. As proceedings are live it would be inappropriate to comment further, other than to state that both Mr and Mrs Sheridan maintain their innocence and are determined to fight this. There will be no further statements or interviews and we would ask the media to respect the Sheridan family's privacy.

Under different circumstances, the last point might have provoked wry smiles from the assembled media pack but this was a sombre moment. Details were sketchy. Tommy and his supporters were uncharacteristically tight-lipped, while the Crown Office would confirm only that the couple had both been indicted for perjury, with Tommy facing an additional charge of subornation – in other words, seeking to persuade or induce someone else to lie under oath.

'FROM BIG BROTHER TO BIG BOTHER,' chuckled the *Daily Record*'s front-page headline but the Crown Office was deadly serious. The indictment meant that there was no turning back. Tommy and Gail would either have to confess to serious criminal offences or face them down in a court of law. This wasn't breach of the peace for protesting at Faslane or a civil offence arising from defying a court order. This was one of the most serious offences on the statue book – one that, in theory, can carry up to a life sentence under Scots law. Perjury was rarely prosecuted but, when it was, it signified that the prosecution was confident of securing a conviction.

None of the others had been indicted but neither had their charges been dropped. Tommy and Gail had already appeared in court on petition back in March 2008. That immediately triggered a timetable – within twelve months, the Crown Office would have to either indict the pair or drop the charges. But the others were left dangling. They had been charged but had never appeared on petition – which meant there was no ticking clock. It looked like the Crown Office was leaving an escape route open for them as a bargaining lever to persuade them to talk truthfully.

Despite everything, I felt sympathy for these people. Their behaviour had been politically illiterate and morally questionable. Ironically, their recklessness had been based not on courage but on cowardice. In the white-hot atmosphere within the SSP in the summer of 2006, it was easier to succumb to Tommy and his rabid disciples than to resist the hysteria. Now, in the cold light of February 2009, with Tommy's credibility and support base diminished by his antics, they were looking less like selfless heroes and more like hapless human sacrifices laid out on the altar of hypocrisy. I felt particularly sorry for Gail. I had never figured out how much she knew. At worst, she had stood by her man. Misguided? Maybe, but she had probably just taken the line of least resistance.

Whatever anger I might have had in the past towards Tommy had gone, to be replaced with a mixture of pity and contempt. This was a man without remorse, without heart, without soul. His socialism was skin-deep, his compassion as phoney as canned laughter. Strip away the pious words and the practised facial expressions and you were left with a zombie. But, as any fan of late-night horror movies will testify, zombies are pretty relentless creatures. And this one wasn't about to lie down and go to sleep – not just yet.

Instead of withdrawing from public life, he carried on as though he had been charged with a speeding offence. Over the next year or so, he would stand for election under three different party labels. And, in the meantime, he devised other schemes to divert attention away from his legal troubles. In May, the *Daily Record* reported that he had 'laid down a challenge to Scots celebrities to fight him in the boxing ring'. Apparently, he had been lined up to top the bill at a celebrity charity boxing bout but no one else was interested. Rather desperately,

Tommy told the paper, 'I'm putting the challenge out there and will promise to take on whoever comes forward, no matter what size, shape or ability they are . . . I hope some well-known Scot will come forward to take up the challenge.' Eventually, he found a Radio Clyde DJ George Bowie to take up the offer. It wasn't exactly Ali versus Frazier – YouTube footage of the bout shows two lumbering middle-aged blokes, heavily protected with helmets, feebly pawing the air with all the grace and dignity of two elephants competing in *Strictly Come Dancing.*

In the European elections in June, he was number two on the Scottish list for a new UK-wide coalition with the text-speak title of NO2EU. Just before the election, he made a move that would startle even some of his closest allies. In a statement carried on the Solidarity website, he called for a rapprochement with his sworn enemies in the SSP.

> Despite our bitter relations with the SSP leadership I believe we should appeal to them and all other left and progressive groups and unions to join this Platform and campaign in a united fashion to maximise the left and progressive vote in Scotland at the Euro election on June 4th.

On the face of it, this was a volte-face of seismic proportions. In the 2007 Scottish council elections, conducted under the single transfer-able vote system, he had explicitly refused to call on Solidarity voters to give their second preference to SSP candidates. In the simultaneous Holyrood election, an internal Solidarity memo set out the twin aims of the party's election campaign – first, to get Tommy Sheridan elected in Glasgow and, second, to siphon enough votes away from the SSP in the rest of Scotland to ensure it lost all its four seats. Tommy and his Solidarity party had preferred to see Labour, Lib Dem, SNP and even Tory MSPs elected in place of the 'class traitors' and 'scabs' of the SSP.

Some of us now suspected he was driving forward his own hidden agenda. As the novelist William McIlvanney once remarked, 'There is nothing so divisive in Scottish politics as a call for unity.' Tommy knew that, after the electoral batterings suffered by both sides of the split, many activists would be attracted to the idea of a step back towards reunification, especially against the background of the biggest crisis of capitalism since the 1930s. But he also knew that his dizzying U-turn would place those he had maligned as liars, fraudsters and forgers in an impossible position. Far from a genuine bid for unity, this looked a calculated attempt to disrupt the SSP and, crucially, to isolate the old leadership of 2004, who would be key witnesses in any future perjury trial. If he could help engineer some kind of split in the SSP, it would be easier to undermine their credibility. With Tommy, nothing was ever straightforward.

Most SSP members knew instinctively that the shattered edifice could not simply be put back together with superglue. A quick-fix repair job might produce an instant improvement but, in the not-so-distant future, as the truth emerged, the walls would come tumbling back down, burying us all in the rubble. And there was an added complication. How could we discuss unity without first discussing the split? And how could we discuss the split without discussing Tommy Sheridan's central role in the whole debacle? Our legal advice was stark – with a live criminal case in progress, any discussion about Tommy Sheridan and his behaviour would leave us open to contempt of court proceedings. Our hands were tied. Until this toxic case was over, there could be no serious debate over the future of the Scottish Left.

It looked like we would be stuck in this state of limbo for a long time to come. The first preliminary hearing, originally set for February 2009, was delayed several times before it finally took place on 13 July. By that time, the European election had come and gone. With Tommy second top of their Scottish list and despite the coalition's backing by the RMT trade union, NO2EU had crashed into twelfth place with under 10,000 votes. The SSP had fared only marginally better, coming tenth with just over 10,000 votes. In 2004, the united SSP had polled 60,000 votes. With the free market economy in meltdown, we should have been celebrating the biggest surge forward in the history of Scottish socialism. Instead, we were all trapped in the wreckage.

As Tommy and Gail arrived at the High Court in Edinburgh for the July preliminary hearing, they were greeted by a small band of supporters brandishing Defend Tommy Sheridan placards. Inside, the details of the perjury charges were read out in public for the first time. The seven-page indictment set out a list of sixteen false statements Tommy had made under oath during the defamation trial. These covered the visits to the swingers' club, his confession to the SSP executive, the incident in the Moat House Hotel and his relationship with Katrine Trolle. There was no reference to the Fiona McGuire allegations presumably because the Crown Office wasn't confident that it had enough corroborating evidence to prove the facts of that dispute beyond all reasonable doubt.

Up until this point, no one had been quite sure what the second charge – attempted subornation of perjury – was all about. The indictment cleared up the mystery. In June 2006, a few weeks before the trial, Tommy had met Colin Fox in the Beanscene coffee shop on Holyrood Road. There, he had presented him with the handwritten statement addressed to 'Colin and Richie' that would later be discovered by Lothian and Borders Police during the raid on his home. Tommy had tried to persuade Colin to sign the statement and commit perjury by corroborating, under oath, the fictitious version of events set out in the statement.

What came as more of a shock was the case against Gail. The indictment stated that she had lied seven times in the witness box. Among the other items removed from the Sheridan household during the police raid back in December 2007 were Gail's diaries, whose entries contradicted the evidence she had given in court. Further investigation revealed that she had misled the jury on a number of points. She had not been at home with her husband every weekend during November 2001 and September 2002. She had been working that Friday night in November 2001 when Tommy had phoned the Cupids club. And, on the night of the Moat House incident in June 2002, she had not been with Tommy and Andy McFarlane as she had stated in court. Nor did she have a conversation with Katrine Trolle at the SSP conference in 2005.

Now Gail was in serious trouble, aggravated by the fact that she stood to make plenty of cash from Tommy's defamation victory. Personally, I was never convinced that Gail had set out with the express intention of committing perjury for financial gain – it was more likely that she had started off believing Tommy's fantasy version of events and had then been gradually sucked in to the quagmire without realising what was going on until it was too late to get out.

The publication of the indictment blew apart the facade of ultra-confidence that Tommy had projected from the start of the police investigation three years earlier. He had always taken the concept of positive thinking to absurd extremes. Optimism was one of his attractive qualities, especially to those who knew him only superficially. He always looked on the bright side of life and had the ability to transmit his enthusiasm to others around him. But his super-confidence frequently defied reality and crossed the boundary between self-belief and self-delusion. Pessimism was for losers, he believed. For him, the ocean was always knee-deep. If he was plunging down a cliff face, he would still be brimful of optimism. Despite the odds stacked against him in what he called this 'mother-of-all battles to clear my name', he had managed to convince himself and others around him that the case against him was going nowhere. He had told an unreported press conference back in December that he had inside information that the Crown Office would drop all charges on Christmas Eve. The timing, he explained, was to stifle any media furore over the costs of the investigation and the waste of police resources.

For all Tommy's political cunning and PR savvy, he had shown himself to be out of his depth when it came to outwitting the law. He had left behind a trail of evidence including handwritten notes, diaries, telephone records and emails. As master criminals go, Tommy wasn't quite in the Macavity class.

Gail was represented at the hearing by Paul McBride, a politically ambitious young QC who had resigned from the Labour Party three months earlier to become an adviser to the Conservative Party. Tommy's QC, the eccentric Donald Findlay, was a more traditional Tory and a hard-line unionist with strong links to Rangers FC. But, in a hint of what perhaps was to come, Scotland's most famous lawyer was absent from the preliminary hearing, his place taken by defence advocate Tony Lenehan. As expected, both Tommy and Gail pled not guilty to all charges. The trial, expected to last for up to three months, was scheduled to start on 11 January 2010.

Rumours were now swirling around legal circles of a rupture between Tommy and his flamboyant QC. On 25 September 2009, the *Daily Record* broke the inside story – or at least Tommy's version of the inside story – via Mark Smith. The report stated that Tommy had fired Donald Findlay by telephone while the lawyer was in holiday in the Far East. It was a chance for the subeditors to give a new twist to an old headline: 'TOMMY DROPS HIS BRIEFS – AGAIN!' Findlay's replacement would be Maggie Scott, a QC who had defended Abdelbaset Ali al-Megrahi, the man convicted under controversial circumstances of the Lockerbie bombing. So what was all this about?

True to form, a 'source close to the case' was quoted as saying, 'There have been no big bust-ups nor differences of opinion. But Tommy has come to the opinion that his cause may be better served by changing his team now rather than later.' So far, so evasive. The source added, 'Tommy has been most impressed by how she [Maggie Scott] has dealt with Megrahi and admires her modern outlook.' The explanation was resoundingly unconvincing. Few people would dream of casually changing their QC two years into a serious criminal case as though they were switching their car insurance provider.

At a further preliminary hearing in October that year, the judge agreed to postpone the trial to allow Tommy's new defence team time to prepare their case. A further hearing in December failed to set a new trial date. By this time, it looked like the Sheridan perjury case might outlast *Coronation Street*.

Tommy's final two forays into electoral politics opened with blazing fireworks then fizzled out like sparklers in the rain. Launching his campaign for the Glasgow North East by-election – called to replace Michael Martin, the Speaker of the House of Commons, who had resigned amidst the MPs' expenses scandal – Tommy claimed that he could win the seat. He presented himself as the most experienced by far of all the candidates, with eight years' experience as an MSP and eleven years as a councillor under his belt. He also received extraordinarily supportive coverage in the *Daily Record* which ran six major articles sympathetic to his campaign, each accompanied by large photographs and headlines such as 'Help Us Ban Airguns For Our Wee Boy', 'Send Junket MSPs to Oz In Shackles' and 'Tommy: Give Me a Shot'. During the heyday of the SSP, before the Cupids crisis, we could only have dreamed of such favourable publicity in Glasgow's biggest-selling daily newspaper.

Yet, when the ballot papers stacked up, the result was a shock. For the first time ever, Tommy had lost his deposit, polling just 794 votes, four per cent of the total. Speaking on the BBC, the polling expert Professor John Curtice pointed out that, just four years earlier, Tommy Sheridan would have been guaranteed at least 20 per cent of the vote in any Glasgow seat. Some Solidarity supporters, though, turning the dark art of political spin into a parody of itself, claimed a victory because Tommy had outpolled Kevin McVey, the SSP candidate. It was desperate stuff as, for all his skills and talents, Kevin didn't have Tommy's fame, his electoral credibility or his sycophantic press coverage.

Undeterred, Tommy stood again in the general election of May 2010 in his home territory of Glasgow South West. This time, he stood as the candidate of the Trade Union Socialist Coalition, a rehashed version of NO2EU. It was the sixth party label Tommy had stood under in 15 years, possibly setting some kind of Scottish or even British record. In a Westminster election dominated by the three big Westminster parties, no one expected Tommy to win. But he had once taken a sensational 20 per cent of the vote in this seat in a general election then, for eleven years, had represented a big chunk of the constituency as a councillor. His right-hand man, Keith Baldassara, had come second here with ten per cent of the vote in the 2001 general election and, two years later, had won Tommy's old council seat outright in a first-past-the-post election.

By 2010, given the catastrophic twin crises of the banking collapse and the stench of corruption surrounding Westminster, the electorate should have been queuing up at the polling stations to vote for someone with Tommy's track record and anti-capitalist credentials. Instead, his old voters deserted him in droves. In his one-time stronghold, he crashed into fifth place with just three per cent of the vote. It was worse than anyone could ever have predicted. Across Scotland, the left-wing vote was split almost exactly down the middle between the SSP and the self-styled Trade Union Socialist Coalition. Each had stood in ten constituencies, avoiding a head-on clash in all seats bar one, but the total vote had been under 7,000, compared to over 70,000 back in 2001. The Scottish Left had paid a heavy price for Tommy Sheridan's defamation victory over *News of the World*.

Tommy Sheridan was now damaged goods – but so too was the post-Sheridan SSP. The party and its members had behaved honourably from start to finish but that fact had been concealed from the wider public. Unbelievably, some elements in the media were still treating Tommy as a saintly martyr who had been crucified by heathens. In one article, published on the STV website in late 2009, senior journalist David Coyle wrote:

A proper firebrand, a radical in the mould of John Maclean, a man of the people who did time for his beliefs. But then the brothers and the sisters turned on Tommy, hoping that they could steal a bit of his thunder and chisel out a wee bit of fame for themselves. Political crimes of the decade that was.

Coyle had been the features editor of the *Daily Record* when the paper ran its £20,000 series of interviews with Tommy and Gail Sheridan in the days following the defamation case and it seemed he was still as gullible as ever. When the SSP tried to reply, the party was advised by lawyers to stay tight-lipped or face the prospect of contempt of court proceedings for breaching sub judice rules. Since his first court appearance on petition almost two years earlier, Tommy had been protected by a legally enforceable wall of silence.

Eventually, at yet another preliminary hearing in March 2010, a new date was set for the trial. It would start on 21 September 2010. At least it might be over before Christmas – but, then, that's what they said about the Afghanistan war back in October 2001. Since the start of the police investigation, Britain had lived under three different Prime Ministers and the serial killer Peter Tobin had been arrested, tried and convicted in three separate murder trials.

By this time, the list of Crown witnesses now stood at 230 – 60 more than had given evidence at the Chilcot Inquiry into the Iraq War. They included Rosemary Byrne, Jock Penman, Graeme McIver and Pat Smith, the four Solidarity members who still had perjury charges hanging over their heads. It appeared that the Crown Office was effectively inviting them to either recant on the evidence they had given during the defamation trial or commit double perjury.

Two further preliminary hearings, in July and early August 2010, were shrouded in secrecy. Tommy's legal team had, despite a challenge from the BBC, successfully argued for reporting restrictions prohibiting any press coverage of the hearings, other than the bare facts of the date and venue. With the media silenced, Tommy's legal team battled for three days to disallow key prosecution evidence, including the videotape of his confession and the corroborating testimony of voice recognition experts. Because the tape had been filmed without his permission, this was, his legal team argued, a breach of Tommy's privacy.

During his defamation battle four years earlier, Tommy had trampled all over the privacy of innocent people. Under cross-examination, he had pressurised several women into revealing intimate details of their sex lives. He had even cited one woman's medical records and had falsely accused another woman of having a conviction for fraud. As well as reeking of hypocrisy, his plea for privacy smacked of desperation. A few years earlier, he had derided the tape as a spliced and doctored 'concoction'. If the tape was indeed a fake, why would he want it banned as evidence? Surely he would have demanded the opportunity to expose this fabrication in order to illustrate the depths to which his enemies were prepared to stoop to destroy him?

The judge, Lord Brailsford, ruled that the videotape and all other disputed evidence would be admissible. Tommy was now looking like the king on a chessboard surrounded by enemy pieces with just a handful of pawns left to defend him. But still he refused to be toppled. Behind the scenes, defence lawyers requested a further delay. The judge and Crown Office agreed to push back the start of the trial by a further fortnight, until 4 October.

In a further twist, Gail's legal team sent out letters to 150 Crown witnesses asking them to provide a precognition statement. On the face of it, this was bizarre. Gail had been indicted 18 months earlier yet her lawyers had waited until the eleventh hour before seeking statements. And what was the point of interviewing scores of SSP witnesses whose evidence was unrelated to the charges against Gail Sheridan? I had already given a lengthy precognition, over two days, to Aamer Anwar, Tommy's solicitor, but none of it was relevant to Gail. Adding to the mystery, it transpired that one man would be conducting all the interviews – Gordon Cumming, a recently retired Strathclyde Police Chief Inspector, who had been in Special Branch and the CID. At this late stage, why not hire a team of precognition officers to race through the witness lists speedily as possible?

It seemed a strange way of proceeding. Perhaps it had been Gail's lawyers who had asked for the two-week delay because they were starting to realise that this case was contaminated. Maybe now her defence team were trying to save Gail from her husband and from her own naivety. If she continued lying all the way to the High Court, she could end up in Cornton Vale, separated from her five-year-old daughter, with her life in ruins. Had this former Chief Inspector been specifically assigned to confirm that the case against Tommy was rock solid? Was this about piling the pressure on Tommy to plead guilty to at least some of the counts of perjury he had been charged with? Maybe then the Crown Office might be inclined to drop the charges against Gail.

From the start of this whole affair, I was convinced that she had been duped into colluding with Tommy's cover-up. She may have been fed snippets of sanitised information and probably suspected that he had indulged in a few flings. But it was doubtful whether she would have been complicit in this cover-up if she had known for a fact that Tommy had frequented swingers' clubs and participated in threesomes with his brother-in-law. Far-fetched though it may have seemed, she probably wanted to believe that Tommy was indeed the victim of a shocking conspiracy.

Many people had suffered torment as a result of Tommy Sheridan's six-year crusade to turn fiction into fact. He had used his media connections to publicly trash the reputation of scores of good people. He had manipulated the weak, placing them in the firing line to protect himself. He had inflicted carnage on the socialist movement. But nothing could compare with the twilight world that he had created for Gail.

28

Autumn 2010

Trial of the Decade

In the film *Carlito's Way*, Dave Kleinfield – a corrupt, deceitful lawyer played by Sean Penn – sums up his personal philosophy thus: 'There is only one rule: you save your own ass.' His client, Carlito, a reformed gangster played by Al Pacino, has a different code of honour: 'There's a line you cross, the point of no return. Dave crossed it. Now there's no coming back.'

By the autumn of 2010, most of his oldest political allies knew that Tommy Sheridan had long since crossed the line of no return. To 'save his own ass' he had tried to annihilate the reputations of everyone who refused to submit to his will. No lie had been too outlandish, no smear too vile, no tactic too underhand. Scotland's most famous socialist had shown himself capable of the kind of ruthless selfishness usually associated with cold-blooded capitalist tycoons.

Yet even at this stage, he could salvage some honour by taking responsibility for his own behaviour and apologising. Even Bill Clinton, following the Monica Lewinsky revelations, achieved some measure of redemption by accepting censure for his behaviour.

Tommy would sooner eat his own right hand than swallow a slice of humble pie. Nonetheless, he could still take the Jonathan Aitken road rather than the Jeffrey Archer route. After being exposed as a perjurer during his libel trial against the *Guardian*, Aitken had wisely cut his losses and confessed. He received an 18-month sentence, in contrast to the four years meted out to the more gung-ho Archer. Inevitably, Tommy would take this right to the wire. But I suspected that he might then pull back and engage in a damage-limitation exercise. It would mean a public climbdown, but in private, 'friends of Tommy Sheridan' would brief the media that here was an innocent man sacrificing his own liberty to protect his wife and child from the ordeal of court.

A week before the new trial date of 4 October, Tommy still refused to blink. Meanwhile, Gail's legal team was in a state of growing alarm. This wasn't some adolescent game of chicken. Round the next bend lurked a high speed collision – and their client was strapped in the front passenger seat beside the driver. Even in the unlikely event that they could persuade Gail to break ranks with her husband and enter a guilty plea, she would still go to jail; under Scots Law, perjury carries a mandatory custodial sentence. At best, Gail's lawyers could plead for clemency, but because of the seriousness of the crime – compounded by the £200,000 the couple had stood to gain from the defamation trial – the judge's hands were tied.

There was one way out. If Tommy could be persuaded to plead guilty to at least part of his indictment, the Crown Office might consider dropping the charges against Gail, and possibly the others who still had perjury charges hanging over them. Even when they have cast-iron evidence that a crime has been committed, the prosecution services in Scotland have the discretion to decide that it would 'not be in the public interest' to proceed. In taking such a decision, they weigh up a list of factors, including the impact on victims, the motivation of the defendant and the likelihood of their re-offending.

Behind closed doors, the Crown Office put an offer on the table that 99 per cent of people in Tommy's situation would have devoured like a starving dog thrown a string of sausages. If he was prepared to plead guilty to the Cupids-related counts, the prosecution would delete those sections of the indictment relating to the Moat House sex party. This would then allow them to drop the case against Gail, which was based strongly on the alibi she had provided for Tommy that night. The prosecution would then look for a maximum 18-month sentence, guaranteeing his automatic release after nine months. He could even be eligible for release with an electronic tag after just five months, under new legislation introduced in 2006. By any standards, this was lenient and exposed the absurdity of the claim by some of his supporters that Tommy was a political martyr, persecuted by the state as part of an ideological war.

But Tommy's messianic sense of destiny overrode everything. This was an all-or-nothing fight to the death. If he could pull off a second sensational courtroom triumph, he would become a legend. And if he failed, at least he would go down in a blaze of fireworks, screaming defiance as he went. Despite the weight of evidence against him, he seemed convinced he could win, especially with Gail by his side. Any compassionate jury, he figured, would be reluctant to jail both parents of a five-year-old child, especially as there were no dead or injured bodies to avenge. To acquit Gail, the jury would have to give her the benefit of the doubt over the alibis she had provided for her husband – and that in turn would increase his own chances of walking free. Hard-bitten lawyers, used to dealing with some of Scotland's most violent criminals, were appalled at the callous cynicism of a man prepared to use his wife as a human shield.

The Trial of the Decade, as it was dubbed by the tabloids, opened on a bright autumn morning. Outside the new High Court building in Glasgow, a scrappy band of Solidarity supporters gathered alongside the photographers, reporters and TV satellite vans that lined the narrow lane tucked behind the city mortuary, their banners calling for Rupert Murdoch and *News of the World* to be put on trial instead of Tommy Sheridan. In their fevered imaginations, these starry-eyed disciples had decided that this was David pitching himself against Goliath rather than a corrupt politician out to destroy truth, subvert justice and annihilate the reputations of anyone who dared to defy him.

The Cult of the Great Leader was back in full swing, with self-proclaimed Trotskyist sects such as the SWP and the Socialist Party setting the tone. I had known many of these people personally.

For all their revolutionary chest-beating, few of them had ever seriously tangled with the law. Now they demanded that dozens of SSP witnesses offer themselves up as sacrificial lambs for the greater glory of Tommy Sheridan. Their version of socialism was straight out of *Animal Farm*, and their view of solidarity was a throwback to the Stalinist show trials where broken men falsely confessed their own guilt to appease a megalomaniac. For all their socialist sanctimony, their morality was no different from that of the political, religious and financial institutions which had, over the decades, covered up corruption, abuse and greed to protect their own power.

The SSP had never wanted any of its members to be hauled through the courts. But we never had any choice in the matter – other than send dozens of people with jobs and families to jail for up to two years for contempt of court. For the best part of a decade, we had been trapped in a toxic legal quagmire, thanks to one man's cowardly refusal to accept the consequences of his own behaviour. Tommy's demagogic ranting against Rupert Murdoch and the *News of the World* might go down well in some circles, but it was a smokescreen. Out of over 40 witnesses who would be called to give evidence by the prosecution during this perjury trial, only a couple were employed by the newspaper. The vast majority were lifelong socialists, defending their party and their cause against a barrage of lies and slander.

This time round, those members of the SSP who had been called as witnesses were clear in their own minds about what they had to do.

During the defamation case, we were all still members of the same party and we had been reluctant witnesses, providing only the bare minimum of information, under protest. It had been the legal equivalent of a work-to-rule. The full scale of Tommy's treachery had only revealed itself during and after that 2006 courtroom battle. Now we knew that we were up against Tommy the Terminator, a man quite prepared to orchestrate the biggest miscarriage of justice in Scottish legal history and put dozens of innocent people in the dock for crimes he had committed. This would be a no-holds-barred fight to the finish.

It took Tommy just one week to sack his QC. 'To lose one parent may be regarded as a misfortune; to lose two looks like carelessness,' said Oscar Wilde. To lose three QCs looked like downright madness. But there was method in it. Tommy knew he would never be able to win this case on the basis of evidence alone. Yet there was another way. His experience in the Court of Session had taught him that juries can be emotionally manipulated. Tommy may have failed to complete his law degree, but he was an accomplished actor with the ability to press sympathy buttons and even turn on the waterworks as and when required. Which meant he must move out of the dock and engage directly with the jury.

With access to an unlimited legal aid budget, he had hired Maggie Scott and her assistants to carry out the complex, painstaking work of assembling his defence case. It had required a level of expertise and intellectual depth that neither Tommy himself nor his solicitor, Aamer Anwar, possessed. In advance of the trial, she and her team had done a thorough job, sifting through masses of evidence, including police statements, transcripts of testimony from the Court of Session, press cuttings and SSP internal documentation to uncover irregularities and inconsistencies that could be used to trip up prosecution witnesses.

But once the groundwork had been done and battle commenced in court, the main man was clearly itching to take over. No way could he be content to remain a spectator at the Tommy Sheridan Show, forced to sit it out mutely in the dock, day after day, for three long months.

The only surprise was that his patience ran out quite so quickly. The first week wasn't a good one for him. But it wasn't Maggie Scott's fault that the first seven witnesses stood by their statements.

Barbara Scott, Allison Kane, Colin Fox, Allan Green, Felicity Garvie, Duncan Rowan and Carolyn Leckie had all attended the infamous SSP executive meeting of November 2004. Most of them had since moved on; apart from Colin, they were no longer involved in the central leadership of the party. They had all pretty much lost contact with one another over the years. But they were all crystal clear about what had happened that Tuesday night six years before in a small room in a backstreet Glasgow office.

New evidence, never heard in the Court of Session, was presented during that first week. The jury were shown the handwritten notes Barbara Scott had handed to the police after the defamation trial, along with the A4 notebook from which she had torn out the pages, the ragged edges fitting together precisely. The Advocate-Depute, Alex Prentice, had also played the George McNeilage video tape. This was the first time the full recording had been broadcast in public. Back in 2006, the *News of the World* had carried some clips on its website and on a telephone hotline, the quality of the recording degraded by background interference. But this was the original tape – 40 minutes of free-flowing conversation, the sound quality impeccable and the distinctive baritone of the former MSP and Celebrity Big Brother contestant ringing out as clear as a church bell on a silent Sunday morning.

To round off a difficult week for Tommy, the Saturday morning newspapers seized on a remark made by Carolyn Leckie during her cross-examination and splashed it as a front page: 'It's disgusting that Gail is having to sit through this'. It was a throwaway comment but it touched a raw nerve and summed up the feelings of millions. Over that weekend, rumours of a rupture between Tommy and his legal team began to circulate.

When the court reconvened on Monday morning, the public gallery gasped audibly as the judge announced that Tommy Sheridan had sacked his QC, along with her two junior counsels, Shelagh McColl and Gillian Brown. Tommy told the court that he had 'lost confidence' in his legal team – apart from his solicitor Aamer Anwar – claiming that Scott had 'failed to follow my instruction'. The judge advised him strongly to find another advocate to represent him, but that was to misunderstand the strategy. This had nothing to do with Maggie Scott – it was all about Tommy Sheridan. The court was adjourned for three days to allow him time to prepare. High drama was guaranteed.

Tommy's first clash was with Jo Harvie, an ex-editor of the *Scottish Socialist Voice*, now working as a journalist with the Red Cross, who faced him down with quiet courage and dignity. Rosie was moving beyond words. She reminded Tommy that her mother had once worshipped him, yet had gone to her grave hearing him call her daughter a liar. Tommy was 'an ego on the rampage' said Rosie – 'and you're actually starting to believe your own lies'.

Back in 2006, Katrine Trolle had been the most devastating witness by far. She had never been paid a penny by *News of the World*. Under threat of contempt of court, she had been compelled to give painful and humiliating evidence because she had been identified to the newspaper by Duncan Rowan, with the apparent collusion of his then friend, Steve Arnott. Now she had to travel over from Denmark to be publicly cross-examined, in excruciating detail, by a man with whom she had once been sexually intimate. Forced for a second time to fight for her integrity, Katrine supplied some additional evidence which had not been presented at the Court of Session. She had drawn a sketch of Tommy's bedroom, including a frilly, flowery quilt and a wedding photo above the bed. She described a white plastic Christmas tree and a sunbed in a nearby room – which there had been at the time, notwithstanding Tommy's denial of ever having owned such an appliance. She also described in detail the interior of the home of Andy McFarlane, where she had been lured into a threesome. There were fairy lights around the headboard in his bedroom, a Christmas tree on the landing and a small white dog in the house. The Advocate-Depute later showed her a newspaper photo of Tommy holding the same white dog in his arms.

Katrine acknowledged she had got the Cupids date wrong in the Court of Session. In response to Tommy's repeated accusations that she was a 'conscious liar', Katrine stated: 'I am guilty of getting dates wrong, guilty of being naive, guilty of thinking you had charisma, guilty of having sex with you, but I am not guilty of lying in court.' Anvar Khan had also been unable, during the defamation trial, to pinpoint the exact date of the visit until she later examined phone bills and other records. The mix-up over dates prompted me to think of events I had attended around the same time, to test my own memory. I could recall attending a Bob Dylan concert at the Scottish Exhibition and Conference Centre in the first few years of the millennium. I could remember most of the songs he sang, the atmosphere, the clothes he wore – but try as I might, I couldn't remember whether it was 2001, 2002 or 2003, let alone the month. To me, then, it seemed credible that these women may indeed have had difficulty pinning down the date of a murky event years before – especially one they would clearly now prefer to forget.

Within that first week of defending himself, Tommy made two serious tactical blunders. First he demanded that the seven witnesses who had already given evidence and been cross-examined by Maggie Scott be recalled so that he could interrogate them himself. Those who had already appeared in court now had to psyche themselves up for a second round, this time against a bare-knuckle fighter with his teeth bared. They were ready for him.

Tommy's second mistake was to initiate a court order against the *Sunday Herald* to get the affidavit that I had signed back in November 2004. He didn't know the newspaper was no longer in possession of the document; a week or so before the start of the trial, editor Richard Walker handed over to me an envelope containing the only two copies of the affidavit in existence. By now, the document had effectively expired. Under Scots Law, there is a three-year deadline for taking out a defamation action, which meant that the affidavit, which had been signed to provide legal cover for a newspaper story in late 2004, was redundant by the end of 2007. I had the option of disposing of the document, which had not yet been cited as evidence. But I knew that to destroy the affidavit would only fuel Tommy's conspiracy theory against the SSP and allow him to spin new suspicions of a cover-up.

I trusted the professional integrity of the two *Sunday Herald* journalists involved, Richard Walker and the investigations editor, Paul Hutcheon, and that they would never reveal their sources even if threatened with a jail sentence. But I also knew that Tommy would have no compunction about locking up journalists in pursuit of his multiple vendettas. As a member of the NUJ, I wasn't prepared to put any journalist in the firing line. Just as importantly, I wanted the opportunity to dispel some of the myths about this affidavit and explain why I had acted to protect the SSP by signing the document under oath back in November 2004. Although it lacked the personal detail contained in the SSP minutes, it was consistent with our account of the discussion that had taken place, and would undermine Tommy's claim that, sometime in 2006, we had retrospectively falsified the history of that fateful executive meeting.

When, on the Friday morning of the third week, the Crown Office agreed to take out a court order on Tommy's behalf against the *Sunday Herald*, I informed the court that I had the document; after a frantic drive across the M8 – while the court was adjourned – I handed over the papers. That afternoon, during his cross-examination of Allison Kane, Tommy suggested that my actions had been 'cynical in the extreme'. Allison, who hadn't known anything about the affidavit, replied calmly: 'I understand why he did it. These were exceptional circumstances and exceptional measures were taken by all of us. He did what he did to protect the party. You had scurried off and spun a web of lies to the press. If he was cynical, so were you.' Tommy had shown the affidavit neither to the witness nor to the jury. That was left to Alex Prentice, the Advocate-Depute, who projected the document onto a screen and asked Allison to confirm the accuracy of its contents, which he went through, paragraph by paragraph. Yes, she replied repeatedly. It wasn't the whole truth, and to protect Tommy's privacy, I had deliberately omitted his confession to visiting Cupids, but it was enough to confirm that our version had been consistent for four years. No wonder Maggie Scott had judged it best to avoid this mystery affidavit.

Towards the end of her cross-examination, Allison told Tommy: 'You must be the unluckiest person in the world because everybody you have met in the last 20 to 30 years is either lying or conspiring against you.' By now, the trial was turning into a headline-writer's dream, as the quotes flowed like whisky at a clan gathering. Carolyn Leckie summed up the essence of Tommy's case with a quote, aptly from a Carry On Film: 'Infamy, infamy they've all got it infamy'. Frances Curran asked him: 'Is that your defence, Tommy? Liar, Liar, Pants on Fire?' and went on to suggest that 'the biggest crime you committed was that you sold out the people who voted for you.' Richie Venton, another long-term friend and ally, accused him of 'mind-boggling recklessness', while Allan Green compared him to Jeffrey Archer – 'going to court to prove lies are truth and truth is lies'. Rosie Kane told him 'Your ego was on the rampage. You were a kamikaze then and you are now.' Colin Fox said: 'You have a Svengali-like influence over your supporters – they'll say black is white and white is black if you tell them to.'

In return, Tommy was ready to resort to any smear to discredit his old comrades. He accused Richie of being a 'trained liar', on the grounds that he had been expelled from the Labour Party in the 1980s for his membership of the semi-secret Militant tendency. By any standards, this was pretty unprincipled stuff. Tommy himself had been expelled from the Labour Party in the 1980s for his involvement with Militant. Four of his own defence witnesses had also been Militant members. When he went down the same line of questioning with me, I reminded him that, 20 years before, I had been the first to challenge that culture of secrecy by calling for Militant in Scotland to be relaunched as an open political party. I could see the eyes of some members of the jury glazing over as they were taken on this detour down into the dimly-lit underground tunnels of Marxist factional history.

More duplicitous still was Tommy's self-righteous denunciation of George McNeilage for 'creeping into people's homes and robbing them as they were asleep in their beds'. This was a reference to George's convictions for housebreaking more than 30 years before, when he was barely a boy of 16, growing up in poverty in a family of nine children. Since then, George had devoted much of his life to breaking young people away from crime, drug abuse and anti-social behaviour and the two men had become so close that George had invited Tommy to be the best man at his wedding, and Tommy had reciprocated when he tied the knot with Gail. During rancorous exchanges between the two former friends, the court was adjourned while Lord Bracadale advised George McNeilage to get legal representation as he would be facing contempt of court proceedings. During my testimony, both Tommy and I had received warnings from the judge after a series of hostile exchanges. But as the *Scotsman* court reporter pointed out, 'the animosity between Sheridan and former political allies was nothing to the atmosphere generated by Mr McNeilage's appearance in the witness box. Pure unadulterated hatred was in the air. If looks really could kill, the carpets of Court 4 would have been awash with blood'. A few weeks later, while the perjury trial was still underway, George made a private appearance before Lord Bracadale, where he pled guilty and was fined for contempt of court. Because of reporting restrictions, the incident was never covered in the media.

Meanwhile, Tommy retreated from his initial cover story for the George McNeilage tape. When the recording had first emerged, Tommy admitted that his voice was on the recording, but suggested that it had been spliced. He also hinted that the secret intelligence services had fitted him up, telling the *Scottish Mirror*: 'When the history of this story is written, I think you'll find MI5 were certainly involved.' At the time, he was widely ridiculed for this apparently random outburst, but there was a calculation behind it. If he was going to claim the tape had been pieced together from snippets of unrelated conversations, then he would also have to explain who had obtained these recordings and how. By suggesting that secret intelligence forces were responsible, he was on safe ground, knowing his assertion could never be proven or disproven. Some people might even believe him. But splices on a video or audio tape are easy to detect, and by now no-one, not even Tommy, was disputing that this was a continuous recording. So he conjured up a new explanation, denying point blank that his voice could be heard anywhere on the tape. Without a shred of evidence or a word or explanation, he accused me of writing the script and recruiting an unidentified actor to impersonate him. He also claimed tape had not been made in November 2004, but *after* the libel case in the summer of 2006.

What the jury did not know was that a few weeks before the trial opened, Tommy's legal team had tried and failed to persuade the judge that the video recording should be ruled inadmissible as evidence, under the Human Rights Act. If Tommy knew that this tape was a fake, he would surely have welcomed its presentation in court, as evidence of the ridiculous lengths to which his political opponents would go. Neither did the jury know that Tommy had been positively identified as one of the two men on the tape by voice and imaging experts. Their evidence was never made available to the court because of a new legal ruling made by law lords in late October, three weeks into this trial. The Cadder Ruling – named after Peter Cadder, who had successfully appealed his conviction for assault – barred any evidence from being presented in court that had been obtained by police without a solicitor present.

Back in December 2007, on the day of Tommy's arrest, Lothian and Borders police had recorded an interview with him which they had sent to linguistics laboratories, along with the tape. The voice experts had found that the range, pitch, timing and intonation of the voice on the McNeilage tape was identical to that on the police recording of Tommy's interview. Police forensics had also photographed his right hand, and his head from different angles, before sending the material for expert analysis. Using computerised 3-D imaging techniques, experts had positively matched these photographs with stills on the video tape. But under the new ruling, none of this evidence could be heard in court.

If this really had been a political conspiracy orchestrated by a cabal of SSP members, it would have made the Mafia look like an adolescent street gang. We had forged documents, fabricated evidence, perverted the course of justice and committed collective perjury in the Court of Session. We had concocted a video-taped confession that had fooled the world's foremost forensic experts, altered hard drives and made entries in Tommy's diary in his own handwriting. We had faced down an intense, four-year investigation by police and prosecution services, and framed innocent people for the crimes we had committed. Then we had gone to the High Court in Glasgow for a repeat performance, this time with ten new witnesses in tow, to back up our fictitious version of events. Along the way, not one person had broken down or changed their evidence. This was one helluva plot. As I told Tommy during my cross-examination: 'JK Rowling could not make up the stories you've made up – this is Harry Potter and Lord of the Rings combined.'

Somehow, we had also managed to conjure up other witnesses, with no connection to the SSP, to corroborate our lies. Gary Clark, for example, who had known Tommy since they started primary school together. Gary and his family had been put through hell over the past four years because of a one-off mistake he had made back in 2002. At the time, he had been separated from his wife and was drinking heavily and suffering from depression. In court, he pinpointed the exact date of the journey he had made down the M6 to Manchester in his own car, with Anvar Khan, Katrine Trolle and Andy McFarlane. Tommy had been in the driving seat, both literally and figuratively. Gary couldn't remember all the details of the Cupids visit, but he was in no doubt that he had been to a Manchester sex club in late September 2002 with the man now trying to face him down in court.

Then there were the two women from Glasgow who backed up Anvar Khan's testimony that she had an affair with Tommy. One woman, Susan, testified that she had gone to Anvar Khan's flat in the West End of Glasgow with Tommy and Andy McFarlane. Another woman, Elizabeth Quinn, a 70-year-old retired head teacher, had lived next door to the *News of the World* columnist, and the two women remained friends after Khan moved to London. When she returned to Glasgow, Anvar Khan would sometimes stay over in her former neighbour's spare room. Ms Quinn told the court that on the afternoon of 11 August, 2003, she arrived home to find Anvar and Tommy coming into her living room from an adjacent bedroom. She had 'absolutely no doubt whatsoever it was him. I was stunned. I thought it was very stupid behaviour.' Elizabeth Quinn was living in California when she heard the verdict of the defamation case. 'It was like hearing that O.J. Simpson was declared innocent – it was a bit of shock,' she told the court. She contacted the police in Scotland and told them, 'I think I may have some salient information.'

Another witness, Tony Cumberbirch, described how he was working behind the bar on the night of Friday 27 September, 2002. Tommy Sheridan had signed his own name in the register, which the barman was later asked to remove by a Scottish friend. He described 'a group from Scotland, which included Tommy Sheridan, two other lads who were drunk, and two lasses, one foreign, Scandinavian, another darker-skinned'. Another woman, Pamela Tucker, testified that she had invited Tommy Sheridan back to her house after meeting him in Cupids. The woman, originally from Glasgow, recognised Tommy instantly. She described 'two girls and a gentleman' with him; 'one of the girls was slim with reddish hair, the other, I think her name was Anvar'. It was also revealed that Tommy's diary contained the phone number of the Manchester swingers' club, next to the name Ian Johnston, CWU branch secretary. A baffled Communications Workers Union official from Manchester called Ian Johnston was called to testify – he did not know Tommy Sheridan and hadn't the faintest idea why his name was in the former MSP's diary alongside the phone number of a swingers club.

By late November, six people had sworn under oath that they had either been with Tommy in the club or had seen him there. Five people had corroborated Katrine Trolle's testimony that she had been involved in a relationship with Tommy. Another five witnesses had backed up Anvar Khan's story. More than 20 SSP witnesses from all over Scotland, including teachers, care workers, journalists, NHS workers, a law lecturer and a criminal justice social worker, had testified that they had heard Tommy confessing to having visited the Cupids swingers club. A number of other witnesses, due to give similar evidence, were dropped by the prosecution to avoid duplication and to speed up the trial. The jury had heard the voice of Tommy

Sheridan on a video tape confessing to visiting Cupids and to having had affairs with Anvar Khan and Katrine Trolle. His telephone records proved that he had telephoned the two women regularly, including the evening before the swingers club visit. He had directly phoned Cupids several times, and had entered the name and the phone number of the club in two separate diaries. And according to Allison Kane, Tommy had been AWOL from an important SSP event in his Glasgow constituency on the specific night in question.

Media and legal circles were now ablaze with speculation that Tommy was about to run up the white flag. The morning after he had finished cross-examining me for the best part of two days, Tommy had told the judge that he was 'emotionally and physically exhausted' and was given an extra day to prepare for his confrontation with George McNeilage. The day after he had finished with George, he failed to show up. As Gail sat alone in the dock, Judge Bracadale told the jury, 'Tommy Sheridan is unwell.' The trial was adjourned for a further three days while Tommy, said to be suffering from high blood pressure, made an appointment for 'rigorous cardiology tests'.

Yet it would be a mistake to underestimate this man. In the words of one journalist he had 'balls of steel and a street intellect that is utterly formidable'. That was probably a fair description but it didn't paint the whole picture. By this time, many of us who had been close to Tommy in the past were convinced that we were dealing with a disordered personality.

In a BBC documentary shown back in 2006, on the heels of the defamation trial, Tommy's mum, Alice, had fondly recalled that, as a young boy, he would spend endless hours moving toy soldiers around an imaginary battlefield. That just about summed up his sense of himself in adulthood. In the strange universe he inhabited, Tommy Sheridan was a superior being and everyone else was there to submit to his will. In retrospect, what we used to laugh off as excessive vanity masked something more malignant: an extreme form of grandiosity and a narcissistic sense of entitlement that meant he was to able to use, abuse and discard people for his own ends without a glimmer of guilt or remorse. The ice in Tommy's veins that allowed him to take monumental risks might give some middle-class professionals a vicarious thrill, but those of us who had tangled with him up close knew the difference between real courage and absence of emotion. He could fake tears and feign compassion, but where other people had a conscience, he had a black hole.

Having come this far, Tommy wasn't about to throw in the towel. He came back out of his corner fighting. And, unlike his opponent, he wasn't constrained by the Marquis of Queensbury rules.

29

December 2010

Day of reckoning

'From a scratch to the danger of gangrene,' says an old Russian proverb. Tommy's long march to the High Court on perjury charges had begun as a tawdry little cover-up. But over days, weeks, months and years, the Tower of Lies had grown higher and higher until it made the Empire State Building look like a lamppost.

The day Matt McColl took the witness stand it looked like it was all about to come crashing down. The Renfrewshire businessman and former football coach had gone into hiding during the 2006 defamation trial to avoid being called as a witness. He had been interviewed four times by the police during the perjury investigation and each time denied that Tommy had been with him and others in the Moat House hotel the night before his sister-in-law's wedding. But four weeks into the trial, he suddenly came clean. He gave the procurator-fiscal in Glasgow a statement confirming that Tommy Sheridan had been present that night in a suite that he had booked in the Moat House hotel – now the Crowne Plaza – alongside, amongst others, the groom-to-be, Andy McFarlane, and a mystery woman from Birmingham.

This was a vindication of Anne Colvin and Helen Allison, whom Tommy had for years maligned as liars. In the Court of Session in 2006, Tommy had cross-examined the two middle-aged women and furiously denied that he had ever before set eyes on either one of them. They were gold-diggers and fantasists, according to the then MSP. But now a key witness, with no connections to either the SSP or the *News of the World*, had come forward to confirm that Tommy had duped the Edinburgh jury. McColl testified that he had met Tommy and Andy McFarlane in the Baby Grand bar near Charing Cross, then met up with the others in the riverside hotel. The Advocate-Depute showed the jury Tommy's diary for that year, which contained an entry for 14 June, 2002: '9 p.m. Baby Grand – carry out' then 'stay with Andy scrabble till 3 a.m.'. This should have been the final straw for Tommy's beleaguered defence. But suddenly everything started to go awry for the prosecution.

The first warning signs came during McColl's cross-examination by Gail's QC, Paul McBride. The flamboyant courtroom performer had all but given up trying to challenge the truth of the Cupids allegations. He had conducted brutally humiliating cross-examinations of Anvar Khan and Katrine Trolle. During the first few days of the trial he had also tried to discredit Barbara Scott and Allison Kane. But when the two stood their ground, he had no further questions for any of the remaining 20 SSP witnesses. But the Moat House chapter could be fatal for his client, so he set about Matt McColl with the verbal equivalent of an AK47.

'Hadgie', as he had been known to Keith Baldassara, responded with a mixture of evasion and cantankerous defiance. Had he followed the trial closely, he might have understood that there was no hiding place for witnesses in this courtroom. He refused to reveal the identity of his long-term partner, with whom he had attended Andy and Gillian McFarlane's wedding the day after the Moat House incident. He was hardly being asked to divulge a state secret, but he told the court: 'You can ask me till I'm blue in the face – if it gets me into trouble, then so be it.' Only after the court was adjourned and the businessman threatened with contempt of court did he finally answer the question. McBride then moved in for the kill, asking McColl a series of questions about his relationship with the woman from Birmingham. During subsequent exchanges, it emerged that the pair had initially met at another swingers club in Manchester, the Adam and Eve club. This information was only extracted from McColl after he had been caught out trying to conceal this part of his history.

After Paul McBride concluded his cross-examination, the Advocate-Depute asked for an adjournment. Helen Allison and Anne Colvin had waiting in two separate witness rooms for two days. There were other Crown witnesses too: Martha Rafferty, their lawyer; Jackie Whyte; the woman from Birmingham; and several members of the hotel staff. When Anne and Helen were told 'you're no longer required as witnesses – you can now go home and you don't need to return', their first reaction was relief. They assumed that Tommy had finally decided to cave in. They were stunned when they discovered the reason for this sudden reprieve.

The decision by the Crown Office to drop the Moat House chapter was a surprise not just to Helen Allison and Anne Colvin but to everyone who had followed the defamation trial four years earlier. The two women had been powerful and credible witnesses, and their oral evidence had been backed up by telephone records. Since then, other witnesses had come forward, some of them reluctantly. Matt McColl had clumsily tried to cover up his own private affairs under oath, but that did not negate the substance of his testimony. It looked as if the Crown Office had planned all along to remove the Moat House allegations, not because of lack of evidence, but because it would clear the way for them to drop the perjury charge against Gail. Many people suspected that they had only indicted her in the first place to put pressure on her husband to negotiate a deal, thus avoiding a protracted and expensive High Court trial. But Tommy, now a regular poker player, had called their bluff. No normal person would have taken such a gamble – not unless they were either blameless, or heartless.

There were several compelling reasons why the Crown Office would now want to drop the charges against Gail. First, there was no public interest in sending the mother of a five-year-old child to jail, even if she had knowingly committed perjury to protect her husband. Second, if Tommy was using Gail as a human shield, it made sense to remove that shield. And third, taking her out of the picture would also remove her experienced and accomplished QC, Paul McBride, from the scene.

There was one problem. As things stood, Gail could not be called to give evidence by her husband; under Scots Law, a defendant cannot call his or her co-accused as a witness. If the charges were now dropped against Gail, it was likely that Tommy would put her under pressure to take the witness stand. Most observers believed that her testimony had swung the jury in the defamation trial, and the Crown Office was not inclined to open the curtains on a repeat performance. Instead, they chose to keep her in the dock until the defence rested.

A week later, at the start of December, the Advocate-Depute announced that a further raft of allegations would be dropped, including the stand-alone charge of subornation, which lacked corroboration. It looked weak and gave the impression that the prosecution case was in disarray. The aim of the Crown Office appeared to be to simplify a complex case and focus the jury's attention on those parts of the indictment they believed had already been proven beyond all reasonable doubt. Clearly, they believed that the charges relating to Cupids, Anvar Khan and Katrine Trolle were solid. But I suspected that they were underestimating their opponent, and that Tommy would mount a concentrated onslaught on the remaining allegations. By apparently raising the bar for proof of perjury to a level that looked higher then the Murrayfield goalposts, the prosecution was unwittingly assisting Tommy to galvanise his witnesses and perhaps also bring some new ones on board to muddy the waters.

Up until now, his defence had consisted of a torrent of slander, smear and character assassination directed against prosecution witnesses. Tommy understood the old advertising truism that nothing beats repetition. Over and over again, he thundered indignantly against witnesses he claimed had been paid for their stories. 'Isn't it the case that when your paper waves wads of cash around, people forget about the truth?' he asked one *News of the World* journalist, who replied: 'You should know, Mr Sheridan – you took £30,000 from the *Daily Record*.' 'That's a lie,' retorted Tommy. It wasn't a lie, but it wasn't quite accurate either. Tommy and Gail had actually been paid £20,000 for their story, plus thousands more in an all-expenses-paid four-night stay in a plush hotel.

In contrast, none of the six people who testified that they saw Tommy Sheridan in Cupids had sold that information to the *News of the World* or any other newspaper. Neither had any of the 25 people who had heard Tommy confess to visiting the club. Nor had the two witnesses who had confirmed Katrine Trolle's testimony, nor the two witnesses who had backed up Anvar Khan. Indeed, Katrine Trolle had refused an offer of a substantial sum of money to sell her truthful story to *News of the World*. Of 35 prosecution witnesses who were not direct employees, only two had ever been paid by the newspaper – George McNeilage, for the video tape, and Anvar Khan, who had been paid £2,000 for the initial article about Cupids, which had not even named Tommy. The only person involved in this trial or in the original defamation case who I knew for sure had invented a story, and sold it to the press for cash, was Tommy Sheridan.

The stench of hypocrisy grew even more rank as he thundered indignantly against tabloid intrusion into the privacy of celebrities and politicians. The shady news-gathering methods of the *News of the World* had become a matter of public controversy in the run-up to the perjury trial. In 2007, Clive Goodman, the royal editor of the newspaper, and Glenn Mulcaire, a private investigator, had been jailed for illicitly accessing the mobile voicemail messages of James Pinkerton, a member of the royal household. One of the casualties of the scandal had been the UK editor of the *News of the World*, Andy Coulson, who was forced to resign his position. With Coulson's elevation to the post of Downing Street Director of Communications following the 2010 general election, the fire was rekindled. Now sections of the media, notably the *Guardian* – one of the few newspapers whose hands were clean when it came to the use of private investigators – were calling for a new police investigation into Coulson's role in the affair.

For Tommy, the timing was perfect. Coulson had been editor of the *News of the World* at the time of the defamation trial. He had travelled to Glasgow to view the George McNeilage tape and had authorised the £200,000 payment for the recording. By taking out a court order against the Metropolitan Police, Tommy's legal team had also obtained notebooks found in Glenn Mulcaire's possession containing his phone number, home address and a mobile phone pin number. These connections allowed Tommy to portray himself, once again, as the little guy doing battle with the giant media corporation.

One of Tommy's favourite quotes was from Bob Monkhouse: 'Once you've mastered sincerity, everything else is easy.' Tommy had a PhD in sincerity. He now presented himself as a white knight on a mighty charger, protecting individual privacy against the ruthless dirt-digging of the tabloid press. 'You don't care who you hurt and how many lives you destroy,' he told Bob Bird and other *News of the World* witnesses, at times dabbing the tears from his eyes. Yet to protect his own privacy, Tommy had ripped open and laid bare the most private lives of dozens of others. He knew that every allegation he made in court, whether true or false, could be reported in the media under the rules of absolute privilege. Nothing was off-limits as he used his courtroom power to expose decades-old convictions; illicit affairs, both real and imagined; drug habits, both legal and illegal; and personal medical records. The action he had begun back in 2004 had by now wrecked marriages, destroyed careers and damaged some people's mental health. These were mostly private individuals who had never courted publicity, nor cared to enter a courtroom, but had been forced to suffer public humiliation and degradation at the hands of a man prepared to do anything to cover up his own furtive activities.

Audaciously he cited Andy Coulson as a defence witness, along with the Metropolitan Police Superintendent, Phil Williams, who had been the Senior Investigating Officer of the inquiry that led to the jailing of Mulcaire and Goodman. Tommy possibly believed that he might be the man to bring down Coulson, by flushing out information under oath that could force the resignation of David Cameron's top aide and perhaps even lead to criminal charges. It would be a spectacular coup. Even if Tommy himself was eventually convicted, he would be remembered not for perjury but for nailing the Prime Minister's right-hand man. But what was intended as a spectacular blaze of pyrotechnics turned into a damp squib. If Coulson had anything to declare, he wasn't going to do it in the High Court in Glasgow. He ridiculed the idea that Tommy had been singled out for political vengeance at the highest levels of the Murdoch media corporation, insisting that before the 2006 defamation case, the MSP had never registered so much as a blip on his personal radar.

As it happened, six weeks after giving evidence, Coulson did resign his position as David Cameron's press aide. Some media commentators speculated that his appearance in the witness box in the Tommy Sheridan trial had been one of a number of reasons for his decision. By a quirk of history, while Coulson was in Glasgow, a group of student protesters against tuition fees attacked a vehicle in Central London carrying the Prince and Princess of Wales to the theatre. It was a major embarrassment for the Government, but their chief spin doctor wasn't in town to handle the fall-out. It was a taste of what could lie in store for Coulson: with a number of lawsuits in the pipeline against the *News of the World* over phone hacking, it looked like the newspaper's former editor would be spending a lot of his time in courtrooms giving evidence.

Following Coulson's testimony, Superintendent Phil Williams told the Glasgow jury that Tommy's details had been part of a huge hoard of material found in a bin bag in Glenn Mulcaire's garden, which included contact information for around 3,000 people. It also transpired that the four-digit figure written next to his telephone number, which Tommy had insisted was his personal pin number, was in fact the generic default Vodafone voicemail code, 3333. This wasn't exactly top secret information; as a highly accessible MSP, Tommy's contact details were known to every political journalist in Scotland. The Metropolitan police investigation, which included analysis of Mulcaire's telephone records, had found no evidence that the private investigator had ever attempted to access Tommy Sheridan's mobile phone.

For the jury, this had been yet another bewildering detour. The murky world of private investigators and tabloid journalists might be worthy of a public inquiry, but had no bearing on whether or not Tommy Sheridan had lied in court under oath. His subliminal message seemed to be: 'even if I have committed perjury, these people have also been involved in criminal activity, so I don't deserve to be convicted.' Neither the Advocate-Depute nor the judge attempted to rein Tommy in. The prosecution allowed him to wander off down irrelevant highways and byways for hours and even days at a time, without challenge. While he set about destroying the reputations of innocent people who had committed no crime, they stayed silent and allowed him to get on with it. When he initiated court orders to obtain evidence, they sped up the process by getting the material for him. When he requested an adjournment to prepare, they made no objection. It was a deliberate strategy, designed to avoid giving the defence any grounds for a future appeal.

In a surprise move, Tommy announced that he would not be taking the witness stand. He was within his rights, but it smacked of cowardice. Over two months, he had grilled over 40 prosecution witnesses, including the seven who had already been cross-examined by Maggie Scott. None of these witnesses had the luxury of refusing to give evidence. Some of them had to endure two, three and four days of cross-examination at his hands. Now he was refusing to face the Advocate-Depute. It was the best of all worlds. Tommy could lead his own witnesses, cross-examine Crown witnesses and deliver a closing speech to the jury without the inconvenience of having to explain the multiple inconsistencies, contradictions and gaps in his defence case. It was a cunning move. But it did throw up the obvious question: if he really was the victim of a far-reaching conspiracy, then why would he not take the opportunity to face down his accusers?

Instead, he relied on a final parade of Solidarity members and some close friends and family members. They included the same group of former SSP executive members who had contradicted our evidence in the defamation trial, four of whom had since been charged with perjury. Other witnesses solemnly testified that this was not his voice on the tape. Two witnesses even gave him contrived alibis for the night, eight years earlier, when he had gone to Cupids. A close friend, Thomas Montgomery, suddenly came forward after having what he called a 'Eureka moment' when he remembered he had been watching the Ryder Cup golf match with Gary Clark on that September Friday evening. Andy McFarlane, who had failed to give evidence at the defamation trial, now stepped up to say that he too had been watching the Ryder Cup that night with his wife Gillian, who corroborated his story. Andy claimed that he had never before mentioned this to Tommy, even though he had been named on his brother-in-law's indictment, published in July 2009, as having been in Cupids on the specific date in question.

It was all rather incredible, and rendered even more suspicious by the refusal of virtually all of Tommy's witnesses to give any statement to the police or the procurator fiscal in advance of the trial. If these people really did believe Tommy had been the victim of a diabolical conspiracy to frame him up, they would surely have been less reticent about coming forward to clear his name. I had eagerly responded to Aamer Anwar's request to provide a precognition statement and had spent two days in his office answering every question he threw at me. A number of SSP members, including myself, had also cooperated fully with Gail's lawyers. The defence had full access to the statements given by prosecution witnesses to the police. In contrast, defence witnesses had no legal obligation to give police statements, which put the Advocate-Depute at a serious disadvantage when it came to testing evidence.

By now, few people in Scotland truly believed that Tommy was an innocent man. If the jury stuck to the facts and the evidence, this was no contest. But other factors could come into play when the jury made their decision. Sympathy and compassion, for example, might influence some jurors – especially at this time of year, a few days before Christmas. People who want to believe something will grab hold of any little morsel to feed their conscience, and Tommy may well have done enough in that final phase of the trial to provide any juror reluctant to convict him with a few welcome crumbs of doubt.

Before the final summings-up, the Advocate-Depute made an announcement which managed to be simultaneously sensational and predictable. Gail Sheridan, he declared, was acquitted of all charges. He pointedly told the court that her QC, Paul McBride, accepted that the prosecution had led 'a sufficiency of evidence' against Gail. The prosecution would not be proceeding with the charges against her, not because they believed her to be innocent, but because it was 'not in the public interest'. It was the right decision. Whatever her motives, she had taken enough punishment over the years as a result of her husband's callousness, recklessness and egotism.

Throughout the trial the Advocate-Depute, Alex Prentice, had been as low-key as Tommy was flamboyant. In his closing speech, he calmly took the jury through the various strands of evidence, ridiculing Tommy's suggestion of 'a grand conspiracy to frame him' by former rivals in the SSP: 'That particular proposition is just fantasy.' He played the George McNeilage tape once again, but instead of focusing on the voice, concentrated on the content. How would anyone but Tommy Sheridan know the details of his conversation with *Daily Record* journalist Paul Sinclair on the concourse of Waverley station on the day of his resignation? How would they know of the text message of sympathy sent to Tommy from Kevin McVey around the same time? Why would *News of the World* be involved in concocting a video in which Tommy denied ever having met Fiona McGuire, thus 'rubbishing its own headline story'? If Tommy Sheridan never swore – as some witnesses had claimed – why would Alan McCombes and Keith Baldassara script a video in which he repeatedly uses obscene language? Why would Alan McCombes have included in the script a

foul-mouthed tirade about his own marital break-up and his relationship with 'that c*** Leckie'?

As well as weighing up the evidence, the jurors should also 'use their
common sense and life experience'. He asked: 'Why on earth would
Katrine Trolle want to come here and tell you about intimate things
and sexual behaviour to a busy court full of strangers?' And why
would Gary Clark, Tommy's lifelong friend, tell the court 'with great
courage' about his visit to Cupids? And if this was all a conspiracy to
bring down Tommy Sheridan, why would the plotters have dragged in
Gary Clark and Andy McFarlane, neither of whom had any connection to the SSP? Why had he scribbled in his personal diaries
references to Cupids and the phone number of the club? Why had
he made multiple phone calls at suspicious times to Gary Clark, Andy
McFarlane, Katrine Trolle and Anvar Khan? The Advocate-Depute
dismissed much of the defence evidence as 'irrelevant'. Underlining
the weight of prosecution evidence, he told the jury that he could not
deal with every point because that would take an inordinate amount of
time. He still managed to speak for two and half hours.

Tommy's closing speech lasted even longer – in fact, twice as long.
For reasons best known to himself, he chose to speak from the dock,
looking diagonally towards the jury from a distance rather than facing
them direct and close up at the lectern. His speech was, by all
accounts, a powerful piece of rhetoric, a tribute both to his oratorical
skills and to his meticulous preparation. It was also a dazzling
exhibition of his capacity for deceit. He was a master of sophistry,
the art of verbal conjuring which relies on trickery. It was all part of the
cut and thrust of political polemic, where opponents can test and
question each other's arguments. Now Tommy drew on all these skills
to disarm the jury.

Tommy also had the demagogic ability to make the most sweeping,
unsubstantiated assertion sound like an undisputed scientific fact. He
told the jury that this was 'the first ever perjury case in Scotland arising
from a civil trial'. It was false and he knew it. In 1999, for example,
seven Strathclyde police officers were prosecuted for perjury following a private civil action in the Court of Session, though all of them
were found Not Guilty. But Tommy knew that the jury wouldn't
know that – and he had the last word. He exploited the failure of the
Crown to provide forensic evidence authenticating the George
McNeilage tape. Again, it was deliberately misleading. Like most
people in Scotland, the jury would be unaware of the Cadder Ruling
and would be oblivious to the fact that, behind the scenes, the Crown
had been forced to shelve their forensic evidence. 'Why have the

prosecution failed to produce any expert witnesses? Where is the forensic analysis of the tape?' Tommy knew there was an explanation for the omission – but there was no explanation for his own failure to bring forward an expert witness to pronounce the tape a fake.

By now, it was difficult to work out what Tommy believed and what he didn't believe. He had repeatedly used the phrase 'a conscious liar' to malign witnesses whom he knew to be telling the truth. He had concluded my cross-examination by denouncing me as 'a cool, calculating liar.' Maybe this was just a form of psychological projection. Maybe he had actually convinced himself that he had never been to Cupids; never made an admission to the SSP executive and dozens of other people; never had an affair with Katrine Trolle or Anvar Khan. Or perhaps he was just an extraordinarily talented fraudster who believed he had the ability to bend, shape and mould reality to his will, like a child playing with plasticine. Either way, it was a sobering realisation that this man, who had once personified socialism in Scotland and been respected in all quarters for his integrity, could lie to Olympic standard, and without so much as a blink.

Curiously for a man who portrayed himself as a radical scourge of the establishment, he pandered shamelessly in his final speech both to conservative family values, and to the culture of deference and hierarchy that still pervades the judicial system. He talked of 'prosecution witnesses who showed contempt for this court' and contrasted their 'demeanour' with that of defence witness, 72-year old Duncan Boyle: 'He was respectful of the court and showed he was one of the old school by calling the judge sir.'

But his trump card was emotional blackmail. He had begun his speech by telling the jury: 'My life is at stake. I have a wee girl and a loving wife at home, and if you decide to convict me I will be separated from them for a considerable time.' He ended his speech in tears as he begged the jury to acquit him. 'I don't fear many people, ladies and gentlemen. But I'm frightened of you because you can do something the *News of the World* will never be able to do. You could separate me from my wife, you could make me break my promise to my daughter that I'd spend Christmas with her.'

The following day, Thursday 23 December 2010, the jury deliberated for six hours before delivering its verdict. By all accounts, Tommy showed no trace of anxiety as he played cards in the court cafeteria and chatted with family and supporters. The first hint that things were looking ominous for Tommy came shortly after three o'clock, when the jury requested that one phrase in one of the counts – the allegation that Tommy had sex with Katrine Trolle in his home –

be deleted from the charge sheet. It sounded like a particle of consolation for Gail, to spare her feelings. But it was bad news for Tommy.

When the verdict came through I was with Carolyn, Rosie Kane, and Rosie's daughter, Nicola. My feelings were mixed. I was sad for the past, the memorable days when Tommy and I had stood shoulder-to-shoulder during the anti-Poll Tax campaign, the rise of Scottish Militant Labour, the creation of the Scottish Socialist Party. But most of all I was relieved. Although Nicola Kane had insisted that the verdict would definitely be guilty, Carolyn, Rosie and I felt that the jury might have been left dazed and confused by Tommy's emotive oratory. But to their credit, they had resisted the temptation to dodge a difficult decision. I wasn't interested in revenge; only in justice. If the verdict had gone the other way, the reputations of many decent, honourable people would have been stained forever. Democracy itself would be subverted because a cloud of suspicion would always hang over the Scottish Socialist Party. Worst of all, Tommy Sheridan, a man without principles, without scruples, without basic human decency, would be reborn as a political hero. The genuine socialist Left in Scotland would be set back by a generation.

Redemption and forgiveness have to be part of any progressive political philosophy. Everyone has their weaknesses and failings, their moments of shame, their episodes of guilt. 'To step aside is human', wrote Scotland's national poet, Robert Burns. Our problem was that we were dealing with someone almost inhuman; someone for whom the normal rules of humanity were a sign of weakness; someone so consumed by self-adoration that he would be prepared to destroy anyone and anything that stood in his way.

Indeed, within hours of the jury's decision, Tommy was once again ranting hatred against those who had stood up for themselves and their party. The language of some of his supporters bordered on incitement to violence. One vowed on the internet to 'make it my mission in life to hunt down these scabs like wild animals'. Some people really did still believe that Tommy had been framed. If so, I could understand their rage. If his accusations against us had been truthful, we deserved to be branded with infamy.

But most of his political associates knew that he had lied his way through the last six years. In a strange sideshow to the trial, some of Tommy's political allies had pleaded with us to join with them in a socialist alliance or coalition to fight the Holyrood elections, even as their leader spat venom in court against the 'liars, forgers, conspirators and perjurers' of the SSP. Between early October and late November,

Frances Curran and Kevin McVey attended, on behalf of the SSP, a series of three meetings in Glasgow to discuss the proposals. Also in attendance were representatives of Solidarity, the SWP and the CWI, including at least four defence witnesses. They refused to explain how they could reconcile this call for unity with their public denunciations of a party which they alleged had orchestrated a monstrous plot to frame up and imprison their leader.

The SSP was created to bring about socialist unity in Scotland. But before unity must come trust. It cannot be forged through duplicitous wheeling and dealing with groups who continue to justify corrupt political gangsterism. Some of these people had taken a wrong turning back in 2004; but instead of retracing their steps, they had kept right on walking until they were thoroughly lost. One of the great taboos in modern politics is to admit you got it wrong. Those who supported Tommy Sheridan will, I suspect, never accept responsibility for their own part in this monstrous debacle.

The SSP is not beyond criticism. Many of us, individually and collectively, made mistakes along the way. But these were honest mistakes, made by people trying to do the right thing to protect a political movement. In any case, on all the main decisions, we called it right. In the two court cases, the SSP never had the luxury of opting out. We had a straight two-way choice: either do the right thing or do the wrong thing. We did the right thing and we did it for the right reasons. Whoever else happened to be on the same side, or on the opposing side, was a matter of moral and political irrelevance.

The taunt that by opposing Tommy Sheridan, we were supporting the *News of the World* was just a variation on a rusty old insult that would have embarrassed an intelligent ten-year-old. For opposing Britain's war effort during the First World War, the Scottish and Irish socialists John Maclean and James Connolly were accused of being in league with the German Tsar. For opposing the tyrannical regime of Josef Stalin, Marxist dissidents in the old Soviet Union were denounced as agents of capitalism and fascism. For opposing the NATO bombing of Serbia in 1999, Alex Salmond was labelled by some Labour politicians as 'the Toast of Belgrade.' For opposing the invasions of Iraq and Afghanistan, the anti-war movement was pilloried by sections western liberal intelligentsia as an ally of Al Qaeda, the Taliban and Saddam Hussein. The CWI group – now the mainstay of Solidarity – should have known better than to indulge in such silly polemics. When in the past they opposed the paramilitary campaign of the Provisional IRA, they were attacked relentlessly by some sections of the Left as supporters of British imperialism, unionism and loyalism.

A little knowledge is a dangerous thing. Some of Tommy's followers, especially south of the border, clung to the infantile belief that his legal case was an extension of the class struggle, and that the SSP had sided with the forces of darkness. But whether through ignorance of the facts, or simple cowardice, none of these critics were prepared to spell out the alternatives. Perhaps we should have defied the law and served lengthy prison sentences to keep a pathological liar out of jail? Or, to restore Tommy Sheridan to his rightful position as the infallible, supreme leader of socialism in Scotland, we should have committed collective perjury, confessed to a catalogue of crimes that we had never committed and hung our heads in shame for evermore?

Tommy Sheridan's future was now in the hands of Lord Bracadale. Like most people in the SSP, I wasn't interested in retribution. Tommy had at last been exposed as a fraud and that was what mattered. If some people still chose to support him, that was up to them, but at least they couldn't be duped unless they wanted to be duped. His conviction cleared the names of those whose reputations he had tried to trash. I hoped that even now he would do the right thing. It was in everyone's interests that he personally set the record straight. It would end the surreal debate that was still rumbling in some quarters over his guilt and innocence, and allow people to focus on the more serious questions thrown up by this experience. For him, it would mean a lesser sentence and the salvaging of at least a little dignity. If he carried on protesting his innocence 'until my dying breath', as he had once threatened, it could only undermine any genuine campaigns that might arise in the future against real miscarriages of justice.

But no. Instead, he talked of lodging an appeal and gave the impression that he would never let this go. He had become 'the liar who can never let it lie' as one columnist put it, one of many journalists who had finally turned on Tommy after years of giving him the benefit of the doubt

One thing was for sure: the floodgates would now open, probably after his sentencing. I had known since November 2004 that the Cupids trips were just the tip of the iceberg. We had only ever dealt with what we had to deal with. But there were plenty more stories out there that had never yet reached the media. A few of us knew more than had ever been publicly revealed and had kept it all under wraps. Far from being moral commissars, the SSP leadership had been laissez faire in the extreme about Tommy's activities; too hands-off some might argue, given the seriousness of some of the allegations. But it wasn't our place to come forward with private information. During the two court cases and the police investigation, we had stuck strictly to what was relevant. We had acted to protect the party when we had no other option, but we also had a duty to protect the confidentiality of innocent people.

Tommy had left a trail of misery in his wake – women he had used and abused; political allies he had betrayed; friends he had drawn into his hidden world before throwing their privacy to the wolves of the mass media. Gail had suffered most of all. She pledged to stand by her man outside the court following the verdict and pointedly thanked 'our real friends, who have stood by us'. But many people suspected it was all a charade, and that it was over between the couple long before the court case. In public, she blamed the *News of the World*, Lothian and Borders Police, the Crown Office and the SSP for her misfortunes – everyone except Tommy – but what she really felt, alone and in private, could only be guessed at.

This whole saga had been folly on an epic scale. It was a dismal and strangely symmetrical farewell to a colourful era. Tommy Sheridan rise to national fame had begun the day he was led from the High Court in handcuffs to serve a jail sentence after breaking the rules of the judicial system. Along the way he had become a swashbuckling political hero, revered by tens of thousands and respected by hundreds of thousands more. Tommy had seemed like the genuine article. Here was a man who devoted his talents to the greater good of society, to the cause of equality, to the emancipation of the poor. Then it had all turned malignant.

His slow-motion downfall, over six painful years, had been a political as well as a human tragedy. Tommy Sheridan betrayed the hopes and dreams of thousands of people, from unemployed teenagers to World War II veterans, who over the years had stood on freezing street corners, emptied their purses, climbed tenement stairs, knocked on doors and marched on demos to help build the movement that had catapulted him to fame and glory. By the time he went to jail for perjury, the one-time idol of the Poll Tax campaign had inflicted more damage on the Left in Scotland than Margaret Thatcher and Rupert Murdoch combined.

Epilogue

Before announcing the sentence, Lord Bracadale paid fulsome tribute to Tommy Sheridan. 'On any view you were a highly effective and hard-working politician. You supported individuals in the community, both in the parliament and in the street; you were able to use your undoubted powers of oratory to press home your cause; you led the Scottish Socialist Party to considerable electoral success; and your contributions to the anti-Poll Tax campaign and the abolition of warrant sales will become part of the fabric of Scottish social and political history.'

The respectful testimonial was intended to convey the message that this was no political prosecution. He reinforced the point by declaring that Tommy's previous convictions would be disregarded as irrelevant. 'But the only appropriate sentence, as you yourself recognise, is imprisonment . . . You brought the walls of the temple crashing down, not only on your own head but also on the heads of your family and your political friends and foes alike. You were repeatedly warned by the comrades that it would come to this . . . In all the circumstances I impose a three-year sentence.' Tommy's Solidarity party rushed out a press release denouncing the punishment as 'barbaric and draconian'. It was a stereotypically over-the-top response. I imagined that some of them would be privately disappointed at the leniency of the sentence. They wanted a martyr but Lord Bracadale had failed to deliver.

More telling was the grinning photograph of Tommy taken through the window of the prison van transporting him to Glasgow's Barlinnie Prison. His own verdict on the sentence had earlier been summed up in two words: 'Fucking result!' The judge's decision meant that he would be eligible for automatic release after eighteen months, and even earlier with an electronic tag. Because he was deemed 'low-risk', he would serve most of his time in an open prison, with regular extended home visits. Tommy Sheridan wasn't going to be Scotland's Nelson Mandela.

In his fifty-minute mitigation speech Tommy had begged for clemency. He used his mother's battle against cancer, his father's mobility problems, the health of his wife and the welfare of his young daughter as reasons why he should be spared a lengthy jail sentence. At no stage did Tommy confess his guilt. But neither did he plead his innocence. It was a strangely obsequious speech for a man who claimed to have been fitted up by a conspiracy of enemies in politics, the Scottish government, the legal system and the media. Why would he not come out all guns blazing, roaring defiance, declaring war to the death against this monstrous miscarriage of justice?

Instead, he told Lord Bracadale, 'The whole impact of the clang of the prison gates is the real punishment. I accept custody is inevitable and I will not try to deflect your Lordship from that. The very fact of my custody and the tarring of my public standing is a deterrent in itself.' This wasn't going to go down in the annals of Scottish rebel history alongside Thomas Muir, who before being sentenced to fifteen years' transportation to Australia, told the High Court: 'I am careless and indifferent to my fate. I can look danger and I can look death in the face, for I am shielded by the consciousness of my own rectitude. I may be condemned to languish in the recess of a dungeon – I may be doomed to ascend the scaffold. Nothing can deprive me of the past – nothing can destroy my inward peace of mind, arising from the remembrance of having discharged my duty.'

But then, the great eighteenth-century reformer was prosecuted for sedition, not for committing perjury to cover up a sex scandal.

Outside, from the steps of the High Court, Gail delivered a short speech. 'The real reason Tommy has been imprisoned today is because he has fought inequality and injustice with every beat of his heart.' It sounded to me like it had been scripted by her husband, a Rod Stewart fan. More startling than the trite and predictable message was her performance. This was Gail doing a Tommy Sheridan impersonation, right down to the facial expressions, the mannerisms and the calculated pauses.

Sometimes it's hard to sustain sympathy, even for a victim. A few months earlier, Gail had been in psychological meltdown, on one occasion locking herself in the ladies' toilet in the High Court and screaming abuse at her husband outside. He had coldly exploited her for his own protection and had played no part in her acquittal – that had been down to the compassion of the hated Crown Office and the negotiating skills of a Tory QC. Maybe she was still loyal, or maybe she was only pretending to be loyal for pragmatic reasons. There was no hint of grief – only a glint in her eye which suggested relief that it was all over and she could now move on.

The Scottish media, a large swathe of which had indulged Tommy after his 2006 defamation victory, had turned hostile. An editorial in the *Sunday Mail* described him as a 'delusional sociopath' and ridiculed his 'laughable self-image as a great socialist hero, like jailed Red Clydesider, John Maclean'. It went on, 'Mr Sheridan, we have heard about John Maclean, we have read about John Maclean. You are no John Maclean.'

In the *Daily Record*, the provocative veteran columnist and agony aunt Joan Burnie made a gracious and poignant apology to Rosie Kane: 'I was once downright nasty about Rosie, when she became an MSP and took the oath dressed to go to a disco. But she had total commitment to those she represented – and Sheridan. She believed in him. She trusted him. Her tragedy is that, unlike so many politicians, she is an incorruptible who refused to lie for him. Rosie's a good woman and to see her now traduced by Sheridan and his acolytes is shameful.'

But there were still some people around who just didn't get it. Some male broadsheet columnists of a certain age continued to hold a torch for the disgraced politician, though their batteries were almost flat. Many *Guardian* readers in England must have been left baffled by the paper's selective reporting of the perjury trial. Whether a reflection of the London broadsheet's chronic indifference to Scotland, its disdain for the *News of the World*, or a combination of both, it focused almost entirely on Tommy's diversionary detours into the world of tabloid phone hacking and private investigators while neglecting the spectacular story of deceit, corruption and self-destruction at the heart of this case.

But the worst was yet to come. Speaking at a 'Defend Tommy Sheridan rally' in February, George Galloway attacked SSP witnesses who had given honest evidence at the trial as 'cowards', 'traitors' and 'flea-infested rats'. It was guaranteed to send the shattered remnants of Solidarity into raptures. By this time George was looking for footsoldiers to back his Holyrood election campaign. Three months earlier, in the middle of the perjury trail, he had declared his intention to stand for the Glasgow regional seat, without even waiting for the jury to torpedo Tommy Sheridan's own ambition to return to Holyrood. In the pages of the *Daily Record*, I threw down the gauntlet, challenging Galloway to an open public debate on the facts of the Tommy Sheridan affair. 'Either put up or shut up,' I demanded. George shut up, pausing only to repeat an old Tony Benn line: 'Never wrestle with a chimney sweep because you can't come out clean.' It appeared to me a pretty lame excuse, especially coming from the man who had in the recent past challenged right-wing Republican US senators to public debate.

The Tommy Sheridan story stands as a screaming warning to those who value personalities over principles. In these days of economic mayhem, savage warfare, climate chaos, rampaging inequality and raging revolt against tyranny, ideas matter more than ever. No-one wants to see politics dehumanised. But the message is bigger than the messenger and politics is a more serious business than *Big Brother* or the *X-Factor*.

For a generation of Scots, Tommy Sheridan had symbolised the noblest qualities of humanity. He had spoken the language of love, equality and solidarity. But the words had meant nothing. He was a fraud. Had he been corrupted by fame and power? Or had he just used the cause of socialism to achieve fame and power? Probably a bit of both. But either way, his actions decimated the left and shamed socialism. Thousands were contaminated by the experience, their idealism corroded, their souls hardened by cynicism.

Yet despite everything, the Scottish Socialist Party survived the typhoon. It might be battered, bruised and bloodied – but it's still standing, still fighting for those who have been abandoned by main-stream politics, and still advocating the case for independence and socialism. Of the 2004 executive of SSP, only a few remain in the central leadership, which is how it should be in any vibrant organisation. The majority, including myself, have since voluntarily stepped down from the frontline to make way for a new generation. After years of political bloodletting, culminating in the battle royale fought out in the High Court in Glasgow, it will take time before the party recovers its electoral strength. But the politics of integrity have prevailed over the politics of celebrity.

For those of us who were at the centre of what sometimes felt like a Gothic hallucination, the Tommy Sheridan crisis was a tough and painful six years. It did though give us insight, knowledge and under-standing. Nonetheless, many who endured that experience might be tempted to sympathise with the words of the Anglo-Irish poet, William Butler Yeats: 'If suffering brings wisdom, I would wish to be less wise.'

Sources

The information upon which this book is based comes from a range of sources, including newspaper and online archives; SSP minutes, documents and bulletins; interviews; and the author's own personal recollection.

Chapter 1
A Time To Rage, Tommy Sheridan and Joan MacAlpine (Polygon 2004)
Evening Times, 9 October 1999; 'Which Side Are You Really On, Tommy?'
I'm Not The Only One, George Galloway (Allen Lane 2004)

Chapter 2
Evening Times, 31 May 1988, 'Militant Poll Tax Plot – Extremist Group in City Power Bid'; 'How Militant Are Using the Tax in Bid for Power in Glasgow'; Driving Force'
A Time To Rage, Tommy Sheridan and Joan MacAlpine (Polygon 2004)
Financial Times, 2 April 1990; 'All the Main Parties Blame Extremists for Poll Tax Violence'
Evening Times, 1 October 1991 'Victory'
Daily Record, 7 March 1992; 'Downfall of a Dodger'

Chapter 3
Guardian, 8 March 1990 (Tommy Sheridan profile)
The Scotsman, 12 February 1996; 'Rainbow Left Unites Under the Red Flag' (Ian Bell)

Chapter 4
Daily Record, 30 April 1999; Tom Brown's Campaign Diary
The Herald, 1 May 1999; TV review (David Belcher)
Evening Times, 11 September 2000; 'George Square Ice Rink Plan Comes Under Fire'
Scottish Mirror, 19 December 2002; 'Two-Faced' (Tommy Sheridan)
The Herald, 30 August 2002; 'Inquiry into McLeish Pledge on His Golden Handshake'
The Scotsman, 8 August 2006; 'Revealed: Tommy Sheridan Made Me Loyalty Swinger' (Robert McNeill)
Sunday Herald, 11 April 1999; 'Well Red' (Denise Mina)
Socialist Review Issue 226, January 1999; 'Scotland's Road to Revolution'

Chapter 5
New Statesman, 29 January 2001; 'Waging War on Wee Ally McBeals . . .' (Tim Luckhurst)

Daily Record, 30 October 2002; 'No Whore Like An Old Hoor' (Paul Sinclair)

Daily Record, 11 December 1998; 'Thomas on Tommy – Face to Face with the Man Who is Last of the Red-Hot Socialists' (Tom Brown)

Chapter 6
Scotland on Sunday, 12 August 2007; 'At Home with Tommy Sheridan'

Daily Record, 26 January 2001; 'We Asked MPs and MSPs to Tell Us the Next Line to Some of The Bard's Most Famous Works'

The Express, 2 June, 2004; 'Off the Leash'; 'Felicity Will Fiz in EU Poll' (Dorothy Grace Elder)

Sunday Herald, 27 April, 2003; Allan Taylor's Diary

The Sun, 16 April, 2003; 'Scotcha! On Wednesday'

Chapter 7
News of the World (Scotland), 31 October 2004; 'Married MSP Is Spanking Swinger'

Daily Record, 25 June 2004; 'Humble Pie – Minister Grovels after He Goes Missing for Lunch'

Daily Record, 24 May 2000; 'How Many Tenants Are You Kidding, Wendy?' (Tommy Sheridan)

Sunday Herald, 21 November, 2004; 'In Sacking Tommy Sheridan, the SSP Are In Danger of Sacking Themselves' (Iain Macwhirter)

The Mirror, 7 January 2004; 'King of Rings' (Tommy Sheridan)

Daily Record, 17 2001; 'Tommy's Too Right Wing'

East London Advertiser, 21 December 2006; 'Stamp Out Strip Clubs'

Chapter 8
SSP EC Minutes, 9 November 9 2004

Handwritten notes created at 9 November 2004 meeting by Barbara Scott, minutes secretary

Daily Record, 11 November 2004; 'Sheridan to Quit as Leader of the SSP' (Paul Sinclair)

Sunday Mail, 24 November 2002; 'Scots Back Our Fight for Freedom of Speech – HRH *v* Sunday Mail'

Chapter 9
The Sun, 12 November 2004; 'Scandal? Say It to My Face – Sheridan Rumours Rap'

The Mirror, 12 November 2004; 'Sexgate: Damned Lies – Tommy Slams Those Sex Scandal Rumours'

Evening Times, 11 November 2004; 'Tommy's Being Dead Brave . . . He's Giving Up the Leadership for Me and Our New Baby' (Brian Currie and Sheila Hamilton)

Sunday Mirror, 14 November 2004; 'What a Spanker, Tommy' (Tom Brown)

Sunday Herald, 14 November 2004; 'A Lesson in Why Politicians Should Ignore Journalists' (Iain Macwhirter)

Scottish Mirror, 12 November 2004; 'It's All a Bit of a Mess, Mate' (Ron McKenna)

Sunday Herald, 14 November 2004; 'Sheridan Was Forced Out by His Own Party' *(Paul Hutcheon)*

News of the World, 14 November 2004; 'Whips, Zips and Handcuffs'

News of the World, 14 November 2004; 'Sheridan Is Finished . . .' (Douglas Wight and Andrea Vance)

Chapter 10

Statement from SSP Executive, 14 November 2004

The Scotsman, 17 November 2004; 'No Public Backing for Sheridan amid Confusion in SSP'

The Herald, 17 November 2004; 'The "Late Tommy Sheridan" Finds Himself Alone in the Party Crowd – Unity a Fragile Commodity as Socialist Colleagues Gather to Discuss Leadership' (Tom Gordon)

Scottish Mirror, 18 November 2004; 'Lovers Plotted to Axe Tommy'

Sunday Herald, 21 November 2004; 'In Sacking Tommy Sheridan, the SSP are in Danger of Sacking Themselves' (Iain Macwhirter)

I'm Not the Only One, Allen Lane 2004 (George Galloway)

News of the World, 21 November 2004; 'Tower Of Lies'

Sunday Herald, 21 November 2004; 'Sheridan Ally: We Won't Build "Tower Of Lies" – Senior SSP Figure Fails to Back Former Leader'

Handwritten notes created at SSP Special National Council Meeting, 27 November 2004, by minutes secretary

Statement from Tommy Sheridan issued at end of SSP Special National Council Meeting, 27 November 2004

Chapter 11

Sunday Mail, March 30, 2003; 'Sheridan: I Won't Back Our Troops: Nazi Claim Sparks Outrage' (Lindsay McGarvie)

Scottish Mirror, 9 April 2003; 'What I Never Said about the Troops' (Tommy Sheridan)

Scottish Socialist Voice, 15 June 2001; 'The Scores on the Doors'

News of The World, 4 May 2003; 'Opinion – New MSPs Must Use Power Wisely' (Euan McColm)

News of the World, 14 March 2004; 'Opinion – "Winner: Tommy Sheridan"' (Euan McColm)

allmediascotland.com, 22 April 2009; Scottish Press Awards nominations

Evening Times, 6 September 2005; 'Everything We Do Revolves around Our Gorgeous Wee Giggly Gabrielle' (Sheila Hamilton)

Spiked, 6 July 2006 'Don't Tinker with the Libel Laws – Scrap Them' (Helene Guldberg)

Guardian, 13 September 2010; 'Wayne Rooney's Infidelity Exposes Law's Misogyny' (Gill Phillips)

Chapter 12

Sunday Herald, 30 January 2005; 'And in the Red Corners' (Alan Crawford and Paul Hutcheon)

The Mirror, 14 February 2005; 'Fox Fit For Fight' (leader: 'Voice of the *Scottish Daily Mirror*')

Evening Times, 2 March 2005; 'If I Believed He'd Cheated, Tommy Would Have Been Heid First in the Clyde . . . And I'd Be Speaking to You from Cornton Vale' (Sheila Hamilton)

Sunday Herald, 1 May 2005; 'A Cunning Measure to Gain a Measure? The Scottish Radge' (Tom Shields)

Sunday Herald, 28 August 2005; 'Door Isn't Closed' on Sheridan Comeback – Actor Mullan's Criticism Sparks Debate over Future of Scottish Socialists' (Paul Hutcheon)

Chapter 13
SSP EC Minutes, 9 November 9 2004
SSP EC Minutes, 14 May 2006

Chapter 14
Open Letter to SSP members from Tommy Sheridan, 28 May 2006
Sunday Herald Seven Days, 29 January 2006; 'Pillar of the Community' (Peter Ross)
Daily Mail, 31 May 2006; 'No Quick Fix to End the Curse of Knife Crime' (Allan Massie)

Chapter 15
Sunday Herald, 28 May 2006; 'Revealed: Secret Record of Meeting that Felled Sheridan and Led to Imprisonment of SSP Official' (Paul Hutcheon)
A Time to Rage, Tommy Sheridan and Joan MacAlpine (Polygon 2004)
The *Mirror*, 21 April 2004; 'Beckham Is Blame Free' (Tommy Sheridan)
The Socialist, 1 June 2006; 'Crisis in the Scottish Socialist Party' (Philip Stott)
The Herald, 30 May 2006; ' "Poisonous" Feud as SSP Official Goes on the Attack – Sheridan Accused over Open Letter' (Tom Gordon)

Chapters 16
Press and court agency reports
Verbatim notes taken during the defamation case; 4 July 2006–4 August 2006 (Pamela Currie and Carol Haney)
Daily Record, 5 July, 2006; 'Champagne Tommy, a Club Called Cupids and a Hotel Threesome'
The Sun, 5 July 2006; 'Chief Whip'

Chapter 17
Press and court agency reports
Verbatim notes taken during the defamation case, 4 July 2006–4 August 2006 (Pamela Currie and Carol Haney)
Scottish Mirror, November 15, 2004; 'Former Hubby Brands Fiona "A Liar" ' (Richard Gray)
Sunday Mirror, 6 August 2006; 'Tommy Case Hooker Lied that She Was Dying from Cancer . . . So I Married Her' (Stuart Paterson)
Aberdeen *Press and Journal*, 5 January 2008; 'Sheridan Saga Husband Admits: I Lied'

Chapter 18
Press and court agency reports
Verbatim notes taken during the defamation case, 4 July 4 2006–4 August 2006 (Pamela Currie and Carol Haney)
Evening Times, 15 November 2004; 'Sheridan Pledges to Sue over Affair Claim'
News of the World, 8 April 2001; 'Irish Probe £2m Heroin Haul Link to Licensee' (David Leslie)
The Mirror, 26 October 2002; 'Scot on Trial over £1 million Drug Find' (Orlaith Delaney)
Interviews with Anne Colvin and Helen Allison (January 2011)
The Herald, 4 January 2007; 'Witness not Allowed to See Results of Sheridan Investigation' (Tom Gordon)

Chapter 19
Press and court agency reports
Verbatim notes taken during the defamation case, 4 July 2006–4 August 2006 (Pamela Currie and Carol Haney)

Chapter 20
Press and court agency reports
Verbatim notes taken during the defamation case, 4 July 2006–4 August 2006 (Pamela Currie and Carol Haney)
Jeffrey Archer: Stranger than Fiction, Michael Crick (Fourth Estate, 2000) [Chapter 20]

Chapter 21
The Express, 5 August 2006; 'Sheridan's Victory Leaves Bitter Political Aftertaste' (leader)
Sunday Express, 6 August 2006; 'There's Always a Place in Politics for Mavericks' (leader)
The Sun, 8 August 2006; 'Let Him Be' (Bill Leckie)
London Review of Books, 17 August 2008; *Short Cuts* (Andrew O'Hagan)
Sunday Mirror, 6 August 2006; 'Exposed: Cancer at Heart of the SSP' (Ron McKenna)
Sunday Mirror 13 August 2006; 'Party's Over, Comrades' (Anna Smith)
The Herald, 9 August 2006; 'Muppet Marxists Who Couldn't Take the Heat' (Iain Macwhirter)
Revolutionary Witticisms of Colin Fox, Rosie Kane and Carolyn Leckie MSPs Word Power Books 2005 (ed. Gregor Gall)
The Herald, 8 August 2006; 'A Sheridan Show Can Only End in Lost Ratings' (Ruth Wishart)
The Guardian, 8 August 2006; 'G2: A Win For Machismo: Tommy Sheridan May Have Emerged Victorious from His Libel Case But All the Women Involved Came Off Badly . . .' (Julie Bindel)
Scotland on Sunday 6 August 2006; 'The Real Losers in The Sheridan Trial' (Magnus Linklater)
Sunday Mail, 6 August 2006; 'Poker in My Heart: Tommy's Fury'
Daily Record, 7 August 2006; 'I'll Destroy the Scabs Who Tried to Ruin Me'

Chapter 22

Sunday Herald; August 6 2006; 'Sheridan The Inside Story' (Neil Mackay talking to John Aberdein)

Amande's Bed, John Aberdein (Thirsty Books 2005)

Sunday Times, 27 August 2006; 'Mullan Taunt Widens Split on Sheridan' (Alistair Mackay and Eva Langlands)

I'm Not The Only One, George Galloway (Allen Lane 2004)

The Scotsman, August 15 2006; 'Now Comrades Will Have to Be Put to The Nail Scissors' (Robert McNeill)

Sunday Herald, 6 August 2006; 'The SSP – A Party in Crisis' (Paul Hutcheon)

The Fight for the Truth, SSP internal bulletin, summer 2006 (Alan McCombes)

The Herald, September 4, 2006; 'Solidarity Wins On Decibel Count But SSP Defeats Sheridan's New Party for Vitriol Levels'

Chapter 23

Information based on interviews with activists in Pollok; extracts from video tape as transcribed and published in *News of the World,* 1 October and 8 October, 2006; and testimony presented in the High Court, Glasgow November 2010)

The Mirror, 4 October 2006; ' "When the History of This Story Is Written, I Think You Will Find MI5 Were Certainly Involved" – Tommy's Amazing Video Claim' (Mark Smith)

*The Herald,*10 October 2006; 'Sheridan Confronts Ex-Friend over Video Claims' (Robbie Dinwoodie)

Chapter 24

The Herald, 8 August 2006; 'The Secretary, The Notes And The Police'

Sunday Times, 6 August 2005; 'Sheridan Case: Police Start Perjury Inquiry (Jason Allardyce)

Scottish Socialist Voice, 25 August 2006; 'Tommy Admitted That He Confirmed Sex Club Visit to EC Meeting' (letter to *Your Voice*)

The Herald, 23 March 2007; 'Police Inquiry After "Bug" Found In Sheridan's Car – MSPs Researcher "Stumbles Across" Suspicious Hidden Device' (David Leask)

The Scotsman, 23 March 2007; 'Police Inquiry into Bugging Fear as Device Discovered in Sheridan's Car' (Louise Gray)

Daily Record, 23 March 2007; 'Sheridan: Who Put Spy Cam under My Car Seat?' (Lee-Ann Fullerton)

Evening Times, 24 March 2007; 'Police Say Sheridan Bug "Worked" '

Sunday Times, 25 March 2007; 'Sheridan "Warned of Sleaze Plot" ' (Tom Gordon)

Daily Record, 28 March 2007; 'Letters –Your View: "Tommy's Bugbear Cheek" ' (Charles Gray)

Scottish Mirror, 24 March 2007; 'If the *News of The World* Is Involved in a Plot to Bug My Car I Wouldn't Be Surprised' (Mark Smith)

Scottish Left Review, issue 37, November/December 2006; 'The Future of Socialism' (Gordon Morgan, John McAllion)

Scottish Mirror, 19 January 2007; 'Tommy Poll Is Seven Heaven' (Mark Smith)
Evening Times, 28 April 2007; 'The House of Sheridan' (Sheila Hamilton)
The Scotsman, 20 April 2007, 'Election Diary' (Alba)

Chapter 25
Guardian, 9 August 2007; review, 'The Tommy Sheridan Chat Show' (Brian Logan)
Sunday Times, 5 August 2007; 'An Evening with Political Failure' (Allan Brown)
Sunday Herald, 12 August 2007; 'Sheridan – Socialist, Politician, Celebrity' (Stephen Phelan)
The Times, 6 August, 2007, 'Critics Show No Mercy to a Socialist on the Fringe' (Ben Hoyle and David Lister)
Scotland on Sunday, The Review edition, 16 December 2007; 'Turkeys – The Tommy Sheridan Chat Show' (Chitra Ramaswamy)
Sunday Mail, 13 May 2007; 'Police Want to Nail Tommy for Perjury' (Steve Smith)
Sunday Herald, 20 May 2007; 'Police Investigate "Bribery" Allegation in Sheridan Case' (Paul Hutcheon)
Sunday Herald, 2 September 2007; 'Police Grill Actor over SSP Motion to Destroy Private Details about Sheridan' (Paul Hutcheon)
Sunday Herald, 3 June 2007; 'Police Find SSP Official Who "Fled in Fear of His Life"' (Paul Hutcheon)
Sunday Express, 5 August 2007 (Maggie Barry)
The Times, 31 July 2007 'Can Tommy Sheridan Bury His Gristle and Sleaze Reputation by Turning Chat Show Host?' (Dominic Maxwell)
Sunday Times, 1 April 2007; 'Sheridan "Sex Party" Witness Sought by Police' (Tom Gordon)
Sunday Times, 22 April 2007; 'Sheridan "Orgy" Claim Checked' (Tom Gordon)
Evening Times, 17 December 2007 ' "Furious" Sheridan Vows He'll Fight to Clear Name – Defiant Former MSP Says He Will Beat Perjury Rap'
The Herald, 22December 2007; 'Socialists Deny They Are on Point of Walking away from Solidarity' (Robbie Dinwoodie)

Chapter 26
Daily Record, 18 December 2007; 'Sheridan's Wife Faces Perjury Charges Too' (Tom Hamilton)
Daily Record, 23 February 2008; 'Gail Sheridan's Fury after BA Suspend Her over Booze Probe' (Tom Hamilton)
The Scotsman, 25 February 2008; 'Scotland Has the Right Balance on DNA but not on Investigation' (Lesley Riddoch)
Daily Telegraph, 21 February 2008; 'Dark Days for Tommy Sheridan and Justice' (Alan Cochrane)
Daily Record, 25 February 25; 'I Would Defend Tommy Even If I Thought He Was Guilty, Which I Don't' (George Galloway)
Daily Express,14 February 2008; 'What's All This Then?'
The Mirror, 22 November 1999; 'Voice of the Mirror: Jail Him'
Daily Record, 20 July 2001; 'Liar Liar the Sleazy Arrogant Cheating Thieving

Lying Rat – Archer Jailed for Four Years over Libel Trial Perjury and
Bogus Alibi'

Sunday Herald, 22 July 2001; 'Libel Laws Should Be Next in the Dock' (Iain
Macwhirter)

Guardian, 17 December 2007; 'The King of the Swingers?' (Iain Macwhirter)

The Socialist, 11 June 2008; 'Stirring Rally Backs Tommy Sheridan' (Jim
McFarlane)

The Sun, 4 July 2008; 'Carry on Swinging, Sheridan' (Yvonne Bolouri)

News of The World, 14 December 2008; 'Sheridan's in the BB House' (Euan
McColm)'

Press Gazette, 4 April 2008; 'Tommy Sheridan Loses Talk 107 Radio Show'
(Paul McNally)29

Chapter 27
What's Going On, Mark Steel (Simon and Schuster 2008)

The Socialist, 2 January 2009; 'Tommy Sheridan in Celebrity Big Brother'
Statement from the Socialist Party/CWI

The Herald, 7 January 2009; 'Why Do They Sacrifice Careers for Television's Shilling?' (Ruth Wishart)

Daily Record, 23 January 2009; 'Bar-L Helped Me Survive BB' (Tommy
Sheridan)

Daily Record, 28 January 2009; 'From Big Brother to Big Bother' (Tom
Hamilton)

Daily Record, 25 May 2009; 'Tommy: I'll Take on Any Scots Celeb'

The Herald, 13 July 2009; 'Sheridan Perjury Case: Full Indictment'

Daily Record, 25 September 2009; 'Tommy Drops His Briefs Again!'

Sunday Herald, 29 April 2009; 'Tommy Can't Resist the Pull of This
Popularity Contest' (Vicky Allan)

Sunday Mail, 18 January 2009; 'Yes But No Mut' (David Taylor)

Chapter 28
Press and court agency reports
The Sheridan Trial Blog: http://sheridantrial.blogspot.com (James Dole-
man)

Chapter 29
Press and court agency reports
The Sheridan Trial Blog: http://sheridantrial.blogspot.com (James Doleman)

The Sun, 24 December 2010; 'The Liar Who Can Never Let It Lie' (Bill
Leckie)

Daily Record, 28 January 2011; 'Rosie Is the Woman Truly Wronged, Not
Gail' (Joan Burnie)

Daily Record, 5 March 2011; ' "Flea-infested rat" snaps back at Gallo'